A SEARCH FOR MAN'S SANITY

A *SEARCH* FOR

MAN'S *SANITY*

THE SELECTED LETTERS
OF TRIGANT BURROW

WITH BIOGRAPHICAL NOTES

PREPARED BY THE EDITORIAL COMMITTEE OF

THE LIFWYNN FOUNDATION : WILLIAM E GALT

CHAIRMAN : FOREWORD BY SIR HERBERT READ

NEW YORK : OXFORD UNIVERSITY PRESS

1958

© 1958 by Oxford University Press, Inc.

Library of Congress Catalogue Card Number: 57-7994

Second Printing, 1958

Printed in the United States of America

FOREWORD BY SIR HERBERT READ

Foreword

I AM not quite sure with what justification I, who am neither a psychologist nor an American, have accepted an invitation to write a foreword to this volume which is the intimate record of an American psychologist's 'search for man's sanity,' but possibly from the distant standpoint of Europe, and with what I trust is a poet's appreciation of human values, I can see the true stature of one whose greatness has been for a long time hidden from his compatriots. It was D. H. Lawrence's review of *The Social Basis of Consciousness* in *The Bookman* in 1927 which first drew my attention to Dr. Burrow's name and work, and from that time I was an attentive reader of all he published. By a happy coincidence, ten years after first hearing his name I was to become a director of the firm that was publishing his works in England, and from that time onwards I was in personal contact with a man for whom I had conceived an unlimited admiration.

I describe this admiration as 'unlimited,' but there was always with me, as with Lawrence and many others, the problem of Dr. Burrow's style. The hasty reader was apt to condemn it as impenetrable jargon, but I soon realized that it was a language with its own semantic rights—even a language with a beauty of its own. Nevertheless, I was insistent in my demands for a clarification—even for a vulgarization—of the important truths that it expressed. Dr. Burrow did make heroic efforts towards this end, and *The Neurosis of Man* was the result. But I did not feel, nor did the public at large, that the required transformation of his style had been effected.

It was with great interest, therefore, that I heard that a volume of Dr. Burrow's letters was to be published, for I knew that his epistolary style was a model of clarity and even rose to eloquence. Here might be the necessary intermediary between the public and the scientific works, for in addressing himself to a wide variety of personalities, Dr. Burrow had surely modified his scientific rigour and come out to meet our lay incapacities. I have not been disappointed. This book, by revealing the man, explains his work. Step by step we see his doubts of orthodoxy being formulated, his own hypotheses being developed and put to the test of experimental verification. I find the book very moving, both as the record of a scientific pioneer, and simply as a narrative of intellectual heroism.

Dr. Burrow began as a faithful pupil of Freud, and for twelve years practised Freudian analysis. For one important year he studied with Dr. Jung. But increasingly he became dissatisfied with the Freudian position (especially as maintained by Freud's followers), and Jung did not supply the key to the problem which, by 1923, had become uppermost in his mind. He always claimed that he had remained faithful to the principles that he had early learned from Freud, and he was obviously disappointed when Freud, far from appreciating the application of these principles to a new field ('the field of the behaviour of the organism as a whole'), misread and almost wilfully misinterpreted his endeavours. Freud subsequently admitted his misunderstanding, but ever jealous of any deviation from orthodoxy, he remained fundamentally indifferent to Dr. Burrow's extension of psychoanalysis to the social sphere. This indifference no doubt influenced the attitude of the scientific world in general. One word of approval or encouragement from Freud would have made an immense difference to the general acceptance and diffusion of Trigant Burrow's main thesis.

That thesis, in its main clause, is surely something very simple, very comprehensible, and overwhelmingly important. It points to the anciently recognized truth that man is not a detached particle of life, pursuing a separate orbit, but that we are part of one another. From that fact it follows that the analysis of the individual can never be completed without a consideration of the group of which he is an organic part. His very resistances to analysis are *social* resistances, and it is these social resistances, buried deep in the unconscious, that must be exposed. But just as personal resistances, which are the concern of orthodox analysis, cannot be successfully handled through mere discussion and theory but must be investigated by a special technique, so, Dr. Burrow maintained, the social resistances must be investigated by a special technique, and this could be only a group technique. The individual could not be separated from his social organism if the analysis was to bring to light unconscious social processes which are part of his social as distinct from his individual personality. Dr. Burrow therefore devised a technique of group analysis, and this was to be his distinctive contribution to the development of psychoanalysis and to the possible improvement of human behaviour in a corrupt world. The potential benefits of such a social therapy are so great that they deserve not only the attentive consideration of every responsible citizen of the world, but far more official attention than has yet been given to them.

It is not for me to comment on Trigant Burrow's theories—there is sufficient comment in the pages that follow. The writer of these letters was a man who could enter sympathetically into the viewpoint of his correspondents, and as a result he was impelled to explain his theories in a variety of ways, some of them perhaps deceptively simple. I particularly commend his letters to Sherwood Anderson, D. H. Lawrence and Leo Stein. There is a passage in one of the letters to Lawrence which seems to me to reveal very clearly the delicacy and understanding with which Dr. Burrow approached the mysteries of human experience. 'I do know what you mean, and I am heartily with you, I think, in your feeling about religion. But isn't it with religion as it is with love—love that cannot endure to hear its own name so much as whispered? "They put their finger on their lip, the powers above. They love but name not love."' In a letter to Anderson he speaks of 'the ugly tools with which I have had to work—the awkward scientific terminology inseparable from my narrow, laboratory training.' In these letters the ugly tools are set aside, and between the lines where the thought is nameless we submit to the communication of truths that are eternal.

Herbert Read

PREFACE BY THE EDITORS

Preface

WE are too close both in time and association to attempt a definitive appraisal of Trigant Burrow. It must remain for the future to evaluate the importance of the role he played in bringing about an altered frame of reference in respect to the pressing problem of human conflict. Without reservation, however, we may say that the problem engaged his interest whole-heartedly and that he devoted to it a lifetime of thought and research. The need of new insight in regard to human behavior was not for him a detached or theoretical problem. It was inseparable from his daily life and activities.

The present volume consists for the most part of letters selected from Dr. Burrow's correspondence which we feel should be regarded as an important part of his writings. They present the feeling and the thinking of a man who became embroiled in the stress of a day-by-day analysis of normal interrelational behavior. Even his most casual notes sprang from a deeply rooted feeling for human contacts in every walk of life, and they give revealing intimations of his approach to man's problem. Many people have remarked on the striking grace and simplicity of Dr. Burrow's letters as compared with his more formal writings, and this leads us to feel that his correspondence may appeal to those who have looked upon his books and monographs as a too formidable assignment. The late Professor Herbert E. Cory(1) once wrote Dr. Burrow:

From the first letter I ever received from you—I think at Berkeley—to this last I have always been deeply impressed by their natural poetry, a poetry that is far more poetic than one finds anywhere except in the most distinguished poems. I hope that all your friends will treasure an abundance of them. They stand in most interesting contrast to your scientific monographs. Not that these latter should be any different. They are quite admirable of their kind, just what they should be. . . . By all means go on with those. But I hope that some day the sort of thing you do in your letters will emerge in a sustained volume, some sort of simple, meditative record of yourself, your community, and your more geographically distant friends who, assuredly, will always remain, in their wayward fashion, members of that same 'beloved community.'

It is, of course, only arbitrarily that one may separate a life into different periods. The periods interweave and interrelate in a way that makes all such divisions artificial. For example, Trigant Burrow's continued interest in the process of attention can be traced throughout his days. The relation of attention to the problem of behavior remained focal with him from the time of his Ph.D. dissertation (1909) to that of his last paper (1950), though there were many significant developments in his views regarding the attentive process.

While realizing the intimate interrelatedness of the various phases, we may say, nevertheless, that Dr. Burrow's life and work showed four major emphases. The first phase, ending with his thirty-fourth year (1909), was characterized by his search for a métier. It was not until he was working for his doctorate in psychology that the spark was ignited that led to his decision to devote his life to advancing the new understanding of behavior and its disorders developing through psychoanalysis.

The second phase of Dr. Burrow's life (1909–23) began with his

(1) Professor of Liberal Arts at the University of Washington.

studies with Carl G. Jung in Zürich. During the next ten years he built up a large private practice, took an active role in founding the American Psychoanalytic Association, and made original contributions in this field. He formally initiated his group-analytic studies in 1923.

The third period (1923–32) was marked by the development of and researches in group- or phylo-analysis. The conceptual stirrings leading to this period go back for several years. Dr. Burrow had for some time been dissatisfied with the emphasis which psychoanalysis placed upon an individualistic assessment of human behavior. Disorders in behavior were for him essentially social or interrelational, and demanded observation and study in their dynamic group setting. This viewpoint was given pragmatic meaning in the association and mutual analysis entered into by Dr. Burrow and his student associate, Clarence Shields, out of which grew a research method for analyzing behavior in a group or social setting.

The fourth period (1932–50) cannot be sharply differentiated from the third. Studies and modifications in the technique of group-analysis continued, but interest now was centered more definitely upon the internal physiological changes accompanying external behavior. Instrumental studies were also undertaken of respiration, brain-wave patterns, and eye-movements and their relationship to behavior phenomena.

Most of the letters in this volume relate to the third and fourth periods. From the first phase only a few letters to his wife and young son are included—illuminating vignettes from another, more sentimental age. The second period is represented by the distinctive series of letters written to his mother during the year of study with Jung. Unfortunately little else is preserved from these early days, but beginning with the year 1922 there is a wealth of material. From this point on it is easy to follow, through his correspondence, the significant events and developments of Trigant Burrow's life and studies. As his interest becomes more and more deeply involved in group-analysis, his letters reflect the unceasing effort entailed in his laboratory approach to everyday living; the lack of articulation with his colleagues; the domestic and financial problems of a man forced by the terms of his research to question even the closest human relationships; the gradual easing of his associations as he begins to relate emotional problems and social conflict to internal patterns of tension; his growing competence in setting aside the 'normal' pattern of wishful thinking in favor of an orientation that encompasses man's native solidarity of feeling; his final envisagement of the future of a science of man's behavior.

The letters are arranged chronologically in fifteen chapters. The biographical text which introduces each chapter or is incorporated in it is intended merely to orient the reader in respect to happenings not covered in the letters. Much of this biographical material is in Dr. Burrow's own words—from his published writings or elsewhere—and wherever possible the editors have left it to the letters themselves to tell the story of his days. Deletions are indicated, and for the most part have been made to avoid repetition.

In the course of his investigations it devolved upon Dr. Burrow to make a thoroughgoing study of 'normal' interrelations. As a result, he was called upon to shatter many cherished prepossessions regarding human behavior, and to make some of the most unwelcome statements of our time. Those who were not acquainted with him may conceive of Dr. Burrow as wholly different from what he actually was. Unusually sensitive to the moods of those about him, he was in constant contact with their concerns and experiences. He seemed always willing to set aside his interests of the moment and enter fully into those of his companion. Indeed, he made them his own, and took hold with enthusiasm upon the project or problem presented to him. With his sympathetic understanding he combined an abounding sense of humor. His relationships show a marked continuity over the years. In a world plagued with divorce at every level—domestic, industrial and international—his professional and family associations remained steadfast in spite of differences that appeared at times to rock them to their foundations.

Through his prodigious correspondence—only a small part is reproduced in this volume—he kept in touch with literally scores of people, some who would seem to most of us mere casual contacts: friends and associates of his children, chance traveling acquaintances, a young gardener who had worked on the grounds of his home in Westport and to whom he wrote regularly during the young man's four years as an R.C.A.F. pilot. He was always more interested in an individual's capacities than in his shortcomings. For though Dr. Burrow constantly stressed the divisiveness and antagonism of 'normal' man, such observations were made against the background of his feeling for the fundamental health and integration of the human species. This feeling brought him close to his kind, and made it possible for him to sweep away many of the artificial barriers which separate men, and to implement his sense of affiliation with his fellow man.

A keynote to Trigant Burrow's life was communication. He kept in touch, whether by telephone, by letter, by book, or by paper. He wrote frequently whenever separated from the circle that formed an intimate part of his life and days. His many papers read at psychoanalytic, psychiatric, psychological, and sociological meetings were primarily motivated by the urge and obligation he felt to communicate his concepts and findings to his colleagues.

In his group investigations Dr. Burrow was consistently concerned with defining the underlying impediments to man's co-ordination. He says,

... the communication requiring adjustment lies at a deeper level than the customary affect-reactions involved in mental and verbal forms of interchange. It lies deeper than the mere exchange of ideas and affects through the symbol of language. It is this deeper level of communication and contact that phylobiology specifically envisages. For this level embodies the articulation and continuity basically uniting the organisms of the species as these organisms are merged in their common interaction with the environment. (2)

In view of his natural ease of communication it may seem paradoxical that Trigant Burrow's writings have so often been criticized as obscure and difficult of comprehension. Perhaps his own words about the writing of *The Neurosis of Man* will be enlightening.

. . . It should be as distinguished in form as it is distinctive in substance. But to be daily embroiled in the devastating task of recognizing one's own part in an ugly, crippling community defection, and at the same time put into beautiful, balanced form one's scientific formulation of this disfiguring behaviour-process—one's own and everybody else's—is truly no light undertaking. It is all very well for the 'artist' to skip lightly over the most inartistic, the most crudely naïve and unconscious expressions of his organism's relation to the environment, and yet compose exquisite nocturnes, paint lovely landscapes, or write line after line of melodious words in graceful cadence. But the task—the internal task of phylobiology in which composition and composer are its inseparable materials, its indispensable media, calls for the artist of far broader perspective, as well as a far deeper sensitivity to life's basic values. Am I equal to this task? Hardly. But however awkward or fumbling the effort, there is no choice. . . . (3)

Consistently aware of the general social trend to carelessness and inattention, Dr. Burrow took pains to counteract its effects both in himself and in those about him. He was meticulous, for instance, in regard to everything he wrote—papers, books, business letters, general correspondence. He was rarely satisfied with any piece of writing until he had worked it over a number of times. Keenly sensitive

(2) *Science and Man's Behavior—The Contribution of Phylobiology*, edited by William E. Galt, Ph.D. and containing the full text of *The Neurosis of Man*, New York, Philosophical Library, 1953, p. 424.

(3) *The Neurosis of Man—An Introduction to a Science of Human Behavior*, London, Routledge and Kegan Paul; New York, Harcourt, Brace, 1950, pp. xv-xvi.

to words and their delicate shades of meaning, no expenditure of time or effort was too great to find the right term or the apt phrase. Manuscripts were thoroughly checked before being submitted for publication, and on more than one occasion the workmanship of his productions brought grateful comment from editors and publishers. Yet in spite of the care he insisted upon, Dr. Burrow was never bogged down in a welter of detail but kept the task at hand moving along. 'There is no tomorrow' was a favorite axiom with him.

He was thoughtful in matters of health and physical welfare, not only for himself but for others as well. He did not smoke, and was completely uninterested in the use of alcohol. Throughout his life he looked characteristically younger than his age. As he passed the Biblical threescore years and ten his mind was keen and resilient, and his feelings and interests ever broadening in scope. Although keeping closely in touch with national and international developments and aware of their tremendous significance, he did not take part in political activities. For him these were alien to his scientific interests. They represented conflict between one part or faction and another, whereas he was concerned with identifying the elements responsible for partition and factionalism throughout mankind.

All through his life he was interested in music, poetry, the dance, and the theater. Some of his friends and correspondents felt that by nature he was as fully the artist as the scientist. In any event he was attempting to bring about a unification within man of the feeling of the artist and the knowledge of the scientist. In the last sentence of his last paper he says: 'There must come about somehow, and quickly, the understanding of man and his behavior. This is the great science, as it is the great art, that awaits the recognition of man in this hour of his acutest crisis—the science and the art of human behavior.'(4)

The task of selecting the letters and preparing the biographical

(4) 'Prescription for Peace' in *Explorations in Altruistic Love and Behavior: A Symposium,* edited by Pitirim A. Sorokin, Boston, The Beacon Press, 1950 pp. 93–117.

notes for this book has been carried out by the Editorial Committee of
The Lifwynn Foundation. This committee has consisted of William
E. Galt, Ph.D., Hans Syz, M.D., and Charles B. Thompson, M.D. of
the Scientific Staff; and Alfreda S. Galt, Aimée Guggenheimer, and
Alfreda P. Sill. As chairman of the committee, Dr. Galt carried the
major portion of the editing, and his untimely death in February 1955
was an immeasurable loss to this undertaking as to the entire program
of The Lifwynn Foundation. The editors wish to acknowledge the
assistance of Flora A. Guggenheimer who, before her death in 1952,
took an effective part in the original screening of Dr. Burrow's voluminous correspondence. The vital interest of the late Clarence Shields
in the inception of this project gave impetus to its development.

We are grateful to Kevin Wallace for reading the book in manuscript and for his helpful suggestions; to Charles K. O'Neill for his
constructive counsel in connection with placing the manuscript; and
to Mrs. Florence A. Weingartner whose sympathetic interest made
her secretarial assistance especially valuable. We wish to thank also
the many friends and relatives of Dr. Burrow who kindly made his
letters available or sent their recollections of his early life, particularly the Reverend Terence J. Boyle, S. J., Miss Elizabeth Dickson, Mrs.
George A. Gunther (formerly Mrs. John D. Burrow), the late Dr.
David R. Lyman, Mrs. Adolf Meyer, the late Mrs. Frank Nash, Mrs.
Francis Pope, the late Dr. George M. Stratton, Miss Rosalie Thornton,
Miss Virginia Watson, and Dr. Cornelius C. Wholey. Especially must
we acknowledge our debt to the late Mrs. Trigant Burrow for her
unfailing interest and help in the early phases of this project; to the
late John D. Burrow who, while still a boy, recognized the significance
of his father's letters and was the first to urge their publication; and
to Mrs. Emily Burrow Syz who worked with us on many aspects of
the volume and whose sensitive feeling contributed greatly to it.

We who have had the privilege of compiling this book have found
it a stimulating and rewarding assignment. It was the good fortune of

each of us to enjoy a close association with Trigant Burrow during his lifetime. The opportunity to renew contact, through his letters, with his broad human feeling and scientific integrity has been a significant and valued experience for us all.

The Editors

The Lifwynn Foundation
Westport, Connecticut
March, 1958

Contents

A SEARCH FOR MAN'S SANITY

CHAPTER 1

YOUTH AND MARRIAGE

The earliest of Trigant Burrow's letters available are the first he wrote to Emily Sherwood Bryan, the girl who later became his wife. At the time of their meeting he was twenty-seven years old. Having completed his formal medical training, he was sharing a home in Baltimore with Dr. Cornelius C. Wholey, a former classmate at the University of Virginia. They were pursuing postgraduate work at The Johns Hopkins Medical School, and Miss Bryan was a student nurse at the Hospital.

Baltimore, Maryland
December 30, 1902

Dear Miss Bryan:

Can you, Miss Metcalf, Miss Higginson (whom Dr. Wholey met) and your brother come over Saturday evening? We want you to come ever so much only *you* must and will, I know, explain to your friends that we've no amusements to offer as inducements such as cozy-corners and pianos such as you grand people have, but that we'll try to be ever so good and interesting ourselves if you'll just come.

Now do come along, and drive a bit of the sombre bachelorness out of our life for just one evening in the week.

And with our greetings and best wishes for the New Year,

I am very sincerely yours,

Trigant Burrow

Baltimore, Maryland
[Undated]

My dear Miss Bryan:

You just don't know how I hate to deny myself the delight of another such walk as that last. And today would be fine for it too. But alas, that everlasting 'paper' of mine is scheduled for this afternoon at the Journal Club, which is held from three to five o'clock, so I have to disappoint myself.

I should enjoy that walk more than anything I know, and this stupid paper less than anything I know, so that I think I'm right heroic not to cut the whole meeting and go gallivanting across-country with you as I want to do. I'm in a truant mood today anyhow. However I shall certainly be over at eight Saturday evening, and I hope we can arrange a 'tramp' then.

If a kind Fate should cancel the meeting of the afternoon's Journal Club (tho' I'm not counting upon any such lucky stroke of hers) I shall come tearing over to the Hospital to claim that walk.

Should anything occur tomorrow evening—lecture or anything and you would not want to miss it, remember that I know you are a trained nurse and that you are privileged to break an engagement whenever it suits you—provided of course it isn't for a moonlight stroll with another man.

Hoping to see you then tomorrow evening,

Very sincerely,

Trigant Burrow

The next spring Miss Bryan returned to her home in Cambridge, Maryland, for a visit with her parents and her eight older brothers and sisters.

Baltimore, Maryland
June 19, 1903, Saturday noon

This day matches my mood so well I almost flatter myself it was
designed especially for me, it is so grey and sombre-hued. You
are just having a grand time by now, aren't you. They've gotten
you back for a while and are fairly gloating over you of course,
happy in their rich possession if it is only a *loan*.

The whole morning I've been trying to write and finally have put
by the task as quite hopeless. It is all so mechanical and dry. The
incentive is too remote and altogether I'm convinced I'm a useless
old thing anyhow. What inspiration ever yet came on an invitation! It is futile to sit and wait its coming. To seat oneself at a
desk and bid oneself *write* is about as stimulating as to betake
oneself to a 'tea' and command one's self to *speak*. Besides the
habit of my mind has been cumulative all these years. It has been
receiving the ideas of others and now to produce something requires reversing the engines completely. All which irrelevant
theories must be intensely interesting to you. Have to fuss tho',
can't help it. You may as well accept the role of victim gracefully
and be patient.

Have you ever read Ibsen's play, 'The Doll's House'? It is a very
subtle work of art and I think, as I recall it, that there is a right
wholesome lesson in it. Anyhow a lack of frankness and understanding between two people leads to a right tragic crisis. See the
drift? You and I must be candid and not refuse to face anything
that helps toward an honest understanding of each other. As it
stands you are quite muddled as to my spiritual feelings, and
haven't a bit good opinion of me in that relation. And I so much
want your opinion of me to do me justice and not seize upon
conclusions that aren't quite fair to me. Perhaps from *your* standpoint, when I have cleared up my position for you, as best I may,
you will even think less well of me *spiritually* than you do now,

but even *that* were better than a wrong opinion of me. So I mean
to be at any cost perfectly frank with you. On questions as fundamental as that we must be honest with ourselves. This isn't
meant to be grandfatherly, however much so it sounds. If you
just wouldn't think me posing as eighteenish. *I'm not.* I hate it
more than anything I know. I don't mean to say for an instant
that I'm not eighteen in very many respects. I know that I am,
and I'm glad of it. One's teens give life a flavor all its own. But it
is the posing I dislike. Of course I do pose some for the world.
I think everybody does. A man can't take the world into his confidence. But I don't pose for *you*. *You* may have all my secrets if
they are worth while enough to you. Now is that posing? I think
it's right generous. Why won't you be as much so and say you
didn't really mean it—that you just hadn't any grass to pull and so
just attacked me instead? Goodbye. Have a *good* RESTFUL time.

As always,

Trigant Burrow

The letter to follow was written nearly a year later, and it is obvious
that in the intervening months their mutual affection had deepened.

New York City
February 4, 1904
Thursday morning at ten thirty

Listen to me my dear little girl. Remain at home. Forget the
remoter duty of your hospital training, however great that claim
may be upon you, and give yourself completely to the immediate
duty of home where your real heart is.

If you've gone already, your father having changed decidedly for the better, or if for the same reason, you have conclusively determined upon going, don't let this letter of mine come in to perplex you. It is all right. You've acted for the very best. But if it isn't presuming of me to try to make your duty clearer—to try to make plainer to you the way it lies, let me urge you to remain at your father's side. The duty at the hospital is very secondary to the duty at home. This is a more sacred thing, it is a part of you. Something essential—something primary and so, paramount to all else. I am not underrating the duty of the brave, self-sacrificing work you've undertaken, it's all fine and splendid and immensely important and one of the biggest things in your life—*the* biggest thing until this moment—when an immediate, critical need summons you away from it. The outline of your duty is probably obscured by the thought that because it is harder to leave home, therefore it is braver and better that you should go.—Not always, my darling. It is a very natural confusion—the difficult thing is usually the test, but not always. Sometimes the duty lies where the heart lies, and you mustn't allow reason to be confounded by it when it is so.

Of course the whole picture of conflicting feelings with all the varying circumstances that enter in and color it, isn't instantly plain to me in one swift glance as it is to you. I view the thing at a great distance and so miss much of the detail. You must allow for that and not let my opinion (if I can call it such) cloud your better judgment. I simply want to save you acting from some half-measured sentiment—I want you to make very sure that this feeling of haste and impatience to accomplish your hospital training is not rather a prejudice—a sort of vague indefinite *bias*, prompted more by nervousness and impulse, than by a solid, rounded, careful process of reasoning.

I think I know so much, don't I, where in reality I probably know nothing about it. Well, I shall be quiet now, or talk of something where the data warrant my talking—as of the play we're setting in motion.

The Lenox Library did not supply the demand—we wanted some modern plays, so I shall meet Miss Laura(1) today at 3 o'clock at the Astor Library. We are at a loss for plot or plan, and I fear it will be a long time before the actual writing is begun.

According to the program we heard Tristan and Isolde last night. It was very grand and beautiful, but somehow I was not nearly in so receptive or appreciative a mood as when in Germany. America is no place for music. How can a lot of nervous, fretted, enterprising, money-hunting people get, in a few hours, into the spirit of a soul-searching Wagnerian *motif*. It is impossible. I shall wait till *we* are in Germany, glad of living, glad of the days, glad of all and everything and so in the spirit of music and art and charm of every human kind.

Don't be fretted, dear, by my officiousness—that's my impudence but you know best.

With dear love,

your Trigant

In the spring of 1904 Miss Bryan completed her hospital training and returned home. Dr. Burrow, who was ill in Baltimore at the time, wrote her mother shortly afterwards, saying in part:

I am afraid it seems to you a hard thing, Mrs. Bryan, that I should come to you just now when the long coveted hope of having your daughter home with you once more has been at last fulfilled, and should ask that you let me take her from you again, that for the future you give her life and her happiness into my keeping. But I want to feel you will try to think of it a little differently because of my earnest wish that you let us include you too in our happiness now and always, that you will not think of it as something apart from you, but rather as something which must be really your own, if our gladness is to be complete.

(1) Laura Spencer Portor (Mrs. Francis Pope), an essayist and life-long friend of Dr. Burrow's, who was assisting him on plans for a play.

Miss Emily will have told you something of our plans—the little while abroad and ultimately life in the country, a thing I have always wanted and which has been at last conceded me, now that the strain of study has, for the present, interrupted my work. My immediate thought now is to get well and I am sure I shall be quite myself again in a short time.

Miss Bryan and Dr. Burrow were married at her home on August 9, 1904. The ceremony was performed by her father, James Lawrenson Bryan, who was not only a physician and educator but also an Episcopalian clergyman. Dr. Burrow's mother, Anastasia Devereux Burrow, was a devout Roman Catholic, and out of respect for her feeling the Episcopal service was followed by that of the Catholic Church. Immediately afterwards the bridal couple set sail for several months of travel abroad.

The young Mrs. Burrow was an unusually attractive girl with large brown eyes and a wealth of chestnut hair. A gay and popular member of her social group, she was thoroughly in earnest when it came to her work. Her interest in nursing had developed as she accompanied her father on his medical rounds—an interest intense enough to outweigh the prejudice of those days against nursing as 'an occupation for ladies.' As a result of her childhood on the shore of Chesapeake Bay, she was an experienced sailor, but her outstanding accomplishment in the field of sports was as a horsewoman. In later years Dr. Burrow enjoyed telling of the contest at the Maryland Hunt Club in which she was one of two women entered in a field of twenty-three. To the consternation of all she won the first prize—a silver flask filled with bourbon!

Dr. Burrow shared her love of this sport, having learned to ride at an early age. Later during youthful summers at White Sulphur Springs he became an expert horseman. Indeed his enjoyment of riding, tennis and dancing was to continue throughout his life, and his performance was always marked by an easy grace born of conscious discipline and respect for the techniques involved.

* * *

Trigant was born in Norfolk on September 7, 1875, the youngest of four children. His mother, a woman of no little determination, defied her doctor's orders and, under the covers, scribbled the following note to a girlhood friend:

Dear Sophie:

Will you with yr. husband stand God-parents for my little boy, born this morning? Answer by return mail. I have them baptized always in eleven days. Will provide proxy here. Pray for yrs. with love.

Anastasia Burrow

107 Wolt St.
Norfolk, Va.

P. S. Select for me a pretty & uncommon name.(2)

Trigant's older brothers were Devereux and Alan Giles. He was especially devoted to his only sister, Inez, eldest of the four, and her death from tuberculosis during his twelfth year was the first great sorrow of his life. In view of his later studies and the observation they entailed of his own subjective reactions, it is interesting that he noted even at this early age something of the nature of grief. For the sure knowledge that his pain would pass was, as he reported in after years, the most agonizing element in this boyhood bereavement.

Dr. Burrow's mother was a woman of culture and keen intelligence coupled, as has been indicated, with an indomitable will. Though known for her dry wit, she was subject also to moods of silent withdrawal when her cold remoteness could chill the stoutest heart. Her passionate devotion to the Catholic faith was a guiding force in her life. Mrs. Burrow appears to have taken a more active part in the rearing of the children than did her husband. Certainly, she occupied the more dominant role in the case of her youngest son.

In marked contrast were the interests of her husband, John W. Burrow, a wholesale druggist widely read in scientific fields. In that period

(2) The name selected was so uncommon that it was frequently mispronounced. Being French, it is pronounced Trē-gañt. The surname, incidentally, is accented on the second syllable.

of hand-prepared drugs the practice of pharmacy demanded a high degree of technical skill and knowledge. 'Dr.' Burrow was not infrequently called into consultation by physicians for guidance in choosing medication for their patients. This participation in the world of medicine undoubtedly strengthened his own natural interest in science. It is significant that Mr. Burrow was said to be the first man in Norfolk to own the works of Darwin.

A Protestant by birth, Mr. Burrow did not subscribe to narrow, conventionalized beliefs, and many people considered him an agnostic. His broad interests and his sensitivity to the trend of scientific progress exerted a powerful influence on Trigant. This influence may account in part for the fact that early in college days at orthodox Fordham University, the young student found that the dogmas of the Catholic Church began to lose their significance for him. His interest tending increasingly toward the field of science, he began to question the basis of what is called spiritual belief. As letters in this volume indicate, he never held an attitude of disdain or cynicism toward organized religion. His respect for religious insights was sincere but he looked upon them as representing merely a symbolic attempt on the part of man to reach a more co-ordinated type of experience and behavior. As he wrote long afterward, 'What is needed in this disordered world is living in and by the principle of unity that abides alone in the prevailing order and consistency of the surrounding universe.(3) In his mature years he threw himself with passionate conviction into the task of demonstrating as a biological reality the essential harmony between man and man, and between man and his environment. But during his years at college he felt only that religious tenets lacked essential meaning for him.

Despite the pain and disappointment this break with her religion must have caused his mother, she did not permit it to mar the devotion between herself and her son. She entered fully into his interests, stood by him during the years of his professional training, and encouraged him in his long search for his life's work.

Anastasia's relationship with her husband was quite different. A painful rift developed between them, and as the boy grew into adolescence, the conflict became more pronounced. Although for the sake of appearance the family continued to live under one roof, the breach

(3) *Science and Man's Behavior*, p. 162.

was never healed. Trigant was thus poignantly confronted at an early age with the problem of human conflict—a problem that was to become for him the subject of lifelong study.

Trigant grew up in Norfolk where, in spite of the rigid code of social manners in the last quarter of the nineteenth century, there was for children little of the physical restriction now necessary in our car-infested streets. He and his companions wandered freely through the nearby meadows, and in the long summer evenings played the interminable games of childhood. By his own accounts and those of his contemporaries he was a roguish and mischievous child, and his mother must often have been hard pressed by the pranks he described in later years with great humor.

An excellent student, the boy received his early education in local private schools, and at the age of thirteen he was sent—perhaps because of the marital discord at home—to St. Francis Xavier Academy in New York. His mother, however, spent much time in that city, and his father would frequently stay at a neighboring hotel where he and the boy would lunch together and afterward explore the wonders of New York.

In describing Dr. Burrow as a youth, a friend, Elizabeth Dickson, wrote of him: 'I don't know anyone who was more entertaining to me than Trigant! He was so witty and original and kept us "in stitches" all the time I was with him.' It was at the Dickson home in White Sulphur Springs that the Burrow family spent their summers, and Miss Dickson says of the days there: 'He was very fond of horseback riding and we had many delightful rides together. Then we used to have many drives in "top buggy days"—and Trigant was always *most* entertaining. In the evenings we nearly always danced the Virginia reel—and such fun as we had!'

In 1890 young Burrow entered Fordham where his older brother, Alan, had already been studying for two years. He pursued the Classical Course and on his graduation at the age of nineteen received awards of distinction in Latin Verse, English Verse, and History. Years later a classmate, Reverend Terence J. Boyle, S. J., wrote of him:

When Trig came to Fordham we were impressed by his talent and accomplishment and by his imperturbable refinement which was so characteristic of the old time southern gentleman. He had a very good singing voice and was one of our outstanding singers in those days. He was up among the leaders in his studies throughout his college course.

In connection with his musical capacities it is interesting that Burrow had that rare endowment, perfect pitch. He had been a boy soprano in his mother's church in Norfolk and his singing figures in the earliest description we have of him. His cousin Mrs. Frank Nash writes:

The only thing I recall about his childhood was his wonderful voice. My very earliest recollection of him was of his rocking away in his shoo-fly horses and singing at the top of his voice. I suppose he was about three years then.

Another of Dr. Burrow's continuing interests was the drama. There is the letter to his fiancée written in 1904 in which he referred to his plan to collaborate on a play with Laura Spencer Portor. Although he completed only one such manuscript—early in his psychoanalytic practice—there was never a time when he did not have the makings of a play in mind. His technical writings always crowded this project out, but later letters show that the theater held a perennial fascination for him. A high point of his college life was the evening when fellow-students, enthusiastic over his performance as young Arthur in *King John*, carried him around the campus on their shoulders.

Following his graduation from Fordham in 1895, Trigant spent a year in Norfolk pursuing pre-medical studies. This arrangement was probably made because of the precarious state of his father's health which began to fail about this time. Mr. Burrow died in October of the following year and that same fall his son entered the Medical School of the University of Virginia.

'Could anything be lovelier than the University of Virginia and at this season of the year!' he wrote to a friend one autumn years later. 'There were, of course, the basic buildings when I was there—the Rotunda, the lovely "Lawn" with its colonnades, and the East and West Range. But we were a very primitive institution of learning, with the dusty Albemarle roads and the coteries of winsome, lackadaisical colored boys ever within call to bring up one's horse of an afternoon. It was rare that I did not ride out into the surrounding hills during the lovely autumn and spring days.

'My room was on West Range and was, I think, number 45 or 47. It was just at the end of one of the units, with a lane between it and the southernmost one. I used to take my meals at Professor Thornton's charming home. It was formerly the home of President Monroe and tops Monroe Hill. But the lovely old trees and the charming wisteria vine that covered the front of the house are no more. It seemed distressingly barren when I passed through the University some years ago.

Burrow's days in that gracious environment were quiet and studious. With his warm human feeling and radiant good humor he was naturally well liked, although, as one of his classmates put it, 'he had no time for our devilment.' Professor Thornton's daughter, Rosalie, recalls him as 'a most stimulating companion,' and adds:

Naturally I saw a good deal of him and we became good friends. He taught me to ride, sitting a side-saddle, the only way a woman should sit a horse, so he thought.

Another taste we had in common was music. He was very musical and loved to accompany himself at the piano and sing the sentimental songs of that day. He had a wonderfully keen sense of humor and always had an apt story for every occasion.

He was a most devoted son. He and his mother exchanged daily messages, I think, throughout his whole stay at the University.

At the opening of the first semester he met Cornelius C. Wholey with whom he later roomed. Young Wholey had serious trouble with his eyes, and always said that without Burrow's help he could not have earned his medical degree. For hours his friend read to him from medical texts, cheerfully relinquishing many social engagements. They achieved high standing in their studies and following graduation both were asked to return to the University to serve as demonstrators in biology. The next year, 1900, was spent in Europe. In Munich they served for a short time as assistant physicians in obstetrics at the University Frauenklinik. Moving on to Vienna, they continued their training at the Allgemeine Krankenhaus. It was here that their interest in psychiatry was first aroused through courses with Wagner von Jauregg and Krafft-Ebing. After visiting important medical centers in Berlin, the young men spent the remainder of the year bicycling through the British Isles, and visiting France and Italy.

On their return to America they settled in Baltimore where, with his father's help, Wholey bought a small house and began the practice of medicine. Meanwhile he and Burrow took postgraduate courses at The Johns Hopkins Medical School—bacteriology under Welch and pathology under MacCallum—made rounds with Osler, and worked in the neurological dispensary under Henry M. Thomas. In addition, Dr. Burrow was studying English literature in the academic department of the University. He was still seeking an absorbing interest. A general medical practice did not appeal to him, nor did he feel a dynamic urge to become a specialist in any of the established fields. As Hazlitt puts it, he needed 'a casting motive to incline the scale,' and several years were to pass before he saw a clear path ahead. It was at this juncture of his life that during a dance at the medical school he noticed an animated group of young men in a corner of the room. Curious to discover the center of attraction, he joined them and found it to be the charming student nurse, Emily Bryan, to whom the first letter in this volume is addressed.

CHAPTER 2

PSYCHOLOGICAL STUDIES

In *The Neurosis of Man*, Burrow describes the moment in which the dominant interest of his life took form.

One morning years ago at a session of the philosophical seminar at Johns Hopkins, Professor James Mark Baldwin was speaking of the field of mental disorders, and I recall his mentioning the names of Charcot, Janet, Forel and other prominent European psychiatrists. But he said that none of them had as yet 'ignited the spark' requisite to bring about an understanding of the basic cause of mental disease. This interested me, and I remember that I then and there recorded the pledge to devote my life's work to the effort to contribute what I could towards igniting this spark necessary to throw light on the nature of abnormal mental conditions. I had just enrolled for my doctor's degree in experimental psychology and I straightway decided that my doctoral thesis would deal with a problem in the field of attention.(1)

At this time the first laboratories of experimental psychology were being established in the United States, largely by men who had studied with Wundt in Leipzig. 'Attention' was a focal point of interest of the new science both because of the emphasis on this topic in Wundt's laboratory and because it was the first of the 'higher mental processes' to be subjected to experimental study. Dr. Burrow's interest in the subject was to continue throughout his life and culminate in a new orientation in respect to the process of attention.

His first study in this field was undertaken in 1906 when he began working for his doctorate in psychology at The Johns Hopkins University under Dr. George M. Stratton. In addition he served as Assistant in the Department of Psychology. Dr. Stratton gives his impression of the young man during this period.

Trigant Burrow is the central figure in memory of my students at The Johns Hopkins University in the first decade of our century.

(1) *The Neurosis of Man*, p. 78. See note 2, p. xviii and note 1, p. ii.

The young man was eager to learn the ways of a psychological laboratory and gave himself to a problem agreed upon in consultation with him as to his own leanings. It required of him a re-examination by repeated experiments, under various carefully-controlled conditions, of Wundt's 'Complication-Versuch,' using the well-known apparatus of the Leipzig laboratory. This he carried through to findings that added to our scientific understanding of a puzzling phenomenon of attention.

But better than his experiments well done, was the young man himself, the rare person to whom I soon became strongly and enduringly attracted. He had then what I appreciated more and more from our later intercourse through many years, a quite careless nicety and strength, an unobtrusive independence enveloping and giving quality to what he thought and said. His whole mind and bearing revealed the benefits, the character of his human surroundings from childhood on—benefits which he made his own and to which he added from his creative powers.

On their return from their wedding trip, Dr. and Mrs. Burrow had lived for several months at the home of his mother in Norfolk, and it was here that their son, John Devereux, was born on May 11, 1905. During that summer Dr. Burrow went house-hunting in the environs of Baltimore. With today's prices in mind, the following letter to his wife reads like a dream.

Ellicott City, Maryland
July 18, 1905

Dear Brownie:

I have just written Devereux a postal to say I've a place in view, as he told Neil [Wholey] he'd like to go himself to Upper Falls upon his return to Baltimore. Now listen, dearie, but say *naught* outside. The house is shaded, large trees, porch across the front, another at side, (landlord will make the two continuous), water in the house, hot as well as cold, Latrobe [stoves] (two), interior arrangement difficult to excel for our needs, right *in* the country, but acceptable neighbors upon all sides (none nearer than from your house to the boat-landing I should say), there is a spring, a dairy, a hennery, an elegant stable, house as far from road (Macadamized) as from your house to Lucia's, and this road an excellent one. Infinite closets in the house, which cancels the necessity of wardrobes. A bath. I think the landlord would put in adjunct conveniences if requested. Oh yes, a hog-pen too, and a cool, 'accessible' cellar, dandy for storing food. ... All the rooms impress you as bright, and the house is *dry*. Former tenants hated to leave. Mr. Reynolds eager to have us neighbors. *Another* big consideration—the landlord is a nice, honest, old country man, whom Mr. R. knows well. He confided to Mr. Reynolds that he liked me and wanted me for a tenant.

PRICE—$15.00 per month

What think you, dearie. Have I not some discernment? Another thing—it will appeal to you but *don't say I said it*—my heart, as well as head, desires this place. *I know you'd like it.*

Think I'll leave here Thursday evening for Cambridge. Since lunch Neil and I have been out here in the shade, high up above the valley, enjoying the breeze. Neil reading while I write.

Oh! The place is 50 acres, but we can take only sufficient for a garden or as much as we like. There is every desire to accommodate us. I am delighted.

I must let this go now to catch the mail.

Dear love for Brownie and the Boy. Delighted at his gain—a half pound!

Love to Mother. So glad she is with your mother. Read her what I've written, relating to the house.

Bye bye. Nap, nap, nap; don't forget your nap!

And the oatmeal water! Try to bring yourself to give it to the lad twice a day. Just determine to do this, howsoever difficult. Bring your *will* to bear.

Love to all,

Trigant

Needless to say, Mrs. Burrow yielded to her husband's enthusiastic description of the house at Upper Falls which they occupied for several years. During that time Burrow was working closely with the keen experimental psychologist, Knight Dunlap. The following letter was written from Norfolk where Dr. Dunlap was a guest at the Burrow home.

Norfolk, Virginia
January 26, 1907, Saturday, midnight

My dearie:

. . . Constantly I keep in my mind—in my heart the thought that it is not long—just two days and we shall see each other again—when I shall return to you and to our darling boy.

I wrote you this morning just as we were leaving for Cape Henry—had a very successful day and a mighty strenuous one! Dr. Dunlap did so enjoy the oysters, then we came home again, brushed up and dressed for dinner. Miss Bessie, Miss Daisy and Dr. Hancock were here for dinner. Dr. Dunlap very soon ingratiated himself with them all. Mother was so delighted with him from the first. He thinks the house is lovely and constantly remarks upon some new beauty that greets his eye. After dinner we went to the theatre—Edeson in 'Strongheart'—it is *fine!* You'd *love* it. We walked home in the cold night air, sat and talked before the embers in the hall and now have come to bed—Dunlap in our room and I here.

We had *such* a bully lecture from Dr. Dunlap—everybody carried away with him! He's quite the sensation!

Mighty happy visit—something 'on' every minute.

Everybody inquires of *you*.

Till Tuesday morning then, and always,

Your devoted Trigant

Much happiness was brought to Dr. and Mrs. Burrow by the birth of a daughter, Emily Sherwood, on January 11, 1909, at which time they were living in Baltimore. Dr. Burrow's relationship with his children was always characterized by deep affection. In the early days, it was also marked by the type of sentimentality shown in the following letter to his four-year-old son.

University Club, Baltimore, Maryland
Sunday, April 25, 1909, 7.30 p.m.

My darling little Jack—

What wouldn't Father give in this moment to take his little boy on his knee and hug and kiss him and tell him about Pegasus, and the fun we are going to have next summer and *everything!*

Do you ask Mother sometimes for Father and wonder when he is coming to see you and Mother and Little Sister and Grandma and all? And are you a good little boy these days, making Mother happy and taking good care of her and of Little Sister?

As I write, it is your bed-time—the time Father used always get that sweet goodnight kiss, with Jack's little arms about his neck and I tell you Father misses it. If we were all home together now as in the winter time, Mother and Father would have said good-night to you and returned to the library for a quiet little talk together. Telling how happy we are, and how grateful, and all that we hope to do for our Jack and Little Emily.

I wish you'd tell Mother to be looking out for a place for us to go next summer near New York for we must all be together. Don't *you* say so? *I* say so!

Well goodnight, little boy! It is eight o'clock and Father must get back and to work. I thought of you this afternoon. Father went out to the park at 4 o'clock and walked till half past six. I had a *fine* walk! But I wished for my darling boy. Kiss Grandma and Mother and Little Sister for Father. Nighty night.

In June 1909, Dr. Burrow received his Ph.D. degree from Johns Hopkins and was elected to Phi Beta Kappa. That summer, having moved his family to a small house in Flushing, he began psychiatric work under Dr. Adolf Meyer at the New York State Psychiatric Institute on Ward's Island in New York City. It was while he was thus engaged that—betwen acts at one of New York's theaters—he was introduced by A. A. Brill to two physicians who were lecturing in this country at the time: Sigmund Freud and Carl G. Jung.

CHAPTER 3

THE YEAR WITH JUNG

The meeting at the theater marked the beginning of a significant and absorbing experience. For a few months later, encouraged by Adolf Meyer, Burrow was on his way to Zürich for a year of psychoanalytic study with Jung. What influenced his choice of Jung rather than of Freud is not known. Certainly Dr. Burrow's letters in later years show his prior allegiance to Freud. But we must not forget that in 1909 there had not yet occurred the rift between Freud and Jung. They stood for the same thing, and the choice did not carry the implications it would have later on.

At this time psychoanalysis was still in its infancy. While it had gained notable recognition abroad, it was as yet an untried field in the United States, virtually unknown to most medical men in this country. So that Dr. and Mrs. Burrow were confronted with a doubly formidable project. In addition to the doubtful contingencies of his taking up a new and controversial specialty, there was involved all the difficulty of a year of life abroad with two young children. Jack at this time was four and a half, and Emily an infant of nine months. The venture also entailed an expenditure quite beyond the Burrows' slender means. However, by selling some real estate inherited from his father, and adapting to the restrictions of a very limited budget, Dr. Burrow was able to take advantage of what seemed to him a golden opportunity. With keen anticipation he and his family sailed for Europe in September 1909.

Burrow was not disappointed. He found the contact with Jung stimulating and rewarding, and the warm friends that he and his wife soon made in the new environment contributed to the enjoyment of their stay in Zürich. He wrote regularly to his mother, describing something of his days, his interests, and his enthusiasm for his teacher. The following selections from these letters tell the story of this fruitful year.

Zürich, October 8, 1909

Dr. Jung is *my man*. I am delighted with him. Besides being a brilliant psychologist he is a most picturesque personality. I sat spell-bound during the entire conference, held in his esthetic study overlooking the beautiful Zürich Lake. Our next meeting was called for this afternoon at 5:00. Dr. Hoch and I met at the boat and went to Küsnacht together—a 20-minute boat ride. On our arrival Dr. Jung suggested that we take our talk out on the water. We were quick to agree to the suggestion and a moment later found us sailing across the lake while Jung descanted upon the psychology of the various psychoses. It was very interesting listening to this wonderful man relating with his characteristic ardor his theories and discoveries in the realm of his interest. It is good to know that I have done the right thing in coming over here, and I believe it is to be the year of my life. ... Dr. Jung this afternoon introduced me to his wife who also speaks English and he has invited us both to call. ... I had a postal from Dr. Baldwin.(1) They have taken an apartment in Paris for the winter and he wrote me asking me to let him know if he might be of service to me in any way here or elsewhere and expressing the wish that we meet at some place before we return to America.

October 19

And now what is all the time *uppermost! I am perfectly delighted with Jung.* Our journey to Zürich is more than vindicated! Now listen! You must have felt these many years of your loving hope for me, that there has been a talent, an interest, an aptitude—what you will—a tendency to penetrate into certain types of character,

(1) Professor James Mark Baldwin.

which however wide of the strictly medical concern, with its knife and stethoscope, has not been without signs of significance for the handling of suffering humanity. You must have felt how apart this strange keen interest has been from conventional medical standards. You must have felt my own pain and disappointment and embarrassment when at every turn, no matter what heart and enthusiasm I brought to each new direction of endeavor, I was ever confronted with the same old uninspiring, unimaginative mechanical physical tools and physical problems. 'Happy,' says Carlyle, 'is the man who has found his work!' How desolately I read and used desolately recall those words! For to my unspeakable misery I had all along *not* found my work. But a new day has dawned and I *have* found my work. With every word from Jung I realize the fellow-spirit behind them! At times it is as if it were I and not he who speaks, so identical is the process of reasoning with my own; and here is the man to whom Europe and America have stopped to listen! So you may judge the comfort and encouragement I hug to my heart at this revelation! And it is a comfort which we can share as one, for the way I have trod you have tread with me step by step and always the desolation of my heart in this unfound work of a life has reëchoed in your own and so it is good that we may stand together and hail the dawn of the new day! Judge of my happiness!

Among those who with me are sitting at the feet of this Swiss Seer is Dr. Hoch, who succeeds Dr. Meyer at Ward's Island when the latter enters upon his appointment at the Hopkins. Dr. Hoch and I have, to my flattering surprise and pleasure, really found in each other a sympathetic and congenial friend, and I count it another of the good things that have come to me in this experience that I have met him here. Dr. Hoch and another of the quartette of disciples go to Munich tomorrow for three weeks, and I shall be yet more closely associated with my learned preceptor. As uncertainly and fearfully as I have tread in these last years, it will come to you as a surprise that I feel with Jung not the *slightest* timidity, and that will make all the work with him so great a joy.

Zürich, October 27, 1909

We had our first misfortune the other day, which cost us $10.00—not so heavy a sum you will think in U.S. currency, but an enormous outlay in its Swiss equivalent of 50 frs! We were made awfully nervous over it and it meant to me *days* of unrelenting depression. The circumstance was we engaged board in another pension and then the day we were to move in we discovered that through a mistake of mine we had calculated the expense here (Pension Fortuna) wrongly—that it was 3 frcs. a day less than I had said, and so we greatly preferred to stay, it being so wholesome and comfortable for us all. The other landlady, though, insisted upon 50 frcs. damages, and everybody said it was too much and we contested and did all we could and finally were warned by our friends that she might take it to court and get even more and that as we were strangers in a strange land we had better pay it, which finally we did, and it was an awful wrench to give out $10.00 for *nothing*. It was very clear to me that my depression and general unfitness was out of all proportion to the *exciting* cause and that there was doubtless a predisposing cause lying deeper down. So I resolved to go to Jung and he said immediately that the trouble lay deeper and that he agreed with me and recommended treatment. So I am going to his office an hour each day, and hope to be greatly benefitted after his analysis and psychotherapy. He said as Dr. Barker(2) said that my own neurosis would be the greatest assistance to me in handling others, and he also said a thing that delighted and encouraged me very much—that he had early recognized in me a readiness to grasp his psychology, that my questions showed my aptitude for this method and teaching.

(2) Dr. Lewellys F. Barker, at that time Professor of Medicine, The Johns Hopkins University School of Medicine.

Zürich, November 21, 1909

Much time of course is actually spent with Dr. Jung, and then there is an enormous amount of reading to be done—all in German —and so I seem quite cramped for time. . . . Last night and this morning I attended with Dr. Jung, Hoch and others an important medical meeting. Saw and met many noted men, among others August Forel, who asked me to become a member of the newly chartered society of psychologists and psychotherapists and to push it forward in America.

December 11, 1909

This afternoon Dr. Jung and I went to a café together as we often do. We all went for a sail and Dr. Hoch and I left the boat and took dinner at a Swiss inn beside the lake and later walked home. You see my environment is very congenial and happy.

We hugely enjoyed the opera the other night—'Der fliegende Holländer'—the pretty accessories being not the least of my enjoyment—the preliminary dinner, the drive to the theatre in an up-to-date brougham with two men on the box, the velveted proscenium 'loge' and all the rest—I thoroughly liked it and shall not again find it in me to occupy my pitiful place in the gallery with the stoic resignation of old. Me for the smart appurtenances!

I had a very nice letter from Dr. Barker, saying he hoped I'd 'bring back to us many new things from Zürich and Vienna.' It was very friendly.

The children's splendid condition is an occasion of constant congratulation for us. Jack is so well and Emily well and very pretty and *so* good and sweet. Such a seraphic smile as she has!

The other morning Jack was in my bed during my accustomed morning bath—an ice cold baptism in an ice cold room. 'Lord,' he said, 'Grandma wouldn't stand that!' A view in which I heartily coincided.

You will see that I don't write letters any more. It is impossible. The work has become *all*—and I just can't get the leisure for a long, idle talk.

Next Christmas we shall surely all be together, and I long for the time. Write me all about Christmas at home—what presents you get, who came to see you, etc., etc.

Zürich, January 3, 1910

We climbed the Zürichberg (Zürich mountain), I hauling Jack on his sled and Brownie and Fräulein pushing Emily in the splendid little sled our friend Mrs. Field gave her. It was such a *glad* day. The day before too was a joy. Brownie, Jack and I went to Zug, took a funicular to the summit of the Zugerberg and from there climbed to the top of yet a higher peak, whence a never-to-be-forgotten panorama of the Lake of Zug with the Rigi and Pilatus in the distance, upon one side, and the Lake of Aegeri with its wee little village and the snow clad Bernese Alps far in the distance. Such a spectacle! The air was fresh and keen and we three fairly ran like elfins from knob to knob, bounding over boulders and revelling in the sheer physical activity.

We returned then to Zug, went down on the quai and watched the sun set behind Pilatus that cast a deep shadow upon the placid lake. It was an afternoon of joy and beauty. ...

In the evening we heard the opera of Mignon, *beautifully* given, for 80 cts. each. Wednesday night we hear Verdi's Rigoletto. And next Saturday night we hear La Traviata. We go first to the Schwarzenbachs' for dinner and to meet the star of the evening

(Miss Scheider who sings Marguerite) and then to the opera, and so ends a very happy Xmas and New Year's recess.

Some evening this week we are to go to the Fields. This afternoon Dr. Hoch, Dr. Amsden and I spent in the Café Metropole, our favorite haunt.

Zürich, January 22, 1910

Now this is important. Mother, *please never* say to any one that I am interested in the *insane* or visiting an insane asylum. I am in so far interested in these conditions as their study throws light upon the mental state existing in the minor neuroses, neurasthenia, hysteria, obsessions and the many inter-mixtures of these types, etc., etc., *but* no one, especially *no one in America*, wishes to believe there is any analogy, however remote, between a neurasthenia and a true insanity, but the fact is a morbid psychology underlies and is at the root of both, however broad the chasm that separates them symptomatically.

In the light of newer conceptions in psychiatry, for which Jung is largely responsible (after his preceptor whose genius has introduced the newer psychology—Freud, of Vienna), the differentiation of the mental state to which we give the inadequate Greek name—neurasthenia, and the condition to which we give the Latin dementia praecox—is one of *degree* largely. Now if I am regarded as an alienist (psychiatrist) patients with neurasthenia and the ilk, believing (because they've been taught to believe) that neurasthenia belongs to the domain of the organic disorders, aren't going to consult me. They aren't willing to believe their condition allied even remotely to the severer mental disorders and they are in view of the prevailing teaching quite justified in their attitude. But it is precisely this attitude that I wish to meet—this need—this lacuna that I wish to fill. I am therefore treating the *functional* neuroses—what is commonly called 'nervousness' and my treatment is wholly psychic or psychological, and my method that of mental or *psycho*-analysis and subsequent education.

Never then identify me in any one's mind with a physician who handles insanity for *in truth* the cases I am to handle are much nearer the normal than the insane, but their pathology is *psychic* and hence of the trend of insanity.

If you are ever again in New York soon, do go over to Ward's Island—'The Institute,' (East side of 116th for ferry going every half hour) and see Dr. Hoch and you will like him so much. Write him a note in advance and say frankly you're seeking the interview with him because you had heard of him through your son, and because you'd like so much to have a direct account of me from him. He is *so* nice.

Société de la Musée de Zürich
February 23, 1910

Since writing to you I have discovered this delightful library, and here in a quiet corner I work every day. Things go on pretty uniformly. For the last week it has been the spring time, and the pleasant air seems to whisper of the glad renewal of life and color once more.

I am busy on an article I hope to have prepared in about a month, in which I am giving some account of Freud's and Jung's psychoanalytic method.(3) My idea is to identify myself early with this new school of psychology and so bring my name before the profession and the public.

I look forward so happily to setting in upon my work next fall! As soon as I have patients it will be such a stimulus to interest. The field is practically empty for psychoanalysis—I am the first man

(3) 'Freud's Psychology in Its Relation to the Neuroses,' *American Journal of the Medical Sciences*, 1911, vol. 141, pp. 873–82.

of American birth to take up this work, and the second man in America—the other being an Austrian(4) in New York. I don't mention Hoch because he does institutional work. You know psychoanalysis is only adapted to the educated classes and I do feel that besides having the adequate training for the work I have what is more important—the instinct. Altogether the outlook is all that can be desired.

Zürich, March 6, 1910

Two things impressed me in your comment upon Dr. Meyer's papers. First that you do not find them unreadable. *Neither do I,* but so general is the feeling that his writings are obscure that I felt always it would have sounded like bragging to have said I understood him. Secondly—that you would say you agreed with his views, did it not sound *presumptuous,* that too was exactly my feeling.

No, you must look up the articles of Freud's and Jung's. Ask Dunlap to guide you.

Zürich, March 7, 1910

The curtain of today has risen upon an exquisite snow-scene, which is the more interesting in its contrast to the spring-like setting of the act which has been presented during the last week. It is a welcome return of the pleasant Swiss Winter.

Sister is walking! For some days she has been attending a course of instruction in the art, and on Sunday was graduated with distinction. May her little feet tread ever the primrose way!

(4) Dr. A. A. Brill.

This reminds me of our little comedian. Jack's latest conquest is the butcher's daughter, age 3½. She is a dear little girl and comes often into the yard to play with Jack. Yesterday afternoon as I started out, I came upon them walking the garden path—Jack's protecting arm about her. Seeing me, he said, 'I like to put my arm around the *kleines mädchen* but she is a dirty thing.' Never guessing, in her unfamiliarity with her suitor's language, that her personal hygiene was being impugned, her seraphic smile continued undimmed by the insult.

Later in the afternoon 'das kleine mädchen' betrayed signs of insubordination, so that my lord (the woman is given little quarter 'in the country') had recourse to physical redress. The difficulty was soon adjusted however to the satisfaction of both parties but my little lad was inconsolable all evening fearing 'what Father would think of his striking a little girl.' Fräulein sought to comfort him and even promised that if Father asked nothing she would say nothing. But the frank little soul found no comfort in the hope of evading the issue—and as soon as I entered the door his loud earnest voice greeted me with the unmitigated acknowledgment of his guilt. 'I hit the little girl, and I hit her hard and made her cry, but I'm sorry I did it, Father—I'm sorry I did it!'

The cherubs are just going out for their daily outing, the preliminary of which is always feeding the gulls on the lake.

Brownie received your good long letter yesterday, one from Miss Jeanie(5) (Albion, Baltimore) and a fine long one from Lucia.(6) So you say she's not coming abroad this year because 'Reggie is not a girl.' So far as I know the technique of modern surgery has not as yet developed adequate operative interference for meeting a demand of this kind and then even if it had there is no certainty that Reggie would acquiesce in the arrangement. How much more

(5) Mrs. Burrow's sister.

(6) Lucia Smith (later Mrs. Frank Nash), a cousin of Dr. Burrow's, who felt she must stay with her parents, not having confidence in her brother Reginald to give them the proper care.

wholesome—tell Lucia from me—to meet the world of reality squarely and frankly than to indulge in fantastical alternatives. Nothing was ever yet completely pat and as it should be. Conditions must be overcome by the strength of personality.

Indeed I have thought very seriously about Lucia lately. I have come to know that the typical insanities are due to a maladjustment of the individual to the world of reality and to the bad mental habit of withdrawing more and more into a world of phantasy. The inadequacy continues without serious disorder until the psychic blow is dealt—the grief, disappointment or whatever form the internal conflict may take, and then the mind, having no outward resources to turn to, no interest, no wholesome activities with which to occupy itself, lapses inevitably into a hopeless psychosis.

The situation with Lucia ought to be fairly faced and *measures taken in time,* and the old humdrum, torpid, inverted existence of 319, with its tiresome round of daily duties and its flat, unenlivened routine forever put an end to and that *at once.* When the curse falls there will be little solace in the remembrance of these empty, futile, narrow days. To go down to sorrow and humiliation for a noble cause is tragic enough, but where no worthy end is subserved, where it is matter merely of a pathological affection, it is too horrible! Alas! That most people never see their sorrows *coming* and so forefend them, but always view them from the other side when they are past and there's no mending. Lucia ought to come over here this summer, despite Reginald's sex and the one hundred other reasons which the pathological fancy can conjure for its own morbid purposes, and she ought to come in order to preserve herself against the tragedy of a hopeless mental breakdown.

Zürich, March 13, 1910

This has been such a beautiful and such a rich experience for us both—I can never have done with my thanksgiving for having spent this year in Europe. When I am in Italy I am going to take up Italian—merely to learn its pronunciation, something of the grammar and to read the Italian periodicals of medicine and psychology. Taking it up only playfully—for not more than two hours daily, I am sure that with my reminiscences of Latin and my current knowledge of French, I shall make a respectable headway with it and that I can begin next winter to read the Italian journals.

When I sing the refrain of 'Dearie,' at each 'Dearie,' Sister says 'Uhm?' This is an entirely original performance with her. She is the cutest thing!—an out and out mother's baby too. Walks all around and is so bright and coy and happy. Her signal of greeting is quite the most enspiriting thing I know—a beaming countenance full of mischief and mirth and repeated shouts of 'Hey, hey' that fairly make the welkin ring.

An odd thing about Jack—I don't know whether I've told you. He hasn't I think at all the musical ear I had at his age, but I suspect a better musical gift. The only airs that catch his interest are the classical ones and those he can produce are also this sort—for example the air he best knows is Walter's song from Wagner's Die Meistersinger. Whenever I hummed it he asked the name and then one day reproduced it with perfect correctness. For the rest one hears chiefly improvisations, which, while not altogether coherent, do not I think outrage the accepted canons of harmony. The words are characteristic, 'Oh, my little sister, you are so sweet. I love my dear father and mother,' then one loses the thread to take it up again at a 'gangplank' or the like!

Zürich, April 24, 1910

Read half of my paper to Dr. Jung, who is much pleased with it. Shall read the remainder this week. The American Vice Consul is going to typewrite it for me; and I hope to get it off very soon.

If you will get the April number of *The American Journal of Psychology*, by addressing Miss Florence Chandler, Clark University, Worcester, Mass., and enclosing $1.50 you will have Freud's and Jung's lectures delivered in America last summer and from them you will obtain an excellent idea of the new field of psychoanalysis.

Zürich, May 8, 1910

This past week has been a quite gala one for us quiet folk. Monday night, as I wrote you, 'Chanticleer,' Tuesday night to dine at the Schwarzenbachs', Thursday to dine and go sailing with Jung, and then one or two other events which I do not in the moment recall.

My paper isn't yet in the hands of the typewriter. So many little details, addenda, and corrections, references, etc., etc., but it is about finished now and I shall be glad to get it off to Dr. Barker.

We land in Hoboken in the afternoon of August 22, and if we can catch the N.Y.P. & N. that evening shall be in Norfolk morning of August 23.

CHAPTER 4

PSYCHOANALYTIC PRACTICE

AND BROADENING PERSPECTIVES

The next ten years constituted a period of intense professional activity. On their return from Europe in the fall of 1910, Dr. and Mrs. Burrow rented a large house, 707 St. Paul Street, Baltimore, which also provided space for his office. Public interest was just beginning to turn to psychoanalysis and the broadening concepts of behavior it embodied. As one of the first to introduce this dynamic method in America, Burrow met with the heartening response he had anticipated while abroad. But practically no letters remain from this period, although there was correspondence with Freud, Jung, and various psychoanalytic confrères, as well as with students and patients. He wrote in longhand, and systematic correspondence files were not kept in his office in the early days. Thus the reader must depend upon editorial comment and upon Dr. Burrow's later reports for the story of these years.

As will be recalled, Burrow had written his mother from Zürich that he felt he had the 'instinct' for his new work. He was indeed richly endowed for it. He possessed a brilliant mind, an effortless graciousness, and the capacity to establish a ready rapport with the people he met. His delicate touch in the psychoanalytic situation, his warmth and humor, his steadfast insistence on the community responsibilities of his patients were deeply valued by those who came to him for treatment.

During these years Burrow had the stanch support of Adolf Meyer who had first advised him to study with Jung. Dr. Meyer, the newly appointed Professor of Psychiatry at Johns Hopkins, was organizing the Henry Phipps Psychiatric Clinic there. Appreciative of the young physician's background and capacity, he assisted him in every way to establish himself professionally. Burrow was a member of Meyer's staff at the Phipps Clinic and Assistant in Psychiatry at the University School of Medicine.

From the outset Burrow was active in organizing and extending psychoanalysis in America. He was already a member of the American Psychological Association and of the American Psychopathological Association. In May 1911 he joined with several others in the field to found the American Psychoanalytic Association (1), serving as one of its first councilors, and later as president. As subsequent letters indicate, Burrow took a leading part for many years in the affairs of the two latter organizations, and was a frequent speaker at their meetings. The first of his fifteen papers before the American Psychoanalytic Association was read in 1912 and the last in 1927, while the twenty-four papers he delivered before the American Psychopathological Association spanned the years 1913 to 1944.

Although the threat of war interfered with the project, Burrow planned in 1913 to broaden further his professional background through an analysis with Sigmund Freud.(2) The differences between Freud and Jung had by this time alienated them from each other. In spite of his original enthusiasm for Jung, Burrow questioned the validity of some of his assumptions. Later he discussed their various positions in his paper, 'Notes with Reference to Freud, Jung and Adler,' which concludes, 'I shall not believe that the breach is an irreparable one. It would indeed be a calamity if Jung's genial perspectives have misled his splendid genius into an irrevocable disagreement with the clear, steadfast, disinterested observations of Freud.'(3)

The circumstances of his life during these years reflected the success of Burrow's practice. He moved his office to Mt. Vernon Place in 1915 (later to the Tuscany on Stony Run Lane) while the family home was established at nearby Ruxton. In the course of his search for a name for this country place Burrow happened upon the word later associated with his behavioral studies. In his Anglo-Saxon dictionary which he

(1) The other founders were Ralph C. Hamill, August Hoch, Ernest Jones, John T. MacCurdy, Adolf Meyer, J. J. Putnam, G. Lane Taneyhill, G. Alexander Young, *Zentralblatt für Psychoanalyse*, January 1912.

(2) In response to Burrow's letter, Freud wrote (November 6, 1913): 'Of course I remember you very well from the time we first met at Hammerstein's Roof Garden and from your contribution to the Internationale Zeitschrift, and it will give me satisfaction if I can do something for you through an analysis. I am especially honored by your confidence in me.'

(3) *The Journal of Abnormal Psychology*, 1917, vol. XII, pp. 161–7. See also letter to Freud, pp. 76–9.

had opened at random he found the word 'Lifwynn,' meaning the joy of life. It is indicative of the mood of this period of their lives that he and Mrs. Burrow decided on this name for their home.

At the same time another family base was being created in a setting which afforded much joy throughout the years. During the summer of 1915, Dr. and Mrs. Burrow and the two children spent a short vacation with Alys Bentley, the teacher of music and dancing, at her unique camp at Merrill in the Adirondacks. This salty, indomitable woman was one of the first American exponents of rhythmic dancing as a means of self-expression, conducting large classes at her camp on the shore of Lake Chateaugay. But her wide interests encompassed far more than the dance. Her rare humor, her sensitivity and vitality appealed to creative workers in various fields, and Camp Owlyout became the center for many of the artists and writers who visited the lake—Geraldine Farrar, Waldo Frank, Louis Untermeyer, Cissie Loftus, Marcella Sembrich, and others.

It was at the Bentley camp that Burrow came to know Sherwood Anderson in 1916, and in the course of long walks in the woods they held the conversations which the latter dramatized in his story 'Seeds.' (4) In a paper written some ten years later, Burrow refers to these same talks when he speaks of 'having spent the long hours of a summer afternoon arguing with Sherwood Anderson as to the merits of the psychoanalytic aim. Anderson argued that human life was not a thing to be delved into with surgical probes—that it was not to be got at that way. Needless to say, I argued as stoutly that the surgical probe was the most wonderful of all human inventions and that it was the only way to lay open to health and growth the sick personalities of our human kind.' (5)

Before their first visit to Merrill ended Dr. and Mrs. Burrow had bought a tract of land on the west shore of Lake Chateaugay. The following year they built a bungalow on this property and from then on spent the summers there. But not even the yearly move to this isolated spot interfered with Dr. Burrow's practice. Never a devotee of the psychoanalytic couch, he at first conferred with his patients on

(4) *The Triumph of the Egg*, New York, B. W. Huebsch, 1921, pp. 21–4. Further details of Burrow's acquaintance with Anderson are contained in letters to William L. Phillips, pp. 558–62.

(5) 'Psychoanalytic Improvisations and the Personal Equation,' *The Psychoanalytic Review*, 1926, vol. XIII, p. 173.

a rustic bench by the lake shore. Later, a charming little study was added on a height overlooking the water. As more and more patients followed Burrow to his summer retreat, staying at various camps around the lake, a special launch was required to carry them to and from their appointments.

To Dr. Adolf Meyer   Merrill, New York
Baltimore, Maryland   July 16, 1918

Dear Dr. Meyer:

I have been trying to get back the ms. of the paper 'The Origin of the Incest-Awe,' that you are good enough to want to see. The copy I have is not fair enough to send out and I have been unable to have a paper made from this. I am very anxious to have your idea in regard to this thesis as certain men who have been over it feel that it helps clarify certain things. If I should fail to get the paper to you within a few days, it will be because of the circumstances I have mentioned.

I hope your plan of being in Plattsburg for a part of the summer may materialize and that you will come to us for whatever spare days you may have. Payne drove over the other day just for a few hours but is coming again some week-end.

You will like, I think, much that this lake offers and we will like nothing better than having you.

I am having such a good summer. There are analyses only every alternate day (except for Mr. X. who is on this side of the lake): the other days I write a bit, do a bit of chores about the place and play—just play with all my heart, and I can't tell you how good it seems to have days in which not every hour is 'appointed.' I am sure this respite allows me to bring a better quality to the analytic work.

I hope so much that you will come and that I may talk with you. I want to tell you just where I stand now in regard to the work. I feel that the past years have given me a certain 'equipment' that I must use to the most helpful ends and in this hope I shall want your idea as always. . . .

I hope Mrs. Meyer and Julia will find farm life to their liking. Please remember me to Mrs. Meyer. (I wish she too would read the Incest paper.)

Hoping to see you soon,

Faithfully yours,

Trigant Burrow

While meeting the heavy demands of his practice, Burrow was also, as indicated in this letter, developing new formulations in the psychoanalytic field which he was regularly presenting at professional meetings. In his *History of Psychoanalysis in America*, Clarence P. Oberndorf cites among the four 'most noteworthy and original among American contributions before 1920 . . . Trigant Burrow's emphasis of a "primary subjective phase" in the infant chronologically preceding the Oedipus situation.'(6) In a chapter devoted to this new concept, Dr. John T. MacCurdy presents with special emphasis Burrow's 'principle of primary identification' as well as his penetrating interpretation of homosexuality.(7)

In a letter which appears in its entirety later in this volume(8) Burrow describes the inception of this early formulation:

'In the midst of my psychoanalytic work I suddenly came upon

(6) *A History of Psychoanalysis in America*, New York, Grune & Stratton, 1953, p. 133.

(7) 'The Primary Subjective Phase of Burrow,' in *Problems in Dynamic Psychology*, New York, The Macmillan Company, 1922, pp. 188–205.

(8) To Mrs. William F. Dummer, December 19, 1935, pp. 311–14.

what appeared to me a phase of organic sensation and awareness that antedated the infant's earliest objective appreciation of its surroundings. (I remember so well the moment, and the patient—a teacher, by the way, and a highly subjective woman.) I called it the organism's *primary subjective phase* and spoke of the infant's *primary identification with the mother.* This was the inception of a direction of thought and investigation with me of which all my later work has been the fuller development. There was no doubt with me that there existed between the infant and maternal organism a *tensional rapport* (I did not call it that at the time)—a total physiological continuity in sensation and reaction that underlay the entire developmental life of the organism and that was quite different from the tensional modifications brought about with the infant's adaptation to its environment *and to its mother* through the process of outer objective awareness (the employment of the symbol).

I wrote at that time a paper which I called "The Preconscious or The Nest Instinct" and read it at the meeting in Boston of The American Psychoanalytic Association in 1917. . . . '(9)

There were other papers about that time in similar trend, among them 'The Origin of the Incest-Awe,' 'The Genesis and Meaning of Homosexuality,' and 'Character and the Neuroses' for example, which tend toward this same underlying scheme as the basis of the organism's mental and social development.(10)

These papers show that in the early phase of his psychoanalytic practice Burrow's outlook was constantly broadening. Another indication of this growth was his increasing recognition of the social implications in nervous and mental disorders. Gradually he was coming to sense the ultimate inadequacy of a merely individual approach to these conditions. His observations led him to the conclusion that 'normality' in the behavioral field does not represent a basic criterion of health comparable to that existing in other branches of medicine.

(9) See *The Biology of Human Conflict—An Anatomy of Behavior, Individual and Social*, New York, The Macmillan Company, 1937, chapter IV.

(10) 'The Origin of the Incest-Awe,' *The Psychoanalytic Review*, 1918, vol. v, pp. 243–54; 'The Genesis and Meaning of "Homosexuality" and Its Relation to the Problem of Introverted Mental States,' *The Psychoanalytic Review*, 1917, vol. 4, pp. 272–84; 'Character and the Neuroses,' *The Psychoanalytic Review*, 1914, vol. 1, pp. 121–8. A manuscript of Dr. Burrow's, elaborating this thesis is now being edited for publication.

As early as 1914, in 'The Psychanalyst and the Community' he wrote:

After all we are of one tissue. We have but to look about us at the so-called normal persons composing the community to see that life masquerades no less under the disguise of social make-believes than under the symbolic subterfuges of the neurotic individual. The difference is that the artifices of the social community, being collective, unite its members, so to speak, by a common language, while the neurotic isolates himself through the extravagance of his metaphors. ... Society, too, has its elaborate system of defense-mechanisms, its equivocations and metonymies, its infantile make-shifts and illusions.(11)

Sensing the latent capacity of mankind for co-ordination and health, Burrow was deeply concerned by the evidences of widespread social discord and antagonism. Yet, as he always maintained, his formulations would have remained on the theoretical level had it not been for his meeting with Clarence Shields and their joint effort to analyze within themselves—as part of the community of man—the factors responsible for human conflict.

In describing his impression of the young man on their meeting in 1915, Dr. Burrow later wrote:

I had not before met anyone with whom I could not enter readily into the customary social give-and-take exchange. I had not before known a man or woman who was not socially accessible in the ordinary sense and yet who was sane. I had of course known many people who were accessible socially and sane, and many who were socially inaccessible and insane. But here was a man whom I could not bring to think either with me or in opposition to me on the accustomed basis of interchange. There was here no common ground. This was a phenomenon which during all the years I had devoted to the study of human behavior I had not come upon before. For the first time in my experience I had met a stranger. The circumstance baffled at the same time that it intrigued me. I was curious to understand this man. I wanted to understand an expression of behavior that defied the behavioral categories.

(11) *The Journal of the American Medical Association*, 1914, vol. LXII, pp. 1876-8.

Clarence Shields' background was in marked contrast to that of Dr. Burrow. A Pennsylvania-German, Mr. Shields had grown up in a farming community and graduated from a small college nearby. Retiring and diffident in social situations, he found contentment largely in wood and field, until the sudden death of the young girl who was to have been his wife thrust upon him the realization of his own profound emotional insecurity. He gave up his job as surveyor and after some months of drifting took up a position as companion to a psychiatric patient whose family happened to be intimate friends of Dr. and Mrs. Burrow. More and more impressed as the months went by with the innate authority and intuitive wisdom of Clarence Shields, these friends came to feel that a meeting between him and Dr. Burrow, so gifted each in his own way, might prove stimulating and rewarding to both.

The two men complemented each other in many important attributes. Mr. Shields' simplicity and repose, his rapport with living nature, his resourcefulness in many tasks, from the details of office organization to cabinet-making, balanced, as it were, the more active, outgoing attitude toward others characteristic of Dr. Burrow. While appreciating wholeheartedly the significance of Burrow's contributions to psychoanalytic thought, Shields was uninterested in mental concepts as such. Instead he approached the problem of behavior from the basis of an organic integrity of feeling that gave him a delicate awareness of emotional falsities. It was this quality which Dr. Burrow prized so highly and which led him to speak of his co-worker in later years as 'my distinguished associate, Clarence Shields.'

This was the man with whom Dr. Burrow embarked upon a study of the behavioral disorders of social man that ended only with his death. The study had its inception in 1918 during Mr. Shields' analysis. As Dr. Burrow described this occurrence in the preface of his first book(12), 'Having years ago been "analyzed" in preparation for my work in psychopathology, I had been for years duly "analyzing" others. It unexpectedly happened one day, however, that while I was interpreting a dream of a student-assistant, he made bold to challenge the honesty of my analytic position, insisting that . . . the test of my sincerity would be met only when I should myself be willing to accept from him the same analytic exactions I was now imposing upon others.

(12) *The Social Basis of Consciousness—A Study in Organic Psychology*, The International Library of Psychology, Philosophy, and Scientific Method, New York, Harcourt, Brace; London, Kegan Paul, Trench, Trubner, 1927, pp. xv–xvii.

As may be readily judged, such a proposition seemed to me nothing short of absurd. Had I not been "analyzed"? Needless to say I had heard this proposal from patients many times before, but while my reaction to the suggestion in the present instance was chiefly one of amusement, my pride was not a little piqued at the intimation it conveyed. So with the thought that in the interest of experiment it could at least do no harm to humour for a time the waywardness of inexperience, I conceded the arrangement.'

But not long after they had reversed their roles as patient and analyst Dr. Burrow discovered that 'my "resistances" to my self-appointed analyst, far from being negligible, were plainly insuperable. . . . Whatever empirical interest the situation may have held for me at the outset was now wholly subordinated to the indignation and pain of the position to which I had been brought.

'What calls for more vital emphasis, however, is the fact that along with the deepening, if reluctant, realization of my intolerance of self-defeat, there came gradually to me the realization that my analyst, in changing places with me, had merely shifted to the authoritarian vantage-ground I had myself relinquished and that the situation had remained essentially unaltered still. This was significant. It marked at once the opening of wholly new vistas of experience. In the light of its discovery I began to . . . see that the student before me, notwithstanding his undoubted sincerity of purpose, presented a no less personal and proprietary attitude toward me than I had held toward him and that all that had been needed was the authoritarian background to bring this attitude to expression. With the consciousness of this condition I saw what has been for me the crucial revelation of the many years of my analytic work—that, in its individualistic application, the attitude of the psychoanalyst and the attitude of the authoritarian are inseparable.

'As from day to day this realization came more closely home to me, and with it the growing acceptance of the limitation and one-sidedness of the personalistic critique in psychoanalysis, my personal self-vindication and resistances began in the same measure to abate. At the same time the analyst too, Mr. Clarence Shields, came at last into a position to sense the personalism and resistance that had unconsciously all along actuated his own reaction. From now forward the direction of the inquiry was completely altered. The analysis henceforth consisted in the reciprocal effort of each of us to recognize within himself his attitude of authoritarianism and autocracy toward the other. With this automatic relinquishment of the personalistic or private basis and its replacement by a more inclusive attitude toward the problems of human consciousness, there has been not alone for myself but also for students and patients a gradual clearing of our entire analytic horizon.'

There was to follow 'the travail of much painstaking research,' as Dr. Burrow expressed it, but he and Mr. Shields did not abandon the larger frame of reference implicit in their experiment. They stuck to it through thick and thin, through the alienation of friends and colleagues, the financial anxieties resulting from the interruption of Dr. Burrow's practice, and above all through the initial period when he lacked the full understanding and sympathy of his family.

However, as he wrote later in *The Neurosis of Man*:

... My only serious loss was a quite voluntary one, but one for which I was amply recompensed in the interest that led me to incur it. I refer to my enforced recognition of the existence of a social neurosis and of my personal share in it. This, I cannot deny, was a serious wrench for me. For having now to adopt an altered basis of inquiry, it was necessary that I forswear completely my psychoanalytic practice and set out anew. Not only this. But, as will be readily understood, the necessity of reckoning with man's ineptitudes in feeling and thinking and doing, as these ineptitudes were daily registered within myself, entailed an acutely painful process.(13)

Dr. Burrow was compelled by the terms of his problem to question all aspects of human relationships, no matter how close the bonds from the accustomed 'normal' point of view. 'Our criterion of investigation,' he says in his Foreword to *The Neurosis of Man*, 'demanded the consistent discrediting of all our habitual "manifest" social expressions. It demanded that in the interest of a common interrelational reorientation the motives of human relations as they exist today be granted no quarter. We had lowered the barriers surrounding the personal sympathies and confidences we had thought to be bonds, and found that inter-human relationships which we had believed were close and dependable were everywhere shifting and insubstantial. In the process of phyloanalysis, however, these relationships became far closer, far more dependable and secure.'(14)

(13) *The Neurosis of Man*, p. 324.
(14) Ibid. p. xv.

Consider in this connection the following note to his wife and the contrast it presents to earlier letters to her.

Baltimore, Maryland
April 23, 1919, Good Friday, 5.30 p.m.

Dear Brownie:

I found your note under my pillow and I want to send this little word of answer. We are not—you and I—living up to what is best in us. There is so much possessivism, unconsciousness—too little personality and growth. Your words to me will mean so much more—mine to you will mean so much more when *we* are much more than we are today. Not more in virtue, in conformity and outward consideration, but in the acceptance of the large element of the unconscious, the sentimental and the infantile in our relation to each other. We have talked of love for fifteen years and we have not known—either of us—not realized the rudiments of real, free, clear, fearless love that is the acceptance in each of his own personality.

Instead of contributing to the lives of each other we are constantly thwarting the lives of each other and therefore of our children.

We need to see this. Because we are really not futile, routine mechanisms, we are individualities—personalities, and we need to come into our own. That is understanding and that is the only love that is real or that can mean anything real to either of us.

I hope you will have a good trip. Give my love to Mrs. Bryan and all and to Emily.

With love to you,

Trigant

A letter during the following year to his son, now fifteen years old and away at boarding school, also expresses the new orientation.

Baltimore, Maryland
October 22, 1920

Dear Jack:

I was so glad to have your letter today. I do not know that there will be time to answer it now—someone is coming in to see me—but I want to talk with you until he comes, and I will return to you later.

It is not easy to speak understandingly through a letter of the fears you experience at night. We could come so much closer to their true meaning in talking to each other. It is wholly mental. There is no ground for distrusting your physical strength. Unconsciously you are looking for the care and protection you are accustomed to expect from your mother. And yet that is not the whole account. Plenty of people have had solicitous mothers who have not become nervous. Nature seems to demand of a certain type of people that they *be* that which they *are*. Now the world of normality—the confederacy of behavior and conformity called 'everybody'—demands precisely that we be what we are *not*—that is that we *pretend* and truckle to 'public' sentiment, it not being realized that public sentiment is itself a thing of fear—a fear to think one's own thoughts, to admit one's own feeling. If one entertains a private feeling which is counter to the public mode of thought and one has acquired a fear of the public thought, his feeling is repressed, denied and this causes a conflict within him. He is not at peace with himself. Now not being at peace with oneself is the essence of fear or worry. When one is alone—when there is no diversion as at night in the quiet, this worry or fear-state needs exploration—it needs to discover a place where it may lodge, as it were. Since one does not realize one's conflict, one's mental expression, one looks for a cause and finds it in the most immediate occasion that may be associated with fear. So naturally you fix upon your cough to account for it. As the cough fills the bill, one tends naturally to hold on to it and so it is made to do duty as it were for the real cause of the fear—one's conflict within one's own life. You said to me for example: 'I ought to want to read.' Here is the essence of conflict. 'Ought' and 'want' are mutually contradictory. If you *want* to read, reading is for you a joy. If you *ought* to read, reading is for you a penalty—an infliction. A joy cannot be a penalty, nor a penalty a joy. Yet you try to affiliate the two in your mind which is, as it were, attempting to *force* to flow what can only *flow*—'want' or interest being flow, and 'ought' or penalty being force or compulsion. This is a small item, I know. But when you crowd your mind with whole days of such items, it means days of conflict or repression—the outer thing, the public thing or the 'ought' (fear), replacing the inner, private thing or 'want'— that is joy and fulfillment of your life.

Perhaps this is not wholly clear. But you will think it over. The visitor whom I expected was good enough not to come and so I have had the longer time with you. I must go though now. It is dinner-time.

Yes, ask Mr. Green to let you and Pat have a table apart, and ask him if that will be agreeable, explaining that he is our care-taker.

Goodnight,

Father

P.S. I am glad you are growing to like the French. Here is another instance. You like it 'because you are keeping up with the class' and 'because you begin to understand it.' To keep up with the class removes occasion of conflict—there is flow, harmony. To understand it joy, fulfillment. But if you could not keep up with a class through no fault of yours, it would be harmonious to accept your limitation and not worry because of outside (public) opinion.

The influence of Burrow's altered trend on his relationship with his patients is illustrated in the following letter.

Baltimore, Maryland
August 11, 1920

Dear Mrs. T.:

I have your two letters—one crossing mine, the other in answer to it. It is not that Clarence and I are turning from you. It is that you have sought unconsciously to turn from us. I understand your pain—it is my own—the pain of the lesser, personal self in its opposition to organic growth. Pain though is everywhere the signal that advertises some alteration—some obstruction to productive function. Where the organism's self is the seat of pain, the organism is itself offering obstruction to its own function—to the function of its entirety as entirety. Where we are ourselves the pain-centre, we ourselves are the unconscious defenders of our pain—of the obstructive process of which we are ourselves the centre and the source.

And when there is some one to be with us—to understand and with us to allay the angry assaults of pain's blind self-defenses and through him to let us come into our organic completeness and strength in the unification of understanding, there is no longer any need to hold to the pain and separateness of conflict. More and more I feel how simple and quiet it all is. How our complications are our own complicating.

There is need that we recognize the delusion of all division. Division, separation, resistance is the meaning of all our pain. You know this so well. But it is to accept it. It is to accept the daily, hourly accumulation of evidence of our efforts of distinction, of differentiation and impatience, to trace the organic breach between the petty wants of our sophisticated external living and the deep needs of our permanent, inherent life. But you know. Not any words of mine can say it. It is to make your knowing your own organically, through your self-analysis and fearless acceptance. Little people all of us—we are so futile in our dividedness!

No more.

Sincerely yours,

Trigant Burrow

It was in the winter of 1920–21 that Burrow temporarily gave up his psychoanalytic practice. He wrote Dr. Meyer, January 6, 1921: 'It has certainly seemed good to have this space I am taking these days for a better acquaintance with myself. Already I feel it will not be unprofitable. I hope you know how much it meant to me to go straight to you with what seemed to me at first a quite desperate, if inevitable, decision.'

That fall after nearly a year of concentrated research, Dr. Burrow resumed his practice with Mr. Shields as his assistant.

To Dr. Adolf Meyer   Baltimore, Maryland
                                       August 10, 1921

Dear Doctor Meyer:

I am glad to be able to write you definitely at last that I shall resume my work on the first of October. I find that what I have aimed *at* I can after all only work *towards* and that whatever the limitations it is time now to return to my place and offer what I can.

It will mean much to me to talk over with you the endeavors of the last months. I have been trying to state in writing as clearly as I can what seems to me the basic occasion of the failure of analysis —our exclusive emphasis of the personal to the utter neglect of inherent social factors. I have found it a difficult thesis but I am hoping to complete it in a few weeks, as it should be the basis of my work from now forward.

Mrs. Burrow is hoping to see you, Mrs. Meyer and Julia at Lake Chateaugay some time this month. We both feel that the activities of the lake have much to give Julia and I am glad to have all of you know our play-ground.

With kind remembrances to Mrs. Meyer,

Sincerely yours,
Trigant Burrow

CHAPTER 5

'OUR COMMON CONSCIOUSNESS'

The summer of 1921 brought the opportunity for a renewal of the acquaintance with Mrs. Sherwood Anderson who was again visiting at Lake Chateaugay.(1) The word she carried back to Illinois of Burrow's effort to re-appraise established psychoanalytic interpretations, and to analyze the habitual social mood, aroused the sympathy of her writer-husband. He responded with characteristic generosity initiating an exchange of letters marked by an honesty of communication that was evidently refreshing to both men.

Palos Park, Illinois
September 11, 1921

Dear Trigant Burrow:

Tennessee has come back from the Bentley camp and has told me something of you, the first news of you I have had for a long time. The news she brings me is amazing and at the same time peculiarly satisfying. How much I wish now that we lived in the same part of the country and could be friends. I have for so long a time been thinking of you as a successful man and that has made it difficult for me to approach you. I am afraid too often I have been in my thought of you a little sarcastic.

(1) Tennessee Mitchell, Mrs. Sherwood Anderson.

My difficulty lay in the fact that I continually thought of you as one who believed they had found truth. What I thought to be your truth I could not accept for myself and perhaps I was angry at the thought that you could accept it. I have thought of the science to which you have given so much of your life as one that could very well do wonders in making life and its difficulties more understandable but that one person could in any way cure the evils in life for another seemed to me impossible.

Perhaps I in some way wanted you to be an artist and to have an artist's point of view. What twisted notion I had I can't get clear for myself.

At any rate I know now, from what Tennessee has told me of your conversation, that all the thoughts I have had of you these last few years have been unfair and untrue. What a struggle must have been going on within you. Will you forgive my stuffy thinking.

Tennessee spoke of a book you want to publish. I would be delighted to write to my own publisher, Huebsch. When will the book be ready? Is it, as I suspect, an account of your own struggle? Will it be a book that we, who have not studied your subject as you have, can understand?

Will you not tell me what you can of the book so that I may write intelligently to Mr. Huebsch. Also tell me what you care to of yourself and your own plans.

With love,

Sherwood Anderson

The book, then called 'Our Common Consciousness,' had grown out of the early group studies. The following correspondence, beginning with the reply to Anderson's warm-hearted letter, deals largely with this manuscript.

Baltimore, Maryland
October 9, 1921

Dear Sherwood:

It would indeed be good if we might be closer neighbors. It means so much to me though that you have such neighborliness of spirit toward me. That you have been sarcastic in your thought of me in the past years could not have been otherwise, it seems to me. My own life, as I look back upon it, has been one long, bitter, self-centred sarcasm. It is a habit of thought that tends to cling to me still, closing me out from clearer things. I work with it. For years I have worked with it. But to work with a tendency which in its nature one does not want to work with, because one has come to like the easy automatic habit of it, is a tardy process. It is this that I would be glad if you would accept with me, until I can better understand. So you see you have not, objectively speaking, been unfair to me. I *have* wanted to be a successful man—worse still I have been a successful man and this thing of my success—this thing of the approbation of others has meant more to me than my own essential life. In this sense you have been more true to me in refusing to accept me on this artificial, 'successful' basis. It seems so good to realize this and to speak frankly of it to you.

About the book, without having intended it, I have already given you the substance of it in what I have just written you. It will be such a help to have your introduction to Mr. Huebsch, but I want to be frank with you as to the difficulties, notwithstanding that I persist in my feeling that somehow there may be found the publisher who will be sympathetic to the aim of my thesis and to whom the spirit of it as it touches human life will mean more than its market 'value.' From what Tennessee said of Huebsch it seemed to me that I might find with him just the coöperation that is needed. Do not conclude that the book is of its nature not saleable. I can well imagine there being a real demand for it, especially as other writers—I have D. H. Lawrence chiefly in mind—have already sensed my tendency from earlier papers of mine and have spoken sympathetically of my trend, but all I mean is that I would so like the question of its commercial possibility to be subordinated to that of its inherent, human quality.

This very thing you speak of as having stood between us—my attitude of one who had found truth and would graciously dispense it to the less fortunate—is typical of us Freudians. It is this *theory* of life we have all been employing to keep ourselves aloof from the *actuality* of life, the while we point authoritatively to the illusion or neurosis of the other fellow, that it is the chief purpose of my essay to acknowledge. In its present development psychoanalysis is not democratic, it is autocratic. Personally I feel that there are many who, like ourselves, feel its inadequacy from this angle. I think the number of such is steadily increasing. So that if my book does aim at overturning the altar, there will not be lacking those who will accord with the movement.

It seems to me that the thesis to which you gave expression under the art-form of 'Marching Men' is inherently identical with this that I have put under the title of 'Our Common Consciousness.' With this thesis of our commonness—of the essential fellowship of man, it does seem to me fitting that the book be published in the simplest way. For this reason I would so prefer to omit the customary attachment of my University degrees and to waive any mention of official connections etc., letting the paper stand without any such personal exploitations as usually accompany the 'scientific' treatise. I know you understand my feeling in this. But while it does seem to me farcical to write of the artificiality of 'distinction' at the same time that I ornament myself with egoistic encomiums, will a publisher sympathize with me in this rather exceptional attitude for the so-called professional or academic writer?

You ask when the book will be ready. It is practically written now. There is need of certain smoothing out of sentences here

and there and some little addition. But this could be done and the
paper ready in two weeks certainly. It is not so much an account
of my own struggle as the outcome and the expression or the
acknowledgment of it. It has seemed to me that there should follow
some time the detailed account of my story, but while it is a
personal record in the spirit of it, in the data of it it does not
attempt to permit an intimate account of myself. To the question
whether the book is one that 'we, who have not studied your
subject as you have, can understand,' I can only say that I think it
will be clear to the personalities to whom it is addressed—the artist
and the neurotic, or the expressed and the unexpressed. To the fat
woman, with the Pomeranian doggy, whom we knew that summer
at Merrill, it will be Greek—decadent Greek. But perhaps this
quotation from the paper itself is the best answer to your question:
'To speak fearlessly and with freedom to the few who are fearless
and free enough to understand means far more to me and will, I
believe, prove ultimately far more fruitful in making clear the
real meaning of our human need than any recourse to statements
muttered with bated breath and trimmed to suit the fear-ridden
prepossessions of the collective mind as it tends in its blind autocracy to dominate the clearer vision of us all.'

As to my own plans, I must wait. You see I have turned aside from
the habitual path of analysis as a 'profession' and it has left me
somewhat in the lurch. I want now to make this statement of my
feeling of the right of personality only and confess my belief in
the menace to personality of psychoanalysis as I and the rest of
us have employed it, if I can find the sympathetic publisher of my
statement. My plans depend so much upon the issue of this thesis.
I do not see why there may not be a helpfulness of approach to
the unexpressed through the actual expression of my own life, after
I have laid aside theoretical truth as a profession. I do not know.

Do you think Huebsch would read the paper himself or would
he depend upon the professional analyst for an opinion? It would
certainly be detrimental to its acceptance by Huebsch if he depended upon the conventional Freudian for a decision.

Whatever the outcome I am grateful to you for your willingness to help.

My love to you and Tennessee.

Trigant

Baltimore, Maryland
December 1921

Dear Sherwood:

The same—the very same! Miss Madge Jenison. There is not any question though of my permitting her to doctor my manuscript (unless in the matter of spelling or punctuation); in its essential matter I could not permit any one to alter it—I couldn't permit myself to do so. Not but what the handling could be much improved, but this essay has really nothing to do with *excellence*. I want to talk to you of this. You see I did not personally write this thing. It was, as it were, dictated to me, and I was in spite of myself forced to set it down. I can't tell you how I stood out against it, just bitterly defiant. It was life pushing itself through and my part was a sort of enforced submission to it. What is written here will be clear, I think, to the artist and to that other form of response to the life-urge in man that is the furthest extreme of the artist's expression—namely the artist who is unexpressed, I mean the neurotic.

What I think of with most hesitation is the ugly tools with which I have had to work—the awkward scientific terminology inseparable from my narrow, laboratory training. I have been roundly scored on this ground by very capable men. I have chiefly in mind Edward Carpenter and his critical reaction to what he called my 'scientific jargon.' He is quite right. But the point is that if the laboratory is not picturesque nor its symbols prepossessing, it is in the laboratory that I have passed the travail of the days that have been my life and for me to repudiate the symbols of its language would be artificial and untrue. I cannot alter that. Do not suppose that the laboratory students will approve of this record. I know very well that it may cost me my connection with the University but I cannot alter that either. I do hope that Huebsch will publish my book, but I could better afford not to publish it at all than to force in it any concession external to it. It is this that you will best understand. And then there is this. It is in its psychological or biological implication that I have come to sense something of the fallacy of my own pride and there are, I do not doubt, many others whose lives, like my own, have been unwittingly forced into the same fallacy through the same biological misconceptions that have frustrated my own life. It is probably only such an approach to life as this book of mine seeks to embody that could ever reach this class of people. As I write you, I see that it is so much more your hospitality that I want than that of Huebsch or the public and that is because you are the artist and the artist, I believe, is he for whom the neurotic must wait for his real understanding and release.

The thought of your coming East and the possibility of seeing you certainly seem good. I never get to New York somehow; but I might get over for a day or two while you are there. What I am hoping is that your tour south may include a stop-off in Baltimore. I should demand forthwith that you come to us for a visit, had I not had to give up my home because of the altered condition of things relative to my work. (2)

We have an apartment near here and it is convenient in every way, as it is close to the respective schools of the juniors and at closer hand for Brownie's enterprises. ... So we shall hope to see you and Tennessee in Baltimore and we can have some cozy meals at least at our new quarters.

(2) The Ruxton home was rented for several years.

The manuscript will surely go off to Huebsch this week-end or Monday of next week (19th). I'll drop you a line though and mention the day of its mailing. If any change in your plans let me have word. As it now stands you will be in Chicago until the 18th and then you go to New York to be with Jerome Blum, 154 W. 11th St., for two or three weeks.

I am hoping to see you.

Yours always,

Trigant

To B. W. Huebsch   Baltimore, Maryland
New York   January 29, 1922

Dear Mr. Huebsch:

Your letter of the 27th came in yesterday. The conflicting reactions of the two readers toward my book is no surprise to me. There will be people of no mean intellectual gift by whom the book will be quite misunderstood and in certain quarters it will undoubtedly arouse very fierce criticism. I have faced this fully. It does not disconcert me. On the other hand there is the assurance of an equally strong faction of no less intellectual attainment to whom my book will come, I believe, as a welcome response to a long-felt need.

I don't know whether your own personal experience has brought you in contact with the large and increasing number of people seriously interested in the problems of psychoanalysis to whom Freud and his individualistic psychology has not proven wholly adequate. It is this audience to whom my book with its more inclusive social outlook especially addresses itself.

As Miss Madge Jenison is one of those who has read my thesis and who has for some years followed the trend of my studies,

I have written her asking her, if possible, to see you and make clear to you better than I could in a letter just what place in our present-day thought my book aims to fill and to give you some idea of the audience on which it may count.

If it is not presuming I am going to ask you to be so good as to further as far as possible the prompt review of my book by your readers. Its early publication would mean much to me. Besides students of my own there are many persons to whom this thesis has been promised as the result of the years of research of which it is the culmination. I would appreciate therefore whatever expedition you can bring to your decision in regard to its publication....

Sincerely yours,

Trigant Burrow

To a colleague

Dr. John T. MacCurdy   Baltimore, Maryland
New York   March 8, 1922

Dear MacCurdy:

I was so glad to hear from you this afternoon, after such a long time. I would like to see you. It has been in my thought that I should see you at the meeting in Washington, in May. You have always been hospitable to my theoretical ruminations and your understanding reception of my trends has often meant much to me on these occasions.

I am sending straight off to you the reprints of four papers, three of which refer quite at length to the primary subjective phase. In the paper on homosexuality the theory is quite fully set forth but I cannot accord entirely today with the deductions that follow in that same thesis. The thesis itself in which this primary identification principle was developed—'The Preconscious or the Nest Instinct'—I have never yet published. The fourth paper that I am sending may interest you as it has to do with the theory of psychoanalysis as contrasted with its actuality. In the others I have marked the passages that refer to the idea you have in mind.

I shall be interested to see your book. (3) I have just lately finished writing a little book myself but the publishers 'do not find their way to understanding it,' they say. It is really a development of this theory of a primary organic continuum in its societal implication. I have never thanked you for your book on War Neuroses which you were good enough to send me and which I and others have read with much interest.

With good wishes,

Sincerely yours,

Trigant Burrow

To Sherwood Anderson   Baltimore, Maryland
                                                  March 11, 1922

Dear Sherwood:

I keep putting off writing you, thinking I'll surely have something to write about the book. But there is still no word of its acceptance. ... I am really not discouraged though. The real ordeal was writing the thing. Having done that somehow, the matter of its acceptance or rejection seems comparatively small.

I will let you know whatever happens. I can't help feeling that if Mr. Brooks(4) had not intercepted your plan to have Paul Ro-

(3) *Problems in Dynamic Psychology*. See note 7, p. 41.
(4) Van Wyck Brooks.

senfeld read the book, things would have gone differently. Mr. Brooks' position was, you remember, that Mr. Rosenfeld had not kept up with the literature of psychoanalysis. So much the better. Academic knowledge of psychoanalysis is itself a neurotic symptom—I mean this very seriously—and it is Brooks' limitation as it is the limitation of the whole academic lot of us. As if psychoanalysis were life and not a mere compartment in life! I flatter myself that as Mr. Rosenfeld has understood you as sympathetically as he has without the aid of a score in front of him, he would have understood me. If he can understand the poetry he can understand the prose. People will permit the intuitional element into art-forms of reality but they still deny it to its scientific form. If I can only count on a publisher's *intellectual* understanding of the thing it will never be printed. I do not understand it intellectually myself. The process of its making was not an intellectual one. It could not have been. It was for me the most real of feeling experiences straight through.

I'll let you know. I wish I could see you. Write some time.

Here's seeing it through!

As always,

Trigant

To Dr. Adolf Meyer Baltimore, Maryland
Baltimore, Maryland March 29, 1922

Dear Doctor Meyer:

You were good enough to wish to have a résumé of the researches in analysis that have occupied me for the past two or three years but I fear I have burdened you unduly in leaving my manuscript with you all this while, particularly as I know how very many demands there are upon your time.

It has become clear in the light of the last few months that the book is much embarrassed by personal limitations of my own. For all its plea for personality I find myself still hugging the illusion of sponsorships invoked in support of fears that are the very antithesis of personality in the interpretation for which the thesis supposedly stands.

This will mean considerable alteration yet if it is to find its way ultimately to publication.

If you will kindly let me have the copy that is with you I will ask Jack to stop by for it tomorrow evening.

With good wishes,

Sincerely yours,

Trigant Burrow

To Madge Jenison   Baltimore, Maryland
Dobbs Ferry, N. Y.   April 15, 1922

Dear Miss Jenison:

Your letter came an hour ago. You have certainly been good. . . .

If the idea appeals to you of spending June or July in the country near here and letting me talk with you of the ideas you have brought together in your books and plays, I shall be very joyfully at your disposal. Or if you'd rather wait till the fall I shall be glad to go over your work with you then. Of course I know nothing of the art of literature, as you are aware, but if our talking together would help your aim let's talk together by all means.

As to my book, I do appreciate all your efforts and intercessions for it but my mind is quite clear now as to the need of my definitely recalling the manuscript for the present and resuming a ground on which I can feel myself at home. Perhaps my work can never find its way to publication but I can at least be at home in regard to it and that means infinitely more to me....

I have three papers finished and am beginning a fourth on the relativity of consciousness as a whole and of the misconception that is current with us because of our personal and arbitrary basis of interpretation. I should like to have you see these. I thought to call the series 'A Philosophy of the Neuroses.' They are 'intellectual' enough to satisfy the most vicarious and will, I think, pave the way for the presentation of the thesis that is *not* intellectual nor possible of intellectual manipulation by any process. As a paving stone take this for example: 'The conception of the relativity of consciousness is from our present individualistic viewpoint a most difficult one. The conception is not one that is possible of comprehension on the basis of the static and absolute principle of consciousness that is our present mode of envisagement.' And this: 'It involves no less a task than that of placing the fulcrum of one's mental operations upon a basis that is outside the sphere of one's individual consciousness.' Surely this will make clear that the burden of its comprehensibility does not rest solely with me and people need to study the thesis for themselves subjectively and not keep crying to me to 'say it with flowers'!

... When I have finished the shorter thesis I am now working on, I'll turn again to 'Our Common Consciousness.' I have grown clearer myself in this interim and can take hold of it with a surer hand when I come to review it.

Do get away Thursday for a good rest. Am only sorry you are not to be in Baltimore County, Maryland, rather than in Seneca Falls, New York.

With good wishes and hoping to see you later,

Sincerely,
Trigant Burrow

The manuscript was returned as Burrow requested, and five years were to pass before it was finally published. When it did appear after much revision and expansion, it was under the title, 'The Social Basis of Consciousness.'

Meanwhile in that spring of 1922 Dr. Burrow was interested, as always, in discussing his thesis with those sensitive to its implications. The next letter is to a high-school student who later became a lifelong associate.

To William E. Galt   Baltimore, Maryland
Selma, Alabama   March 31st, 1922

Dear William:

You are doubtless hard at work again at your studies by this time and are looking forward to your graduation in June.

I have thought of your comment at our last talk—that it did not seem to you possible that there should exist so complete a unity between any two people as the unity that exists in the common function of one's two hands. Your skepticism is most natural under the circumstances but I think you and I have pretty definitely agreed that the 'circumstances' are very far from natural, owing to the habituations that have come to play so significant a part in human life as it is now understood. It is, I think, to these circumstances which are now a part of the system about and within us that is due our skepticism.

As a part of the system we favor the system. We doubt the simplicity that underlies life because we are already caught up in its complexity. Because of the system of competitiveness about us our doubt is really prompted by our prior self-interest. But you have probably thought it out for yourself before now.

I know you were glad to get back to your school athletics again.
With good wishes,

Sincerely yours,

Trigant Burrow

To Dr. John T. MacCurdy   The Tuscany, Stony Run Lane
Cambridge, England   Baltimore, Maryland
                                                May 21, 1922

Dear MacCurdy:

Your letter came yesterday. The paper on 'Psychoanalysis in
Theory and Life' was published in the *Proceedings of the International Conference of Women Physicians*, Vol. IV.(5)

I wish it had been possible to have you see the fuller development
of the identification basis that has been the outcome of three
years daily analysis of my own reactions. I don't know whether
I mentioned to you this analytic experiment upon myself. It has
certainly altered my outlook and simplified my own life and that
of others with whom I have been working, even though it may
never gain a hearing amid the general audience. Perhaps we may
talk of it some day.

The meetings in Washington were the usual thing. Personally, I
felt more the absence of Hoch than the presence of the others. It
was good to see Clark again.

(5) Republished in *The Journal of Nervous and Mental Disease*, 1926, vol. 64,
pp. 209–24, and included as chapter 1 in *The Social Basis of Consciousness*.

I insist on your effacing 'The Washington' and 'Mount Vernon Place' from your memory and noting carefully my address of the past four years, above!

As always,

Trigant Burrow

P. S. I have left unsaid how glad I am that the reprints seem worth-while matter to you.

As their mutual analysis continued and developed, Dr. Burrow and Mr. Shields frequently came to the kind of impasse that quite generally occurs in human interchange: the point where the conflicting sense of 'right' of the individuals involved forces either a complete break or a superficial compromise. However, committed as they were to study the motivation underlying human discord, they held firmly to their course. But they were coming to feel more and more the need for a larger experimental group to enable the examination of interrelational impediments on a broader scale. This group they felt must consist of both normal and neurotic individuals and provide a test tube, so to speak, for an intensive study of the basic factors responsible for human conflict, in both its individual and its social aspects. Such an enlarged group composed of Dr. Burrow's associates, students, and patients, as well as the members of his immediate family, was first formed in the summer of 1923. It consisted of some twenty persons who lived and worked together that summer at Lifwynn Camp, as the Adirondack property was now called. From then on, the camp served each summer as a setting for the research endeavors of the group. The composition of this group changed from time to time but many of the original members continued work through the years and formed the nucleus of The Lifwynn Foundation when it was established in 1927. An early participant was Nelly Hölljes, R.N., whose later intensive study with Mr. Shields was a significant contribution to the larger research undertaking.

The expansion of the investigation further accentuated for Dr. Burrow the break with the customary pattern in which the personal life—the interests of 'home' and 'family'—are kept distinct and insulated from behavioral studies. No longer was he husband and father first and laboratory investigator second. On the contrary, the emotional involvements concomitant to the social role of husband and father furnished material for analysis in the laboratory of human behavior. This consistent application was characteristic of Burrow, and led Kurt Goldstein to write to him years later: 'You are one of the few scientists who make one feel that for him life and work are closely related.'(6)

Adjustment to this new orientation was no easy task. 'It need hardly be pointed out,' Dr. Burrow said, 'that to this intimate group that constituted my home, nothing could have conformed less to their idea of exciting entertainment than an experimental research into the behavioral ineptitudes of the Hominidae! As our interest had always been just the joy of life as we knew it, an unsolicited analysis of personal and social reactions was the more unwelcome.'(7)

But Dr. Burrow's family stood by. In the face of unavoidable misunderstanding, the essential core of their relationship was too sound—his feeling too deep and generous—to allow of alienation.

To understand the significance of these pioneer group studies it is necessary to recognize that the term 'group' referred primarily to a biological principle of behavior rather than to a conventionally assembled collection of individuals. As Burrow wrote on one occasion:

I have at no time thought of groups as a landscape gardener thinks of an arrangement of trees, or an educator, of a class of students. Biologically, such grouping is purely extrinsic and artificial. No inherent principle binds the individuals composing these arbitrary units. Such groups represent but a fortuitous collection of heterogeneous elements. In my use of the term group, I have had in mind from the outset a biological group and a biological principle of behavior ... It is because of this organismic principle of behavior underlying our researches that in the course of time I discarded the term 'group-analysis' in favor of the term 'phyloanalysis.'(8)

(6) Letter, December 31, 1948.

(7) Author's Foreword, *The Neurosis of Man*, p. xix.

(8) *The Neurosis of Man*, pp. 91-2.

From this point of view there could be no one person in the group who, more enlightened than the rest, undertook to advise and counsel his colleagues. Rather the group as a social unit undertook its own a-nalysis. 'A feature of central importance,' Dr. Burrow wrote later, 'was the circumstance that the investigation included me and my psycho-logical assistant, Mr. Clarence Shields (I had only his assistance at that time) equally with patients and students. As it appeared to me, there was everywhere—not only in my patients but in everyone—some basic inadequacy in adaptation.'(9)

These quotations highlight essential differences between Burrow's position and that of the various group therapies which developed later. The primary aim of phyloanalysis, moreover, was investigative rather than therapeutic. Yet these early studies, which introduced the then unfamiliar idea of analytic work with groups, undoubtedly helped to pave the way for the subsequent development of group psychotherapy.

A more fortunate environment than Lifwynn Camp for the initiation of the experiment could hardly be imagined. The simple living con-ditions made for concentrated study with a minimum of interruption. The property could be reached only by boat two miles across the lake, and there was no telephone. Yet, in spite of this seclusion, mail came and went regularly and it was in no sense difficult to keep in daily contact with the larger community, or to receive occasional visitors.

As time went on new cabins were added until there were a dozen or more set among the woods on the lake shore. The dining room and kitchen comprised a separate unit, while the original bungalow served as a large and comfortable living room. Here the group-meetings were held, and in the evening by the light of kerosene lamps, the campers gathered around the big fireplace for music, reading, or other recreation.

Mrs. Burrow took charge of the household management with her characteristic energy and efficiency, while the various tasks involved in the operation of camp and office were shared by the students. When emotional situations arose—irritation, aggressiveness, dependence, for example—they were handled as material for objective analysis. The laboratory sessions might occur spontaneously at the dining room table or wherever any group of students was engaged in some common enterprise—preparing a meal, painting a canoe, stacking wood, and

(9) Letter, June 21, 1935, to Dr. William M. Malisoff, editor of *Philosophy of Science*.

so on. There were also the more formally scheduled group-meetings, all directed toward unmasking the covert motivations to overt behavior expressions. The first summer a major project was the reading and discussion of 'Our Common Consciousness.'

Dr. Burrow greatly loved the deep quiet and the bracing atmosphere of Lifwynn Camp. It was ever a joy to him to have this setting for his work as well as for relaxation and play. From a wilderness the camp was gradually transformed into a place of exceptional beauty. Interested in it as an enlarging development, especially for the benefit of young people, Dr. Burrow, with the aid of other campers, eventually added a tennis and a badminton court, a croquet ground and soft-ball field, and created a place which was a continual source of pleasure to his family and associates. As for his own feeling he summed it up in a letter to his wife in 1943: 'How lovely the lake is this morning—this cool sweet morning. Not a ripple on it and just a light haze over the mountains. Lifwynn Camp is the earth's choicest spot for me.'

CHAPTER 6

ALTERED ORIENTATIONS AND THE
PSYCHOANALYTIC COMMUNITY

In 1921, the year of Burrow's break with the security of his professional life, he received an encouraging letter from the historian, James
Harvey Robinson. 'I am confident that your estimate of the normal
as a pestiferous neurosis is all too true,' he wrote. ' . . . I have been
teaching graduate classes in Columbia University for toward a quarter
of a century, and am sorely afflicted with the unreality of practically
all that passes for education. It is one gigantic conspiracy of repression.
I gave up my job, as I understand that you are giving up yours . . . I
hope that you will develop your thesis more fully. We are on the verge
of a revolution in our thought about man analogous to that which over-
took natural science early in the seventeenth century. All the older
psychology, politics, history and sociology are as little pertinent and
as archaic as scholastic natural science was to Descartes and Galileo.'
  Some time later Burrow wrote:

To James Harvey Robinson   Lifwynn Camp, Merrill, N. Y.
New York   September 5, 1923

My dear Dr. Robinson:

Three years ago, when I withdrew from my work, you were good
enough to write to me. It was a moment of very great difficulty
and uncertainty. I had not a clear course before me. There was

not the courage of conviction. So that your thoughtfulness meant very much indeed to me and I have thought many times of your consideration.

In the time that has passed there has been the necessity of much new endeavor. In the midst of the groping I began after a while to write. Since then things have been growing clearer from month to month until of late I have begun to sense something of what it has all meant.

After somewhat more than a year I went back again to my work—in the same place, amid the same conditions, with much the same people. The externals were unchanged and yet something had been definitely altered. About this time your book(1) came into my hands and with it a renewed stimulus to my own work. It seemed good to find trends that are as revolutionary as yours handled with such clearness and authority. In the last weeks I have completed a book in which I have tried to make clear the results of my own self-inquiries. It is off now in search of a publisher, but the chances of finding one seem doubtful to me in view of the generally unacceptable character of its matter.

It is because I wanted you to know of this outcome of my experience in these last years that I am writing you now and because in the midst of the uncertainty and trepidation of the moment in which I last wrote you, I must have said only half adequately how much your letter meant to me. It is to express the realization of what I could so dimly sense then that I am sending to you this word of my appreciation today.

Very sincerely yours,

Trigant Burrow

(1) *The Mind in the Making*, New York, Harper & Brothers, 1921, 235 pp.

The manuscript Burrow refers to in this letter was the expanded version of 'Our Common Consciousness.' At the same time other writings were under way which reflected his altered trend of inquiry. The first to set forth fully the new position was 'Social Images Versus Reality'(2), read before The American Psychopathological Association in 1924. 'The community,' Burrow says in this paper, 'occupies the central position within the social unconscious that the mother-image occupies within the individual unconscious. . . . But if the social image represented by the community possesses the same underlying psychology as the mother-image, then this social image can have no more relation to the reality of the social organism than the image of the mother has to the reality of the mother-organism.'

This challenging statement was soon followed by a paper entitled 'A Relative Concept of Consciousness'(3), in which the author introduces his concept of 'the organic mass consciousness of man to which the personal systems of men, single and collective, are but relative.' He says: 'As this organismic conception of consciousness is relativity itself within the subjective sphere, its encompassment can no more be apprehended in the scheme of evaluation represented by Freud and his predecessors than the relativity of the physicists can be apprehended on a static Newtonian basis.'

As indicated in his letters, Burrow did not regard his studies as a repudiation of the principles expounded by Freud but rather as an extension of these principles to the social organism. Though this view was not widely shared by his psychoanalytic confrères it was to this group that Burrow looked for an understanding of his thesis.

He continued to take an active part in the affairs of the American Psychoanalytic Association and was elected its president for the year 1925–26. In this capacity he delivered a paper entitled 'The Laboratory Method in Psychoanalysis, Its Inception and Development'(4) at the Ninth Congress of the International Psychoanalytic Association at Bad Homburg, Germany, in the fall of 1925.

(2) *The Journal of Abnormal Psychology and Social Psychology*, 1924, vol. XIX, pp. 230–5.

(3) 'A Relative Concept of Consciousness—An Analysis of Consciousness in Its Ethnic Origin,' *The Psychoanalytic Review*, 1925, vol. XII, pp. 1–15.

(4) *The American Journal of Psychiatry*, 1926, vol. 5, pp. 345–55. In this paper Burrow presented his concept of the societal origin and implications of the neuroses, and discussed his group-method of analysis.

His continuing interest in the psychoanalytic method is shown in the following letter to Sigmund Freud.

To Professor Sigmund Freud   Lifwynn Camp, Merrill, N. Y.
Vienna   July 4, 1924

My dear Professor Freud:

It has been a very long time since I have written you—not since the months immediately preceding the outbreak of the war. Perhaps you will most easily remember me if I recall that at that time I had in mind the possibility of going to Vienna with a view to undergoing an analysis from you. This was the purport of our correspondence at that time. Of course with the onset of the war my plans were brought abruptly to an end.

My determination to write you now was prompted by a statement made to me when I was at Atlantic City a few weeks ago attending the annual meeting of the American Psychoanalytic Association. At the outset let me say that of late the air here in America has become rife with tendencies that seem to me largely subversive of the basic principles of psychoanalysis. My feeling is that consistency with these principles demands that this tendency be boldly challenged by the representatives of psychoanalysis. It is in this conviction that I am taking the liberty of writing you now.

The circumstance was this: At this meeting a paper was read by Dr. Rank in which he advocated a new procedure in regard to the technical conduct of psychoanalysis—a procedure by which the analyst definitely assigns a period at the termination of which the analysis shall peremptorily cease. I was wholly unprepared for such a statement, particularly coming from a psychoanalyst of Dr. Rank's reputation and experience, and I confess that the proposal appeared to me as a most unwarranted and amazing innovation.

Upon the conclusion of the session I was among those who sought Dr. Rank in order to ask questions that had not been brought out in the discussion that followed his paper. The question I asked was: 'What is Freud's attitude toward this proposed change?' Dr. Rank's reply gave me to understand that you were by no means unfavorable to it. As I understood him, he said that you had been absent from your office for six months owing to illness, but that you had recently returned to work and that you intended giving the new plan a trial. I know that Dr. Rank would not have made this statement had he not felt warranted in doing so; and yet in view of what I know to have been your long-standing tradition in this regard I find it difficult for me to credit it.

I admit my resistance to the implications of this statement and I concede that my attitude may not be wholly dependable because of the amount of affect with which it is laden. But granting this, I still find myself unsympathetic to so radical a departure from the attitude of non-interference that has always characterized the position of psychoanalysis toward a patient. I am perhaps the less sympathetic because of my lack of accord with certain kindred adaptations that have become increasingly prominent of late in different quarters. As in Switzerland, so within a certain element in this country, what was once psychoanalysis is no longer psychoanalysis. It is for the most part a judiciously considered modification of the clear and uncompromising principle in which it originated. In the hands of such interpreters psychoanalysis has wavered in its course, and in its hope of placating the many it has hesitated to meet the need of the few. Not that psychoanalysis has not undergone much conscious and valuable modification in the brief years since its inception. I do not know of anyone who has been more ready to admit the faults of your method than you have been wherever it has appeared to you inadequate or mistaken.

But modifications of psychoanalysis offered in the interest of truth are very different from modifications that are offered with a view to making terms with the critics of psychoanalysis.

I remember that in the very early days of psychoanalysis objection was raised against it on the ground that such a method of treatment occupied too long a time. Your reply at that time seemed to me all-sufficient. No one, you said, had ever questioned the validity of the orthopedist's method of correcting a distorted limb because of the length of time required to do so; why then all the outcry because of the length of time required for adjusting the distorted mind? I can readily conceive that there are conditions which make the treatment, as it is at present, *needlessly* long. If so it seems to me that what is needed is the analysis of these conditions, in which circumstance they will automatically adjust themselves. But to shorten a course of treatment because it is long seems unintelligent to me. It seems merely shifting from one unconscious condition to an equally unconscious alternative—a point I attempted to develop at this same meeting in a paper entitled 'Our Mass Neurosis.' (5)

I know, of course, that those who advocate limiting the duration of the analysis have invoked the theory that the analysis represents for the patient psychically the entire period of his intra-uterine life, that in the fanciful attitude of the patient toward the analyst this experience is again relived symbolically and that accordingly it should proceed symbolically to its logical interruption at birth. This theory, I know, is quite in line with your own early conceptions, as with those of Ferenczi. And if you happen to recall earlier papers of mine, written between the years 1914 and 1917, ('The Genesis and Meaning of Homosexuality' and 'The Origin of the Incest-Awe,' both published in the Psychoanalytic Review), you will agree, I am sure, that I would be the last to deny Dr. Rank's theoretical basis. But surely it is not the part of the analyst to corroborate the phantasy-life of a patient! Else of what worth were the analysis? . . .

(5) *The Psychological Bulletin*, 1926, vol. 23, pp. 305–12.

I do not wish to be misunderstood. I do not mean for a moment to imply that I regard the position of psychoanalysis as beyond criticism. Not at all. But I feel that the answer to such criticism is more analysis and not less, that what is needed is yet deeper and wider study of the mechanisms and reactions into which you were the first to penetrate rather than a curtailment of our analytic responsibility through recourse to short-cut simplifications.

As I see the amendment suggested by Rank it is just another feature of an increasing program for trimming the method of psychoanalysis to the public whim. It is part of an insidious tendency toward unconsciousness that has entered our own ranks and is little by little leading psychoanalysts themselves to capitulate their ground. I am speaking to you without reservation. If I may not speak frankly to you, to whom may I speak frankly?

These tendencies to innovation, first expressed by Jung and his pupils, are preëminently adapted to the susceptible type of social hysteric for which a large element of our American population is only too justly reputed. I am the more interested just now in the modified tendency of outlook among psychoanalysts because of a book I have just completed in which I have attempted to discuss the social implications of the neurosis from a viewpoint that includes the reactions collectively of psychoanalysts themselves as a special form of a social or mass unconscious within and about us.

In my book I have openly expressed what I feel are our psychoanalytic limitations. As far as my own personal limitations and unconsciousness permitted, I have tried to show to what extent psychoanalysis has been restricted in its outlook by a too narrow interpretation of its applications and I have tried to indicate what seem to me its wider possibilities of growth.

In view of the probable publication of my book within a short time I am the more interested to know directly from you whether it is true that you are disposed to consider the adoption of the 'new method of psychoanalysis,' as it is called, or whether you were incorrectly quoted when you were reported as having expressed

your intention of trying the new method now advocated by Dr.
Rank and his school.(6)

May I say in closing that I deeply regret to hear of your having
been ill. I do not yet abandon the thought of making at least a brief
visit to Vienna some time in the not too distant future. I look
forward at that time to the privilege of seeing you again.

With my high esteem and kind regards,

Sincerely yours,

Trigant Burrow

To a young relative   Lifwynn Camp, Merrill, N. Y.
                                                        September 1, 1924

Dear J.:

I have your letter and assure you that the earlier one requires no
apology. There is a great deal to say and I know that letters are
inadequate.

(6) In reply Freud wrote that he believed Dr. Burrow had 'developed concerns
which fortunately are not justified.' It is interesting to note, however, that
the rift between Freud and Rank which occurred in 1926 is ascribed to this
innovation. In speaking of it Karpf says: ' . . . it was precisely this theory of
Rank's, as developed in his *Trauma of Birth,* which precipitated so much
defensive controversy in the movement that it eventually forced an unwilling
break between Freud and Rank.' (Karpf, Fay B., *The Psychology and Psychotherapy of Otto Rank,* New York: Philosophical Library, 1953, p. 10.) In
regard to Rank's new conceptions Sachs reports: 'Freud tried for a while to
mediate but with little success since the gulf between Rank's new opinions and
the psychoanalytic theory became more and more evident.' (Sachs, Hanns,
Freud: Master and Friend, Cambridge, Massachusetts, Harvard University
Press, 1944, p. 160.)

It does seem to me that I need in justice to you to make myself clearer in what I said about the absence of conviction with you. You see, the neurotic personality (and that is everybody) is unconsciously dependent upon mental images which have no substantiation but which have been artificially induced in him through the mental images of the people in closest contact with him. It is a *social condition.* I am only too glad to meet your need in the utmost way in which I am capable but I am not meeting your need if, in trying to let you see your unconscious mental dependence, I at the same time invite in you an attitude of dependence upon me. If, for example, you are in a position to be in Baltimore quite independently of me—that is, without any arrangement or assistance of mine, I am prepared to have you come in and work with me and with our group in just so far as your time and ours will permit. This may seem harsh to you, but anything else would seem harsh from my point of view.

You were utterly dependent all your life upon your father and your family. Your father was all his life utterly dependent upon his father and his family. It is so the world over. I believe that a new social order is on the eve of its beginning. We cannot lament with the individual. We can only go forward with the race and let enter upon this newer outlook whatever individuals there are who will, who *must.*

Far from being different from everybody else, you are exactly everybody else. You are right. Your depression is a disease with you, but it is common to society at large.

With love to all,

Devotedly,

Trigant

To Dr. Isador H. Coriat   Lifwynn Camp, Merrill, N. Y.
Boston, Massachusetts   September 4, 1924

Dear Coriat:

I want to tell you how sorry I was that you should have had to go away before we could have had another talk. Our contact this summer seemed after all so fragmentary, but with my own days so definitely scheduled, it just was not possible for me to be with you more, as much as I should have liked to.

My secretary sent Jones' letter to you last Friday.(7) I wish we might have discussed this. It is not possible to do so by letter. To me the strong note in Jones' discussion is that of business and I am not very apt at this, though I do not mean to discredit the objective necessities of the case as Jones sees it.

What I should have liked to talk of with you is the aspect of his letter that is of importance to me from the altered basis of our group work. While it is not a condition that can be blamed in any way, it does seem to me quite outrageous that psychoanalysts are themselves as neurotic and as confused as their patients and that unconsciously they are using the conflict of their patients to divert attention from their own. I think it quite perverts the central aim of our work for us to pretend any longer that the neurosis is not a social condition and that we ourselves do not share equally with our patients in it.

It is not possible for me to stand alone in my work. I do not wish to. And if I did wish to, I could not. Its whole meaning is its inclusiveness. I do not know whether other psychoanalysts are prepared to challenge their own personalistic and objective basis as I have

(7) Ernest Jones, editor of the *International Journal of Psycho-Analysis*.

been forced to challenge mine. I know you understand from the talks we have had this summer that my position leaves me no other course than to call to every sincere worker in our field, as in allied fields, for recognition and support of the new conceptions to which the concentrated labor of several years in group analysis has led me.

I do not want to burden you or anyone else with unwelcome responsibilities—I know you have your own—but neither can I permit myself to refrain from drawing attention to obligations which I feel that others share in common with me. This position explains the absence of accord on my part toward the general tenor of Jones' letter. My feeling is that the work that has opened up to me and my associates is of a larger scope than that for which Jones seems to stand. Knowing from you your own interests in the broader economic and sociological aspects of psychoanalysis, I do not feel that in saying this I am thrusting upon you a viewpoint that is alien to your own. It seems to me that the real interest of psychoanalysis is not in the direction of Jones' appeal and that if we are to preserve its traditions in their wider development, we must stand together for interpretations that are larger than our own hitherto individual scope. I hope you will consider these things and that our talks this summer will not have been a temporary incident in the ultimate thought of us both. . . .

Dr. Syz(8) returned to Baltimore yesterday to the great regret of us all. We shall all be leaving though about the fifteenth. Just now the weather here in the mountains is very delightful. I only wish you could have remained longer. . . .

With remembrances from Mrs. Burrow and myself to you and Mrs. Coriat,

Sincerely yours,

Trigant Burrow

---

(8) Hans Syz, M. D., an early participant in the group studies, later an associate of Dr. Burrow's. Syz is a Swiss name, pronounced 'Seets.'

To Gail Gardner   Baltimore, Maryland
New York   January 15, 1925

Dear Miss Gardner:

May I send to you and Miss Doing(9) New Year's greetings in
the form of two papers I have recently published? I don't know
whether their thought connects up with your own general formulations but I wanted you to have them because they are part of
a larger thesis that has come to be of much meaning to me in my
altered outlooks.

Baltimore had a rare treat Monday night in Jeritza's concert. She
sang to an overflowing house that received her with unbounded
enthusiasm. We were reluctant to leave at the close of her long
recital. Emily commented the only thing lacking was an open fire
and a seat on the floor as it is in camp. Friday night we are booked
for Toti dal Monte and I am, of course, all eagerness.

Please thank Miss Doing for the notice of Mr. Imandt's recital
sent at her request. I must write him in a few days. We are hoping
to have him play in Baltimore next winter. What about you? Are
you singing in public this winter? Jeritza sang Schumann's
'Widmung.' It brought back very pleasant memories to us all.

With good wishes to you and Miss Doing from all of us,

Sincerely yours,

Trigant Burrow

(9) Gail Gardner and Ruth Doing had a camp on Lake Chateaugay for the
teaching of rhythmic dancing.

To Dr. Alfred Adler Baltimore, Maryland
Vienna January 25, 1925

Dear Doctor Adler:

I am heartily ashamed at not having replied long ago to your very
kind postcard to me. Dr. Syz has spoken of his visit to you and of
what he felt to be the points at which our interpretations seemed
to make contact. I have had in mind your kind interest to have me
send a paper for publication in your journal, but the very deep preoccupation of the last years in writings which attempt to set forth
my general thesis has rather kept me from contributing articles to
the general psychological journals. Of late, however, I have published two brief papers that give some hint of my trend. I am
sending these to you in the hope that they may be of interest.

With my kind regards and best wishes,

Very sincerely yours,

Trigant Burrow

To Professor Sigmund Freud Baltimore, Maryland
Vienna January 28, 1925

Dear Professor Freud:

I was very glad indeed to have your letter last summer in answer
to my inquiries and to know your reaction to my general misgivings.

While I feel sure of Dr. Rank's personal devotion to you, I still
cling to a certain obstinate suspicion with respect to recent psychoanalytic innovations. As I hear these new theories promulgated I
cannot but mark the overcharge of affect that invariably ac-
companies their presentation.

But I am writing you today to call your attention to reprints of two recent papers that are the outcome of several years' intensive research with groups of students in the problems of psychoanalysis in their social implication. This extension of the individual analysis to groups of students seems to me to give an added confirmation of your numerous formulations with respect to the individual. . . .

I should be very glad if these papers may seem of interest to you.

With my kind regards,

Very sincerely yours,

Trigant Burrow

To Sherwood Anderson
New York

Baltimore, Maryland
January 29, 1925

Dear Sherwood:

I don't know how it has happened that so long a time has passed without any interchange of messages between us. But here I am anyhow as good as new and I wish I might have from you a message of like purport.

Nobody liked my book so that I added another to it and then apparently they liked it still less. The last years, however, have entertained me no little in the opportunity they have offered for intensive research with groups of students in our common social reactions. It has introduced a much needed democratic element into our former tendency toward restriction and overspecialization. I hope we may talk of these things some glad day. In the meantime I am sending you reprints of two recent papers. They are part of the larger work I hope some day will find its way to the publisher.

I wish I might have some direct news of you. I am ashamed to say that I have not yet read your latest work and the one that will undoubtedly be of greatest interest to me, though I am fortunate enough to own it. The days allow me little leisure outside of the work's demands. I hope that some day I may see your face once more.

With love,

As always,

Trigant

To a friend
Louise Collier Willcox(10)
Norfolk, Virginia

Baltimore, Maryland
February 1, 1925

Dear Mrs. Willcox:

I haven't written you in all these weeks and have not thanked you for your courteous card of Christmas greeting. Mrs. Burrow and I appreciated very much your thinking of us.

Since I wrote you I have been in New York to give an address and while there stopped in to see Mr. Wells.(11) He was in Europe but Miss Virginia Watson was there, whom, as it turns out, I had known forty years ago when we were children together at the Atlantic Hotel in Norfolk!

I had a nice day in Norfolk about two weeks ago sitting and holding hands with Mother as in the old days. I cannot wait to get back

(10) Mrs. Westmore Willcox.

(11) Editor of Harper & Brothers.

to her again. The next time though I hope she will be better so that I can spare a moment from her side to run in and see you. Inez told me of your being so much better which sounds more like you than anything I have heard for a long time. I am looking forward to your article on 'Experience.' I am rather chary of seeing my portrait by your hand. A kindly hand but it has misinterpreted me so. . . .

With my kind regards,

Always sincerely,

Trigant Burrow

To a former patient

Baltimore, Maryland
February 11, 1925

Dear Miss W.:

If you are not sentimental, if in your human relationships you are not actuated by secret motives of righteous, religious self-interest that loves to look and talk kind, to the end of procuring for yourself a pleasant sense of benevolence and merit, then I fear that no effort of mine to translate my thesis into A.B.C. for you would be of avail.

It has been the slow—because painful and unwelcome—realization of this furtive, personal, unconscious incentive underlying the outward expressions of our lives, and marring in us all truth and wholesomeness, that has brought together those of us who compose this group in the joint, concerted effort to understand in our united organization this subtle and destructive tendency existing unrecognized in each of us as a single and separate individual.

It is significant, I think, that the one thing you found in our talks last spring to be untrue and unacceptable was the one thing which discredited you and your attitude toward others and that this sick quality of which you say you do not partake has been found by those of our group to be a quality common to us all.

I think that the earnest individual—the individual of sensitive feeling and intelligent outlooks—must come to put aside all personal criteria. I think he must come to see that the unwelcomeness of a statement is not only *not* a disproof of that statement but on the contrary that it offers the stronger evidence in support of it.

The trouble has been all along that the individual has stood alone. Alone he can only defend himself. He can only set up an opinion of himself that tends desperately to offset the falsely derogatory opinions which, as a child, he sensed toward him on the part of those around him.

I do not think the individual need be alone. Neither do I think he need comfort his loneliness with the false flatteries and assurances of those who are the expressions of an equally mistaken loneliness. Loneliness, long enough entertained, becomes a fetish. It is a painful guest of whom we would not be rid because we know no other. Fetish-worship is intriguing but it is without intelligent, thoughtful warrant.

This needless and destructive and quite subtly egotistic loneliness of the world generally is an absorbing theme with me. If I have obtruded unduly upon you this thought that is the preoccupation of my own life, I hope you will not lay it to any wish of mine to alter outlooks of yours that you prefer to leave unchallenged, but to the overwhelming tendency to express most earnestly what I have myself come most earnestly to feel.

With my kind regards,

Sincerely yours,

Trigant Burrow

To a friend   Baltimore, Maryland
Dr. Hanford Henderson(12)   February 13, 1925
Washington, D.C.

Dear Hanford:

No 'morning' or 'afternoon' would be long enough to satisfy my
eagerness to see you. Won't you come over Sunday and spend as
many days as you will? You mustn't have any feeling of being an
interruption. Brownie and I are so completely at home with you
that if there are necessary engagements we shall just leave you
with a book—probably my book—until we can rejoin you.

Let me know what time we may meet you Sunday. We dine at
1:30, but come either in the morning or afternoon whichever is
convenient to you. But let me know, if possible, so that we may
meet you at Union Station.

I am more happy than I can say at the thought of seeing you again
so soon. With love,

As always,

Trigant

To Mrs. Howard S. Gans(13)   Baltimore, Maryland
New York   March 10, 1925

Dear Mrs. Gans:

It meant very much to me to have your letter and to know of your
interest in the papers. If there can be a response like yours from a

(12) Dr. Henderson was an educator and author, and one of the first leaders
in the children's camp movement.

(13) President of the Child Study Association of America.

few thoughtful people, I feel it will be the beginning of better things in our attempt to deal with the problems of human behavior. May I say that during these last very arduous years of enforced reconstruction of principles that had come to be, as I thought, basic with me, I have often felt that you would be among the first to sense whatever value these newer formulations may hold. So that your letter is like an answer I had long awaited.

It happens that I may be in New York to give a paper before the Academy of Medicine on the twenty-sixth of this month. I shall be the guest of Dr. Pierce Clark, who plans to have me go with him Friday to Stamford. (14) I won't be able to remain longer than that day at Stamford as I must be back in New York to meet some engagements during the week-end. I shall be very glad indeed to see you and to meet the small group of which you spoke. I wish our coming together though might be very direct and informal. If we could discuss things as students together, I should feel at once that I was upon home soil and in this more intimate way I feel that there may be the beginning of something of common help to us all.

But I do hope that in addition there may be the opportunity of talking with you of the outlooks that have come to be of very much meaning to me. I am sure you are quite right about the need of a briefer statement of my thesis before the larger and more technical work can expect to gain an audience. . . .

Looking forward to seeing you,

Sincerely yours,

Trigant Burrow

(14) Psychoanalyst who had a sanitarium where he specialized in the study of the psychogenic aspects of epilepsy.

To Dr. L. Pierce Clark   Baltimore, Maryland
Stamford, Connecticut   March 31, 1925

Dear Dr. Clark:

Nothing quite so nice has happened to me in a very long time as this visit I have just had with you. I got back late Sunday afternoon feeling quite renewed in spirit and refreshed toward outlooks generally.

It was too bad you had to leave the theatre the other evening. There was no falling off toward the end—the final act was masterfully done.(15) Miss Yurka rose to a superb height. I have never seen a higher order of interpretation. It was like the Russian players translated. Ibsen always brings fresh inspiration, and I am quite full of the idea of a play which I should like to see tackled as a group creation.

I liked so much the atmosphere of your group home at Stamford. I felt a nice spirit of unanimity among your co-workers and students there. The response my paper(16) met among them and at the Academy encourages me to go on with further writing in the same vein. I have thought of your suggestion about the possibility of the Atlantic. As I think it over, though, I cannot imagine it getting by that stolid Atlantic front. It needs a good deal of revision, however, and if later it seems at all a likelihood for the Sedgwicks, I will ask you to write Mrs. Colby. As Harper's have asked me for a paper I thought possibly this might be suitable for them, but I don't know.

(15) The Wild Duck.

(16) 'The Heroic Role—An Historical Retrospect,' *Psyche* (London) 1926, vol. VI, pp. 42–54.

Saturday morning I saw Harcourt. He is going to consider the
small book of which I spoke to you and I am to hear from them in
about a week. I do hate so this business of going about and trying
to sell my wares.

It was an interesting unit I found in the members of the Federation
for Child Study that met Saturday afternoon at the home of Mrs.
Howard S. Gans. They seemed much interested in the group
activities we are pursuing here and at Lifwynn Camp.

I am looking forward to the names of the books you are going to
let me have. I wonder if you have yet gotten to *Wuthering
Heights*. As psychiatry, Kraepelin is not to be compared to it.
Heathcliff affords material for a ripping analysis. I am so glad too
that you haven't yet read *The Soul of Man under Socialism*. It is
pleasant to call your attention to at least a few things that have
meant very much to me. I am sure you cannot help but care for
this essay. I wonder if you know Carpenter's books—*Love's Coming of Age*—with reservations, *Pagan and Christian Creeds, Civilization, Its Cause and Cure*, and *The Intermediate Sex*. You would
be particularly interested, if you have not yet read it, in Coomar-
aswamy's *The Dance of Siva*, particularly in his chapter 'Sahaja.'
I should think it might be well to have on your bookshelf at Stamford Olive Schreiner's *The Story of an African Farm* with its bi-
sexual conflict, and also her *Woman and Labor*, Loti's *An Iceland
Fisherman*, and Witter Bynner's *The New World*. I wonder if
Mr. Eunecker(17) (I doubt if I spell it correctly) knows these
books.

What is foremost in my mind is your visit to us when you come
to Washington for the American Psychopathological meeting.
As that meets on Thursday, I should like so much if you could
return with me and spend at least the week-end. We can probably
have some good motoring at least. If you don't know this country,
you will probably enjoy the very varied scenery it presents. So I
am counting on you to plan to be with me for as many days as you

(17) T. E. Uniker.

can give us. Of course, if you find it more convenient to come before the meeting, we would love to have you then. May not our group count on an informal talk from you? Perhaps we could have two or three such conferences during the days you are with us! May I suggest your taking up the articles which you let me see in manuscript Friday morning and that after hearing you read from these, we make their matter the basis for discussion. This is only a suggestion, and if it would in any way be a burden during the time of your recess, don't consider it for a moment as I would like your visit to us to be just as free and unhampered as mine was to you. . . .

I hope you will remember me to your daughter and to your son. I wish you would remind your son again for me of Darwin's *Expressions of the Emotions in Man and Animals*. Will you tell your daughter that Mr. Stead was not a stranger to me after all. One of the students reminded me that she had shown me just the other day a very interesting letter from him from England. I hope you will give my greetings to those in association with you at Stamford.

We are looking forward with more pleasure than I can say to your visit in the spring. With my kindest regards and appreciations,

Faithfully yours,

Trigant Burrow

To Professor Sigmund Freud   Baltimore, Maryland
Vienna   April 3, 1925

Dear Professor Freud:

I appreciate very much your letter with its comments upon the two reprints I recently sent you.

Your letter, though, has left me not a little puzzled and I can not but feel that you will welcome my wish to speak to you quite frankly of it. In regard to your criticism of my paper on 'A Relative Concept of Consciousness' and your feeling that I have failed of my task in attempting to correlate mental processes with laws operative within the physical universe I have nothing to say. Perhaps you are right.

With regard to the second paper, 'Social Images versus Reality,' I feel that I have been placed at a distinct disadvantage and as no one, I think, has suffered from a similar embarrassment more than you have, there is probably no one who will more readily sympathize with my position than you. It seems to me that the great disadvantage under which your own work has labored has been the misinterpretation from which it has suffered. Statements made by you in clear and unequivocal terms have been definitely misrepresented and ideas have been attributed to you time and again for which you could not have been justly held answerable.

I find myself in a like case in regard to your criticism of my paper, 'Social Images versus Reality.' You quote me as having said that the mother-image 'bears no relation whatever to the early associations of our childhood.' I do not know whether you read my paper first hand or whether it was submitted to you in abstract form. But I do want to state most emphatically that my article contains no such statement as this you have quoted, and to judge the merit of the paper upon this basis is hardly fair to me.

I not only did not make this statement but I made the directly contrary statement of this over and over again throughout the paper. For example: 'The image, in short, which every individual carries in the locket of his unconscious is the image of his mother. It is this image which he treasures throughout life as beyond price. From Freud we have learned the far-reaching influence of the mother-image upon the affective life. But there is the need to recognize that the mother-image becomes the underlying criterion of every judgment that the individual forms. Its impress is the emotional substrate of all the thoughts and activities of his life.'

As nearly as I can discover the passage to which you refer, the actual statement, page 233, reads that the 'mother-image bears no relation whatever to the mother-organism.' My distinction between the mother-organism and the mother-image is clearly explained. If this distinction cited throughout the paper—the distinction between the *impression* the mother *suggests* and the *reality* that the mother *is*—has been understood, you will realize that I could not have made a statement as utterly unwarranted and as utterly contradictory of the experience of every psychoanalyst, including myself, as this statement you attribute to me. Such a statement, I assure you, would seem to me as puerile and absurd as it must seem to you. If you have made yourself at all familiar with my earlier writings such as 'The Origin of the Incest Awe' (*The Psychoanalytic Review*, Vol. v, No. 3) and 'The Genesis and Meaning of Homosexuality' (*The Psychoanalytic Review*, Vol. iv, No. 3), you will see that I have given my fullest recognition to your outstanding thesis of the significance of the mother-image in its relation to the early associations of childhood and its bearing upon the neuroses and psychoses.

May I say that in attributing to me a position that is identical with that of Jung you again do me an injustice. My attitude toward the social neurosis is definitely analytic, personal, historical, and has been daily subjected to the scientific discipline of actual experiments in group procedure. Jung's position is theoretical and, as you say, impersonal and unhistorical. Far from being identified with Jung's concept, I have wholly repudiated what seems to me to be Jung's wholly mystical and unscientific position. The social images to which I refer are nothing other than the extension socially of the repressed images first described by you in their individual manifestation.

To be quite as frank with you as I should like to be, I really am not so much interested in the mistaken interpretation you have made of my statements as I am in the motive that has led to your attitude toward them. I should be very interested analytically, as I feel you would be also, if you would discover, in what I feel to be in keeping with a spirit of mutual confidence between us, just what has been the underlying occasion of your having so completely and so unsympathetically read me.

From my first acquaintance with your work fifteen years ago, nothing has ever so completely compelled my interest and assent. I have labored diligently through all this time endeavoring to understand human life on the basis of the psychological concepts set forth by you. I have tried earnestly to extend the application of the principles first enunciated by you to the social as well as to individual repressions. In response my efforts are discredited upon interpretations which have no basis whatever in fact. Were there the discrepancy between my own views and those I have learned from you, I could hardly make the statement that is contained in the introduction of a book I hope soon to publish: 'Let me say at once, however, to anyone who may have lacked the opportunity or the candor to verify within himself the essential objective findings of Freud, and who is disposed to read into this thesis a vindication of his personal reaction against Freud's formulations, that he will find this study in no wise adapted to assuage their outrage to his sensibilities. Whatever may be the value of this work, in the spirit of its presentation it is in no sense a personal discrimination against the teaching of Freud but rather it is the acknowledged outgrowth of that teaching.'(18)

In remonstrating, as I do, against your misunderstanding of me, I must not be thought as offering any word of defense. There is no need of any. I do feel that I owe it to myself and to you, however, to forestall, if possible, a misunderstanding that is based upon a criticism that rests not upon what I have said but upon what I have not said, and to give myself and you the opportunity of discovering, if possible, wherein lies the occasion for your discrimination against my scientific endeavors. My own feeling is that your attitude does not bear directly in any way upon the actual material I have submitted you but that it is possibly due to a preconception of me based upon the reports of others.

(18) *The Social Basis of Consciousness*, p. 4.

I know that your days are very full and that it cannot be expected of you that you be familiar with the work and the endeavors of all of your pupils. It is inevitable that you should know many of us merely second hand and by hearsay. I quite understand this circumstance and accept it with entire respect, but I feel sure that where, through inadvertence, I have been incorrectly misconstrued by you, you will be the first to wish me to call your attention to this unintentional misapprehension on your part.(19)

With my high esteem and most cordial greetings,

Sincerely yours,

Trigant Burrow

To Dr. C. P. Oberndorf   Baltimore, Maryland
New York   May 10, 1925

Dear Oberndorf:

I think I did tell you in Richmond how excellent I thought your paper on the Psychoanalytic Movement in America.(20) I don't believe I did halfway convey to you though how much I appreciated the significant place you gave to my own work. I was interested in your feeling for 'A Relative Concept of Consciousness.' It does not seem to have been very generally understood, so that I was the more pleased at your appraisement of it.

In writing you now my thought is to put aside what is commonly called personal modesty and, as chairman of the Association, to

(19) In his reply Freud wrote in part: 'I was mistaken in my judgment of your second article and I am ready to correct my judgment. ... Your paper, "A Relative Concept of Consciousness," disappointed and irritated me, so that I was prejudiced also against your other formulations.'

(20) 'History of the Psychoanalytic Movement in America,' *The Psychoanalytic Review*, 1927, vol. XIV, pp. 281–97.

try to call your attention to what I consider has been the really significant contribution from me. If it is of real value, you will want to bring it before the notice of your readers. From what I have gathered, the impression prevails that very little of original work has come from America and for this reason I am under the greater obligation to bring to your consideration whatever work of mine may seem to fall under this category.

I have chiefly in mind the conception which I call the 'principle of primary identification' as first described in my paper, 'The Genesis and Meaning of Homosexuality' (*The Psychoanalytic Review*, July 1917).

In MacCurdy's book, *Problems in Dynamic Psychology*, on pages 38–39, there is this passage:

Freud has said little or nothing about the development of narcissism. This problem has, however, received most enlightening treatment from Burrow, who traces the steps by which self-consciousness and self-love grow out of the 'primary subjective state' and a primary identification of self with mother. It is peculiarly significant that this, the most original and important contribution to psychoanalysis of recent years, has received no attention from Freud and his immediate followers.

In two of Pierce Clark's papers there are references to this theory of mine. In one, *The Psychoanalytic Review* for January 1923, there is this rather long passage describing my conception:

Only very recently there has been brought forward an intelligent hypothesis to explain the phenomenon of narcism. Many case illustrations might be cited to substantiate this new view which, briefly stated, is as follows: During intrauterine life the child feels that it is a part of the mother and it continues to do so for some time after birth. When the physical weaning period is reached many of these primary traits or manners of feeling continue to remain in a state of identification with the mother. The child then looks out upon the world about him with the feeling-eyes of the mother: he sees his own person as the apple of his mother's eye; he receives her tenderest love and protection. Continuing this state of identification, he looks on this image of himself as the greatest of love-objects. He may gain such a wonderful entrancement of his own worth that he becomes engrossed in this first love. During this phase of development he may take on the mother's likes and dislikes and may never be able to free himself in later life from this attitude. He may go on loving and worshipping his own destiny to such an extent that he may never attain normal emotions toward the opposite sex, or, in exceptional instances, even for others of his own sex (homosexuality). In such a state of narcism he looks upon himself as an all-sufficient god, ever enduring or ever renewing himself by his own will. There are so many phases of the immediate descriptive topography of narcism that one may only venture to point out the enormous importance of the whole subject, which forecasts a very rich fruition in personal¹ and social psychology. But as a general pattern we may say that narcism has its very roots in the mother's passion and temperament, and is modified and screened through the mind and imagination of the child.

Chronologically, narcism antedates the Oedipus complex; the state of identification comes before that of looking upon the mother as the adored object.

This factor of the primacy of the identification principle in contrast to the secondary and objective principle embodied in the Oedipus complex is one that gives particular significance, I think, to my conception of the infant's primary subjective phase. Before publishing his paper Clark sent the manuscript to me but through some inadvertence he does not mention my name in the paper.

In an article of Clark's in *The Journal of Nervous and Mental Disease*, January 1925, page 51, he again cites my theory, and contrasts it with that of Freud.

Besides these there have been very many references in the literature to this primary subjective phase which I first cited in 1913 in a paper called 'Psychoanalysis and Life' and read before the New York Academy of Medicine.(21) If I am not mistaken, you yourself were present at that meeting. It was the following year that I read my paper on 'The Genesis and Meaning of Homosexuality' at the fourth annual meeting of the American Psychoanalytic Association in Albany, but, as I said, I did not submit this for publication until 1917. The theory has been developed by me from

(21) Unpublished.

different angles in the following essays: 'Character and the Neuroses' (*The Psychoanalytic Review*, February 1914); 'The Preconscious or the Nest Instinct' (read at the seventh annual meeting
of the American Psychoanalytic Association, Boston, 1917 and
not yet published); 'The Origin of the Incest Awe' (*The Psychoanalytic Review*, July 1917); 'Notes with Reference to Freud,
Jung and Adler' (*The Journal of Abnormal Psychology*, August
1917).

I think you will feel with me that this conception is a basic one and
that it advanced an entirely new psychological principle. On this
account I think that this piece of work should be included among
the original contributions of our own psychoanalysts cited in your
paper. . . .

On rereading this letter I fear the prominent place I am giving
myself in it may sound very egotistical to you, but I feel sure you
will understand that were it anybody else I should be as glad to
bring forward whatever work might seem to me to veto the
criticism of the Europeans that the Americans have contributed
nothing to psychoanalytic thought.

Looking forward to hearing from you, and with my good wishes,

Very sincerely yours,

Trigant Burrow

To a young relative   Baltimore, Maryland
                                               May 17, 1925

Dear J.:

I have spoken to several of the group of the plan of your coming to
camp this summer in the function of a part-time worker—or with
a semi-scholarship—the terms being those offered your brother

last year, and, so far, the response has been wholly favorable to the idea. . . .

With the Doing Camp closed I fear you would find little congeniality in the direction of music. But there is this. Last summer I asked Mrs. Holtzman(22) about the possibility of group work this summer in singing. Our secretary wrote her several weeks ago —about two weeks to be exact—but we have not heard. Mrs. Holtzman is in Paris. The idea is that she give us the technical work and that I study each student's approach from the psychological end. The project interests me deeply and may offer something of significance to you.

You probably have the impression that I am not interested in having you take up our group work. Nothing is farther from the facts. I don't want to hold out false hopes to you. You, like everyone else, have been surrounded all your life by sentimentality. You don't know anything else. It is inevitable that you think of my work sentimentally. And it is inevitable that, thinking of it so, you will necessarily come into sentimental disappointment. It is not at all that I do not want your participation in our activities. It is that I want only your genuine and wholehearted participation— the only participation possible in work such as ours. I hope you understand, at least vaguely, that our position challenges the entire social system—not as it exists in others and not ourselves, *but as it exists in everyone including ourselves*. The only practical working ground in such a situation is our own fears, our own antagonisms and our own substitutions and pretenses.

As regards your part of the camp work, of course you know that I would not permit you to assume any arduous duties. The chief need is a dining-room assistant and this I rather think will fall to your lot. There is just one point. We expect our group to be on hand at the opening of camp (July 1st) and to remain until closing time (September 1st). This makes for group uniformity both in our analytic work and in the summer courses—French, German,

(22) Florence Lee Holtzman, singing teacher.

rhythms, singing, etc. So I am sure you will realize the need of group continuity in our activities. Should Mrs. Holtzman undertake to give us vocal training, we shall each have to contribute his proportion of the charge. Of course all activities in the camp are included as part of the camp life.

After five interruptions, let me conclude this final installment with the assurance of my happiness to include you in our work, if you still feel interested to undertake it, but again let me say that you must take your place among us upon a wholly self-dependent and equal footing with the rest of us, realizing that a mental attitude of dependence toward life is the root of nervousness as of all evil.

With my love,

Trigant

To Dr. Isador H. Coriat   Baltimore, Maryland
Boston   May 18, 1925

Dear Coriat:

I am looking forward to that promised letter from you. Had it not been that my mother was expecting me in Norfolk Wednesday noon, I should have been so glad to have stayed over and had a talk with you that morning.

A suggestion of Dr. Glueck's that I read a paper at the International Congress [of Psychoanalysis] outlining something of the group-method of analysis, together with my election to the presidency of the American Association, has put in my head the thought of possibly going abroad for the September meeting. Some friends of mine are going over just about that time and have wanted me to go with them. So that if there were still the possibility of offering a paper there, particularly if it would further the work of our own organization [the American Psychoanalytic Association], I would consider very seriously going over for the meeting. Can you tell me to whom I should send the title of the paper, and will you tell me what you think of the project both from the point of view of the possible representation of the American group and from the point of view of presenting the conceptions that are so close to me and of which you and I have had so many close discussions. Do you know who else is going over beside yourself?

Mrs. Burrow is sailing for Europe with my cousin Miss Smith on July 2nd. So that I am the more tempted to go over with the idea of returning with their party.

I certainly will appreciate any advice you could give me from your experience as president of the Association. You will know its needs and can no doubt indicate to me in what way I can render the service I should like to offer in appreciation of so significant an office. It is certainly pleasant to have Stern with his experience and efficiency remaining as secretary. . . .

I am looking forward to your letter. Wish it would have been possible for you to have spent this week-end here with me. We have had some interesting motoring and I feel sure you would enjoy knowing the country surrounding us here.

Please remember me to Mrs. Coriat. With best regards,

Sincerely yours,

Trigant Burrow

To Laura Spencer Portor   Baltimore, Maryland
New York   May 29, 1925

Dear Laura:

Except for your having had grippe, your letter was a real relief. I feared I had been at fault in my failure to keep the appointment with you and had probably put you to real inconvenience because of my lack of punctuality.

I hope it may be possible to see you on our way to camp—on Emily's and my way to camp, on Brownie's way to Europe. She and Lucia are sailing July 2nd. I'll give you ample notice this time. We expect to have a day or two in New York.

As for this grippe you and I persist in having, it is just punishment for our sins! We take drugs for the illness, but utterly disavow the sins. But if you will take a remedy from so weak a vessel as me, let me recommend lots of water for the flu we share admittedly, and for the sins on which we hold our separate monopoly let me recommend a visit to Lifwynn. The water should be taken slowly, the visit to us with the utmost despatch. We are giving up the house for the summer not later than the 15th and mayhap the 10th. As the newsboy once said to you 'Lady, be a sport!'

I do so wish and Brownie so wishes too that you would come.

We'll look for a gay telegram from you tomorrow saying you are coming.

With love,

Trigant

To Dr. Hanford Henderson   Baltimore, Maryland
Washington, D. C.   May 30, 1925

Dear Hanford:

This is the first moment I have been able to sit down quietly and write you. The letter has been in my mind many times when I have gone to and fro and in various intervals of the day.

I have been trying to think it out. I have been trying to think what I might say to you that might be helpful and might not seem foreign and not un-understanding of your pain. I felt after you had gone away that I had been somewhat false to you in regard to your sister—I mean false to myself and to you. From what you have told me of her disease—the nature of it—from what I know of the physicians you had consulted, the quality of the men and their training, I felt that your sister's illness must be hopeless. If I said this to you at all, I said it but half-way and tried to believe there might be some hopeful aspect when I was really convinced there was none. If this is my tendency in your behalf, how much more must it be your tendency in behalf of your sister. I nevertheless think that such an attitude of mind is unworthy of both of us.

I think, Hanford, that you have not accepted the actuality of your sister's illness and the ultimate fatality of it. I think you have looked in the face of a clear actuality and have refused to accept it. I think that is why your heart is 'one big ache.' When I think of your powers, when I think of your equipment, when I think of your love of growth and beauty and human relationships, it seems quite dreadful that any backward look should obscure your own complete joy and activity. After all, there are so many for you to serve. That you should turn all your thought toward a regret for one to whom your service must be denied does not seem right, it does not seem in tone with the nature of things living and positive. I do not know whether it is possible for you to see your course as I see it but it seems to me if anything might put you in the way of interest and gladness, it might be the realization that someone who senses something of your own personality and its need feels, as I do, about the problem that you are face to face with. The tragedy of life is not so much, I think, the sorrows that come to us as the sorrows we will not part with when they come.

I am sorry there could not have been the visit to us. We should not want, of course, to crowd in between you and your sadness. But you must know that we shall be waiting at any time you care

to invite us in between you and what is now your great regret. . . .
With love from us all,

As always,

Trigant

The date of the International Congress at Bad Homburg, at which Dr.
Burrow was to speak as President of the American Psychoanalytic
Association, was close at hand. The following letter was written in
response to a note from his son, now twenty years old, who had suggested that he accompany his father to Europe.

To his son   Lifwynn Camp, Merrill, N. Y.
Baltimore, Maryland   July 24, 1925

Dear Jack:

You no doubt received my telegram yesterday morning and will
be expecting this letter following it.

I would like you for the moment to put everything else aside and
read very carefully and very thoughtfully what I shall attempt
here to make plain to you.

I think the time has come for you and me to be clearly understanding of one another—that the closeness that really exists between us
be fully accepted by us with all the responsibilities and all the
obligations that closeness of purpose entails mutually upon us.

As long as you were a child I tried in my limited way to bring to
you what from every point of view seemed to me best in life
for you. With your manner of receiving what I have endeavored

to offer you I am more than content. You seem to me equipped for a rich and full expressive life as no one else that I know. But I feel that the time has now come for us to stand together for that which we are. You are no longer a little boy. You have no longer a little boy's outlook. The circumstance of your growth and responsibility has merely not yet come home to you with a clear realization. I think you must know that there is nothing in the world that could give me greater happiness than giving happiness to you. But I like to bring you happiness now as one comrade to another and not as one gives happiness momentarily to a mere child.

My going to Europe involves very serious considerations. It is now no longer possible for me to go to Europe in the spirit in which the thoughtless tourist would go, who has in view only the quest of his momentary pleasure. If human happiness in general can best be served through my going to Europe and participating in the Congress at Homburg, I should be, I assure you, not less happy than you at the prospect of such a trip. Where the matter, however, is one concerning happiness in the large it is not for me to decide apart from the responsibilities it has become my obligation and my happiness to fulfill. As I say, the matter of my going is far-reaching and serious in its significance.

It seems to me, if you are interested with me in our possible project of going to Europe, that it becomes your obligation to be with me in order to consider the questions upon which the decision must ultimately depend. The next two and a half weeks must be the decisive weeks with respect to the outcome of the work to which I have given my constant thought for many years. The time has come when the effort that Mr. Shields and I have been making along with our associates and students must take on the definite form of actuality. If the work is to continue, there must be established in the fall a definite laboratory for its continuance. The measures requisite to this end shall have to be determined immediately. There are only a few weeks for the forming of plans necessary to this purpose. This involves many practical details of deep import to all of us.

If I can look for your coöperation in this, it is important that you ask that you be given your vacation at once and that you come up to the Lake and consider with Mr. Shields and me both the position our work now represents in our present laboratory undertaking as represented in the camp as well as the practical questions its continuance involves.

With love,

As always,

Father

To Professor Sigmund Freud   Lifwynn Camp, Merrill, N. Y.
Vienna   August 12, 1925

Dear Professor Freud:

I meant to answer long before this your very kind note that reached me in May. It was very generous of you to write me as you did and I assure you that the spirit of your letter means very much to me. So much of the pain in life may be laid to needless misunderstandings and I am particularly glad to be relieved of any needless misunderstanding between us.

I am looking forward to attending the Congress at Bad Homburg and to the pleasure of meeting you again at that time. I wish there were time to write you fully of the ideas that have of the last years been occupying me in regard to what seems to me the need in the development of psychoanalysis in this country. At least the attempt of my associates and myself has been in the direction of insisting that psychoanalysis is not dependent for its data upon esoteric doctrines but that the data first described by you may be socially demonstrable through a technique comparable to that maintained elsewhere in the laboratories of biology.

It is this endeavor which I have attempted to outline in a paper I am reading at the International Congress. I shall much value your thoughtful consideration of this widened approach that is being made on the part of my students and myself and I hope that our efforts may recommend themselves to you. Our endeavors, I realize, are at present in their merest inception. And naturally the 'resistances' to this social extension of psychoanalysis have been, as you may well imagine, almost overwhelming. But psychoanalysis has not faltered before the resistances of the individual in its approach to the problems of the individual analysis and I think it need no more falter before the resistances of our social confederacies in our approach to the problem of the social mind.

I look forward though to a fuller discussion of the whole matter when we shall meet at the Homburg Congress. (23) With best greetings and my kindest regards, I remain

Sincerely yours,

Trigant Burrow

To Dr. Hans Syz   Kurpark-Sanatorium
Baltimore, Maryland   Bad Homburg V. D. H.
                                         September 5, 1925

Dear Dr. Syz:

It is too late and I am too tired tonight to attempt a real letter. The Congress concluded at noon today. In the main it has been worth while. To present our position here was almost necessary. I mean it was a necessary formality. I do not think many of the Germans were able to follow my paper. They are interested though to read it and I am to send it to the *Zeitschrift*. This I will do in a few days

(23) Professor Freud did not attend the meeting.

—I want to get the right person to translate into German the footnotes referring to Clark's papers. By the way Clark was not very well received. Certainly not to his satisfaction, and left immediately following the session in which his paper was read. Jelliffe in his address made a very complimentary reference to my conception of the social aspects of the neurosis.

The enclosed card will interest you. I was very pleased with Dr. Bally. He understood you were rather unfavorable to psychoanalysis. I explained that I thought you favored it in the sense in which I favor it—as a stepping stone to a broader comprehension of man's feeling and thinking life.

The unpleasant feature of the meeting was Jones' almost crude attitude of resistance to me. He was quite contemptuous and I think made what effort he could to discredit my position with our German colleagues. It is no matter.

There were two 'business meetings.' These were quite painful for me. It became apparent that they were mere political rallies—that psychoanalysis is about to disintegrate with the passing of Freud and that every effort is being made in the use of artificial respiration to keep alive an organization that lacks the vitality of internal coördination and accord.

I shall make our position very clear at the next two occasions—the mid-year meeting in New York and at the meeting in the spring. Psychoanalysis has missed the phylogenetic significance of the mental life and is attempting to maintain itself without this essential biological basis.

I shall send a cable in a day or so. It is not possible to send one from here Saturday afternoon and tomorrow things will probably not be open in Frankfort. We go there early tomorrow morning. Then to Heidelberg, Strasburg and Zürich.

Dr. Eitingon commented on the excellent German I used in the Abstract. I explained that you were responsible for that. I am so glad to have the translation of the paper for the *Zeitschrift*.

We must be off early in the morning so I won't write more tonight, though there is much, much more to say. I would be glad if you would give the utmost thought and time you can to the office and to our work without of course embarrassing your obligations elsewhere.

While Mr. Shields and I will doubtless derive much benefit from our trip our real wish is to be back with you all again.

Yours always,
Trigant Burrow

To Dr. Paul Federn   Baltimore, Maryland
Vienna   October 28, 1925

Dear Dr. Federn:

I want to thank you in a very special way for your very kind letter that reached me two days ago. I wish I could have you feel how very much it means to me that you should have written me in a spirit of so great sincerity. My appreciation is more than I can express.

On first reading your psychoanalytic explanation of the reason for my not giving a simple statement of my results, it was my tendency to deny your interpretation of me and to say that *you* failed to understand me. But what you say cannot be denied. It is quite true. I have tended to hold a quite reserved and sovereign attitude in my writing and to place the whole burden of understanding upon the reader. I shall try to take your advice and shall in the next weeks bring together as best I can some account of the results for which you and Professor Freud have asked. I am giving a paper before the Washington Psychoanalytic Society on November 14th, and shall endeavor to have this paper fill the requirements you have in mind and send it later to you.

I am very pleased that Professor Freud wishes to see my Homburg paper published in the *Zeitschrift*. Any recognition on the part of Professor Freud naturally means very much to me.

I am very glad too to send under separate cover reprints of earlier papers including 'The Genesis and Meaning of Homosexuality' in which I describe my account of the homosexual mechanism. I cannot think that this paper antedates the work of Sadger, but my conception is entirely independent of his. The paper was written and presented in 1914. I can say that the principle upon which my conception rests—the principle of primary identification —was formulated somewhat earlier and received mention in earlier writings, among them 'Character and the Neuroses' which I am also enclosing.

The very circumstance of your interest will, I think, assist me very much in attempting to write more intimately and in detail of the work my students and I have been doing. I begin to see now that the absence of more general recognition on the part of my con-frères has made me somewhat hesitant in writing freely of our work. I do not think I am unduly sensitive in feeling this. John T. MacCurdy has spoken of the marked neglect of my formula-tions in his book, *Problems in Dynamic Psychology*. And Mac-Curdy's relationship to me is in no sense a close one. I feel that his view in this matter is a quite disinterested one. . . .

I want to express again my pleasure in the contact made with you at Bad Homburg and my appreciation of your very sympathetic interest in the endeavors of our group. I hope you have me on your list for any reprints of your own. I am not a handy German scholar, but what I have read of your material has been of great interest and profit to me. . . .

Again thanking you for the sincere expression contained in your letter, believe me with good wishes and kind regards,

Sincerely yours,

Trigant Burrow

CHAPTER 7

THE EXPANSION OF GROUP-ANALYSIS

The reception accorded Burrow's paper at Bad Homburg was characteristic of the response to his contributions during this period in which he was attempting to broaden the psychoanalytic horizon and to introduce the group-method of analysis. Letters of this period reflect the development of interest among social scientists and others, but little understanding was shown by his psychoanalytic confrères. There was bewilderment on the part of some, open hostility on the part of others, and only occasionally an intuitive sense of the need for such work as Burrow was undertaking. He was, however, too keenly aware of the wrench that the new direction of his studies had been to his own cherished prepossessions to harbor resentment of the hostility of his colleagues. Instead, as evidenced in this chapter by letters to several of these men, he asked them to view with him the interrelational situations in which he and they were together involved.

Years later Burrow wrote of the 'pain of the unavoidable break with my professional colleagues.' 'Certainly,' he says, 'no one can lightly wave aside adverse criticism and the loss of the friendly co-operation one has known among his fellow workers. The situation was the more difficult, as in the work I had entered upon it was essential that I forgo old outlooks before attaining the new. Not knowing towards what specific objective I was bound, I had perforce to embark for unknown shores. It was this factor of lottery inseparable from the early stages of my scientific adventure that entailed the greatest hardship. But this uncertainty was in time completely dispelled as our consistent investigations gradually brought our laboratory unit to a realization of the solid and dependable course on which we were launched.'(1)

(1) *The Neurosis of Man*, pp. 324–5.

Since the beginning of the unique experiment at Lifwynn Camp the group studies had expanded. On Dr. Burrow's return from Europe in the fall of 1925, a house was rented on St. Paul Street, Baltimore to serve as a laboratory base for the growing behavioral studies.

These quarters housed six of the students while the others came to the laboratory for meals and for scheduled group-meetings. Both at that time and later many of these meetings were held at the dining-room table. 'It was the common experience of all of us,' Burrow wrote in 1937, 'that at a certain age—at the age of two or three years—having, through our nursery training, become adept in the use of certain symbols, certain social meanings or behavior-conditionings and their attendant prohibitions, we were permitted to enter the larger home circle and to take our place at the family table. In being absorbed thus into the family unit, we were admitted into what is for the individual his first symbolically systematized social group or community.'(2)

Burrow chose this setting, so closely associated with the social conditioning of the infant organism, as appropriate for the laboratory meetings. '... I attempted along with my associates to establish a more or less stabilized group-table or "family-board" replete with all the conventions and paraphernalia to which each member of the unit was "born and bred." For sixteen years we met according to Hoyle three times a day, but with a very different aim from that imbued by the dominating social pattern of interchange to which we had been severally conditioned at the parochial family table. Our purpose was that of applying a method of objective inquiry to reactions and processes which we had until now accepted subjectively on their face value.'(3)

'... it was no simple matter to bring to book this table d'hôte of behavior into which one is inducted during early nursery days. For it was the automatic tendency of every student ... to shy away from his self-allotted task as an element in a primarily integrated unit or social group.'(4)

Participants in the group studies supported the laboratory by their payments for board and lodging, and shared responsibility for the house management. One student, Flora A. Guggenheimer, served full-

(2) *The Biology of Human Conflict*, p. 253.

(3) Ibid. p. 257.

(4) Ibid. p. 259.

time as volunteer housekeeper for the laboratory, a position she held until her death twenty-seven years later. For the most part, however, the members of the group were actively engaged in the community, some in such professional capacities as psychiatrist or nurse, others in industrial or business positions ordinarily unrelated to behavior studies. Mr. Shields continued to assist Dr. Burrow in his office where his talent for organization was a distinct asset. Students joined in common enterprises such as the preparation and editing of anonymous articles and short stories for *Mental Health.*(5) This small journal was published by the Mental Hygiene Society of Maryland of which Dr. Charles B. Thompson, a member of the group, was Medical Director. The sharing of activities and responsibilities afforded the continuing opportunity to observe interpersonal reactions as they presented themselves.

This same fall (1925) Dr. Burrow faced a great sorrow in the loss of his mother who had been in ill health for a year or more. A deep bond had always existed between them, and her death brought to a close a devoted relationship.

To Dr. A. A. Brill   Baltimore, Maryland
New York   November 26, 1925

Dear Brill:

I have not yet acknowledged the reprint of your article 'Schizoid and Syntonic Factors in Neuroses and Psychoses.' This is just to let you know that I have received it and look forward to reading it when things are less pressing.

Since my return from Europe a month ago I have been very much concerned because of the illness and recent death of my mother. I find that when face to face with a loss like this my

(5) These articles were later republished in *Our Common Neurosis—Notes on a Group Experiment* by Charles B. Thompson, M. D. and Alfreda P. Sill (New York, Exposition Press, 1952, 208 pp.).

philosophies quite desert me momentarily and I quite lose heart for the things that are of customary moment to me.

We missed you at Homburg. I had understood that you would be on hand. I hope, however, to see you in New York at the mid-year meeting if not sooner. With my kind regards,

Sincerely yours,

Trigant Burrow

To Louise Collier Willcox   Baltimore, Maryland
Norfolk, Virginia   November 27, 1925

Dear Mrs. Willcox:

...I didn't halfway say what was my real meaning the other evening. I never do. And you went off with some notion about 'spiritual vision' or something that has no reality outside of poetry books. It is all very well to cite the life of Francis of Assisi—but Francis would have been wretched in a group meeting. So would you. That's what I want to be honest enough to say to you instead of being socially insincere as I was with you the other evening when I said automatically that we would be glad to have you with us in camp. So we would. That was sincere enough. But with your knowing and your helpful concern for others you would be unhappy with us, and you would know the fault was surely ours. It is the people who need help for themselves and who accept the humiliation of their need and have the full recognition of it to whom we have anything of interest and renewal to offer. Personally (though you will hate me for saying it) I think all your drive and anxious concern for others is the proud disavowal of your own deep need. By need I do not mean any sentimental personal complaint. I mean something, as you yourself expressed it, 'larger than oneself'—larger than all the selves that ever were rolled into one. That need is not humiliating, but I believe completely strengthening and liberating when accepted by us. . . .

Of course you have the New Testament. 'Except ye become,' etc., etc., etc. But then becoming a little child in these sophisticated days requires the combined efforts of a laboratory of mental and social research. But how foolish of me to be yearning over you this way when in fact you are so splendid!

My regards to Mr. Willcox.

Always sincerely yours,

Trigant Burrow

To a former patient   Baltimore, Maryland
                                                   December 13, 1925

Dear Mrs. T.:

. . . Your expression of interest in the work that has occupied my associates and myself so constantly in the last years means much to me as an expression of your friendliness and thought. This year has at last marked the opening in an objectively small way of the laboratory of research in social analysis which I have long felt to be the need in the scientific approach to the problems of our human pathology. The interruption each year to the concentrated group life and activities of the camp is no longer possible. And so with our laboratory now definitely established (not far from the Tuscany) there is the opportunity for the continued group expression that has underlain the conception of my work in the last years.

I appreciate your expression of interest in our endeavors but that our undertaking is one that you would care to lend yourself to without regard to personal preference and long-accustomed values, individual and social, is hardly a prospect that I can encourage myself to anticipate. But neither do I want to discourage your own or anyone else's inquiry into our group endeavor should the opportunity come to you at any time to do so. In that event I want very especially that you should know that if your husband is no longer in a position to meet the accustomed fee, you are to feel entirely free to come to me at any time without entailing the slightest financial obligation to Mr. T. I am sorry to know that he has been worried about finances.

I hope you will remember me to him.

Very sincerely yours,

Trigant Burrow

To Alys Bentley(6) New York

Baltimore, Maryland January 8, 1926

Dear Miss Bentley:

It was so nice to have that moment with you in New York the other evening and all of us enjoyed the novel experience of dining with you at the Threefold Community House. The vivid coloring of both vegetation and crockery was pleasantly reminiscent of Owlyout and the Lake! Let us hear sometime about the plates.

It was good to have that moment's half talk in the theatre. The play itself, by the way, fades out markedly when viewed in calmer, less immediate perspective. Were there not at the heart of our modern audiences the dull, persistent boredom of their routine lives making them rush out obsessively toward anything offering some promise of 'entertainment,' there would scarcely be one play in a thousand that could stand its ground with them.

(6) See page 39.

Emily has been rushing about in a real round of gaieties throughout this holiday time. When we can talk quietly together I want to speak of the possibility of a visit to New York and of your thought to have her spend some days with you. I know she would love every moment of it if conditions generally fit in with the plan.

I did not tell you how your note at Christmas with its flaming background of color and its deeply understanding message appealed to me as to us all.

With love from us all,

Yours always.

Trigant Burrow

To Cecilia Gaul(7)
Baltimore, Maryland

Baltimore, Maryland
January 12, 1926

Dear Miss Gaul:

I have returned in mind many times to your recent note in regard to Emily. Sometime I would like to talk to you of the whole situation and of the situation generally where children with real feeling, I think, for music are often without interest apart from the instruction they have at the time of their music lessons. I see no other solution than that I just somehow find a way to take up music too. You have set me thinking though of the matter of Emily and her practice and I hope to talk with you about the situation at a not too distant date.

I hope you had a pleasant Christmas. Will you not let me come sometime to your apartment and let me hear you play again? I do miss hearing music often as I used to hear it as a child. The absence

(7) A former pupil of Franz Liszt, Miss Gaul taught music in Baltimore.

of it in my life seems quite abnormal, but I mean to mend my ways and sometime I shall ask you to help me do so.

With good wishes for the new year,

Very sincerely yours,

Trigant Burrow

To Dr. Max Levin   Baltimore, Maryland
The Johns Hopkins Hospital   January 20, 1926

My dear Dr. Levin:

I have your letter asking for information upon the case of Mr. O. I regret to say that I have no data whatever in regard to him. It happened that he came to me after I had abandoned the older psychoanalytic basis of technique. With my altered approach all of the reminiscent material upon which I formerly set so much store has now been completely thrown into the discard, and my entire work with Mr. O. consisted simply in training him to detect in the immediate moment the obvious discrepancy between his observable mood and his alleged mental content indicated by his presumably 'direct' statements. Working as I do with the immediate behavior of the patient before me as my exclusive method of attack upon the neurosis, I have, except for the quite informal story of the patient's general life setting, which you no doubt have in far ampler form, no clinical annotations whatever of the sort for which you have inquired.

I regret that I am not in a position to assist you in the manner that you desire, but I assure you that if in any way I can be of help to you in your view of Mr. O., I shall be only too glad to do what I can. If you would be interested to have me make clearer to you what I have in mind in speaking of the process of direct investigation as over against the earlier historical method of psychoanalytic usage, I hope you will feel entirely at liberty to avail yourself of whatever service this may be to you. If with this idea you think it would be worth while to see me sometime, I should be glad to arrange a time in which we could talk over the situation and discover whatever points of contact might serve to coördinate our respective approaches to the problem which the patient presents.

Very sincerely yours,

Trigant Burrow

To Dr. Adolph Stern   Baltimore, Maryland
New York   February 2, 1926

Dear Stern:

Your letter found me laid up with a second attack of grippe else I would have replied more promptly to it. Thank you for your earlier letter too with the account of Abraham.(8) I much appreciate your giving me these fuller details concerning his illness and death.

With regard to your and Oberndorf's suggestion as to the choice of papers and the selection of men, it seems very thoughtfully chosen throughout except that I am somewhat at a loss to understand your selection of Jelliffe to present the paper which I had chosen for my own subject and had so written Oberndorf on November 21st. The subject I chose was 'the need of the reconcilement of the psychiatric and the psychoanalytic viewpoints.' If it is felt that Jelliffe is better adapted to this presentation than I, it is only necessary to say so and you will find me quite in accord with your feeling. Even though Jelliffe and I chose the same

(8) Dr. Karl Abraham, president of the International Psychoanalytic Association.

subject, it would naturally be treated in an entirely different manner, so that there would really be no conflict; but to choose a subject practically identical with that I chose seems unfortunate unless, as I say, it seems best that that subject be consigned to Jelliffe—a not bad arrangement at all it seems to me. In that event I thought of a paper entitled 'The Need of an Analytic Psychiatry.' (9)

With regard to the suggestion that one session of our meeting be held in New York and another in Pittsburgh, I think the plan quite impractical. For a good many men it is not easy to get away for these meetings. For some the matter of expense is no small item. And to ask the members to make two trips to attend one meeting, one session in New York and the other in Pittsburgh, seems to me is not giving sufficient thought to their convenience. So that I strongly suggest that the meeting be confined to New York. ...

As Secretary of the Association will you not be quite frank enough to say to me that you think my paper undesirable for the meeting in prospect, if this is your feeling, as I would on no account wish to make use of the office of President to force upon the meeting a paper which would be in an unwelcome trend or which would not seem in line with the intention of the joint session.

I hope you people in New York have been less subject to grippe than those of us here. Baltimore is in the throes of a real grippe epidemic.

I would appreciate a word from you at your early convenience.

With best wishes and kind regards,

Very sincerely yours,

Trigant Burrow

(9) *The American Journal of Psychiatry*, 1927, vol. VI, pp. 485–92. This was the paper Dr. Burrow finally gave at the meeting.

To Dr. Paul Federn
Vienna

Baltimore, Maryland
February 7, 1926

Dear Dr. Federn:

Only the circumstance of my having been ill for the past three weeks, due to a quite severe attack of influenza, has prevented my answering until now your very thoughtful and painstaking letter. I want first to assure you how deeply I appreciate the entire sincerity in which you have written me. Far from being unsympathetic to the frankness that characterizes your letter, I deeply value the honest spirit of your criticism....

There are so many matters in your letter which tempt me to a very full discussion of them. But this, I know, is impossible. I do want to say though that certain of your very kindly meant criticisms rest upon a misunderstanding of our position, and these I know you will want me to draw to your attention. Perhaps I must despair of making myself entirely clear because of the peculiar quality of a work for whose essential understanding one is necessarily dependent after all—I no less than others—upon the circumstance of actual experience. I think it is not realized that I have not approached my group experiment with the authority of the physician but with the self-investigation of the student. I find that in the attitude of all my inquirers their approach to me is always on the ground of the medical colleague rather than on the ground of the societal individual whose affiliation with me in respect to our group obligation must rest solely upon our common recognition of our separate pseudo-group moods....

My feeling is that the group work that my students and myself are undertaking is the spontaneous evolution of the individualistic work that originated with Freud, that there has had to be this interval of development and of varying evaluations and permutations before there could have fashioned itself the automatic group investigation to which circumstances have led my associates and myself in the midst of the social unrest and disorder dominant in our American life. All around me here within the circles of my own colleagues there has been for several years only intellectual inquiry and for the most part a certain irritation with me because of what has been my incapacity to transfer to others what has only come to me through the experience of my own group participation. It has been my painful experience that an internal accord is not possible upon any external or self-determined, i.e., individualistic basis. Only the few among my colleagues who have felt *within themselves* the need such as our group endeavor seems to answer have really associated themselves with me in any fully sympathetic and understanding sense. There is today a growing number of my colleagues who are gradually coming to realize that, after all, this work of our group is not *my* work, that it is a societal summons, so to speak, in which I am simply a participant along with others.

I am naturally quite familiar with those writings of Freud of which you speak. But theoretical discussions by Professor Freud or myself or by anyone else, who writes as the colleague analyzing an individual or any group of individuals, do not apply in respect to the particular direction of investigation that is in process among us as a laboratory group. Our whole position rests upon the inversion of the customary analytic relationship in which the analyst stands as critique toward the individual analysand. On the contrary, in our laboratory outlook the united societal consciousness composing our group becomes the critique in respect to the individual, be this individual the medical colleague represented in Freud, or yourself, or myself or anyone else; and, correspondingly, in the interest of his laboratory investigation, the medical colleague submits himself *as a patient* to be investigated by this societal consciousness. I wish it might be possible for me to make clear to you that the analysis of a group *by me*, the individual, or the analysis of a group even by Professor Freud, the individual, cannot possibly interest us as laboratory investigators. In our group approach what can alone be of interest to me as a laboratory investigator is the group's analysis of me. What can alone be of interest to Professor Freud or to you as laboratory investigators is the group's analysis of him or of you. From a laboratory point of view I cannot be interested in Professor Freud's interpretations or of my own when we stand before the group as teachers or physicians. What interests me is the group's interpretation of Professor Freud or of me, when we stand before the group as quite isolated and 'normal' individuals requiring for our essential integrity of personality the coherence of man's original group or societal basis.

May I say that you are quite mistaken when you imply in your letter that our group-method of analysis is intended as a substitution for the individual analysis and that in this course we are unconsciously influenced by our 'resistances' to Freud. In point of fact it is definitely stated on page 11 (German) of my paper (10) that the group-analysis is a supplement—an adjunct—to the private analysis and that, far from being a substitute for the individual analysis, every patient is required to undergo a private analysis prior to his entrance into the group, and that he is at liberty to return at any time to the private analysis while undergoing analysis in its group form.

It may be of assistance to you in understanding my position to know that all of the students who have entered upon the group work had been previously analyzed individually. In addition the development of our group technique has not involved in any sense the abrogation of the qualification of the psychoanalytic method of Freud. On the contrary, far from being an expression of my resistances to Freud, my group experiment was only undertaken after I had devoted twelve years to the exclusive practice of psychoanalysis. In all these years my outlook was confined solely to the individual technique as employed by Freud. . . .

I do not know whether all that I have here written is of any real help or significance. I do know that the spirit with which you

(10) 'Die Gruppenmethode in der Psychoanalyse,' *Imago*, 1926, vol. XII, pp. 211–22.

have endeavored to lend a sympathetic and helping hand to me in my group undertaking has touched me very deeply because of what I feel to be the very unselfish and loyal intentions with which you are guided. Your interest and response are the more appealing to me because of the quite stolid indifference with which my endeavors have been very generally met as yet here in America among my psychoanalytic colleagues.

There is just one other point. If you will glance again at my paper you will find that I have said quite specifically that the resistances met in the group-analysis are really greater than those encountered by the individual in the personal analysis. In the same connection I mentioned too that we do not for a moment eliminate the transference. It is a factor that cannot be eliminated until it is dissolved through a process of analytic assimilation. There are, in fact, as many transferences as there are individuals in our group. . . .

I take for granted that my correspondence with you and the different papers I am sending will be brought to the notice of Professor Freud. In my position as a psychoanalyst and most particularly in my present office of President of the American Psychoanalytic Association I feel under no little constraint both in respect to my colleagues as well as to the lay students of psychoanalysis in pursuing a method of investigation that is the direct outcome of Freud's teaching and technique while lacking as yet any statement from Professor Freud in support of the very earnest endeavors of my associates and myself. But sometime I hope to write to Professor Freud himself and set before him something of the nature of my position. I personally feel that there need be no conflicting element in the situation. But if Professor Freud should not accord with me in this view, naturally I should be obliged to bow to his judgment in the matter. . . .

I am the more sorry for the delay in having this letter go to you because of its postponing too long my expression of my personal sympathy to you in the death of Dr. Abraham. I have not received so great a shock in many days as the news of his death occasioned me. I have, of course, written Dr. Eitingon of my sense of personal loss in the death of our honored President. Resolutions will go to the Berlin group in due course giving expression to the very deep sympathy of our American Association for our European colleagues.

Hoping to hear from you at your convenience and with my kindest regards to you and also to Professor Freud, I am

Sincerely yours,

Trigant Burrow

To Dr. Smith Ely Jelliffe   Baltimore, Maryland
New York   April 8, 1926

Dear Jelliffe:

I don't wonder that you are bored at the idea of serving on a committee, but when I selected you as Chairman I was thinking not of you but of the good of the Committee!

I am sorry to hear of your broken collar bone. What with your grippe and conjunctivitis some time ago and now this untoward accident you seem to have a deep-seated grudge against yourself. Why don't you come down this week-end with Stern and Oberndorf and have dinner with me here following the meeting Sunday morning of the Washington Psychoanalytic Society and let us look into your case? Incidentally, we can then talk over the matter of the educational program of which you have been the unwitting and unwilling Chairman. Come along by all means if it is possible. If it is a pleasant day, the motor trip from Washington here would be worth while.

I am glad you liked my paper. You people are always telling me in how much better terms I might say it, but, hang it, you never say it yourselves!

Hoping to see you Sunday,

Sincerely,

Trigant Burrow

Burrow's application of the challenge of his laboratory to the circumstances of his everyday life is exemplified by the following letter. It was occasioned by the fact that his colleagues, Clarence P. Oberndorf and Adolph Stern did not come to the dinner given in their honor by Dr. and Mrs. Burrow, and sent no message explaining their absence.

To Dr. Adolph Stern   Baltimore, Maryland
New York   April 18, 1926

Dear Stern:

I have your letter this morning, and I shall be very glad to give your message to Mrs. Burrow.

Because of my sense of your and Oberndorf's inherent sincerity, I find myself unwilling to speak to either of you upon any basis other than that of the completest sincerity of which I myself am capable. Frankly, I thought your and Oberndorf's sudden decision to yield to personal influences and dismiss at the last moment the arrangements Mrs. Burrow and I had planned, as we thought, for your pleasure, was a quite undeserved slight. Had you given us the least intimation that we were intruding upon your plans in asking you to dine with us and our friends, you may be sure we would have respected your feeling and would, of course, have withdrawn with entire understanding despite our personal disappointment. As I wrote Oberndorf, I cannot but feel there were factors present in the situation toward which you were momentarily quite unconscious. It is precisely the reckoning with such everyday factors that has become the interest of my associates and myself in our effort to bring human analysis under a more inclusive program.

I concede that my speaking to you in this unreserved manner is quite unprecedented, but I cannot require of myself a less direct manner of adaptation socially than I expect of my patients individually. If you are inclined to resent my speaking to you with the entire frankness with which I have, I can only say to you and to Oberndorf that my frankness is forced upon me through the high regard in which I hold you both.

The letters I am enclosing are more or less explanatory of themselves. As you see, I had told Clark that I would speak to you when I would see you on Sunday. As there was not the opportunity of talking to you, I am sending the letters to you with this.

With my kind regards,

Very sincerely yours,

Trigant Burrow

To Dr. Smith Ely Jelliffe   Baltimore, Maryland
New York   April 27, 1926

Dear Jelliffe:

I have your letter of several days ago and meant to sit immediately down and write you straight from the shoulder. In spite of all your carefully laid plans for your interment I refuse absolutely to have any participation in it. You are altogether too much needed for me to listen for a moment to any project looking to your early sepulture. While grave-lust (if one might so call it) is by no means unknown to me, I don't believe that your ailments are any different from mine. I believe they are a passing mood—you and your lesions—and that you will make as complete and satisfactory a recovery as I begin to see my way to making and that we shall both be granted many long years of our psychoanalytic and other tomfoolery with which to wile away the interval unto the delectable day of our merited euthanasia!

Seriously, though, I know the handicap of a broken collar-bone is no slight annoyance, but your arm will no doubt be out of captivity by the time of the spring meetings and you may even be in better form because of the enforced rest.

By way of diverting your mind at least with troubles of a different kind, I am enclosing a reprint of my Homburg paper. I wish you really would get down into this thing. Unless I am pursuing a false scent, the tracing of this phylogenic implication is as much your job as it is mine. I realize, of course, the shortcomings of all my material until there is really a more intimate acquaintance on the part of my colleagues with the laboratory basis on which these formulations rest.

I was very sorry not to have you with us the other evening but look forward to having you another time.

I wrote Eitingon of your accident and trust I have completely exculpated you for the time.

With all good cheer and my best wishes,

Sincerely yours,

Trigant Burrow

To Professor James Mark Baldwin   Baltimore, Maryland
Paris   May 1, 1926

Dear Dr. Baldwin:

It was very many years ago, in the days of the Philosophical Seminar—so long ago now that you have doubtless forgotten it—that you let drop quite casually some remark about the need for more thoroughgoing research in the field of psychiatry than had yet been established among the students of insanity. You said, as I remember it, that there was need for some spark to ignite the accumulated mass of detached conceptions and fuse them into a conceptual whole. Your words somehow took a strong hold of me. My youthful imagination was deeply stirred because of the forceful way in which you set before us the needed precipitant. I remember that I determined at that moment that that would be the direction of inquiry to which I would devote whatever powers I might have to bring to it.

I speak of this, thinking it may be of interest to you in these after years to know of your part in furthering what has been for me a very untiring endeavor, however poor it may be of fulfillment. From you and Dr. Stratton I came fortunately under the influence of Adolf Meyer, then of Freud and Jung. But always with a sense that there was lacking the necessary coördination in our psychiatric conceptions that you had long ago pointed to....

It would be a pleasure to have word of you sometime and a real account of your days and interests. I hope you will remember me to Mrs. Baldwin and to your daughters.

With my warm remembrances to you, believe me

Sincerely yours,

Trigant Burrow

To Dr. Adolph Stern   Baltimore, Maryland
New York   May 10, 1926

Dear Stern:

You have been very much in my mind ever since your good letter
came and I have wanted to answer it before this. What has been
uppermost in my thought is the very real friendship between us
and the unwillingness on the part of both of us to allow any misunderstanding to mar our essential confidence in one another.
This means very much more to me than I can put into words,
and your letter naturally tends only to make our understanding
the closer still.(11)

You and Mrs. Stern are very kind to want me to have dinner with
you while in New York and I should like nothing better. Unfortunately, it happens that my time is not my own during the few
evenings I shall have in New York or I should certainly avail
myself of your very kind invitation. The last time you and Mrs.
Stern and I sat down to dinner was a memorable occasion, so that
I hope the date is not too distant when we may all gather around
a similar board. I hope, though, to have the pleasure of seeing
Mrs. Stern at the time of the meetings in New York. . . .

Will you let me know who are on the program for our joint session
with the American Psychiatric? It had not been definitely completed when you wrote me sometime ago as to just who would
give papers. I would also be glad to know, as soon as it is convenient for you to write me, where our evening session will be
held. . . .

With my good wishes and looking forward to seeing you soon,

Sincerely yours,

Trigant Burrow

(11) Dr. Obendorf's friendship with Dr. Burrow also continued without a break.

To the husband of a patient Baltimore, Maryland
May 13, 1926

Dear Mr. T.:

I tried to make plain to Mrs. T. when she was here that my position does not admit of any separation between the obligations of a patient to remedy his own emotional condition and the obligations that belong to his or her home life. I tried especially to have your wife know that nothing that was said to her could be withheld from you in consistency with her work with me—that your interest and her interest are bound in one and that I cannot accept any view that challenges this interpretation. I do not know whether I have made clear to her my position. I know that very often in the past Mrs. T. has tended to represent matters to the office in one way and to you in another. Perhaps she has come to a clearer understanding of my attitude by this time. I hope so. But in order to make very certain, I am writing you to let you know that at all times my sympathy and interest are constantly as deep in my thought of you as they are or could ever be toward your wife.

I am certainly sorry to hear of the accident you lately sustained. I have just written Mrs. T. how sorry I was to know that on returning home she found that you had been hurt. After all, our automobiles must be reckoned as great a menace as they are a commodity!

With my kindest regards,

Very sincerely yours,

Trigant Burrow

To Pendleton Dudley   Baltimore, Maryland
New York   May 17, 1926

Dear Mr. Dudley:

I want to thank you for your letter. Naturally, I am pleased at the interest my papers hold for you and was interested too in the questions they brought up in your mind.

Yes, there is no little disquietude among my colleagues as a result of the published writings that have been the outcome of our group findings. I do not reprove myself for this however. The trend of our investigations has been as disquieting for ourselves as for others, and we are quite *with* our friends when they make outcry against the tendency of our disclosures. There is, however, little outcry. There are rather the submerged rumblings that betray the fundamental kinship of our critics with ourselves.

Our thesis, however, does appear to become more and more compelling, and I suppose that as more and more our colleagues realize that it is in no sense directed against them but is intended for their greater freedom of thought and feeling as for our own, there will be a gradual recognition of the quite sober objective nature of our laboratory basis. . . .

With my kind regards,

Sincerely yours,

Trigant Burrow

To Dr. Adolph Stern   Baltimore, Maryland
New York   May 27, 1926

Dear Stern:

You will be as amused as I when I tell you that you have omitted
me from the program for a communication called, 'Speaking of
Resistances.' (12) But I have your letter saying 'you are down on
the program for "Speaking of Resistances".' So you cannot escape
me! But I promise to be brief and I hope not too characteristic. (13)

With kind regards,

Sincerely yours,

Trigant Burrow

To Dr. Harry Stack Sullivan   Baltimore, Maryland
Sheppard and Enoch Pratt Hospital   June 17, 1926

Dear Dr. Sullivan:

Your faith in human nature must be very great that, in spite of
the inadequate formulating on my part of the principle of our
work and the many affect barriers existing socially with us all,
you could still have been so considerate of me as you were at our
last session (American Psychoanalytic Association).

I am taking the liberty of writing you to say that I heartily appreciated the liberal spirit you showed. Perhaps I am the more

(12) Paper scheduled for the meeting of the American Psychoanalytic Association. Published in *Psyche* (London) 1927, vol. VII, pp. 20–7.

(13) Dr. Stern's reply read in part: 'I was not altogether amused at being
informed of my symptomatic act. I rejoice, however, that it afforded you amusement. It jolted me, and made me think a bit.
'You go on the program, as promised.'

appreciative of your feeling in view of the exacting toll lately demanded of me because I have felt compelled to state unreservedly what I have felt to be unreservedly true.

I hope your summer will be a pleasant one. . . .

Very sincerely yours,

Trigant Burrow

To Dr. John T. MacCurdy   Baltimore, Maryland
Cambridge, England   June 19, 1926

Dear MacCurdy:

I want to acknowledge and thank you for your letter of May 18. There is no aspect of your many-sided originality that intrigues me more than your custom of saying disagreeable things to my face and, if rumors are dependable, of making comments out of my hearing which can only lead me to feel that I am not, after all, wholly anathema in your sight.

In regard to all you say I am sure you are right, and in conceding this I am sure I am conceding what represents to every man his highest satisfaction. One cannot do more. Meyer repeats, in other language, practically the same verdict regarding me. Likewise Dunlap, Jung, Freud, Prince and Jones. And, as I say, there is no doubt whatever how right—how unquestionably right all of you are. But then, what is this thing—to be *right*—this relentless claim of each separate individual toward every other? That is what interests me, albeit I am thereby proven so incorrigibly wrong.

With my kind regards,

Sincerely yours,

Trigant Burrow

To Isaac Faulkner(14)   Lifwynn Camp, Merrill, N. Y.
Norfolk, Virginia   July 2, 1926

Dear Isaac:

I do not know what you must have thought of me that you have had no word from me in all your recent trouble. I can only say that I had no word of Nannie's death whatever. Only when Miss Virginia came to visit us and told us did I receive any word of the sad news. I hope you understand my not having written you and there having gone no expression of my feeling on the occasion of Nannie's death. I think you know me well enough though to be assured that I should on no account have let this sad event pass unnoticed by me had I had any knowledge of what had transpired. Remembering Nannie's lifelong devotion to my mother and her faithful attendance upon her throughout so many years, there is no one I hold in dearer memory than your sister.

I hope you will write me and let me know if there is anything I can do at this time to lighten the burden of your loss.

In the meantime I want to enclose this small check in the thought that it may assist you in immediate needs connected with Nannie's illness.

I know that nothing can atone to you for her loss. She was a really beautiful character and in her love and duty to my mother she will be remembered devotedly by all of those who hold my mother in devoted memory.

(14) He had served as butler in the home of Dr. Burrow's mother for thirty-five years.

I am enclosing a self-addressed envelope and will be so glad if you will write me and let me know if there is anything I can do.

With my kind regards,

> Always sincerely yours,
>
> *Trigant Burrow*

To Dr. Paul Federn   Lifwynn Camp, Merrill, N. Y.
Goisern, Austria   July 28, 1926

Dear Dr. Federn:

Your letter reached me day before yesterday and it was a pleasure to have word from you again. ....

With all the work you have undertaken within the last months you have certainly been carrying a heavy program. I am sure you have thoroughly earned your vacation and I sincerely hope it will be a pleasant one.

As I said in my letter of a week or so ago, I appreciate very much the earnest effort you gave to the consideration of my papers, but I am unable to accept the view, expressed in one of your earlier letters, that credits resistances to me in so large a measure unless there is a proportionate acknowledgment of a like tendency to resistances on your own part. I do not feel that resistances are ever one-sided and, when you remove from a paper the statement in which I expressed the view that I knew nowhere in scientific fields of so arbitrary an attitude as that maintained by psychoanalysts, I feel that you were definitely prompted by unconscious motives of self-protection to suppress this unwelcome incrimination against psychoanalysts and that you were not guided solely by the wish to clarify for your readers either my thought or my language. However, I am not of those who think that resistances, which are essentially a mood-reaction, can be for a moment reached and dissolved by any process of 'reasoning'; and I merely mention this to set myself clear before you as being unable to accept your more benign interpretations of the motives back of certain of your corrections of my paper. But this does not lessen my appreciation of your courtesy toward me in giving to my papers the consideration you have given them.

At the last meeting of the American Psychoanalytic Association I read a paper on 'Speaking of Resistances' in which I endeavored to point out the resistances existing socially *among ourselves as psychoanalysts,* and I assure you that this endeavor met with a most cheerless response upon every hand. It was the more convincing to me of how deeply in need are we psychoanalysts of a thorough-going house-cleaning among ourselves.

Dr. Syz, who is here with me, appreciates your kind messages to him. Our laboratory work continues here at my camp in an even more concentrated manner than is possible during the winter when conditions necessarily call for scattered living among our group.

Your mention of the possibility of our meeting and talking things over sometime here in this country is a pleasant one to have in view, but until there is more immediate indication of such a visit, I should feel I was but indulging in pleasant phantasy to look forward at this time with any definiteness to it.

Looking forward to hearing from you whenever you have the inclination to write, and with my very kind regards in which Dr. Syz joins me, I am

Very sincerely yours,

Trigant Burrow

To Max L. Rosenberg(15)　　　　　Lifwynn Camp, Merrill, N. Y.
San Francisco　　　　　　　　　　　　　　　　　August 3, 1926

Dear Max:

I was so glad to have your letter, especially to have it from Oxford, and to feel your delight in it all. Except for a few hours at Oxford last fall, it has been many a day since I have roamed its ways.

I understand all that you say about the writings I sent you—how wrong I am, and that what I am saying today is but the old fallacies decked out in new trappings. I know. It is all so true. ... And yet I keep asking myself what is this thing, to be right?—this which every one is but which is not competent to arrest the great scourges that afflict our common humanity. ... They flourish and increase. And so, until there is something clearer, I must be somehow content to go on in the repeated defeat and humiliation of my wrongness, believing that somewhere there will ultimately be disclosed a place in our human behavior that is neither right nor wrong—a place in which there will be quiet without retirement, serenity without isolation, self-expansion without self-interest or aggression. While I am undoubtedly wrong, I must somehow go on with the inadequate investigations of our group endeavor, knowing at least that to be right, to be this thing which every one is—and all so ineffectually—is really not the answer.

If it will not offend you or seem an intrusion that I should still try to be articulate in the midst of so limited an equipment as our poor human words, may I send you this further effort to clarify my habitual mistakenness in this little essay I am enclosing upon what I call 'Our Mass Neurosis.'

(15) Mr. Rosenberg had been deeply interested in Dr. Burrow's psychoanalytic work. Later he was one of the founders of the Rosenberg Foundation, established for the improvement of living and working conditions in California.

Anyhow it was good and it will always be good to hear from you. I hope sometime there will be the opportunity of seeing you and hearing directly of the splendid trip you have been having with your friends during the last several months.

With my good wishes,

Sincerely yours,

Trigant Burrow

To Laura Spencer Portor   Lifwynn Camp, Merrill, N. Y.
New York   August 18, 1926

Dear Laura:

I have really been more appreciative of your thoughtful and helpful letter than would appear from the long interval I have let pass before writing you.

I do want sometime to get the books on correct writing that you mentioned, but your letter seems to me to serve quite adequately enough as a text. With this thought in mind it has been placed in a special file not only for myself but for the students as well. . . .

Is there not some news of you? Formerly, if your letters lacked, I could always turn to the *Atlantic* and keep in closer touch, but I do not find you there any more and feel often quite at a loss to know what you are doing and of what you are thinking. . . .

It seems strange, but up until now I have never thought of writing as a form of entertainment. I never myself read to be entertained. And so, reading has been more or less a drudge for me except certain occasional, very occasional things. If I wanted to know certain things, if I felt it worth while to know certain things, I would go to certain books and get hold of the things I wanted to know. In the last years I didn't find in the books, even on my own subject, the things I wanted to know, so that the last years have been rather working things out as best I could with what material I could assemble and observe. I suppose this has made my writing rather like uphill work both for me and the unhappy reader. Are not writing and entertainment and beautiful things generally matters for leisure? You see I am trying to encourage myself that some day I shall be able to write clear English because I like to feel that some day I shall have clear leisure to do this. I don't mean idleness at all. I mean just a sense of not being driven. . . .

'I'll tell you what I think'—as I used to say when I was a very, very little boy—I think there is no such thing as leisure for a thinking or sensitive individual under our present unthinking (though at heart not insensitive) social system of thinking and things. And so, all that I can see for us, Laura, is an altered social basis for our human endeavors. And this is what interests me. And this is what takes leisure. And this is the point I want to come to—this factor of leisure and the need of a conscious reckoning with it as part of the technique of a saner basis of living. I often see people with a certain power of detachment that enables them to attain a sense of leisure over long periods and in these periods they put out much effective work. But I would so like, if it is possible, to obtain conditions that will insure constantly this same sense of leisure and yet entail no effort of detachment, that it will be a leisure that is in no sense apart from the organic course of things everywhere. . . .

Brownie's, Jack's and Emily's growing participation in the growing need of our group endeavor has meant very much to me this summer. They have, and very naturally, been so confused by it all. And I have not until lately been half articulate enough myself to explain away what must often have seemed to them, to their great pain and disappointment, a very unworthy discrepancy in my own position toward them. Things seem to clear though somewhat now and I to clear somewhat along with them. . . .

I wish you would let me have some word of Mr. Pope. I saw Dr. Amsden recently and he spoke so very appreciatingly of you.

No more.

With love,

Trigant

To Dr. C. P. Oberndorf   Lifwynn Camp, Merrill, N. Y.
New York   September 7, 1926

My dear Oberndorf:

I had your very welcome note some weeks ago. I too was sorry that there was not the opportunity during the meetings for more of a talk. I appreciate your wanting to see me when I am again in New York. . . .

I have often thought that I must have seemed to you very inhospitable when at the June meeting I replied, as I did, to your question as to the possibility of a delegation visiting our laboratory. I did not mean for a moment to discourage your interest, but such an approach would be meaningless for you. Not to have said so frankly would have been to hold out to you an anticipation that could not possibly be realized in the very nature of our group technique. Group-analysis is an analysis participated in by a group. It is not an analysis performed by a group in front of an individual onlooker—not any more than the individual analysis could be made such an objective enactment for the outside spectator. But all this, I think, will gradually become clearer as still more groups of individuals feel the necessity of bringing their own social reactions to their own objective observation. It is, I think, only in this way that a group-analysis will take its place as a necessary supplement to our present private basis.

Of all the persons interested in our group endeavor the one whose interest and openness of judgment mean most to me is Freud himself. When he senses the fact that I am 'grappling with an important, still unsolved problem,' I am sufficiently heartened to carry my investigations to their ultimate conclusion. In fairness, though, I must add that Professor Freud is as impatient of the theoretical trend of some of my papers as you yourself are. But perhaps we will talk of these things sometime.

If I do not get in touch with you at this time, you will know it is because I am rushed every moment. But if you would be free in the middle of the day and could lunch with us at the Harvard Club, won't you let me have a line at the Hotel Commodore. Dr. Huiskamp, Dr. Syz and one or two others of our group will be there with me from the fifteenth to the twentieth.

With my kindest regards,

Very sincerely yours,

Trigant Burrow

To Dr. Eduard C. Lindeman(16)   Lifwynn Camp, Merrill, N. Y.
Highbridge, New Jersey   September 8, 1926

Dear Dr. Lindeman:

I appreciated very much your expression of interest in the group endeavor some of us are making toward a better understanding of ourselves and our human kind generally. Our analysis in groups amid conditions of daily group living here at Lifwynn Camp has revealed and is daily revealing many unexpected factors which cannot, I think, fail to be of interest in the field of sociology as well as of medicine. Naturally, this daily analysis of normal as

(16) A member of the staff of the New York School of Social Work.

well as of neurotic reactions is leading more and more to quite altered views regarding what was formerly our private basis of analysis.

You were good enough to express the wish that we might meet sometime when I am in New York and I want to say also how glad I should be of the opportunity to meet and talk with you at our leisure. You will be interested to know that I am planning to make the beginning this winter of a laboratory base in New York. It will be a very modest beginning, but, because of the few people there who are interested to work things out among themselves along the same analytic lines adopted by our own psychiatric group, I am interested to share with them the benefit of whatever technique has been thus far developed among ourselves.

I want to say how very encouraging it was to have you express your interest in the papers I sent you. I know that such discussions can give only a most superficial idea as to the real material observed in our laboratory or as to the technique of observing it. . . .

Very sincerely yours,

Trigant Burrow

To Dr. Louis K. Anspacher(17) Lifwynn Camp, Merrill, N. Y.
New York September 8, 1926

Dear Dr. Anspacher:

I am ashamed of myself that I have not written you long ago in response to your own very cordial letter to me of May 14th. As I said to you when we talked on the phone, your understanding and interest in the conceptions I am trying to express are a very real encouragement to me. So often the artist comprehends where the so-called scientist stands in wide-eyed mystification.

(17) Playwright and lecturer.

Brownie and I appreciated so much your and Mrs. Anspacher's wish to have us stop and see you at Ossining. We should have loved it. But, alas, we are frail enough creatures not to be as yet masters of our own time. I concede it is a serious slur upon intelligent people that there should be any mastery over them but their own free spirit. But such is our infirmity that too often the paths that beckon us most pleasantly are just the paths we are least at liberty to follow.

You will understand better the unusual demands upon us of late when I tell you that I am planning to make a beginning—the very modest beginning of a group base in New York this winter.... So you may imagine that there has been a good deal to consider in the way of plans. What I think we will have to come to recognize— I feel that you yourself must have sensed this—is the growing transition among thoughtful people today from a personal to a social basis of outlook, from medicine narrowly conceived to a sociological encompassment in its best sense. I wish I could talk with you but it would be never ending.

We have had a most interesting summer. Jack has taken so dependable a part in our undertaking. Brownie and Emily too are really at heart deeply in sympathy with the fundamental purpose of our group endeavors. Though they did leave for Baltimore the other day at the close of camp quite furious with me, both of them. Where the illusion of the individual's private 'right'—especially the private prerogative of woman—is challenged, there must, I suppose, be a considerable scattering of feathers.

With the prospect of quarters in New York this winter and of having part of my work there, I do look forward to seeing something of you. What do you know about New York apartments— not too expensive because this winter's base will hardly be a permanent one? It is to serve largely as a position from which to look about. If it is not interrupting you, I may phone you when I am in New York and get your feeling about the outlook of suitable sections for our purpose....

Have you your lecture tour pretty well made out for the winter? And what about the new play? I hope we are going to have a visit from you and Mrs. Anspacher in Baltimore this winter. . . .

These hills are so perfect now. I am loath to part with them. But for the prospect of ultimately finding a permanent place in the country for our laboratory work I should be inconsolable at returning to the city at this lovely time of the year.

I had not meant to write you at such length. Your own sympathetic understanding is in no small measure answerable.

Looking forward to hearing from you if not to seeing you and with love to you both,

Always sincerely,

Trigant Burrow

To Professor Sigmund Freud
Vienna

Baltimore, Maryland
October 16, 1926

Dear Professor Freud:

I was indeed glad to have your letter of August 15th which reached me at my camp in the Adirondacks. It heartens me very much to know that you realize something of the difficulty of the work I have undertaken. When you write me that you are interested in my publications and realize that I am 'grappling with an important, still unsolved problem,' I am encouraged to go forward and acquire, if I can, both a better technique of procedure as well as a clearer language in which to describe the practical application of my thesis.

Naturally, it has been my hope that my endeavors in the direction of social analysis might some day find sympathy with you. If there underlies my work a principle that is sound, I cannot but believe that you will welcome this extension of the field of individual psychology. I recently sent you reprints of some further papers, 'Insanity a Social Problem'(18) and 'Our Social Evasion.'(19) Today I am sending you another article which I hope may clarify my meaning—a meaning which, I confess, has been altogether too unclear to myself and which still must wait for further practical investigations before I shall be prepared to state my position without reserve.

I have insisted and shall continue to insist that psychoanalysis is an essentially laboratory method of procedure and that as a laboratory discipline it must be given academic acknowledgment along with other laboratories occupying a place in our university curricula. In a paper called 'The Need of an Analytic Psychiatry,' to appear in January in the *American Journal of Psychiatry*, I have again attempted to draw attention to what seems to me the utter futility of psychiatric or psychoanalytic methods which are lacking in a laboratory basis of observation. It seems to me that psychoanalysis will be liable to the misuses of charlatanism until the universities have demanded a laboratory qualification for the student who undertakes psychoanalytic methods of treatment. . . .

Dr. Federn tells me that the next Psycho-Analytic Congress will have its session at Semmering where you have your summer residence. I earnestly hope to have the pleasure of attending the Congress and of seeing and talking with you at that time.

With my kind regards,

Sincerely yours,

Trigant Burrow

(18) *The American Journal of Sociology*, 1926, vol. XXXII, pp. 80–7.

(19) *Medical Journal and Record*, 1926, vol. CXXIII, pp. 793–6.

To Crystal Herne
New York

Baltimore, Maryland
October 22, 1926

Dear Miss Herne:

I should not willingly intrude upon you in this way—it is my first offense of the sort—but for the very great interest I found in an article of yours I happened to see in the *Theatre Magazine* some weeks ago. The article was interesting to me because I had seen your play, 'Craig's Wife,' and was most impressed both by the play itself and what seemed to me your own splendid interpretation of the part of the neurotic wife. But I should not feel at liberty to write you because of my admiration of your very acceptable characterization of Craig's wife or even at the instance of your article.

The occasion of my writing you is a certain comment in your paper, which I cannot dismiss from my mind without some word to you. Let me say first, as a plea for my writing you, that my own work is that of social psychology, most especially psycho-analysis. As I left the theatre after a performance of 'Craig's Wife' one evening last June, it seemed to me that I had been actually in the home of one of my very own patients, so accurately had you drawn the lines of her domestic pathology. It interested me deeply. Perhaps it is not necessary for me to say that technically I know nothing of the stage. I thought, though, 'here is an artist who knows the clinic, who knows human pathology at close range.' I still feel it must be so. But a few months later I came upon your article and to the sentence in it that is the occasion of this letter to you.

You write that what you cannot understand in the character of Craig's wife is the seeming inconsistency in this woman's showing so meticulous a care for her home, and yet at the same time assiduously keeping all would-be comers out of it. Throughout all of Mr. Kelly's very subtle play this 'seeming inconsistency' is, on the contrary, a most delicately discerning perception. Far from inconsistent, this was, to my feeling as a psychopathologist, the most exquisite touch in the dramatist's portrayal of this very vital character. There is absolutely no inconsistency here. It is, in fact, neurotic consistency *par excellence*. This woman's home was for her a sick phantasy—a phantasy of a privately cherished possession, but a *phantasy*, not a vital reality. Consistent with this phantasy, notwithstanding that she was jealously watchful of every detail in the appointment of her home, she kept the *actuality* of other presences than her own religiously out of it. Is not one's dream the more complete the more one shuts out from it the intrusions of reality? Nowhere than in 'Craig's Wife' is the neurotic's dream more faithfully enacted than in this artificial enclosure so many women call their 'home.' This home, like so many others, was the revery of a dissociated personality. Any outsider was necessarily an unwelcome interloper. Any intrusion was automatically resented. And so Craig's wife was completely faithful to her own realm of phantasy—the only realm she knew—when she gave to her home the unstinted care she did in sheer vanity for its appearance and at the same time shut out its 'appearance' to all comers!

I concede that the clinical picture presented in these dissociated states is not always recognized even by the psychopathologist when the revery makes use of the daily furniture of actuality as did Craig's wife. But there is no contradiction in the seeming discrepancy of this woman's behavior. And, from the experience of the consultation room, I cannot refrain from suggesting to you this added sidelight upon a characterization to which you have given such painstaking study and which, notwithstanding your perplexity on this single point, was, in my judgment, as nearly perfect a drawing as I have anywhere seen upon the stage.

I trust you will understand the spirit of interest that has prompted me to this comment in relation to the problem that confronted you in the very sensitive psychology of Mr. Kelly's play.

Very sincerely yours,

Trigant Burrow

It may be of interest that the letter to Miss Herne was written literally at the moment of Dr. Burrow's departure for New York. His secretary recalls that by the time it was ready to be signed his suitcases were in the foyer awaiting the cab to take him and Mr. Shields to the station.

For the remainder of that fall and the following winter, although maintaining a base in Baltimore, Burrow spent the major part of his time in New York where he opened a professional office.

To Dr. Kimball Young(20)   New York City
The University of Wisconsin   October 26, 1926

Dear Dr. Young:

. . . I want to thank you for your own very kind expression of interest in the things that have been occupying me of late years. I too wish there might be the opportunity to talk more fully with you of the trends that are of common interest to us.

It is a pleasure to know that it seems to you of value to include part of my paper, 'Social Images,' in the book of lectures you mention. I regret that 'The Group Method of Analysis'(21),

(20) Professor of sociology.

(21) *The Psychoanalytic Review*, 1927, vol. XIV, pp. 268–80.

which is with *The Psychoanalytic Review*, has not yet appeared. I would send you a reprint of the German version published in the *Imago* but this was tampered with no little in the German editing, so that I am writing today to Dr. H. C. Syz, who is associated with me in Baltimore, and asking him to send to you a copy of this paper in manuscript.

Perhaps I ought to say that I do not feel entirely at ease about this paper. I have not in mind its matter so much but rather a certain tendency I feel in it to lead to misconception. The other reprints for which you ask, my secretary writes me, were sent you just about the time you wrote and probably crossed your letter. Along with 'Our Social Evasion' and 'Our Mass Neurosis' were sent 'Psychiatry as an Objective Science' (22) and 'Insanity a Social Problem.' I shall be very pleased to have sometime your reaction to these studies.

What I should like so much to make clear to you is that my thesis is not one which has been in any sense *thought out*. Not at all. It is the outcome of an actual analysis of my own social mood. It is physiological not intellectual, and to understand it intellectually is to misconceive its essential physiological meaning. I have not arrived at it mentally—I would have, heaven knows, if I could have—but only through some sort of organic social sense as it has come through in our group or social analysis. But this will perhaps become clearer after a while.

I was indeed interested to know of your talks with Mrs. Dummer. She was among the very first to whom my work appealed because of its social background. She was good enough to write me some years ago and I have hoped sometime to meet her. If you are ever in New York or Baltimore I hope you will let me know.

Sincerely yours,

Trigant Burrow

(22) *The British Journal of Medical Psychology*, 1925, vol. v, pp. 298-309.

To Alvin Johnson, Director   New York City
The New School for Social Research   November 6, 1926
New York

Dear Mr. Johnson:

Your letter of October 11th should have had an earlier answer. It was here when I came three weeks ago but since then I have had hardly a moment at my desk. You have touched upon matters which are, it seems to me, of very vital concern both to sociology and to psychiatry.

What you write of the analogies you have as a sociologist long observed between certain collective reactions and the reactions of the clinically insane interests me very much. But when as a 'layman' you ask me what is the relationship between these more diffuse processes and the deeper invasion of the individual organism, I can only answer that in the face of these problems I am a layman too. Indeed psychiatry seems throughout a lay discipline in its relationship to the social aspects of insanity.

What has been in the last few years of increasing interest to me has been the opportunity of meeting with groups of normal people as well as with confessedly neurotic subjects with a view to developing a psychiatric technique that makes it possible to observe and correlate just such processes as you mention.

You speak of the socially 'infectious' nature of certain processes such as shell-shock and ask what is known about this and where you can find it? The truth is, I do not think this social factor in mental disorders has been explained. If so, I have not seen it. It is just such questions which I think call for the development of a social technique of analysis if we are really to find the answer. I am sorry I cannot be of more help. Your statement, though, that 'the man who is a lunatic in his collective persona may be quite sane in his individual persona' is not one—at least as generally understood—with which I can accord. Certainly if our group studies have afforded scientific evidence for anything, it has been the questionableness of this very widely credited differentiation.

But until there is a larger number of students taking a serious responsibility toward the study of mental states as problems of a social biology in which we are all commonly involved, it seems to me that psychiatry must remain, in regard to its social problems, in its present purely speculative stage.

Let me say again how very much interest your letter held for me.

Sincerely yours,

Trigant Burrow

To Victor V. Branford(23)   New York City
London   November 8, 1926

Dear Mr. Branford:

I have neglected longer than I meant to the letter I promised several weeks ago to send you. The reason is that I have only in the last days found the opportunity for a fuller acquaintance with the very valuable book, *Science and Sanctity*, which you were good enough to send me.

After going through your thoughtful thesis, I find myself particularly sympathetic to its trend. I hope I am not presuming unduly in believing that there underlies the group basis of analysis of my students and myself much the same purpose that you have in mind,

(23) Editor of the British *Sociological Review*.

the purpose, namely, of unifying man's scientific outlook and those aspirations toward self-realization which reside in the deeper stratum of his instinctive moods.

Your plea for a closer coöperation between sociology and psychology means very much to me and is, in my feeling, most timely. Indeed, in a broad encompassment of both, neither can subsist in the absence of the other.

Perhaps sometime it will be possible to talk together of these things.

Again with appreciations,

Very sincerely yours,

Trigant Burrow

To his daughter
Ruxton, Maryland

New York City
Emily's Eighteenth Birthday!
January 11, 1927

Dear Emily:

This is only a birthday remembrance; it is not a gift. There is no gift adequate to express all the joy and love and confidence my heart holds for you. As silent as I have been, as silent as I have had to be in these last difficult years, I would like you to know something of what I feel, dear Emily, when I say that no man ever had a daughter who meant as much to him, who has always meant as much to him as you mean and will always mean to me.

With my love,

Father

Dear Professor Giddings:

Your kind notes of December 4th and January 17th brought with them the refreshing stimulus that has accompanied any word from you in regard to the papers I have sent you from time to time. Nothing has in the last months meant so much to my associates and myself as a certain sympathetic appreciation toward the trend of our endeavors that has come from the sociologists. Our researches both in the individual and in the group have brought even more clearly before us the fact that the problems confronted by the psychiatrist are those which pertain to the social body in the large and cannot be divorced from the field of the sociologist and the educator. Naturally, any recognition of this feeling elsewhere has been for us a most stimulating incentive. . . .

I was much interested in your question as to the possible overstressing of the importance of the social factor in relation to insane states. My own feeling is that this—the social mood-repression—is the exclusive factor in the production of insanity. Of course I need not say that I am speaking only of the psychogenic type of disorder. Naturally, disorders due to structural changes or to toxic incidents are quite excluded.

Your mention of abnormal mentality occurring in individuals through generations, as it has come under your direct observation, is a condition which is certainly not to be denied. Some fifteen years ago a lady came to me, whose mother had been for years in an asylum and subsequently died there. The condition of my

(24) Professor of political science.

patient was diagnosed as dementia praecox, and she was referred to me by Dr. Adolf Meyer. The data which I was able to gather from this lady in regard to her mother, as well as data given by the patient's father in regard to his wife (the patient's mother), in addition to the reports of physicians as to the absence of physical findings, give every indication of the psychogenic occasion for the insanity of the mother. As I reviewed her case, the social factor here seemed to me undeniable. There was a very serious social trauma which existed throughout the early life of this lady. That the condition of the daughter was a definite response to social conditions was most plain. Her case was regarded as one of very unusual recovery. She is holding today an important position socially in her home city and has four children. But I do not think that the restoration that there has been with her would have been possible in the absence of her patient study and recognition of the social element in her neurosis. So much for individuals of two generations.

Now as regards her children. They present no unhealthy marks. The contrary is rather the case with them. The oldest is fifteen. But what I do observe is an undoubtedly sensitive, alert, affective type of constitution. Now my own way of reckoning is to regard this affective, alert, sensitive constitution as the inheritance factor in the situation. But, while this strain of inherited sensitiveness is undoubtedly present, we cannot, I think, affiliate this strain with the factors entering into an individual's pathology, for this same strain is in quite as many persons represented in unusual productivity in the sphere of art and science, provided such an individual finds an adaptation in which he can more or less take his place in the social environment.

People so commonly think of alcoholism as being an inherited condition because one so often sees it passing through a definite family line. I cannot myself conceive of alcoholism being inherited, but I can most easily see how a very sensitive disposition may be inherited and how an individual of this disposition would reach out desperately for some easement for his restlessness and pain. In his discomfort it is natural that he would turn to that recourse which is most handy and which is most readily suggested by his social environment. Is not this situation a good deal like that existing in tuberculosis in which an individual inherits a non-resistant constitution which exposes him more than other individuals to tubercular infection?

If I am not flattering myself too far it does seem to me that, with the assistance of my associates, our laboratory endeavor has made much progress toward unearthing what is probably the specific microgenic event in the causation of mental disorders. The nature of this event, I feel, lies in a certain early inculcated spurious image. This image is general, existing normally as well as in so-called neurotic subjects and it is found specifically in the social relationship that characterizes the reaction of the parent toward the child. I hope, if I must seem sweeping, that I do not seem extravagant. The years of daily experimentation in the reactions *inter se* of individuals comprising social units leaves me no other conclusion than that a nervous disorder is essentially social. In the sense in which I view our nervous disharmonies a certain pathological image-substitution, existing socially, is as definitely the cause of mental disorder as the germ of tuberculosis is responsible for the prevalence of this disease among us. I cannot see how it is possible for us to expect a satisfactory removal of this widespread social incident in our mental life in the absence of a widespread educational campaign. It has been shown impossible to eliminate the cause of tuberculosis in the absence of a program of education among people generally; and I do not believe that in the absence of a campaign of education directed toward the challenge of our social mood that there will be the effective remedy for nervousness and insanity among us.

I am very glad that you mentioned this point in your letter. I do not know whether I have responded to it satisfactorily. If I have not, I should be glad if you would tell me....

Again with my deep appreciation of your interest, I am with kind regards,

Very sincerely yours,

Trigant Burrow

To Professor Sigmund Freud   New York City
Vienna   February 7, 1927

Dear Professor Freud:

I would not have allowed your letter of November 14th to have stood so long unanswered but for the circumstance of a quite long and serious illness that has kept me from my desk for many weeks. In the meantime, I have had word of your having recently been ill and under the necessity to undergo surgical operation. I regret very much to learn of your having had to pass through so trying an ordeal. I trust that by this time you have been quite restored to your usual health.

In replying to your valued letter I do not know what to say. I do not believe there is anything I can say. I shall send to you copies of whatever writings I have from time to time and, if you have the leisure to run through them, perhaps they will assist in making my meaning clearer than I have yet been able to do. My task has not been a light one. I shall go on with it encouraged by the response I have met in the fresh group environment with which I have had contact in New York City.

I cannot but feel that I stand in relation to my work in precisely the same position in which you stood at the outset of your discoveries in psychoanalysis. Every one said 'I do not understand' and placed upon you the burden of their being made to understand.

This burden you could only place back upon their shoulders where it properly belonged. The same material which you had examined, and the same technique of investigation which you had used to examine it, was open to them as to you if they cared to make use of it.

I cannot see that the situation is any different in regard to the group technique and the group basis of analysis which, with my associates, I have endeavored to develop. For sixteen years I have pursued the practice of psychoanalysis in strict adherence with that method as defined by you. Today the tendency is very general among my colleagues to insist that I shall solve for them their difficulty of understanding what I am endeavoring to solve for myself only through a special process of technique. No one knows better than you that it is not possible for the psychoanalyst to win acceptance from his individual patient through mere theoretical discussion and explanation but only through his own affective experience with the method and disclosures of psychoanalysis. In the same way I cannot stand opposite my hearers and explain unconscious *social* processes which are secretly concealed within their own social personality when in their affective life *they do not wish these unconscious social processes explained.*

Those who are interested, and their number is growing, are coming to acknowledge more and more—a circumstance which they must really know, however much their acknowledgment may be repressed socially—that social resistances are no more susceptible of theoretical handling through lecture or discussion than the personal resistances, which you were the first to recognize and confront, have been successfully handled through mere discussion and theory. The matters under investigation with my associates and myself, as with you, are matters of definite analysis and it is as impossible in group-analysis as in personal analysis to legislate human moods.

I am sending you today a paper which may better reach the feeling it attempts to address than other writings of mine. I do not know.

But I send it to you in the hope that the earnest endeavor that underlies it may bring some pleasure to you because of your realization that whatever merit may underlie the work of my associates and myself, it is traceable to the impetus that first came to us from you.

With my kind regards,

Very sincerely yours,

Trigant Burrow

To D. H. Lawrence
Florence, Italy

New York City
February 7, 1927

Dear D. H. Lawrence:

Many thanks for your good letter from Florence of January 12th. I am very glad you felt with me in my paper, 'Psychoanalysis in Theory and in Life.' What you say of my involved sentences is too terribly true. See if my language is not improving in this essay I am sending you today, 'The Reabsorbed Affect and Its Elimination.'(25)

No, nobody listens to me. But I do not expect them to. I didn't listen myself. Circumstances, very unusual circumstances, *compelled* my mood to listen whether or no. And now and then I have the opportunity of compelling by extension this same mood acknowledgment in others. But it is only by compulsion that our willful mood is touched, not by persuasion. Intellectualism simply does not figure for a moment in the process.

(25) *The British Journal of Medical Psychology*, 1926, vol. VI, pp. 209–18.

No, I am not a Jew. I like them and they like me, but racially I am not one of them. My ancestry is chiefly French, though in recent generations depleted with English and Irish strains.

Your letters and their sympathetic encouragement have meant very much to me. You should have stopped to see me on your way from Mexico to England. This winter I am in New York in response to the group interest there on the part of several people. It has been an interesting experience, this fresh contact with a totally new environment and the opportunity to approach it from an entirely fresh mood basis. The response there has been more than I had had any expectation of. New York also has its soberness and its pain.

You are so fortunate to travel as much as you do. I think each year I shall set out but each year there are interests that stand momentarily in the way.

With my good wishes,

Sincerely yours,

Trigant Burrow

To Dr. Adolf Meyer   New York City
Baltimore, Maryland   March 29, 1927

Dear Dr. Meyer:

Your letter of March 17th was forwarded to me here. I was glad to hear from you notwithstanding the occasion of your letter. For some time I have been painfully conscious of what must have seemed to you the obstinate recalcitrance of my attitude and yet I find myself unprepared for this word from you. In answer to your suggestion that my University connection be dropped and my association with you brought to an end, I have only to say that if this is your wish I shall, of course, abide by it without question and assure you that, whatever your decision may be, it will have as always my entire respect.

My only regret is that your suggestion of bringing to a close the years of our association rests upon your feeling that there is the absence of any practical collaboration between us. If, however, I cannot concur in this interpretation I at least can fully concede the propriety of your own position in the circumstance.

If this means the conclusion of my association with you, I do want to say to you how very much that association has meant to me over the years and express the deep sense of my obligation to you. I only hope that, whatever circumstances have arisen to divide our ways, you will know the very high appreciation and regard in which I shall always hold you. . . .

As you say, 'the work with the patient is after all what constitutes the psychiatry.' Of course, though, the patient is a reflection of a social system of which he is a part and if I, as the physician, am a part of the same social system, in so far as there exists a common social involvement between physician and patient it seems important to proceed from a feeling-basis that takes full account of this situation. And so it has been our endeavor to accept with the patient the existence of a general social collusion and to meet him on the basis of this acceptance. This position, I feel, in no way limits, but rather it immeasurably broadens the work with the patient. . . .

With my kind regards,

Sincerely yours,
Trigant Burrow

To Dr. Adolf Meyer   New York City
Baltimore, Maryland   April 16, 1927

Dear Dr. Meyer:

I want to thank you for your letter of April first. It makes the situation much clearer to me and my own course plain. What is especially gratifying to me is the realization of your feeling that whatever the demands of the situation for new adjustments on my part, it in no way touches our personal relations.

Under the circumstances I feel compelled, if it is not a needless formality, to tender forthwith my resignation. The situation, however, which the last years have created, places upon me the necessity of some explanation to the University, not only because of my obligations to the University but because of the obligations of personal integrity, as I feel that the University is unaware of the true status of my position in respect to it.

I must therefore ask you to let me consider the situation in some detail, though I realize the situation is not one that should place upon you a burden which, as I understand it, rests upon the University.(26)

You will recall that, some years ago, quite unsolicited by me, you yourself proposed to me that my duties to the University, as assistant in psychiatry, would be more satisfactorily fulfilled if henceforth I were released from attendance at the Dispensary and instead should give my time to such members of the Staff or to any of the students whom you might recommend to undertake their analysis with me. The arrangement was one that was

(26) In his reply to this letter Dr. Meyer stated: 'It is not and was not "the University" requesting your withdrawal. ... When I spoke of "University" I merely implied an administrative relation. On all the points that have come up, I have to bear all the responsibility.'

most welcome to me and I appreciated that it was consideration for the nature of my work which prompted it.

According to the new arrangement under which I was to perform my duties to the University, I devoted some two years to the careful and very difficult analysis of a physician who was a member of the Phipps Staff, and who was sent to me because of a condition of major epilepsy. The seizures reported in the history and twice witnessed by me in my office left no question of the epileptic nature of the convulsive attacks. While I have had subsequently no direct word from the hospital nor from the patient, the condition, which was one of years standing, was, I believe, permanently relieved and, as I understand, is regarded at the Clinic as a definite cure of epilepsy by psychoanalysis. (Though, it is true, I employed at that time, as subsequently, my own modification of the psychoanalytic method.) Since then, more than three years have passed and the patient has continued in active duty at the Clinic and is an efficient member of its faculty.

Subsequent to this period, I felt under scientific obligation to improve my own technique of therapy. I felt that the entire psychoanalytic field needed thorough investigation and reconstructing. On arriving at this determination, I told you of the necessity I felt of giving up my private practice temporarily in order to devote my time exclusively to research. It seemed to me that research in a field in which there was as much confusion and lack of coördination as in psychoanalysis was a worth-while and indeed imperative undertaking. It is not necessary to call your attention to the sacrifices which were incident to relinquishing my practice and assuming a research task of indefinite duration —the debts I incurred and the necessity which I and my family were under to give up our home and the incidental comforts habitual to us. These are matters personal to my wife and to me and not of interest to the University. I mention them only in order to indicate the earnestness and responsibility I felt toward my undertaking.

The result of these years was the development of a new technique in the analysis of mental conditions, the inception of a laboratory method of observation in psychoanalysis, the publication of a book and of numerous papers as the result of this investigation, as well as the recognition from scientific men of other universities, in this country and in Europe, of the work I have attempted to do. In view of these circumstances, I am unable to believe that the University is wholly cognizant of the actual situation when, in requesting my withdrawal, it offers the reasons for its action mentioned in your letter.

To sum up the situation briefly: The University instructs me that my duties are to consist in my giving to the University what time it may ask for the analysis of individuals connected with it. Following a period of two years of such work, which I understood to be entirely satisfactory, the University determines to send no more officers or students to me and now, without further word or explanation, states: 'The University does not maintain positions which cease to exist in the form of actual duties and services.'

I do not question for a moment the University's right to dismiss me at its pleasure, but when it does so upon terms which imply that I have been content to accept from the University all the privileges pertaining to my connection, the while I have failed to render the services to which I was assigned, I must, in justice to my own integrity, ask for representation that is in accord with the actual conditions.

Somewhat less than a year ago you spoke to me of a pending situation in which you felt you would be unjustly represented in the University. Recalling that situation—though a quite minor incident compared to the present one—I am sure you will understand somewhat my position today and will overlook this otherwise disproportionate intrusion upon you.

I take for granted that I am leaving no question in your mind of my having any wish to retain further connection with the University. My only concern is that I make a clear representation to the University of the circumstances incident to my resignation.

I want to say again how heartily I share your feeling that the situation does not in any way involve our own personal relations.

With my kind regards,

Sincerely yours,

Trigant Burrow

CHAPTER 8

THE LIFWYNN FOUNDATION

During the winter of 1926–27 Dr. Burrow became more and more interested in the greater opportunity for understanding and sympathetic contacts offered in New York. He eventually gave up his office in Baltimore and centered his professional activities in New York. At the same time the informal organizational setup under which the laboratory studies had been carried on was giving way to a more formal structure.

'We are bringing ourselves to the full consciousness that we have and have for some time had in spirit the elements of a foundation,' Burrow wrote to an associate in 1926. 'Instead of my being the healthy psychopathologist to whom the sick and delinquent neurotic turns for help, paying in professional fees for the therapeutic remedies I have to sell, we have been a group of co-workers giving of time and resources very freely toward a common purpose. What is really needed now is more a technique of a foundation as must come with the realization that the foundation is already at hand. Of course, what we have to keep in mind is that what our project entails is a mood foundation and not a money foundation.'

The Lifwynn Foundation for Laboratory Research in Analytic and Social Psychiatry was incorporated in Maryland in August 1927, deriving its name from the Adirondack camp where the group studies had first been conducted in a community setting. Directors were drawn from the professional members of the group, and Burrow served as Scientific Director, a position he occupied until his death. An office was rented in New York, and a house taken in Greenwich, Connecticut, where Dr. Burrow and several members of the Baltimore group took up residence.

Several years later Dr. Burrow wrote, 'As to the Lifwynn Foundation, it is in a broad sense a symbol; it stands for the development of
phylobiology—a laboratory approach to man's behavior that represents
the effort not of one individual but of a group, a community—may I
suggest that it embraces latently a race or phylum—of individuals. And
so in a deep as well as in a broad sense, the Foundation embodies man's
total organic study of man. It is an incorporated organization that
originated in a definite laboratory need and only later came to be appreciated as a community-vehicle for carrying on the study of man
as an integral part of man's community-life. That is, the Foundation
happened; it did not set out with the purpose of doing a piece of work;
the incorporation did not come first but only years later along with
the development of what I had first called group-analysis. . . . The
Foundation is itself a study in developing a laboratory approach to
human behavior. The chief purpose of our organization, I may say,
as the subjective expression of a daily living laboratory effort, is to
learn to discriminate in the practical conduct of ourselves, individually
and as a community, between the human organism's total behavior-
motivation—its primary pattern of reaction—and those secondarily conditioned reactions which represent but partial reaction-responses. But
it is a long story.'(1)

August 1927 brought the culmination of another effort of many
years' standing, with the publication of *The Social Basis of Consciousness*, the enlarged version of 'Our Common Consciousness.' The book
was roundly criticized by many of Burrow's professional colleagues,
but it interested and influenced others, and led to considerable correspondence and contact with such men as D. H. Lawrence, Leo Stein
and later Herbert Read.

Stein expressed his appreciation of *The Social Basis of Consciousness*
in a review he entitled 'Psychoanalysis Psychoanalyzed.'(2) Lawrence
wrote Dr. Burrow in August 1927:

Your book came three days ago, and I have now read it. I found it extremely
good. Your findings about sex and sexuality seem to me exactly it: that's
how it is: and your criticism of psychoanalysis as practiced is to the quick.
I believe as you do—one must use words like believe—that it is our being
cut off that is our ailment, and out of this ailment everything bad arises. . . .

(1) Letter to Dr. William M. Malisoff, June 21, 1935.

(2) *The New Republic*, December 14, 1927.

I shall write a review of your book if I can.(3) Probably even then nobody will print it. But it is most in sympathy with me of any book I've read for a long time. Pardon the egotism—what is one to say! I hope we may meet, really.

Lawrence's interest in Burrow's approach was of long standing, as indicated in his small book, *Psychoanalysis and the Unconscious*, published in 1921.(4) 'Lawrence was much influenced by Trigant Burrow,' Herbert Read writes in *Education Through Art*, 'and in this way some of Dr. Burrow's ideas have been diffused among people who have never heard his name. The sociological emphasis thus introduced into modern psychology has been reinforced more recently by writers such as Karen Horney (*The Neurotic Personality of our Time* and *New Ways in Psychoanalysis*) and Eric Fromm (*The Fear of Freedom*).'(5)

In this same book Read enters into a full and interesting discussion of *The Social Basis of Consciousness*. He says in part:

... If individual and social harmony is to be restored, and cultural growth continued, then we must strive to recover on a physiological and psychological basis what Burrow calls 'the total organism's internal feeling-behavior.' How that can and must be done has been shown by this psychologist in his very significant but little appreciated work, *The Social Basis of Consciousness*.

I have read this difficult book three times ... but always with a deepening sense of its truth and importance. I have also read all the criticisms that were written of it, mainly about the time of its appearance, and, in so far as they were antagonistic, mainly by Freudians. I have the greatest respect, as must already be evident, for the genius of Freud, but I have found that he fails to provide us with an adequate solution for the problem just stated—the cure of our modern mass-neurosis; and at the point where Freud fails us, there I think Dr. Burrow, who is himself a pupil of Freud's, comes to our rescue, and provides us with a solution.(6)

(3) Published in *The Bookman*, 1927, LXVI, pp. 314–17. Republished in *Phoenix, The Posthumous Papers of D. H. Lawrence*, New York, The Viking Press, 1936.

(4) New York, Thomas Seltzer, 1921, pp. 21–2.

(5) Read, Herbert, *Education Through Art*, London, Faber and Faber, 1943, p. 198.

(6) Ibid. p. 197.

For the first few years after the move to New York, Mrs. Burrow continued to live with their son and daughter in Ruxton. Jack Burrow held a position with a bank in Baltimore and Emily was just making her bow to society before going abroad for several winters to study singing and the dance. Mrs. Burrow made frequent trips to New York, and spent the summer months at Lifwynn Camp handling the many details involved in the household management.

During the winter of 1928–29 there was an unexpected financial curtailment. After an auspicious beginning, the New York venture was gravely threatened by the sudden death of an associate who had been contributing generously to the undertaking. The necessity for retrenchment was pressing. The Greenwich property was sold, and Dr. Burrow and Mr. Shields took up their living quarters in the apartment where Dr. Burrow had his private office. Their associates, many of whom were professionally employed in the city, were scattered in the neighborhood.

Such living conditions were not favorable for an experiment demanding the daily observation of social interactions. It was therefore a fortunate development when in the fall of 1929 four members of the Foundation leased a five-story brownstone-front house—27 East 37th Street. This committee rented offices to the Foundation and to Dr. Burrow, besides living quarters for him and the other members of the research group. Space was also later provided for an instrumental laboratory. Administered by certain members of the Foundation, the dining room and kitchen completed the facilities. Here for sixteen years the phylobiological work was carried on.

By 1929 several other groups had been formed in addition to the one representing the original and continuing research endeavor. For several years these groups met with Dr. Burrow or his associates and pursued their independent analysis of individual and social behavior patterns.

The focus of Burrow's interest, however, was beginning at this time to center more and more compellingly upon the physiological substrate of disordered interrelational behavior. He was presenting frequent papers before professional organizations and during the years 1928–32 these writings began to reflect the change of emphasis. While he was still occupied with group-analysis as indicated by the titles of some of his papers(7), others show the emergence of interest in patterns of

(7) 'The Autonomy of the "I" from the Standpoint of Group Analysis,' *Psyche*

internal tension.(8) Similarly, in the letters of this period the reader will find the first references to this theme, later to achieve full expression in his scientific reports.

To William E. Galt   New York City
Lifwynn Camp   June 23, 1927

Dear William:

I am seeing you soon, so will not attempt to answer your letter. The heat is intense and the stone drill intenser and to shut the latter out is to shut the former in. Of the two evils we prefer the former, when we do not prefer the latter! It will be good to get away next week.

Cannot you and Jack so arrange your mutual activities this summer that you can give two hours daily to the typewriter? If you could fill the needs of the New York office—if you had sufficient proficiency in stenography (in 'speedwriting') and typewriting to have a position with us on a half or whole time basis (or perhaps three quarters) it might be practical to take a course or two at Columbia.

(London), 1928, vol. VIII, pp. 35–50; 'The Basis of Group-Analysis, or the Analysis of the Reactions of Normal and Neurotic Individuals,' *The British Journal of Medical Psychology*, 1928, vol. VIII, pp. 198–206; 'So-Called "Normal" Social Relationships Expressed in the Individual and the Group; and their Bearing on the Problems of Neurotic Disharmonies,' *The American Journal of Psychiatry*, 1930, vol. X, pp. 101–16.

(8) 'The Physiological Basis of Neurosis and Dream,' *Journal of Social Psychology*, 1930, vol. I, pp. 48–65; 'Physiological Behavior-Reactions in the Individual and the Community,' *Psyche* (London), 1930, vol. XI, pp. 67–81; 'A Phylogenetic Study of Insanity in its Underlying Morphology,' *The Journal of the American Medical Association*, 1933, vol. 100, pp. 648–51.

A circumstance I want to speak of—if it is possible to write of it clearly—is the unusual direction of your education and training in the last years and the need of giving it practical application, precisely as you would have done had your education during these years been predominantly in the field of pedagogy, letters or mechanics. With you, as with Jack, your whole training has been concentrated upon the *mood*life of man and upon its subjective significance in man's biology. 'Application' in this field means training in the expression of *feeling*. It is too long a story to write of....

You and Jack might think it over.

Sincerely,

Trigant Burrow

To Mrs. W. F. Dummer   New York City
Chicago   June 27, 1927

Dear Mrs. Dummer:

... We have thought in broad racial terms of our biology as it relates to our structural tissues, why be less biological and inclusive in the study of man's social interreactions? As a race are we not woven into a unitary tissue that is as common to us functionally, physiologically as the elements that unite us structurally into a common, unitary species? Really, the closeted conferences with which our analysis of human motives and instincts first began must give way to a broader laboratory method of inquiry that will be sociological in its approach. I am sure it is coming. Even the most devout of the individualistic school are beginning to concede the quite esoteric tendency of the present basis in psychoanalysis. If the papers and lectures I am trying to put forward ever more simply and clearly will contribute somewhat to build a more solid scientific background for the interpretation of our human problems I shall be very happy. It is by no means a task for one individual of very limited capacity, and now that the sociologists and educators as well as a few psychiatrists are beginning more and more to ally their interest with that of my associates and myself, I feel the time is not far distant when the laboratory or group method of analysis will go forward as a definitely organized scientific movement.

I shall always remember and be grateful to you, Mrs. Dummer, for the early interest and sympathy you expressed in our endeavors. It meant, I assure you, very much to me. . . .

Very sincerely yours,

Trigant Burrow

To Dr. Kimball Young Lifwynn Camp, Merrill, N. Y.
University of Wisconsin July 11, 1927

Dear Dr. Young:

. . . I find it hardly possible to answer your letter in a manner that would be satisfactory to us both. The reason is largely that my usages are often quite special and do not coincide with those generally current. You speak, for example, of 'group' as of a collection of people, whereas 'group' in my usage is an organic principle resident not less in the individual than in a collection of individuals. This is a somewhat long story but perhaps some recent writings of mine will make clearer my use of the concept 'group.' A paper to be published in *The British Journal of Medical Psychology* called

'The Problem of the Transference'(9) will help, I think, in this respect and you will find there too the very different meaning of 'transference' as I use the term. Extending it to its fuller social implication externally involves a quite different concept.

You ask about the propriety of one's bringing before a group a private personal problem such, say, as an unhappy marriage relationship. There is never occasion to bring in such reminiscent material, it being the purpose of our laboratory work to observe only the *present moment*—that is, the mood of the present moment as it relates to one's self and to others. For in our finding the immediate moment is the focal point of our human pathology. This may seem strange after all these fruitful psychoanalytic years and it is not possible for me to make fully clear what I have in mind in the absence of your closer personal contact with our basis and its technique. With my patients and students, they observe with me from the outset conditions shared commonly by all individuals and participated in no less by ourselves. Surely one cannot exact less from one's professional colleagues than from the lay student and yet my colleagues appear to believe that there is some other access to the technique and understanding of group-analysis than that obtained through an actual group or internal technique. I am saying this not as one complaining but only in the spirit of helpfulness as far as I see it. You yourself have spoken in your letter of this same need of personal inquiry so that perhaps I am giving the circumstance greater emphasis than there is need to do with you.

Your inference that our procedure has in it an element of 'confession' is a most natural one but all tendency to confession is quite precluded in our undertaking. You ask about the possibility of there being 'items in the human unconscious which are too deep for revelation to a group.' I do not think so. I do not think the unconscious is primarily deep at all. I think the whole story is on the surface and in full view at every moment. We simply do not commonly possess a technique for observing its outstanding obviousness.

(9) *The British Journal of Medical Psychology*, 1927, vol. VII, pp. 193–202.

I hope some recent reprints reached you and that these later formulations may have served somewhat to answer the very interesting and important questions contained in your letter. I see nothing for us but that we sometime talk things over with a possible view to your own actual participation in the group basis of analysis. My hope is that when my own findings are more fully established and my formulations clearer that the method that I have found so very helpful to me both in my scientific outlook and in my contacts with patients may appear less formidable to my colleagues. . . .

With my kindest regards,

Sincerely yours,

Trigant Burrow

To Mrs. H. A. Sill(10)   Lifwynn Camp, Merrill, N. Y.
New York   August 8, 1927

My dear Mrs. Sill:

The letters you sent me—your brother's and your own—reached me only three days ago, as they were delayed two weeks owing to incorrect address. Our post office address is Merrill and not Chateaugay.

In view of the circumstances I would have preferred that you had first obtained your brother's consent before showing to me a letter of his to you. I am returning to you both your letter and your brother's with this.

(10) An early participant in the group studies.

May I say that the basis maintained by you as indicated in your letter, is not one upon which I can enter with you. It is a private basis, and I respect it completely, but it is not the basis of my work, and I am unable to make contact with it at any point. It seems futile to avoid the quite simple recognition of this and so persevere in attempts at an interchange which assumes the reconcilability of positions which are really incompatible.

You and your brother, as far as I understand it, cannot possibly do any other than continue to preserve, each toward the other, his own separate and unchallenged 'I' and, from this privately established criterion, continue to address each other in terms appropriate to this private mood. It is not a thing that can be helped. It is the compulsion authorized throughout the present system of personal and social images, and to complain and want help is merely more image, more private criterion, more exaltation of the separate 'I' that complains. Besides, some days the separate 'I' has its innings and is 'happy' or elated. The happy or elated individual has his individual compensations. Why may he not expect his unhappiness or depression when the organic balance of things demands its adequate tallying of the human account?

Thank you for your good wishes to us all. With greetings to you and yours,

Very sincerely yours,

Trigant Burrow

To Louise Collier Willcox   Lifwynn Camp, Merrill, N. Y.
Norfolk, Virginia   August 10, 1927

Dear Mrs. Willcox:

I want to write and tell you about what seems to me the very fortunate auspices under which my book has at last been published.(11) Professor C. K. Ogden of Cambridge, England, who edits the International Library of Psychology, Philosophy and Scientific Method, was good enough to become interested in my thesis last fall, and, to my great pleasure, on looking through the book, accepted it.

After the many disappointments from one publisher and another, I could not allow myself to believe it was really true that my essay was to see the light, and so I have held off writing you until I should have the book in my hands. Copies of the English edition are now actually on my desk, and Harcourt, Brace writes me that the American edition will be ready on August 18th. I have just written them asking that they send a copy to you with my compliments. It goes to you with very grateful remembrance of all your sympathetic interest in helping me find the right publisher. In the meantime I have prepared still other works which I am hoping to bring out in the next years.

I don't suppose you are in Norfolk at this time. I should like very much to hear from you and know something of your own days and interests. Did I tell you that I had taken an office last winter in New York and this winter am taking on a larger one with my assistant, Dr. Syz. I can't quite bring myself to relinquish entirely as yet my office in Baltimore and still hope it will be possible, with proper assistance, to continue at least some of the work first begun there.

I don't know.

It is lovely here in these hills, and the summer's work seems always to go so much more easily because of the very quiet and restful environment of Lake Chateaugay. . . .

Mrs. Burrow and Emily are having a wonderful time in Europe this summer. They have returned from Italy and have lately been at Montreux. Emily seems somehow to have newly awakened. I don't seem to know this suddenly developed young woman who

(11) See note 12, p. 44.

writes to me now. What is the news of Christine? Is she not yet ready to appear before a Chicago or Metropolitan audience? It has been long since I have had news of you. I hope you will find leisure to write to me very soon. Remember me please to Mr. Willcox.

With my affectionate remembrance to you,

Sincerely yours,

Trigant Burrow

To Dr. C. K. Ogden   Lifwynn Camp, Merrill, N. Y.
Cambridge, England   September 2, 1927

Dear Dr. Ogden:

... I have been thinking a great deal of your *Meaning of Meaning* and of the whole story of word-magic as you have described it. I can't help wondering whether your approach to the study of symbols, and the work I have been attempting in group-analysis are not along convergent lines. If you happened to read a paper I published a year or two ago in *The British Journal of Medical Psychology* called 'Psychiatry as an Objective Science,' you will see what I mean. I hope it is so. It seems to me the ultimate test of any direction of inquiry if it is found that simultaneously others are proceeding with much the same inquiry and with largely related findings, though from a different angle of approach.

Anyhow I want to shape up and send you a paper I have called 'The Autonomy of the "I" From the Standpoint of Group Analysis.'(12) If it seems to you of sufficient interest to readers of

(12) *Psyche* (London), 1928, vol. VIII, pp. 35–50.

Psyche, I hope that you can find space for it in your journal. It really epitomizes our direct procedure in group-analysis, and I cannot see but that the mood-magic (if I may paraphrase your use) we find through analysis to constitute a sort of spell, not only upon neurotics, but upon normals as well, is an emotional equivalent of the mental state represented in the prevalent superstition you have described as word-magic (a magic and delightful usage, by the way!).

I thought that the article in the last issue of *Psyche* by Sir Richard Paget, on 'The Origin of Language' was fascinating. It set moving a whole series of dormant speculations.

It is too early to predict the sort of reception my book will have, but so far I have been rather pleased at the reviews—the few that I have seen from English papers. And apparently there is some inkling of what it is all about! This is more than I had expected, considering the 'mood' basis from which people, especially the intellectuals, habitually 'think.'

It has been a good summer here in these woods. I hope your own summer has been of value, and a rest to you as well.

With my good wishes and kind regards,

Sincerely yours,

Trigant Burrow

To Louise Collier Willcox
Norfolk, Virginia

Lifwynn Camp, Merrill, N. Y.
September 2, 1927

Dear Mrs. Willcox:

That was a nice long letter you sent me, and I have been quite pleased at so great a favor from you. . . .

So you read Dewey and you read me to find somewhere the place that comforts you! Did you ever try—try just for half an hour, say—to be quite uncomforted. Do not misunderstand. When the outlook is dark and one is depressed, it is then that he is fairly lapping up comfort. I do not mean that sort. I mean something very different. Going uncomforted, especially if one might go uncomforted always, is very beneficent. The organism expands and grows and multiplies in effectiveness under its spell. You might go back sometime to the passages that are not comforting. Comfort is empty compared with the deep experience that asks no comfort, that knows quite calmly that there is none, nor any need for any, that man is only complete in being man.

Now go tell God I said *that*!

You don't know how I shall miss these hills when we turn back to the city in two weeks from now. The quiet rhythm and order of the days in these hills lend themselves very gratefully to the study of the problems of our human ways.

I hope we shall meet in New York, and with every good wish for a delightful vacation, believe me,

Sincerely yours,

Trigant Burrow

To D. H. Lawrence   Lifwynn Camp, Merrill, N. Y.
Florence, Italy   September 9, 1927

My dear Lawrence:

It seems good to have at last a moment when I may write you. You have been very much in my thought. Your letter was so heartening and so very kind. I want to say to you first, though, how sorry I am that you have been ill—that you were born ill, born protesting at being born. I, myself, howled about it for one mortal year, they tell me, but the insult did not get deeper into my organism than that. I have been whimpering softly to myself, though, ever since, and I mean to go on whimpering until Man is born (even if only some small bit of the occiput presents) and there is an end of his image and of unconsciousness.

When people are ill, who should be well, I feel I must go to them and do something. As a matter of fact nobody could do less than I if he went to you. I have always disliked medicine—that is medicine as pathology. What knowledge I acquired in the long years of my apprenticeship in laboratory and clinic has left me today with little more than a futile tenderness. Do they take your clothes off and put you in the sun? That's the first thing. But I am sure your own instinct has seen to that. Or perhaps, like myself, you are making a living? That is very bad for you. Not even the sun can reach a man who is making a living. This enforced over-concentration of interest upon the nutritional instinct sets up such rigidities, such artificial tensions in us, there is no breathing right, no right rhythm anywhere, and the scalp binds till the head would break.

Sometime we must feel into these things together—that is all group-analysis is anyway. It is breaking up old adhesions and unnatural contractions within the organism of man. How can men be well if Man is not? And Man is so well essentially. There are just the contractions (habituated now throughout the centuries) with which he shrinks in fear from the anomaly of his own image, his stupid purpose in life apart from the purpose that is life. I do not know why we need permit God to do to us what he did to Adam. Adam had nothing approaching our educational advantages.

I do know what you mean, and I am heartily with you, I think, in your feeling about religion. But isn't it with religion as it is with love—love that cannot endure to hear its own name so much as whispered? 'They put their finger on their lip, the powers above. They love but name not love.' What man can adore and call it adoring!

Yes I am married, very much so. I have also a son, 22, who is this summer with me in camp, and a daughter, 18. Mrs. Burrow and Emily have lately been not far distant neighbors of yours, I think. They were in Italy for a while on their tour of Europe this summer.

But about marriage. What I said of marriage, I said of marriage as ownership. And marriage *is* ownership—let's face it. I think no two people were ever more stupid and reluctant to face this un-savory actuality in their lives than my wife and myself, but we have kept at it, and the deeper understanding and sympathy and confidence that have come of it, I count among the richest mean-ings of the many rich meanings that life has brought to me.

About the 'cut-offness'—I do not want to be tedious and seem to talk to you, as people so often feel that I do, with teasing paradox—but really it is not you who are cut off, but the image *you* have of 'you.' So that your question as to what one is to do about the cut-offness, I can only answer, as far as my experience goes, by saying that this image that is socially reciprocated everywhere must, it seems to me, be dissolved in the common pool of social images that now make for those differentiae among us that are really the projected image of each. If it is not your organism that is cut off—your or-ganism with its feelings and instincts and its unending joy of life—but some purely artificial image, superstitiously sponsored under the traditional mood-protectorate of a primitive fear-ridden so-ciety, what avails it to look to the organism for one's mending? Our mental pathology does not really *touch* our organism. Think of it! All our pathology boiled down reveals at last that there was nothing there. Only images mutually supported by images socially begotten and socially sustained. This social distemper is a social obligation to remedy, and we psychiatrists (myself included) have been all this while but standing in the way.

You are right—one cannot forgive. All our forgivingness is spiritual snobbery. But then for us to say with our minds that forgivingness is stupid leads us from the actuality of a mood that does in fact cherish (as a mood based upon the parent-image must) a deep-seated sense of guilt, or self-blame. If I am stupid enough to blame myself, it is up to me to be stupid enough to forgive myself. A stupid equation, but not so stupid as an equation left unresolved.

I love what you say about my excruciating style. It *is* awful, and you have diagnosed me in no imprecise manner. The as yet unresolved conflict within me between science and art is the thunderous noise one hears on every page as I come laboring along. It seemed to me that in some of my later things my breathing was less stertorous. I hope so.

It is good of you to have in mind the thought of possibly writing a review of my book. It would mean much to me to have your very understanding comment upon it. And I, too, hope very earnestly that we shall meet. After October first my headquarters will be at 67 Park Avenue, New York City.

My daughter is making her debut this winter (she would not miss it) and I shall be much in Baltimore, but my work will be in New York, and I am looking forward with real zest to the winter's interests and to newer and, I hope, saner adjustments.

I do hope you will be well soon and that you will keep in mind how much I enjoy having your good letters.

Sincerely yours,

Trigant Burrow

P. S. Won't you reserve your verdict and not say quite yet that 'men were never fully societal'? Do you know Kropotkin's *Mutual*

Aid, and do you know the passages in *The Origin of Species* from which Kropotkin really fashioned his thesis? It is the subjective sense of this societal and organic interconnection or continuum among us as a species that is really the whole meaning of my position, and group-analysis but the clearing away of the manifold image differentiae that have so separated man from himself.

To a prospective student   New York City
                                                                November 1, 1927

My dear Miss I.:

I had not meant to neglect your letter. It came at a moment when I was just moving into new quarters, and in the last week I have succumbed to grippe.

I don't know now quite how to write you. You say you have read my book but your reading it must have for you a meaning which, at least in a measure, is quite private to you, quite apart from my feeling toward it. I thought if there was one thing I had set down clearly it was the fact that wanting 'for one's self' was itself the very essence of our human pathology. Yet you ask me to tell you how the individual *you* 'can do this thing *for oneself.*' This is surely not to read my book. It is to read the lines perhaps but not the feeling which is beneath the lines and which is the whole meaning of our group position.

I have not myself found, in a personal sense, the solution you seek, so that I am hardly in a position to give you the key to it. Indeed, the circumstance of a group basis of inquiry has made it very clear (however unwelcome at first) that this entity called 'I' with its insistent wants is itself the disorder which for years I too tended to locate in every other quarter. Do you not see that society is throughout nervous—that society throughout has its hidden complexes, its secret repressions with their endless compensations in compromise and substitution? Our position is that society must make itself answerable for its otherwise unanswerable mental states. There must come—indeed there is now rapidly coming—this recognition among certain thoughtful groups, and there will follow among similar social clusters the same group process of analysis.

You may be, like other so-called nervous patients, more restless under the image restrictions that everywhere express society but nevertheless it is not true that the illness is greatest where the restlessness is most acute. The neurosis is a condition of the social constitution and the nervousness of an individual here and there is merely a symptom of this wider social disorder.

You see I cannot give to your pain the personal concentration to which your pain leads you to feel you are privately entitled. I cannot feel that your cry for help comes from the real seat of the disorder. This may seem harsh, it probably does seem so to you, but following the period of research it has been my privilege to participate in along with my associates over many years, if I should take any other course I should be taking the attitude of the physician who administers an opiate to quiet pain when he knows very well there is a constitutional disorder which calls definitely for constitutional methods of repair. If with certain of your own habitual associates you should care to enter seriously and responsibly upon a study of your habitual group processes, I should be glad to arrange that my associates and myself offer whatever possible assistance we may be able to bring to such a study-group. In this event may I ask you to communicate with our Laboratory, 149 East 40th Street (Caledonia 3736). . . .

Very sincerely yours,

Trigant Burrow

To Count Alfred Korzybski   Greenwich, Connecticut
Brooklyn, New York   December 16, 1927

Dear Count Korzybski:

I found your letter at my office yesterday, and what you have written has been much in my mind. So that I want today to turn to it at once and give you what answer I can, however inadequate it may be because of what, I should say, is the fundamental difference in the basic methods employed by us. Do not suppose that I do not take off my hat with profound respect to intellectual giants like yourself wherever I meet them. But I hope that in your greater intellectual capacity you will not be forced to despise me completely if I say to you as I must (if I am to reply to your honest letter with the frankness which you have asked from me) that I am wholly an alien among my intellectual friends (intellectual in method) because of a constitutional incapacity within me to proceed along that way. I would no more pretend to debate with you in intellectual argument than I would attempt to argue in pugilistic terms with Mr. Dempsey. With both of you I should have not only to be carried out of the ring but into it, my complete vanquishment being an *a priori* matter of acknowledgment! I do not want to excuse myself but it is a pleasure to try to explain myself in an answer to your frank letter to me.

Your writings are leagues beyond me. My baffled intellect has not a ghost of an idea what it is all about. I simply have not the 'mind' or mental method competent to grasp it. And you are quite right as to my not understanding Einstein, though I thought I had acknowledged that in my book. Perhaps I did not—perhaps in my very disavowal of an understanding of relativity as a mathematical postulate, I presumed a familiarity with it which I did not possess. If you say that I did, then I am sure I did, and it is to be regretted. The way I 'understand' him is the way I 'understand' you. As I sought to acquaint myself with the meaning of Einstein, I felt that there was that in him which is to me my only interest in any man or his theory. Einstein seemed to look at an object or to face an idea without an anterior conviction respecting it. The method of the *man* rang true. He was, in my sense, physiologically accurate. In a word Einstein *observed*.

I once had the pleasure of hearing you talk. As you talked you compelled my complete sympathy and confidence in your thesis. Much that you said I did not grasp. I was really not so much interested in precisely *what* you said—in your observations, but felt wholly content and at one in the sincerity and accuracy of you as an observer. I might as well make a clean breast of things now that I have started, and take whatever penalty my delinquency calls for. As I see it, the whole stimulus to inquiry of any sort lies in the interest, direct or ulterior, which it holds for the inquirer. Now there is not any objective fact in respect to which I have the slightest interest or competence except as it has a direct subjective application to or use for myself or others with whom I am united by the circumstance of practical daily living. To help me better to say what I mean let me illustrate: Any natural phenomenon is a matter of intellectual interest to any normal individual. This I take to be the fundamental axiom that underlies all education. Yet I do not accept this postulate for a moment. It is to me, and upon the analysis of other individuals I have found it to be also for them, a matter of complete indifference. Such a phenomenon, for example, as the mark made by ink upon paper is, and according to the educator by every token should be, a highly arresting circumstance to the alert child. So little 'alert,' so little adept am I intellectually that I find myself devoid of all interest in this and in kindred objective phenomena *per se*. The observation that ink makes a mark on paper has significance for me only by reason of the circumstance that through it I am enabled to communicate with other people by means of the written word.

If I am not mistaken, there exists on the other hand, a vast mass of subjective facts, the whole significance of which for many people is their aptitude for excluding subjective communication between them. This, I am convinced, is the whole meaning of the 'interest' in psychiatric inquiry generally. These and such reflections have led me in the last years to confine my interest solely to the subjective or mood-life of man. Far from reaching any conclusions through intellectual processes, whatever conclusions may have been reached by my associates and myself have come precisely through the abrogation of the intellectual method. If I or anyone else *knew* something, then I or anyone else could keep it to himself as far as any interest it had for my co-workers and myself was concerned. The quality—the physiological quality, the nature of the attention (sincerity of the observer) which the subject brought to his object has been my sole concern.

And so with your discourse as with your written work, I hope I do not seem less sympathetic—less 'understanding,' if you like, than your more intellectual listeners, when I say that I am not interested in the material you set down, in the observations you make. I am interested to the point of being completely carried away by your thought, by the sincerity of attention (the physiological accuracy) shown by you as a scientific observer.

My gifted psychiatric colleagues repeatedly shake their heads and say to me again and again: 'I do not understand you.' As if I had ever any thought or hope that they would! As if 'understanding' —the projicient, intellectual method—had anything to do with the sphere of my processes or with the investigations proceeding from them. Putting the thing in other terms, I have tried to acquire a subjectively phyletic basis from which there might be adopted a position which permitted the observation of those subjectively isolated manifestations now regarded by each individual as a *bona fide* basis of feeling quite private to himself.

Such expressions from you, however, as 'scientists and specialists which were *born* non-Aristotelians' make me feel your fundamental understanding (I do not mean only 'intellectual') of my position. This understanding is, though, largely instinctive and organic to you. For me to understand your position or Einstein's would call for the special intellectual training which you have had. I have no such equipment. I can only employ what understanding may be native or organic to myself in order to know the sincerity of the process or method of you both. Its details I cannot follow. Its results biologically I think I do somehow biologically, instinctively, sense.

I did not refer in my book to your work nor to conclusions of yours and others which were identical to those to which I also had been brought. Not to do so was awkward for me. It could only appear, I know, ungracious, ungenerous even; and yet I had to forego, what would have been under any other circumstances, my natural inclination, because the circumstance which was of significance for me was not at all the intellectual *result* arrived at but solely the phyletic *method* in which I was subjectively an enforced and reluctant contributor. I meant to convey some hint of this in the opening paragraph of the introduction. It was difficult to say and I did not feel that it could be more than intimated. There were indeed also in my book many reservations similar to those for which you ask the reader's indulgence in yours.

Perhaps after all I have only begun to scratch the surface of the field that has come to be my engrossing interest. There is certainly much to be added to the things I have already attempted to say. I am working on other material now. This I hope will present itself in a way that will somehow at the outset disarm all effort at an intellectual approach to my thesis. As I mark the difference over the years in actual group procedure and see the tendency of its application today as compared to its application, say, even a year ago, I realize how extrinsic I have been in my approach to an essentially intrinsic process.

How you should derive the results which clearly round us up at an identical position of attention or observation, and do so by the physical mathematical route you adopted is a circumstance which it is beyond me, even vaguely, to conceive! But the fact is you have, and my inability to follow your method arising, as it were, *de novo* from the sheer employment of 'higher-order abstractions' does not leave me in less amazed admiration of your results.

It gratifies me more than I can say to have you express your sympathy toward my book. For me this means that you understand it! Your suggestion of an exchange of books between us is most welcome to me. A copy of my book should have gone to you before this. It will be mailed to you tomorrow or Monday.

You are very good to want to see me sometime and I should like nothing better. I am living this winter at Greenwich and am in New York only one or at most two days in the week for group conferences. If sometime later when my hands are not quite so full, I may look forward to getting in touch with you I should be very glad indeed. In the meantime let me extend to you my very cordial greetings for the holiday season.

Sincerely yours,

Trigant Burrow

P. S. One of these days, when I have cleared away the mass of unfinished material that confronts me now, I mean to take up your thesis and study it in detail. Throughout my youth I had, as I later looked back upon it, nothing short of a phobia toward mathematics. My teachers of course did not suspect this internal situation with me. I did not intend they should. They insisted I possessed a more than usual mathematical gift. I was convinced I did not. The conflict, inarticulate and stubborn, is one of the most painful of memories with me. In addition to the neurotic element with myself, I have long thought since that there was concomitantly a neurotic method employed by my teachers—what you call (and it helps articulate the whole matter for me) the tendency to 'first-order abstractions.' With the aid of your thesis I shall go back over the situation some day and tackle it all anew.

To D. H. Lawrence   New York City
Florence, Italy   December 21, 1927

Dear Mr. Lawrence:

I am ashamed of myself that I have not written you before this to tell you how deeply I appreciated the very kind and sympathetic review of my book that you sent to *The Bookman*. It was such a generous recognition on your part and has, I am sure, stimulated no little recognition among readers generally. It was very good of you and I have appreciated deeply your thoughtfulness in this.

You will be glad to know, and perhaps as surprised as I am, that the book is really being read and finding not a few favorable reviews. I had no idea it would be so. In the last weeks I have been trying to make amends for the obscurities and difficulties in *The Social Basis of Consciousness* by putting together material from some more recent notes.

A small group of us is enjoying immensely the winter in the country about Greenwich, Connecticut. I believe I wrote you of our plan in my reply to your good letter to me of last summer. By the way, I sent my letter to Scandicci and hope it found its way to you. For closer acquaintance sake I tried to enter into the questions suggested in your letter to me.

I hope that you are entirely recovered from the illness that was so great a distress to you at the time you wrote me.

This is today no more than a word to acknowledge your kindness in giving so much helpful impetus to a thoughtful reception of my book. I assure you it has meant very much.

With my very cordial greetings for Christmas and the New Year, believe me

Gratefully and sincerely,

Trigant Burrow

.

To Leo Stein
Paris

New York City
December 29, 1927

Dear Stein:

I have just returned from a few days Christmas recess in Baltimore and found at my office there a copy of your book *The A.B.C. of Aesthetics*. I had already gotten a copy some weeks ago and had it in my bag with me. Thank you very much for this personal copy of your book. It should have had an earlier acknowledgment. There is at present no one to represent me at my Baltimore office and I fear your book may already have been there many weeks.

Your review of *The Social Basis* that appeared in *The New Republic* two weeks ago reads most delightfully. It is finely cut and will do much to bring my thesis to the notice of those who may venture along its way. I am most grateful to you for your sponsorship of an endeavor which I realize, and which I know you realize also, is yet far too limited and incomplete.

I am reading your book slowly and carefully. I like so much its leisure manner. It is an aesthetic experience to read it. Your subject never cramps your style as is the case with me. I am hoping that through *The A B C of Aesthetics* I shall learn to hold my pen more loosely hereafter. I read Waldo Frank's review of it. It is very able, of course, but Frank, it seems to me, falls into the way of so

many critics: he seems so much more interested in what he is saying than in what the author has said. Have you seen his articles
on 'The Re-Discovery of America'? The first two essays have
interested me deeply.

Do you happen to know a Korzybski here—the mathematician
who wrote the essay *Time Binding* and a book called *The Manhood of Humanity?* And do you know who Scudder Klyce is?
They are both mathematicians and philosophers who have unfortunately been led through reading my book to assume that I know
something of mathematics or philosophy. I write protesting my
innocence but apparently it is of no avail. I am quite overwhelmed
as I would not presume to match wits with these intellectual giants.
Were we meeting on grounds of sheer physiological measures of
feeling, I should be more at home. But one cannot talk with
these people. They are going to have me intellectual willy-nilly. . . .

You will be amused to know that group-analysis is coming to be
quite the vogue in New York. The popular adaptation has to do,
I understand, with the analysis of collections of people on the part
of a self-appointed arbiter called the psychoanalyst. It is a form of
group-analysis (!) in which the arbitrary position of the analyst
receives the yet wider arbitrariness of a social extension. It is
interesting to speculate what will be the outcome.

With ourselves there is the definite culmination with the New
Year of plans which have been long dormant but which led definitely last September to the formation of a Foundation incorporated under the laws of Maryland. You have guessed aright. The issue
after all is an economic issue. A leader as a central image of private
authority has to be eliminated and our common problem met by
us in common if we are to break through the bonds of a socially
enveloping neurosis. This involves at the last, as you say, an economic situation. I hope to avoid confusing it with the manifest
economies of politics and industrialism. As I see it our economic
problem is primarily and essentially a physiological problem—
physiological, I mean, in the sense of racially physiological. For
certainly there are physiological interreactions among the indi-

viduals of our common species of which scientists have not taken adequate account. It is a long story and a difficult one. In the last weeks I have been feeling about for a way to say it simply and well. Your book, your own simple and clear mood, helps me in this no little but there are adhesions in my own way of thinking which need to be broken up if I am to state the thing as clearly as I'd like.

A circumstance that has to be faced and accepted is the complete absence in the social medium of a respectful attentiveness to what has been a really authoritative effort to investigate that same social medium. You would be surprised to know from how many quarters I have been practically told 'Your way is not my way and therefore it is the wrong way'—('my way' being, of course, in every instance the established, the academic and the apostolically mitred way).

I hope two recent pamphlets reached you. 'The Problem of the Transference,' I think, will be to your liking and may satisfy better the need you feel for a clearer statement from me. What I am really concerned to uncover is *man's economic secret*. It is, I believe, the whole story. It won't be touched by the Communist any more than by the Monarchist. The economy I mean is not a matter of manifest symptoms but of latent, deeply latent physiological impediments to the unitary functioning of man's organism as a race or species. Freud complains bitterly of my reticence but Freud fails to realize that this is a reticence with which he is in full complicity with me. It is, though, not a matter of his speciousness or mine; it is part of a vast social collusion in images of private advantage for which there is no sane physiological warrant in the inherent organism of man. These are things I want to get clear about now and say as clearly and as unreservedly as I can in certain papers I hope to get in shape in the next weeks.

Did you find any relief from seeing Neumann in Vienna? I understand Mrs. Stein's feeling perfectly and think her insistence on your seeing this leading otologist was most wise notwithstanding that you yourself were 'of little faith.'

I hope you have had a good Christmas. What has become of Lawrence? Did he recover completely from the illness of last summer? He wrote such a nice review of *The Social Basis* for *The Bookman*. Perhaps you saw it.

With every good wish for the New Year, I am

Sincerely,

Trigant Burrow

To his daughter   New York City
Ruxton, Maryland   January 6, 1928

Dear Emily:

Your letter is here. In view of your mother's condition and the worry she would be caused through your going to a boarding house here in New York, such a plan would not be feasible.(13) And I should myself not be willing to enter into any plan in which she would not know the actual circumstance. Under these conditions the only alternative is the Laboratory. . . . If it is really an escape from the rush of things in Baltimore that you are seeking I should think that your best course by far would be the house at Greenwich. This would afford you quiet and early hours and yet allow of your being in New York each day to attend to the matters you wish to inquire into on your own account.

If on the other hand there is some ulterior purpose in your trip— some interest apart from rest or matters of enterprise—you would find your life happier and healthier if you could see all such hidden and ulterior recourse as part of a very general social illness—an illness which it happens, by chance, that your father is bending

(13) Mrs. Burrow was confined to her bed with a broken leg.

much effort to bring to the attention of the community through a few intelligent persons like yourself. If you have been cheated by your parents in your childhood, it is hardly justified that you in turn take advantage of them and of others when you have grown up. This is everywhere the spontaneous reaction of defense. It was my own. It was your mother's. But this condition of cheating in the attitude of parent toward the child is a general social condition, and the parent does not himself know that he is cheating. So that the only scientific or, let us say, thoughtful position to take toward the condition is one that sees the circumstance as a whole and proceeds to deal with it accordingly.

It seems to me you are too intelligent to act unintelligently because everyone else is doing so. And I mention this for whatever use you may be able to make of it in the midst of the very sick social conditions into which you have been thrown as part of a social neurosis existing at present everywhere.

This is really not the disciplining parent. I am speaking to you as one whose own life was cheated and who inevitably reacted by cheating the lives of others about him including your own. It is silly for me to resent the circumstance or to deplore it. It is common. And the only thoughtful attitude is one that regards it as common and takes an adult stand toward it that permits a clear and sane observation of it.

This is all now. I do not want to seem lacking in interest in your plans. I think you know how interested I am in anything of real interest to you. I have my obligations though also, and it's this sense of obligation that leads me to suggest your consideration of an attitude in yourself that is not always frank—not frank with your-self—because of what I know are the consequences of such divisions of feeling and of thought within one's own self.

No more. Please wire if you are coming. I'll do what I can.

Devotedly,

Father

To a former patient   New York City
                                        March 26, 1928

Dear M.:

I was very glad indeed to have what you call your 'purposeless' letter. Anyhow in the midst of so much silly purpose abroad in the world, something purposeless now and then is really very refreshing.

There is, indeed, much mistakenness in the world and undoubtedly your parents made their mistakes too. I cannot see, though, that your parents or the rest of the world can be held answerable for their mistakes as though they were naughty children and merited punishment. This is not a clear, scientific way of handling a serious and widespread problem and there is need for an impersonal, unprejudiced 'objective' approach to it. Nothing has been done in science except as man has taken this objective attitude toward his materials. The great inventions of man did not come about through his idle complaining of conditions as they existed. He brought an objective method to the employment of objective tools and out of that he has created the marvelous engines which modern science applies to man's comfort and convenience. The whole history of medicine and of biology has been the abandonment of old superstitious ways of complaint or prayer and turning instead to the application of direct methods of observation of conditions as they actually exist.

This is likewise man's sole recourse in the sphere of his mental life—his thoughts, his wishes and emotions. It is so easy for everybody to say (and everybody in fact is saying it in one form or another) that this person or that person, this circumstance or the other, did or failed to do such and such for him. But such an attitude will bring us to nought. This is to act like children or primitive men. It is to believe in fairies and in evil spirits. It is to make an image called 'God' and place it in the sky rather than make the true principle of life the internal organic integrity of man himself. Christ, the real religionist, knew better. 'The kingdom of heaven is within you' he said. The pseudo-religionists, so many of them so-called Christians, look everywhere else than within them for the peace that surpasseth understanding. But still consulting their 'understanding' they lose all touch with the clear heart of man and the principle uniting him in a common race life, and pursue superstitious images of good and bad. 'This one has done wrong to *me*,' says everyone, 'and should be punished.' 'That one is nice to *me* and should be rewarded.' It is very plain that it is neither 'this one' nor 'that one' but *ME*, the self-important centre of the universe, that is the sovereign guy.

We can bring our essential feeling to bear upon this absurd trick that man is everywhere playing upon himself and this is, it seems to me, the obligation and the privilege of intelligent people among whom, I think you know, I have never failed to include you.

Write to me when you care to. I am always glad to hear from you.

With my kind regards,

Sincerely yours,

Trigant Burrow

To Waldo Frank   New York City
Yorktown Heights, New York   April 26, 1928

Dear Mr. Frank:

I want to thank you for your letter and tell you how much it meant to me. I appreciate more than I can say the spirit in which you have written me. Your letter was forwarded to me from Baltimore else it would have had an earlier reply.

I haven't a word to say in defense of the inept manner in which my book was written. It is inexcusable. The fact that I set out very determined that I should on no account be 'understood' by the shallow reader does not account for the difficulties of style. Neither does the circumstance that it was written against all manner of personal inertia. (I am by habit and training the meekest of conformists). The job was unwelcome to the greater part of me and the telltale of my resistance is its lack of grace and fluency. I was backward about it and the sentences were written backward. I can only feel the more grateful to you, knowing what you must have gone through, that you should have written so generously of what I tried to have you and others feel in common with me.

It was a little more than ten years ago that I, too, met you. It was through your early novel, *The Unwelcome Man*. I seem to have been confined in laboratories all of my life and I have read very little. I read that story though and liked it and like you for writing it. I remember speaking to Sherwood Anderson about it. It seems so long ago now.

This winter I have been enjoying so much your series of articles in *The New Republic*. Their facile language is not wholly lost on me for all my own shortcomings in this regard. What interests me most, though, in the essays is what I sense of a common ground between us. A feeling that has long been with me and of which your letter leaves now no uncertainty. This is why your feeling for my book means so much to me—so much more than I can express in any words. You yourself know what I mean. You express it again and again—the mood of it—in these papers of yours on 'The Re-Discovery of America.'

I am sending you reprints of certain more recent articles. There is in them, I think, less of the impediment of style than in my book. I wish very much that you could sometime find leisure to run through 'The Autonomy of the "I".' None of the papers are adequate or complete. They merely mark a direction. My only hope is that the direction may become gradually clearer with the deepening of our group inquiries.

The symbols of living are such a bore. This 'manifest content' of consciousness we have come automatically to subscribe to has got somehow to give way to clearer, simpler evaluations. The symbols that stand in the way of intrinsic human relationships are becoming really too patent.

Thank you again for your thoughtful and understanding letter. I hope you know how deeply grateful I am to you for it.

Sincerely yours,

Trigant Burrow

To Lance L. Whyte   New York City
London   March 13, 1928

Dear Mr. Whyte:

But for my having been laid up with grippe the last several weeks your second letter with its very kind message would have received an earlier reply. I had just written you when it came. You are most generous and I deeply appreciate the spirit in which you have written me. As you may imagine, my book has not been received with any too great hospitality generally, so that your feeling and Mrs. Whyte's and the very sympathetic comment contained in the letter you received from Vienna mean the more to me. The lines you quote from this letter of your friend interested me very much and it was good of you to repeat them to me. When I am really on my feet again there is much writing that I want to do and

I hope to make amends for many of the shortcomings of this first book. . . .

I am looking forward eagerly to seeing your review of my book.(14) The publishers seem a bit disconsolate over the reception the book has had but, for myself, I have come off so much better than I had at all expected that I am more content than otherwise.

Thanking you again for your very generous sympathy in the endeavors of our group, believe me,

Sincerely yours,

Trigant Burrow

To Dr. Louis K. Anspacher   New York City
Ossining, New York   May 12, 1928

Dear Dr. Anspacher:

I have just gotten back from attending the anniversary of The Phipps Clinic of The Johns Hopkins Hospital. They were good enough to want a paper from me(15) and I was more than glad to have this opportunity to discuss with a specialized and discriminating audience of that sort the thesis that has so engrossed my thought in recent years.

It hardly seemed possible in turning to my letters that your very kind note had not been answered before. You are very good to want Brownie and me to come out to 'Rynstede.' She has just been with me here at Greenwich and begins to seem somewhat

(14) Published in *The New Adelphi*, March 1929.

(15) 'The Basis of Group Analysis,' *The British Journal of Medical Psychology*, 1928, vol. VIII, pp. 198–206.

like her old self again or her young self rather. She had such a serious accident last winter. Falling on the ice in the road near the house she broke both bones of the leg just above the ankle and in addition sprained the ankle badly. So for three months she was in a cast from her thigh to her toes. Imagine the ordeal of this to anyone of Brownie's temperament and coming as it did just in the midst of a whirl of parties incident to Emily's coming out this winter! Brownie is managing though to get about more and more with the aid of a cane (she discarded crutches three weeks ago) and she is also able now to drive the machine and in general is more cheery than she has been for some months past.

I am so interested to hear of your play being now so advanced in form. I must tell you, though, that with your usual generous evaluations of others you greatly overestimate my fitness to offer any really helpful criticisms of your work. Just so it's true to—what shall I say?—to psychiatric type. In O'Neill's 'Strange Interlude' the nice, normal youth who in the end marries the nice, normal girl would not by any stretch of a psychiatric imagination have done anything so nice and normal. The character was throughout a biological anomaly and it just seemed to me as I sat there that the youth had been somehow smuggled from the asylum and in some mysterious way doped temporarily in order to go through with the clinically impossible last scene. You know what I mean. But perhaps with your wiser sense of stagecraft you would feel with O'Neill that what is good psychiatry is by no means good theatre. Of course I don't know about these things technically but the truer development humanly would, I should think, be the most convincing dramatically—at least to the people really interested in true convictions. Anyhow I look forward to seeing your play and I know that I shall enjoy, as I did 'The New House,' its sensitive human sense and its delicate workmanship.

When I learned of Isadora Duncan's death I of course thought of you and of what must be your irretrievable sense of loss not only of an artist but of a friend. You and Mrs. Anspacher will have felt my sympathy even though I did not write you at the time.

I love the picture of you both busily setting 'Rynstede' to rights with the awakening of the new spring. Perhaps when Brownie comes up again on our way to camp you will let us motor out to you for the afternoon.

Thank you again for your very kind comment on my book. Harcourt, Brace has written me that it has been received so very well, far better I am sure than either they or I had expected. . . .

With my kindest regards to you and to Mrs. Anspacher,

Sincerely yours,

Trigant Burrow

To Dr. Havelock Ellis   New York City
London   June 1, 1928

Dear Dr. Ellis:

I have not allowed your letter of December 19 to remain so long unanswered because of any lack of appreciation of its thoughtfulness. I am really a little ashamed of what must seem to you the very debonair allusion in my book both to your own and Freud's epoch-making contribution to the field of the subjective sciences. This must have been just one of many awkward ways of putting things in writing my book. I am sorry. How much of actual objective reality you have brought to thousands of people including myself —people who had been utterly mystified by the immature and uncorrelated concept entertained toward the problem of sex, I fully and gratefully realize. As I read your letter I am deeply appreciative of the spirit of temperateness it expresses in face of my own immoderate and, I fear, high-handed manner.

I think if I were saying it again it would go somewhat this way. While acknowledging without question the objective importance and reality of your findings and Freud's, I should be inclined to lay emphasis still upon the need of an unlimited educational program in respect to these conditions. I cannot see normal or average expressions of sex as any more healthy than the obviously divergent forms. If the impetus lies in mental pictures of self-satisfaction, the whole expression seems to me biologically unsound. The whole moralistic basis of normality, I mean, seems to me unsound. Viewed from an organic basis, morality seems despicable to me—as despicable as immorality, and for the life of me I cannot see but that the whole instigation to sex is prompted now throughout civilization by one of these two organically anomalous alternatives. What I should like to see would be the recognition that your work and the work of Freud applies to all individuals and that it applies to all individuals because all persons are by reason of a universal social repression inevitably committed to a policy either of pseudo-denial or of active substitution in their sex life. . . .

You are very kind to say that you would be glad if we might meet if I should sometime be in England. To see you would, I assure you, be no small part of my interest in visiting England again.

With my kind regards, believe me,

Sincerely yours,

Trigant Burrow

That Dr. Burrow applied the principles of his studies to the realm of his family life is clearly demonstrated in his letters to his son. He had come to view dependence and irresponsibility as inevitable products of a general disorder, and from this basis he met such attitudes in his associates, his family, and himself. At the same time the research effort was actively assisted by the inherent trend toward behavioral health. This essential integrity was conspicuous in young Mr. Burrow and made it possible for his father to write him with unusual directness. Even as a boy, Jack began to save these letters, and while still a young man repeatedly expressed the hope that they would some day be published. He was in no way concerned with the fact that they reflect his own ineptitudes and the difficulties he encountered in the process of growing up. On the contrary he was eager to share with others a significant approach to family and social problems.

The following letter addressed to Jack in Baltimore refers to the medical advice he had received in connection with a somewhat persistent abdominal pain.

To his son   Greenwich, Connecticut
Baltimore, Maryland   June 9, 1928

Dear Jack:

Your letter—so welcome as always—was brought out to me at Greenwich yesterday. The same mail brought a brief note also from Dr. Brown. I shall enclose a copy of it.

Of course I was greatly relieved at your mother's message the evening of my return from Baltimore. The next day I wrote to Dr. Brown and to Dr. Fisher expressing my appreciation of their great consideration of you. Dr. Fisher's whole reaction toward an operation impressed me as being most conservative as well as most inclusive and I feel we owe much to his broad and sympathetic attitude.

My feeling is that the situation, to use the common parlance, is definitely up to you. Not morally, but thoughtfully, scientifically. To follow an unthinking and impulsive program of living that is not hygienic and to expect that there will not be ill consequences of a serious nature, is to adopt an attitude of unthinkingness and undevelopment. No one can live your life for you in the last detail and the more intelligent an organism is naturally, the more uncompromising is its own demand for its own basis of consistent living. Every one will, with the least encouragement, try to live your life for you as an escape from the adult necessity of living their own, and in the measure in which you do not live your own life—the organic life of the race—you are necessarily giving every encouragement to others to do so. But youth has today its unrivaled opportunity. In this dynamic age it is youth to whom we are looking to rebuild a most dull and disfigured world. The older generation is not to be leaned upon. The vitality it boasts of is not real. There is the need that youth awaken to its own strength and to its own intelligence and not render itself impotent and dependent in response to the impotence and dependence of a superstitious social tradition.

The conflict, which you and Emily assume to exist in the attitude of your mother and me toward one another, is not there. The conflict is one that is wholly internal to himself on the part of each of us. Your tendency—yours and Emily's—to 'side' surreptitiously first with this one and then with that one, is merely your own conflict—ever vacillating between your own vain projections of it.

Now to the immediate concern. Your physicians, accustomed as they are, too, only to structural (medical and surgical) disorders, tend to exclude your symptoms from this category. There is though a *cause* for your disturbance and there is strong presumptive ground for believing that this cause lies in the functional or emotional sphere. It happens that this sphere is precisely the domain of science to which your father has devoted no small effort and with results in practical findings not to be easily discounted.

I shall be in Greenwich for the rest of this month—or until June 30 specifically. If you care to come up for two weeks for an entire change of environment and the opportunity of rest and recuperation generally, the opportunity is yours. The firm with which you are working has been most generous in its attitude and they will not unnaturally expect just now that some steps will be taken with a view to restoring your health, so that a leave of absence would not be difficult to arrange. . . . This is only a suggestion but it comes out of much thought as of much feeling for you and for your need. As I say, what you do rests entirely with you. There is an endeavor—an earnest endeavor in progress and it is for this that my office stands. It has to do with the human organism and its right setup as an efficient personality. There is this though: What this endeavor may have to offer to you is one thing you *cannot depend upon*. What you can depend upon is alone what you have to offer to this endeavor.

I have not spoken of my need to have you with me in the undertaking I have tried to promote in the Community. This is personal and wholly beside the point. Your own identification with a larger social outlook and activity can only come of your own need of larger outlooks and responsibilities—and your own intelligent capacity to relate your own functional inhibitions and contractions with an inhibited and image-dependent social scheme of which you are a part.

Were you a child I should not feel it worth while to try to bring these things to your attention; nor would I do so, were you old and deeply inured already to unthinking ways of adaptation. But as you are a man in your very youth with all of life and possibility before you, I speak to you of these things for what they may seem of worth to you.

My feeling in all I have written has been by no means brief or momentary and I have not found it easy to confine my expression within the limits of a few brief words and I hope, Jack, that you will sense something of the spirit in which I have tried to write you—that you will not think of what I have said as written in the spirit of a self-righteous father to his wayward son but rather in the spirit of a comrade strong in youth to a comrade in whose youth he sees a possibility far stronger still.

With all my love,

Father

To one of his students   Lifwynn Camp, Merrill, N. Y.
                                                 August 9, 1928

Dear Miss O.:

Your letter reached me several days ago. I need hardly say how
glad I was to have word from you.

I find myself pausing here and, by way of reply, perfunctorily
gathering in all sorts of items relating to camp. There are, of
course, such items and they are, of course, of interest to us both—
Mrs. Burrow's and Jack's arrival Saturday, Emily's wholehearted
interest in the life and spirit of camp and my delight in this, the
pleasure of Dr. Syz' arrival yesterday (he went over to the White
Mountains en route), Mr. Leigh's(16) out-of-door enterprises
when here and his and William's construction of a really substantial deck-tennis court, the introduction into camp this summer of
the inspiriting game of Ping-Pong, Emily's studies with Mrs.
Holtzman who wants to take Emily back with her to Paris, and of
course, the weather, over which there has been serious contention;
I insisting that the summer has brought a succession of brilliant
days and the opposition led by Miss Flora and William as stoutly
maintaining that we have had little but rain. All this and much
more is of mutual interest but it really is evading your letter and
the difficulty of answering it.

But here's turning to it and meeting it as best I can. 'Pride, humiliation,' shame, contrition! What am I to say? Is there after all *anything*
to say? How can we live by social images and make the basis of

(16) John R. Leigh, an early student of Dr. Burrow's.

our work their disavowal? But in saying this (having already said there is nothing to say) of course I am saying nothing. Here in camp this summer there has been little of this thing of saying—of saying nothing. There has been more a tendency to lean back upon feeling, even though there is as yet very little there.

With regard to taking a position on your own. It seems to me things have been with you, as it is, altogether too much on your own and that, as with everybody else, it has been a merely pseudo-ownership. Besides, who would believe that a position rejected the applicant when the applicant in his secret heart had no intention of taking the position? And who can say that your setting up a corner stand all to yourself isn't prompted more by the thought of your encornered self than of the corner? This is very disagreeable I know but so are you disagreeable—you and your corner with its tray upon tray of tinseled intellectual wares to which feeling must ever take second place. As if feeling could ever take second place. As if even the practical philosophy of the Amoeba does not refute your inverse position. Yours and your cohorts of normality.

I cannot see but that your best course—provided you can leave your corner stand long enough—would be to spend a couple of weeks here in camp in September. Nobody's really going to take your certified intellect from you. On the contrary it is rather to enhance its efficacy. That means, however shy we may be of withholding first place from the normal image, of giving primacy to our untutored and original feeling. What does it matter if you are the best woman in the world when people are looking if you are, like myself, the world's worst when they take their eye off you? There is no circumventing this bidimension. You might think of shutting down your news-stand for awhile and giving yourself a few weeks of psycho-physiological stock-taking wherein 'psycho' means interindividual. . . .

Sincerely yours,

Trigant Burrow

To his daughter(17)

Lifwynn Camp, Merrill, N. Y.
Friday night 10.30
September 14, 1928

Emily dear:

It is good to come back to my cabin and to you. I think of you every minute as the time draws near for your ship to sail. Just an hour and a half!

If *you* understand, if you are with me in my feeling, it means so much more to me to say goodbye to you here, quietly in my cabin —just you and I—than to be in the excited crowd on the dock amid strangers in a strange place. Here I can take you again in my arms as I do now and tell you once more how I love you and how happy I am in the happiness this winter's experience will mean to you. Good-bye, dear, and know that I am with you now and always. Your sweet, brave little message was such a comfort. 'Everything under control. Letter on way. Good-bye, Father. Love and love. Emily.' Nothing could have said more and I shall keep it before me—this word and your dear photograph. Hope my reply to the boat reached you, and my letters. It said, as I remember, 'Telegram received. So glad to have this word. All my love and good wishes for a pleasant crossing. Father.'

And now a last good-bye until a little note of greeting meets you in Paris. Good-night, **dear.**

Father

(17) She was en route to Paris to study singing.

Saturday, September 15

Morning! And your ship is well out to sea. The night was clear and the morning dawned brilliantly over the Lake. I hope you had such weather too. I shall be so eager to have word of the crossing. Next week-end and you will be in Paris! How swiftly the events of the last weeks have passed.

I'll keep you in touch with little incidents of interest to me because they represent the fruit of very much labor, and perhaps a little love.

This winter I have in mind to read some French so that my daughter will not have outgrown me too completely! So now *au revoir*, or as I like better to say: *à bientot*.

Monday morning, September 17

Your letter was awaiting me on returning from Dannemora Saturday afternoon. It was so good to have it. I have read it and re-read it. It means so very much to have it, dear.

I shall tell you of any 'new ideas,' and gladly. This morning I was thinking how it is not now so much a matter of new ideas as a central basis of sensation from which all ideas should proceed. Perhaps though—I feel very sure that as this altered source comes more and more to animate my ideas, the ideas will convey also the *feeling* from which they arose.

You must keep in your thoughts somewhere the sense of my feeling of our common part in life and of the bond that is made between us in the winter's work you are entering upon—*our* work.

Your devoted

Father

To his daughter   Lifwynn Camp, Merrill, N. Y.

September 18, 1928

Dear Emily:

With regard to the trip to Dannemora, it was very disappointing. Wards with rows of beds, kitchens with rows of kettles, halls with rows of cells were all that we saw. There was no personal contact with any of the prisoners. Those we saw passing from the prison recreation grounds to the refectory (dining-hall) were in general unprepossessing in physical make-up—faces bearing degenerate marks and bodies showing poor posture. What impressed us though was the identity of the conditions inside the walls and out. It is walls outside as well as in, walls about the 'good' who aren't in *those* prisons, as well as walls about the 'bad' who are confined in them. So that I thought some day I'll write a play and I'll call it 'Walls,' and it will show how all is *walls* and that the real *wall* is the division between the organism and its more spontaneous function.

I want to write you too of an idea I have for a play that appeals to me strongly—not the plot but the method. It is this: I don't know whether you saw 'Strange Interlude.' I believe not. You know though that the outstanding technical recourse or method in this play is the prominent 'aside.' The play I have in mind is to be only 'asides'—that is, what the character is internally feeling and thinking, and the development of the play will be the development of this feeling and thinking basis. Meantime of course there is the external action or plot—of no significance, casual and commonplace like the average, too average plot in life, but serving merely as a *vehicle* for the internal plot to weave itself upon. For instance, let us take, say, a scene in a physician's office between physician and his secretary, or some scientist or writer at work jointly with a woman writer on a book. They sit with their duplicate manuscripts before them. They turn the pages. They make notes. They look in the dictionary from time to time or go to the shelves for various reference books, &c., &c. But all this is nothing. It is the mere warp. But it is the woof that is of interest. They 'love' each other and their thoughts interchange—their secret thoughts are expressed interchangeably so that a connected and logical conversation goes on *in this internal way* between them.

You see it is all 'aside.' But this 'aside' is, as in *life*, what is really vital in the lives of the persons presented. All the while there 'must' of course continue the quite convincing external plot or vehicle. I like the idea immensely. It is the thought of (I'm lisping!)—I meant to say the *sort* of thing I could enter into feelingly and write with interest and delight. It is also the 'thought' of things you would be interested to help me with. Think the 'thought' over. But let it be as yet *entre nous*, please.

I'd follow out the plan you had to have paints and such drawing equipment in your room. It will be an entertainment in odd hours. I'd get down my thoughts or write an article too from time to time. It is all in your feeling and interest.

Will write soon again.

Your devoted

Father

To Mrs. Burrow   New York City
Ruxton, Maryland   Monday, February 25, 1929

Dear Brownie:

I am sorry my letter to you seemed so unfeeling. I had meant it in
a very different spirit. It does look as though words are necessarily
misleading or that they fail to bring people into communication.
I don't think it is the fault of people but of words and perhaps a
better medium of understanding should come to replace these too
common and too inadequate symbols of one's meaning.

It has been interesting this winter how much fewer words there
have been among those of us here. I have almost talked to no one,
remaining in my room with my work and going down only for
meals and the casual conversation relative to immediate needs and
such practical concerns. The result has been a so much more satisfactory, productive winter, as well as a far greater absence of
misunderstanding or conflict.

In this way I cannot but think that ultimately the barriers to harmonious, united feeling everywhere will drop away and leave us,
confused and benighted human beings, at peace with ourselves
and therefore with others also. To achieve this—to form the
nuclear beginning of a unified basis of feeling among our fellow
beings is the meaning, the only meaning of all the pain and confusion and blind struggle that has gone into the sum of patient
inquiry that this work has endeavored to embody. The conflict I
have inevitably aroused toward me is only a reflection of the conflict that has raged all these years within myself—a conflict due
to an individual's determination to feel clear and understandingly
in face of his own personal unwillingness (backed up by thousands
of years of his race's tradition) to do so. What process of evolution
shall have merged the quite extreme types of 'disposition' of Mr.

Shields and myself into this common task of mutual unwelcomeness is not a riddle to be solved through the measures we commonly compute by. At least it has been a service and a service is a privilege not to be lightly reckoned when its fulfillment—however far distant that may still be—promises to human life all that this agonizing undertaking on your part and on that of all concerned seems to hold out in the ultimate test. Personally I do not see the final resolution far removed. Intelligence is getting too close a grip at last upon data so long hidden from man in respect to his own feelings and reactions. And so I am encouraged to work on.

Emily seems to be managing for herself very well as far as I can judge. Shall probably send my next letter (tonight or tomorrow) to the Rome address, trusting they will forward it from the 'pensione.'

With love to you and Jack,

Devotedly,

Trigant

To his son
Baltimore, Maryland

New York City
March 12, 1929

Dear Jack:

Before going out for breakfast I want at least to begin a letter to you. You are much in my thoughts, as I think you know. This calamity that has come in the midst of our work is part of the inevitable process of that work(18)—our work, yours and mine, your mother's, Emily's and those about us here in New York and those here and elsewhere in no way connected with us. Because

(18) The sudden death of a valued associate.

this work is the community's work, the nation's. It is the work of mankind. There is no narrowing it down to this or that individual or to this or that group. It has been thus confined in the fancy of the individual and of the group. But this has been artificial. The neurosis is society's illness and the task of sanity and health is the responsibility of society—not the society we talk of and place opposite us, but the society that is within us and of which each of us is subjectively an integral part. Never mind my language. Do not try to 'understand.' You do not need to. There is only the need that we be one in our feeling. That is the only understanding. And this is the really significant implication in the events of the past two weeks. It brings our seemingly separate positions—yours and Mother's and mine to a common point. It unites us in a common loss and in a common pain and in the common responsibility to meet them. It forces us to see that we are one and to take our positions as one in representing the principle upon which our work depends. Compared with this realization, everything else loses significance. With this realization I am sustained and inspirited as never before. I can set to work, under this inspiration, with a new zest, a fresher energy, and a perception that is clearer than at any time.

No more now, dear Jack. With love to you and Mother,

Your devoted

Father

To Lance L. Whyte   New York City
Berlin   March 28, 1929

Dear Mr. Whyte:

I meant to write to you this long ago. Your card reached me at camp last summer and I was very glad to have the reference to the passage from Nietzsche's *Joyful Wisdom*. I do not read German fluently enough to read it extensively but I was very interested in this passage you cite from Nietzsche's *Fröhliche Wissenschaft*. I do know something of Nietzsche's writings from translations into English and when I was younger I shared with others of my student contemporaries the general craze for Nietzschean emancipations.

What I should like so to do would be to transpose the social intuition of Nietzsche and other men of his trend into terms of a social physiology. I am sure this statement cannot mean much as a mere statement but I want to work out some more tangible basis for defining the reaction which we now summarize broadly under the term social reaction. In this country everybody talks of 'social reactions' but without any definite biological basis.

I certainly do appreciate your interest in the interpretations toward which I am more and more inclining. I should especially value your feeling in regard to a paper that is scheduled for the new *Journal of Social Psychology* to be brought out by Professor Dewey and Carl Murchison. The paper is called 'The Physiological Basis of Neurosis and Dream'—a rather ambitious title, I fear, for the very sketchy treatment it receives but it is some indication of the direction that seems to me more and more important from the point of view of biology and the medical sciences. (19) A recent reprint, 'The Basis of Group Analysis,' went to you in care of *The New York Times* in Berlin. Perhaps this will help make my position somewhat clearer to you, as you are so good as to be interested.

I want to tell you how much I enjoyed the article by you that appeared in *The New York Times*. I confess to being unable to understand even the more popular expositions on this subject but I enjoyed this brief account of Einstein's new theory at least as an article coming from your pen. . . .

(19) 'The Physiological Basis of Neurosis and Dream—A Societal Interpretation of the Sensori-Motor Reactions Reflected in Insanity and Crime,' *Journal of Social Psychology*, 1930, vol. I, pp. 48–65.

I wonder if you plan attending the International Congress of Psychology at Yale next September. You spoke in a letter last winter of having in mind the possibility of a visit to America and I wondered if it would be at that time. Perhaps you will be offering a paper for the meeting. I sent in a title but naturally the first preference is given to foreign members so that I shall very possibly not be on the program after all. (20)

I don't know whether you are yet back in London but I hope this will find its way to you.

With my very kind regards,

Sincerely yours,

Trigant Burrow

To Professor Jared S. Moore   New York City
Western Reserve University   March 28, 1929

Dear Professor Moore:

Ever since reading in the *Philosophical Review* your very thoughtful review of my book, *The Social Basis of Consciousness*, I have had in mind writing you. I certainly value very much the thought and the earnestness which you gave to the consideration of my thesis. As to its literary style, you are quite right. . . .

(20) Dr. Burrow read two papers before the Congress, 'Emergent versus Deterrent Differentiations in the Evolution of Human Society,' unpublished, and 'The Social Reaction of Right and Wrong—A Biological Approach to Social Behavior,' published under the title, 'Crime and the Social Reaction of Right and Wrong— A Study in Clinical Sociology,' *Journal of Criminal Law and Criminology*, 1933, vol. xxiv, pp. 685–99.

Where I seem to have made myself most deplorably unclear is in the passages that express my attitude toward religion. I am judging from the sentence in your review, 'Religion fares badly with Dr. Burrow . . . ' I had thought that if my book stood out strongly for anything, it was for a conception of religion that is one with the biological solidarity of life. I am sorry if I did not make plain that my quarrel is by no means with religion as the ultimate reality of man's feeling-life but with those pretenses of devotion to truth which now so widely travesty devotion and truth under the guise of empty social images and symbols.

I do not write you this in the thought that my feeling has suffered misinterpretation at your hands. Not at all. My feeling was evidently not put clearly, and naturally has led to a misconception of what my feeling fundamentally is as regards the meaning we call religion.

Thank you heartily for your very able review and for the careful thought you were good enough to give to it.

Sincerely yours,

Trigant Burrow

To his son
Baltimore, Maryland

New York City
April 5, 1929

Dear Jack:

Your letter came this morning. It was so good to have it. I appreciate the spirit of it. You know that.

This afternoon I gave to the joint groups the first of a series of lectures I am giving—the series to be later incorporated into a book I am planning to write.

I do understand the sentiment expressed in your letter and I value it more than I can say. For things to go wrong with me is for things to go wrong with you. I know. It is as one organism. It has always been so with us. I understand.

Can you not feel with me though the dignity of difficulties that are incident to a difficult and dignified endeavor. Other experimenters —research workers— students of new and untried processes—seekers after deeper values and realities have undergone many ordeals. Why should not we? The very difficulty, the very ordeal becomes enspiriting when it is seen in this light. Let us not complain and indulge in depression but rather convert into deeper power and resourcefulness and thought what would be complaint and depression were our task and our obligations not accepted with dignity and a deeper self-respect. But I know you understand. You have always understood and no one more so. There is just the need to make your understanding your very own—a thing within your self, silent and assured and self-contained. I am, if anywhere, within yourself, as you are within me. No outer avenues can ever unite us. Within is the great, clear understanding way.

Good-night. That was a nice letter from Emily, was it not? Tell Mother I received her letter this morning and will answer it very soon. Wrote her yesterday enclosing a copy of a letter of mine to Emily.

Write again.

With love,

Your devoted

Father

To a student   New York City
                                                   July 5, 1929

Dear Miss N.:

Things are crowding so thickly about me at the moment prepara-
tory to leaving that I shall not attempt really to write you. I wanted
merely to complete what I was trying to say to you in the brief
moment on the street yesterday—as my mind keeps returning to
our unfinished theme.

I did not mean 'that you should not be tragic.' What I had in mind
was to somehow keep clear in the midst of all our hectic social
dramaturgy that there is not one individual more tragic than another; that the tragedy is social and that the heart of our social
tragedy lies only in the circumstance that each of us tragic per-
formers believes inevitably (as he looks inevitably only at the
mirror in which he sees only 'himself' reflected) that he—the
organism—is the only tragic and image-isolated figure. When I
said I depended completely upon Mr. Shields I did not mean that
I depended upon his image or he on mine. I did not mean that
I depended on his concern for me or his 'help.' I meant that I depended upon my efforts of internal coöperation with him and you
and others for the unravelling of this human tangle in which our
image-ridden normality has placed us.

Because you are louder in your outcries, more expressive in your
mood intolerance you are not on this account more intolerant or
more outcrying in your need than the rest of us. The tears that I
restrain are as truly tears as the tears that you rain! The trained
tears merely run down on the inside and are not visible to specta-
tors. Human beings just can't longer stand the burden of their
socially imposed isolation however cherished their isolation may

now have come to be. My own feeling is that you handled yesterday's situation with a moderation that shows very clearly that our work—yours, Mr. Shields' and mine along with others—has its place and its definite aim.

Very sincerely yours,

Trigant Burrow

To Mrs. Burrow   New York City
Ruxton, Maryland   July 8, 1929, 11 a.m. Monday morning

Dear Brownie:

You have no doubt been through a painful and trying experience in the last days. Guy looked to you as to no one else in these years of his illness and I know his death has been a deep grief to you. (21)

There has been so much in recent years to cause you worry, and pain, and tension in body and mind, that I would like to talk to you for a moment very seriously about yourself. Does it not seem to you imperative that you have a rest and change of some sort this summer? The physician who treated the last abscess said you lacked resistance. This, it seems to me, is a warning to take very special care of yourself and to build up. The camp affords a good deal, when you haven't the responsibility of things, but if that would entail a certain inevitable worry—just the contact with it— and you would be freer and happier somewhere else, I would like you to go wherever you'd find most rest and refreshment and congeniality. Would it not be well to go first for a visit to the Beach with Lucia. You do not like to leave Jack—I know, but, on the other hand, Jack needs to be somewhat more on his own too

(21) Mr. Guy Bryan, Mrs. Burrow's brother.

and you would both really find more enjoyment in each other, if now and then there were the opportunity to be more to yourselves.

I notice, as people get older and the disappointments grow and there is less physical buoyancy to meet things, that there enters very softly and unnoticed a certain secret comfort in the thought of death. It has seemed to me that with you there has been of late a steadily growing intimacy with such thoughts. Unless one becomes aware of this—this tendency to beckon death prematurely out of one's need of rest—death is hastened with us when there might have been many rich, full years yet. We need to think of this.

You seem to me to have such stores of natural vitality. Your physician has said your resistance is lowered. If you will get a thorough rest this summer, I have no doubt you will come right up to standard and feel like a different person. There is the brighter side looming, as far as this work we've undertaken is concerned. I think we can both feel that.

I am looking forward to the days with Emily. Your letter of Sunday has just come. . . .

With love to you and Jack,

Devotedly,

Trigant

New York City
June 2, 1930

Dear Brownie:

Your welcome letter delivered at eight this morning. No, no, we're not tired, not getting old—never will. We have undertaken, along with others, a difficult piece of research in regard to the basic feelings of ourselves, as of communities of man everywhere. These very feelings which are the material of our vivisection naturally show irritability, fatigue, resistance, depression, unresponsiveness and now even exhaustion. But it is the *wish* in the feelings themselves—the symbol (isolated and privileged), of self-advantage. Does it not mean a great deal to you to know that now I am at least sufficiently unentangled from habitual associations and fixations to be able—to be eager to get out, to take exercise, play tennis, drive and walk? Let's see only the positive side—the physiological side. That is so essentially *your* side—has always been. So a truce to despondency!

Love to you and Jack,

Devotedly,
Trigant

Lifwynn Camp, Merrill, N. Y.
July 11, 1930, Friday evening

Dear Brownie:

. . . It is good to know of the evening at Lifwynn in the moonlight with Emily and of the quiet talk. I know that Emily is 'rare,' so is Jack. But it is not enough. My mother was rare, so was yours. You and I are rare for that matter. It is not enough. Emily and Jack sense with us something far more than this. This rareness—this character-distinction in their generation—is coming to the break-ing-point. They must have a wider, fuller, truer self-realization than this distinctiveness and character and rareness, with all the secretly irreconcilable repression it entails, can possibly afford in-telligent, sensitive, developing natures like theirs. Jack and Emily are far too intelligent and endowed to endure with composure—with sanity—the stupidities—the organic stupidities that are their only expression according to the social interpretations to which they are constantly referred for all their experience today. The situation is impossible for them. I am not speaking with alarm, but only with earnestness. Something is developing in man's feel-ing. It is to be sensed among ourselves. It calls for thought, for application. A new way of thought, a fresh method of application. Jack and Emily occupy a very special, a very critical position in their generation and they have not realized their own mean-ing in relation to it. They have a place that is theirs. They cannot take any other. They do take, are forced to take every other. Of course they suffer. Who does not?—if he has any urge to growth. I realize that suffering is a disgraceful thing biologically—that it means *dis*ease or obstruction somewhere. Man has to find out *where*—to give over his habitual use of temporary narcotics and search into causes.

It is morning and with it a deeper sense of 'What's the use?' Talking to you as I did last night won't avail. The course to under-standing and harmoniousness and life lies in quite another direction.

. . . I'm grateful that some better sense of Mr. Shields begins to reach me some little. We have not known him. We have wished him to be rare, as we would be. What he is though is beyond all rareness, all separateness and distinction of the individual, and we have not understood him. It has not been our fault. There isn't that anywhere. Nowhere is there *fault*. We just haven't under-stood this element of our own organism embodied—ensouled and embodied in Mr. Shields, nor has he understood the social element and its equal promise as represented in our rare and normal selves. But what's the use? These things lie whole and effective only in the channels of feeling. Talking only hints of them. I shall be glad when you are here.

Love all around,

Devotedly,

Trigant

D. H. Lawrence died at Vence in the Alpes-Maritimes in early March 1930. A few months later Burrow wrote:

Lifwynn Camp, Merrill, N. Y.
July 11, 1930

Dear Brownie:

. . . Having hounded Lawrence to death, his persecutors—that is, everybody—are all for making up to him now, so sure are we that his wracked and torn little organism with its feminine soul is too utterly spent and motionless now to make a single further sound in its defense. It is the sentence we shall long continue to pass upon the human anomaly we know as genius—it must burn to death within its own fires. Genius shall not yet be felt and shared as the creative expression of man indivisible and continuous throughout his species. Of course Lawrence had his part in the very persecutions that destroyed him. He was an equal element in the forces that isolated him, for all his outcries and protestations. . . .

Devotedly,

Trigant

To his son
Baltimore, Maryland

New York City
November 4, 1930

Dear Jack:

Your nice letter is still unanswered—the one you wrote at the office in which you spoke of the pleasant quarters you have there. I am writing, now, though, to speak of a matter Mother mentioned. She spoke of your being constantly worried about debts—that they 'worried you to death.' I wish you had felt free to speak to me of your situation. You did mention at camp last summer that you had considerable debts—outstanding bills, I think you meant, but I thought you planned and saw your way clear to paying them all off very soon through a more judicious care of your resources and through greater economy.

I wish we could see certain things with a common mind, from a common viewpoint. Debts are unbecoming; they are ungracious; they are a discourtesy to those in whose debt we stand. Debts mean that some one else's money is in our pocket. That is really not fitting from the background you and I have always held. You see what I mean. It isn't, in the truest sense, aristocratic. It's inelegant, not good form, indelicate. In saying which, I'm saying nothing new to you, nothing with which you are not—have not always been in full agreement with me.

Perhaps you will let me know the full situation in detail. Don't hesitate to be completely frank in writing me. Let us go over the items very fully together and see what we can do. Do this at once, dear. Be quite clear and thorough in your figures. Write plainly. And may I ask that you include also any expenditures which seem to you—and which you feel will seem to me—sheer extravagance. Don't let shyness or reserve spoil the true picture. I'd like to be of help, if I can; you, on the other hand, must let me know the actual situation, if I am to be with you in it.

Mother's visit seemed so short. She was so helpful toward problems of one sort and another while here.

I must be writing to Emily. Guess even a brief word is very welcome to her now and then.

Will be glad when you can find time to come up and see me. I'll be going to Baltimore too when things here aren't as exacting in one way and another.

Have had several good rides this fall and have certainly enjoyed them. It has been a great help. Wish you'd go riding regularly or often.

No more though now. Will count on hearing from you very soon.

With love to Mother and to you,

Always devotedly,

Father

To Professor Thomas D. Eliot(22)   New York City
Northwestern University   November 6, 1930

My dear Dr. Eliot:

. . . Thank you very much for your letter and for your idea of inviting me to give a report of what actually occurs in a group session. I certainly value your interest and your sympathetic appreciation of what we are trying to do. Your feeling that your interest in having such a report is shared by others gives added importance to your request. I hope I may be able to reply to your letter in a way that will make quite clear to you the situation that compels me to decline your very kind invitation and that will at the same time leave no doubt of my sincere regard for the desire

(22) Professor of sociology.

you have expressed nor of my deep sense of indebtedness toward your efforts of coöperation with us.

Let me write you quite fully because, in view of the social ramifications directly involved, there is due you and your colleagues the clearest statement of which I am capable.

It will have been your observation, I am sure, that wherever investigators have arrived at special results in their particular field, it is the natural desire with them to report their findings to those of their colleagues who are working in the same or in related fields of inquiry. I think there can be no doubt that the technique and procedure of group-analysis have resulted in findings which possess scientific interest and social value. If, then, I do not seem disposed to impart to others the specific data derived through the actual procedure of a particular group session, as would naturally be one's scientific interest to do, the indication would seem to be that either there is some defect in my scientific attitude or else that there is lacking with me a conviction or sense of confidence as to my findings.

I think you know that I have devoted no little time and labor to the writing of papers and to discussions on the subject of group-analysis, trying to make clear the principles and methods of our procedure. Surely this would show that I am neither lacking in scientific conviction nor disposed by temperament to be uncommunicative. If, then, we may dismiss the question of personal inhibitions on my part, there is left no other explanation for the absence of the report you desire, and which it would ordinarily be one's scientific interest to present, than the nature of the group procedure itself. This, if my experience allows me to speak with authority, is in fact the true situation. The data obtained in group-analysis—the data being the feeling-reactions of the organism as expressed physiologically in the immediate moment—do not of their nature lend themselves to reportorial account. The immediate physiological moment, when reported in intellectual or verbal symbols, ceases of course to be the immediate physiological moment. Besides there are, in fact, no verbal data in group-analysis. There are no views, no opinions, no ideas that are of the slightest value or meaning in the analysis, nothing that could be given verbatim report. I can tell you *about* the reaction or event *after* its occurrence but I cannot possibly impart to you the event itself, and it is the event itself that you and I and our colleagues are interested in getting the actual sense of in the actual situation.

You see, the reactions that occur in group-analysis are quite aside of—quite apart from the mental or intellectual sphere of our habitual social reactions. That is why no mental, verbal (symbolic) or social report of them is possible. In the social or group setting, verbal material expresses the purely manifest content of the social group and it is only with the latent reactions—the emotional or feeling substrate—that group-analysis is concerned. While a dictograph would record the words of the group meeting, it happens that the words, or the mental content expressed in a group meeting, are the discarded by-products of the procedure, while the underlying feeling-content as physiologically experienced is the only usable material. A dictographic record, therefore, would give to the meeting you propose the *words* or the merely *manifest material* such as in our meetings the demonstrator ignores; a dictograph would not reproduce the subjective physiological tensions and alterations which are the exclusive material of our group investigations.

So that my observation and experience, after a good many years now of daily familiarity with the material and process of group-analysis, is that its data are not to be mechanically reproduced subsequent to the moment of their initial motivation. And this circumstance, may I say, I have repeatedly mentioned in my papers. After all, many years of daily working-contact with data occurring within a particular field of investigation do necessarily afford the investigator a fairly thorough acquaintance with that field. One comes to know its possibilities and its limitations rather clearly. But leaving aside my own statement, I assure you there is not a student who has had actual participation in group-analysis for even so short a period as four weeks who, because, let us say, of a period of enforced absence, would think of asking whether he might not have a report of the meetings that had taken place while he was away in order that he could get a sense of what had taken place during the analytic sessions he had missed. Four weeks or less of actual contact with group-analysis makes clear to him that the understanding of group-analysis is necessarily the result of first-hand procedure and not an experience that is transmissible through subsequent description or report.

As I see the situation it really reduces itself to the simple question as to whether my experience through daily experimentation in a special field over a period of nearly fifteen years permits me to speak with authority in regard to the nature of the data derived and of the conditions requisite to their observation. This question is, of course, one that must be left entirely to the disposition of my scientific confrères.

Perhaps my inability to meet your request sounds unappreciative of your position—of your outstanding interest in group-analysis over many years. I should be sorry if this should seem so. I am really not unmindful of your many expressions of appreciation of what my associates and I are attempting to do in dealing directly with individual and community reactions. Many others of my colleagues have asked for the same type of report as that which you have expressed the wish to have, but we really do know our ground when we state, as I have so often, that a mental or 'after-image' report of our procedure is excluded in the nature of the procedure itself, namely, the observation of actual physiological reactions as they occur in the immediate moment.

After all—and this may be of as much interest to you as it is to me—group-analysis is a sociological phenomenon that is the outcome of definite sociological tensions and exactions in the community everywhere. It is not a process of individual choice but of community evolution. Not a member of The Lifwynn Foundation or its students (I am speaking equally of myself of course) chose the method of group-analysis for their information or instruction. It was with each of us the force of sociological circumstance that required a process that would lead to altered adjustments individually and socially among us. The social and industrial pressure of the times is undoubtedly becoming more acute, the manifest content of social reactions proportionately unstable, and I have no doubt that with the progressively poignant sensitization of individuals and of communities toward the insecurity of conditions socially, politically, and industrially, there will be gradually forced upon wider communities the same internal demands that have been forced upon the small group represented by ourselves. For this outcome it seems to me that you and I and the rest of us can only wait. . . .

You will be interested to know also that there is no material presented in group-analysis which might, for the sake of discretion, require deletion. Apparently a lag of attention, as complicated as this impediment has now become socially, is our only misdemeanor, but how slight and how elusive is this delayed time-interval may only be estimated by the student's difficulty in detecting it.

In closing, let me say that I hope you will not think for a moment that my associates and I are inhospitable to the wish of any individuals or groups to participate in the work we are doing. Wherever scientific groups have indicated their wish to undertake their own group-analysis under the control of an experienced demonstrator, there has been no lack of interest on our part to assist their free and independent undertaking.

In the meantime I shall go on as best I can trying to express in clearer, more acceptable terms the basis of the group work and thus perhaps slowly foster in the community generally an attitude of tentative inquiry toward habitual community processes. As I said, for this we can only wait.

Sincerely yours,

Trigant Burrow

To his daughter   New York City
Milan, Italy   January 1931

Dear Emily:

Do you mind if I think aloud with you a little while. There is just
the one absorbing theme with me, and you and I have talked of it—
felt our way into it as best we could with the limited experience
we'd gathered at the time. That experience grows as experience
does grow through increased contact with the materials before
one—in this instance, *within* one.

I've found assistance this way in the last days. Come close now and
listen. Give your mind—the mind of your organism—a chance.
Over there, let us say, I see an angry man. What I 'see' of course
are certain external appearances—sharp, intense, narrowed eyes,
congested face, heightened breathing, clenched fists, etc., etc.
These gestures are what I *see*. From this I *infer* the anger—from
this I know the man is angry—that he has the feeling of anger
within him. Very well then I do not see—do not observe the actual
state of anger. Now as a scientist, dealing with man's feeling interchange as a social organism, it is necessary to observe actual material. That is how the biological scientist proceeds in the sphere
of his external objective data—that is the method of the chemist
and the astronomer, and so it must be the method of the group- or
phylo-analyst. He must observe also direct material.

All observation hitherto has been dependent upon the external
senses—anger, the feeling, isn't observable through the external
senses—through the ordinary channels of perception. We've just
seen that I only 'infer' the feeling of which I see the external signs.
How do I infer it? Through the relation between such external
signs and the sensation of anger as I have experienced it within myself, or subjectively. Very well, then it is within myself that I would

best observe the sensation of anger. But observation as I have known it has been a projective act hitherto. My external sense—my eye—has observed only what is before it. Like the camera that doesn't take a picture of the photographer behind it, my eye does not see or photograph feelings or conditions lying back of it. Very well then, to see or observe my anger (it might as well be love, or suspicion or greed of course) my position of observation must move back to some point or zone where it will have the anger-feeling in front of it. And so, resting back, as it were, upon the organism's primary sensation as a whole—upon the zone of primary body-feeling, one senses—at first very vaguely and fleetingly, certain sensations *in front of it*, that is, in the region of the head or cerebral zone—particularly in the region within and around the eyes. And he comes upon this extraordinary observation—that all the emotions which he believed to be biological and organic do not occupy his organism as a whole, but are centred around the eyes (chiefly) and are perceptible as certain definite tensions and constraints within that zone! No matter what the emotion—whether pleasurable or distressing—it is now objectively perceived as a sensation of stress about or within the eyes. Now coincidentally with this shifting of the perceptual feeling-zone into the primary body-zone, there is a quiet, inclusive, self-possessed feeling or reaction. One gets a sense of having really never 'seen' (as he thought) anger or love or desire, he gets a sense of the utter artificiality of his relationship to others (and to himself) on the basis of this sort of 'seeing' or 'feeling.' He has been living—experiencing feeling—in front of his eyes, outside of himself, of his organism, where no living or feeling exists. It is really so simple but not without procuring another camera and setting it back where one may get a picture of the photographer—Mr. Man—who has hitherto been taking pictures of everyone else! You and I and the rest of us being Mr. Man.

Well, there is a technique here—a physiological technique. Not a religion, a philosophy, a new 'idea'—but a technique too long unrecognized and unemployed by the organism of man in its estimate of the overemployed brain with its estimate of everything else—that is, everybody else.

As the speaker says in concluding a tiresome paper at the end of a scientific meeting, 'I thank you' (Bow and Exit).

Hope you received Christmas cheque and the record of her master's voice.

Your devoted

Father

To Dr. Goodwin B. Watson　　　　　　New York City
Columbia University　　　　　　　　　March 21, 1931

Dear Dr. Watson:

I haven't yet acknowledged your letter of January 5th in which you expressed the wish to include in your source book reference to my trend. As it happens, the aspects of my work that are of particular interest to me are best focused in certain quite recent papers—some of them already published and others which will appear fairly soon. If these more recently published articles cannot be included in your material, I should like you to have them anyhow and am mailing them to you today along with those of my earlier studies which seem the most pertinent to be included in your summary.

Whatever characteristic feature my work may possess, it had its inception in the principle to which I first referred as 'the principle of primary identification' in the paper called 'The Genesis and Meaning of "Homosexuality." '(23) This was extended to its

(23) Read before the American Psychoanalytic Association in 1914 and published in *The Psychoanalytic Review*, 1917, vol. 4, pp. 272–84.

social interpretation in a paper on 'Social Images.' Then came the group principle and 'The Autonomy of the "I"' with its laboratory implications, and finally Phyloanalysis leading to a closer approach to the phyletic morphology underlying man's feeling life.

I am enclosing a list of the papers and have grouped them roughly in relation to this developmental order. May I ask you to let me have this material again when you have finished with it.

Very sincerely yours,

Trigant Burrow

To Dr. Adolf Meyer   New York City
Baltimore, Maryland   November 16, 1931

Dear Dr. Meyer:

I want to have the earliest possible reply go to you in response to your letter to me of November 12th, notwithstanding that some later moment might offer a more favorable opportunity for writing you as adequately as I should wish. . . .

. . . This is my story in a nutshell: Attempting to remedy sick ideas and emotions with ideas and emotions that are not sick seems to me a quite unfeasible program. Years of long and painstaking concentration upon just one point—upon one single feature of our human behavior—makes it impossible for me to think that mental pathology is measurable in terms of the deviate ideas of one individual as compared with the normal ideas of the community at large. I find myself unable to accord with this generally accepted pedagogic principle. I am led to regard the deviation or disparity, individual and community, as resident within the organism itself. I am led to see the deviation as a disparity between the organism's behavior as now *symptomatized* in certain ideas or emotions and the physiological behavior of that organism as a unitary sum of functions. Let us for the moment leave 'pathology' as you and I have ordinarily understood it; let us return to your letter and my letter, quite disregarding the content of either in the ordinary sense. Let us rather take for granted quite tentatively for the moment that ideas dealing with ideas, emotions dealing with emotions *are* our human pathology. This will help us come nearer to a mutual understanding of what I would like to say. It may pave the way to something more concrete.

If there was a note of resentment in a letter I thought I had written you with feelings of only the deepest cordiality and appreciation; if Dr. Syz took an attitude of emotional criticism toward some remarks once made by you; if Mr. Shields was so involved in affect as once to have dismissed as insignificant an attitude presented by you; if the excited young woman at the lunch table here a week ago shouts out against me, accusing me of using the utmost craftiness and diplomacy in my efforts to maintain the integrity of this or that social unit or group (and incidentally never was truer word spoken!)—none of this on the principle now employed is of meaning. It possesses no dependable basis of experimentation and inquiry. My affect or resentment is the symptom of a condition or disparity circumscribed within my own organism. Likewise for Dr. Syz, likewise for Mr. Shields, and likewise for the student who featured in last Sunday's episode. The condition cannot be socially projected and cannot therefore be met with social measures of interchange and projection—with ideas and meanings.

Since I first took up this work, now many years ago, the affect that has piled up within and about me has been immeasurably intense and insistent. The problem has been forced into the acutest possible issue and sustained at this point day in and day out (night in and night out too) over the years. But it is extraordinary what modifications and adjustments of feeling and expression have occurred within the organism—the organism which, by virtue of the rigid premise of experimentation it has more and more made its own, *shall not speak*, shall not throw the burden of complaint or question upon other speaking, complaining, questioning persons with their habitual basis of interchange and understanding in the projected idea or emotion.

This will be of interest to you. In our effort to get down to an organic basis, to efface entirely the emotional basis that can project itself socially in ideas and words, none of the nice things we do and think were, in our experimental groups, admitted as any evidence of the actual sanity or integrity of the organism. Correspondingly all of the unseemly, cruel, self-satisfying, narcissistic things we phantasy 'but would not do for the world' were placed in the category of things actually done. There was no alibi. Phantasy as something detached, cut off from actual motor dysfunction was for practical experimentation completely unadmitted. But the intolerable shocks of this working premise were slowly preparing the organism for new and unexpected powers of adjustment.

This too can't but help I think. On one occasion—it was in some smoke-filled psychoanalytic lobby, I remember—you were being discussed, and someone remarked that he 'simply could not understand Meyer.' I said, to their bewilderment, 'I don't have to.' Of course I have said this sort of thing to you more than once, but it so applies to the whole principle that is at work with us here. It is not your *idea*, whether written or spoken to me directly, that I understand and derive impetus from. It is the sense of something consistent—this is not the right word—something connected and continuous between the feeling or intention underlying your idea and the feeling or intention that has always seemed to me to direct, to give purpose to your organism in its entirety. This is not saying anything specially significant, I know. But apparently it does become significant where this total feeling occurring within the unit or sum composing the total organism becomes the directive technique of a principle of intercommunication as this principle may be made humanly operative. For Mr. Shields or for Dr. Syz or for me to reabsorb this affect of ours (habitually projected by the individual into the idea or social image where it has for thousands of generations sought vent, appeasement or requital in response to a race-old habit), this is the conscious technique upon which we are at work as a directive social process.

The student who is a newcomer, relatively speaking, to our bivouac and who cries out upon my social premeditations and adroitness, finds no opposition to her opposition, no defense or extenuation, no 'come-back'; her whole emotional content is utterly nugatory. Not what I do or ought to do, as *seen* by her, is her task. But to realize that her invariable preference, her automatic, reflex preference, is outward toward the projected social image, this is her task, as it is mine, Dr. Syz', Mr. Shields'. It is to integrate her own processes so that no 'idea of reference'—no *emotion of reference* really—shall, as it were, slip from under the protectorate of the organism as a whole.

As words all of this is utterly meaningless. As an idea going from a me to a you it takes along no cargo whatsoever. But in the measure in which the underlying principle is your own organically, in the measure in which it is mine organically, it makes for a really powerful social force freighted with no limit of possibility, it seems to me, for social unity and integration on every hand.

I am not very connected in all this, but you have not asked me to be. You have frankly asked me to express rather my quite unformed, unedited, quite immature and groping manner of inquiry. You have asked for my thoughts in process, so to speak. And this thing I have been saying is really the stuff of still another paper I am writing now—the paper they'd have none of at last year's psychiatric meeting.

I fear that by this time though you will have grown deeply sympathetic to the recipient of the letter from the Frenchman who wrote that if he had had more time he could have written a short letter! I am afraid I shall be writing you without end on the present schedule. It only goes to show, it seems to me, the fundamental agreement of principles between us. Incidentally it is so nice in this paper now under way to find myself, while disavowing the whole interideational psychiatric scheme of therapy, at the same time acknowledging my complete indebtedness to you and to your conception of the organism as a whole for the revolutionary position to which my work has brought me. It is so perfectly consistent and true from the background that is essential to us both.

I really must let this go to you now, though, for what it may be worth. It hardly scratches the surface, I know, but at another time perhaps I can write you 'a shorter letter.'

Sincerely yours,

Trigant Burrow

CHAPTER 9

THE PHYSIOLOGICAL BASIS OF CONFLICT

By now many years had been devoted to intensive group-analysis, and Burrow's studies were more and more aligning man's common behavioral impediment—his inability to achieve social integration and rapport—with a physiological imbalance directly appreciable within the organism. Even in the days of his psychoanalytic practice, Burrow had sensed that distortions of behavior were related to disturbances of physiological processes. His increasing emphasis on patterns of internal tension, then, had its continuity with early, albeit theoretical, trends in his work.

In *The Neurosis of Man,* Burrow describes his accidental recognition of 'a most unexpected phenomenon'—a barely perceptible sensation of pressure, stress or tension in the forepart of the head, especially in the region of the eyes.(1) With continued experimentation over a period of years, this sensation became more clearly defined, and proved to be related to a ceaseless preoccupation with the image of the self. 'In this physiological localization of the stress concomitant to the sense of separation or conflict, we were at last "getting warm" . . . We began to discriminate the pattern of ditention, of separation, of private self-interest, from that of cotention or the common, undifferentiated self-interest of man's organism as a species.'(2)

Burrow's first systematic statement about the role of attention in mediating the relationship of organism to environment, and his differentiation of the two contrasting modes of attention characterizing man's behavior appeared in *The Structure of Insanity* published in

(1) *The Neurosis of Man,* p. 114.

(2) 'Prescription for Peace,' p. 107.

1932.(3) His term cotention, designating the organism's primary pattern of integration, was introduced in this book. A concise exposition of his thesis, the small volume reports the observations of internal tensional patterns which had occupied him for several years.

It is evident from his letters that with the shift of emphasis to internal patterns of tension there came for Burrow and those close to him a certain easing of the experimental task they had undertaken. 'Both as individuals and as a group . . . we were now upon wholly new ground. We were faced with a problem of man that had to do directly with the organism, and with its neurodynamic relation to the environment. . . . Disregarding the mental and social factors of partition and sectionalism existing throughout human communities, we had now to deal with an alteration in behavior occurring immediately within the organism of man. We had now to address ourselves directly to tensions and reactions existing internal to ourselves.'(4)

In order to formulate concretely the new concepts and data he was presenting, Burrow began about this time to develop other distinctive terms which will appear occasionally in his letters. 'As from the beginning I have for the most part had to plot my course through uncharted ways . . . ,' he says, 'there has been the necessity to develop what may be the beginning of a somewhat altered terminology. I am thinking in particular of such words as "stereogenic," "phylopathology," "cotention" and so on. As far as possible, however, I have kept to words that are well established in the field of scientific literature, even if I have frequently been compelled to employ them in a somewhat unusual sense.'(5) For, as he explains, 'in my attempt to establish a biology of behavior that recognizes man as an organismic unit apart from our petty ideological differentiations—national, political, religious—I have really been no little cumbered in the matter of terminology.'(6)

In 1932–33 Burrow served as vice-president of the American Psychopathological Association, but he was taking a less active part than

(3) *The Structure of Insanity—A Study in Phylopathology*, Psyche Miniatures, London, Kegan Paul, Trench, Trubner, 1932, 80 pp.

(4) 'The Social Neurosis: A Study in "Clinical Anthropology",' *Philosophy of Science*, 1949, vol. 16, p. 35.

(5) *The Biology of Human Conflict*, pp. xvi–xvii.

(6) 'Prescription for Peace,' p. 100.

formerly in the affairs of the American Psychoanalytic Association. When it was reorganized in 1933, he was dropped from the membership list although a charter member and former president. A letter to A. A. Brill relating to this matter appears among those that follow.

By this time the Ruxton home had been sold, and Mrs. Burrow moved to New York in October 1933, occupying an apartment in a gracious old house on Gramercy Park. Although Dr. Burrow continued the living arrangements necessitated by his day-by-day studies with his co-workers, the apartment provided a welcome base for social contacts and family gatherings. Miss Burrow had a small apartment nearby, and her brother lived at the Foundation headquarters. However, the letters that begin this chapter were written before this move to New York.

To his son   New York City
Baltimore, Maryland   February 9, 1932

Dear Jack:

I've intended writing you for I don't know how long. It's one thing and then another and then still another, and so it goes.

You and Emily and I seem to be pretty much of one cloth—don't know what we want, can't make up our 'minds,' know we've got minds worth making up, but are too distracted by the excitement of our wants to turn seriously to our needs, our personalities, our essential organisms. Well, it's all right. It will all straighten itself out in a little while. What is significant for me in the meantime is that all the nice, clear, quiet, healthy people who call themselves normal are at base of one cloth again with the three of us. It's just that we somehow hold together, keep steadfast in one another's faith and hold together also with all others—the moody, the confused, the neurotic like ourselves, as well as with the steady, the assured, the 'normal' who are at base no less like ourselves, no less confused and moody. Consider this 'world-depression' and how all the old cheerio therapies are failing to work, how the trouble continues its sick symptoms and gives us clearer intimation of the deeper-seated nature of the real disease. We've just got to hold on and wait somehow. I realize that waiting is the most difficult and courageous of all man's tasks. After all, it has been intelligent waiting that has been the chief element in every technique that has led to any significant discovery.

Love to you and Mother,

Devotedly,

Father

•

To Professor John Dewey   New York City
New York   May 11, 1932

Dear Professor Dewey:

You were good enough to write me that the material I have published from time to time has not been without interest to you, so that I am taking the liberty of having sent you today with my very deep regards a copy of a short essay that has just been published and that represents the trend of investigations that have occupied the interest of my associates and myself in recent years. (7) I hope this statement may seem to indicate a trend of inquiry which may prove fruitful along with the many efforts which are directed today toward resolving our very complex problems, individual and social.

Your own labors in this direction are, I am sure, very heavy, but it would mean much to me if you could find time to run through this brief report of our investigations into certain aspects of our human dilemma.

With my high regards,

Very sincerely yours,

Trigant Burrow

To his son   New York City
Baltimore, Maryland   May 13, 1932

Dear Jack:

Your letter reached me this morning with your request for the advance check of fifty dollars at this time and the bill of $27.50 for Maryland Club dues. I am enclosing a check for $77.50 to cover both these amounts.

I do want you to know the pleasure it is to me to be able to assist you in this small way. I do wish you would not ever think of yourself as in any way a disappointment or burden to Mother and

(7) *The Structure of Insanity.*

me. It would really hurt me very much if I thought you could entertain such an idea. Nothing is further from the facts. You are always a source only of comfort and pride to me at all times, and I would like you to know this and keep it with you.

That you should be without active and progressive employment is much on my mind because I know it is a serious trial to you. Before your letter came I was thinking of writing you, wondering what I might say or do that might be of assistance to you. You have so much capacity, so much background. All that is needed is that it be harnessed to the right job. Let me know as promptly as you can what the prospect is with the Standard Oil. That would probably be an excellent connection—the prospect of travel, new contacts, wide awake experiences and a chance to find yourself more and more on your own in every sense, all this appeals to me very much. But I do not set my heart on this and you must not. At the same time we must recognize that you simply cannot remain idle, that it is organically subversive for one of your talent and temperament. We'll just have to get back of the situation together and take radical steps now.

I am glad you are interested in the book. (8) I think too it is awfully nicely gotten up. Yes, it *is* technical, not too technical though for you, and I am glad you are already delving into it. Subject yourself to the reading of it more than once. It really needs a little study—at least certain passages.

This takes you my love and every confidence that there will soon be now the 'break' (I hope my usage is correct) that you are looking for and struggling so hard to find.

Devotedly,

Father

(8) Ibid.

To one of his students

New York City
June 18, 1932

Dear Miss N.:

I have had it in mind for some time to write you. I like the idea of writing because it assures your being held at bay until I have finished what I have to say. And even then there will have to be some interval before you can assemble your reply. In other words I like writing rather than speaking because I have you at an advantage. You can talk faster and on shorter notice than anyone I know with the exception of myself.

I have heard from time to time about your being somewhat pressed for money. Then there were rumors of your salary having been curtailed. This you confirmed in speaking with me the other evening. So I get the general impression that you are in rather straitened circumstances and are no little chafed and discomfited because of it. I haven't a doubt but that your straitened circumstances are due to your own normal or phantasy basis of living. You indulge, in many directions doubtless, the extravagances of a princess. You are 'helpful' far beyond your resources and are a spendthrift, like most of us, where your hobbies are concerned. But all that is your affair, and I am only speaking of it in order that I myself may feel the more clearly how completely your financial expenditures *are* your own affair.

Now to me and what is my affair. As you know, I have lots of money. This wealth of mine is largely in the form of youth, health, vitality and an absorbing interest or rather joy in life. But in addition I have actual money in bank. Out of this abundance I can so easily lend you what money you are in need of. You can borrow from me so comfortably. You do not have to think about such silly strictures as 'interest,' or rent to be paid, for this trifling commodity. You do not have to think of its being 'due' to be paid on a certain day or of its having to be paid back on any day for all I care. And neither do you have to burden yourself with any idea of me as being 'kindly' or 'generous' or as possessing any of the normal merits. That is only meaningless dramatization, as we both know now.

All of which just reminds me that you should study the life processes of the salamander! It seems there is quite a simple and unaffected action of the whole organism with these little creatures, but then parts of them—a forelimb, let us say—take on at times a quite independent, reflex action. These localized and independent departures in function assume betimes, I am told, a quite hoity-toity air. They even assume quite an 'antagonistic' manner of behavior toward the primary total action of the organism. I believe though that, in the salamander and kindred forms of life, these arbitrary and partial activities remain quite 'discrete,' as the biologists say. They do not assume any total or integrated or centred principle of individuality or identity. The total salamander preserves its individuality intact, as I understand it. There are these little side currents—these little eddyings of activity here and there—but 'Who cares?' says salamander. As long as they do not get organized, do not form a union, as it were, they cannot really threaten the vested capital, so to speak, of the central salamander principality.

Man, too, began using these little physiological asides, these partial reactions, these reactions which are unintegrated with the 'total action-pattern.' That was long, long ago though, so long ago that you and I do not remember any more. But as I figure it out, these, at first, quite incidental and insignificant rebel activities began more and more to systematize themselves, to organize, to form trade unions, so to speak. They became specially strongly organized in the region of the cerebrum, and through it these 'partitive' stimuli and responses found a ready inter-connection or inter-change socially. Then gradually the centre of gravity was shifted, or rather the organism began to act *as though* the centre of gravity were shifted. The principle of identity or of individuality was artificially displaced into this localized, cerebral zone of inter-change among us. These partial activities systematized themselves into something called 'I,' and this 'I' constituted the identity that replaced the identity of the organism as a whole. This truancy, this misappropriation of feeling, this displacement of the centre of gravity, or of personality, so to speak, has registered itself in the tissues of the human organism. It is very faintly, very delicately perceptible now of course after all these—heaven knows how many—hundreds of thousands of years of our inadvertent self-ostracism. But it *is* perceptible. This partial, this cerebral innova-tion, this systematization of discrete functions is perceptible as being separate or discrete from the main trunk of man's feeling-life. It is probably some organic protest within the species against this arrogant shift of man's physiological centre of personality or of authority that is the true account of the superficial symptoms we see today in man's social unrest, depression and outer disinte-gration generally.

Well, in all this we seem to have lost connection with our sala-mander. But that's just what I meant to do as I've been writing—to lose connection very gradually, quite imperceptibly with this lower order. For, after all, his situation is a cinch compared with our own. The salamander's physiological mutinies haven't sys-tematized—haven't coalesced to usurp his central, primal sover-eignty. Whereas with ourselves there has been this systematized outlawry, so to speak, among the arbitrary and discrete processes. Then, too, we are not on the inside of the salamander and his inter-neural conflicts. Whereas with the neural conflicts that beset the organism of man we are on the inside—we are ourselves the embodiment of these warring processes. And this is man's subjective rub. He is himself the problem he must now of himself unravel.

So, to return to the economic aspect of our internal situation, if you will let me know what money you are in need of for meeting more comfortably with me the problem of our misadventures in development—misadventures to which the inadvertences in our physiological growth have led—I shall be very glad to send you a check. If I am playful and absurd in my way of putting things, it does not mean less earnestness in my conviction of their significance. Solemnity (praise God!) does not make one any more earnest, and you know me well enough, I think, not to let ineptitudes of manner or temperament with me disguise my real intention.

This set out to be a letter and has become a dissertation. I am sorry. You will have to bear part of the blame, for being the sort of person who makes me feel that I can be at ease in writing you in this way.

It looks as though we shall not be getting away as soon as I had hoped after all. I want to see some things finished up and in their proper pigeonhole before starting off.

Sincerely yours,

Trigant Burrow

To Sally Kirby   Lifwynn Camp, Merrill, N. Y.
New York   July 5, 1932

Dear Miss Kirby:

Coming back here to these hills as I do from summer to summer, I am always so vividly reminded of you and of the time of our first meeting here many years ago. I remember last summer walking across the meadows that stretch before your delightful Swiss chalet and it made me downright homesick for the happy times we used to have in the days when you were there.

It would be so good to hear from you again and to know something of your days and interests during this interval since I have seen you. Brownie had heard of your having been a year or so in China and of having been quite ill. And I was reminded of you very specially the other day before leaving New York upon coming across a little volume of Lawrence's which you were good enough to send me with the comment that 'the only thing you liked about it was what he had said in appreciation of me.' Of course that set me up just where I like to be!

Why can't we see more of the people to whom we are ever held by bonds that are the deeper because they are invisible? For the last six years I have been living in New York, quite unreconciled to all its bustle and whir, and yet finding there the shorter avenues of contact that seem to give swifter activity to one's work and days.

Won't you let me send you a copy of an essay I have recently perpetrated, *The Structure of Insanity*. I can't vouch for its literary interest or dramatic charm, but it formulates the result of certain aspects of a research project which has meant very much to me, and on this account I want you to have it. But first won't you tell me where you are now and how I may reach you. You are such a will-o'-the-wisp, but I shall try to trace you with this as far as the Women's City Club at least and then look to them to find your present whereabouts.

These are difficult times everywhere, aren't they, both economically and politically? But still more tragic doubtless would be a too easy solution and a swing back again from our present period of depression to a no less dependable position of social elation.

What are you reading these days? Do you know Mary Follett's

Creative Experience? I had such a nice letter from her recently. Her book would, I think, interest you if you do not happen to have seen it.

Here's hoping to hear from you very soon and to have good news of you. Brownie, were she here at the moment, would be joining me in all manner of affectionate remembrances.

As always,

Trigant Burrow

To Dr. G. E. Coghill   Lifwynn Camp, Merrill, N. Y.
Wistar Institute, Philadelphia   July 7, 1932

Dear Dr. Coghill:

I received your reprints and needless to say I found the deepest interest in them. Your papers would have been acknowledged earlier but that I have waited until I could have brought up to me here in camp our bound volume of the *Archives of Neurology and Psychiatry* containing your paper, 'The Early Development of Behavior in Amblystoma and in Man.'

The reports of your investigations are of special significance for me because of the analogy they seem to afford to the work I have attempted to do with human groups or communities. I have in mind my effort to bring to objective awareness those restricted subjective reactions which mediate our communication socially through the employment of the symbol.

From the point of view of phylobiology my interest in this problem has to do with the presence of this specialization or differentiation ('individuation') of function *within man himself.*

The salamander, if confronted with the task of reconciling the differentiations which mark the independence of its 'partial action-patterns' from its total, undifferentiated pattern of action, would be approaching the problem from a very different angle or position from that at which you and I now stand as external (mental) observers of its processes.

I am making this absurd analogy in order to bring out the actual situation with which man is confronted in the problem that faces him in the conflicts of feeling and adaptation that exist within himself. In my paper at the afternoon session at Atlantic City (9) I tried to emphasize the necessarily subjective nature of the problem man has on his hands in the obstruction to adequate function or adaptation involved in the psychosis or the neurosis. But as yet it would seem, for myself as for others, an almost impossible task to bring to practical, definitive awareness the essentially internal, subjective nature of our maladaptations, individual and social.

I do not know where, or indeed whether, I shall publish my paper in this country (it was originally written for publication in Germany) but it has been gratifying to make reference to the biological conceptions which have been the outcome of your investigations as offering a helpful analogy to the point I have for years been attempting to bring out regarding this localized differentiation (partial action-pattern) as it exists in man's own internal processes. Naturally I am particularly interested in the Archives article because of the clear indication in your paper that there exists an identical law of neural growth in man and in amblystoma.

With regard to your use of the term 'individuation,' it seems to me most adequate as you apply it. My feeling is that one's meaning is so much a matter of one's own background and that after all

(9) 'The Morphology of Insanity as a Racial Process,' *The British Journal of Medical Psychology*, 1933, vol. XIII, pp. 296–312.

the investigator himself is the best judge of the term that most nearly expresses the meaning of his investigation. 'Individuation' and 'the discrete element' were the terms I chose to differentiate the reactions so designated from processes of 'integration' or 'organic confluence,' when I attempted to express in my book, *The Social Basis of Consciousness*, the organic 'isolation' or 'separation' involved in the tendency to symbol-identity now socially dominant in man—the species of artificial 'segmentation' I later referred to as the 'social substantive "I".' So that naturally I am sympathetic to usages of yours in a field which seems to offer (if not the identical condition) at least analogies to the type of behavior-reaction I have attempted to tackle.

Thanking you again for the reprints and your letter and hoping that you will keep me on your list for future papers,

Sincerely yours,

Trigant Burrow

To Mrs. Burrow   The Windsor, Montreal
Baltimore, Maryland   Wednesday, July 13, 1932

Dear Brownie:

On the spur of the moment Emily and I decided to vagabond in the neighboring Canadian country and came over here in the car yesterday afternoon. Perfect weather, delightful drive. Whither today have, as yet, no idea. As soon as Emily dresses we'll have breakfast and look up the tourist bureau. Expect to return to camp tomorrow afternoon, but we are unfettered by any definite schedule.

It certainly seems good to have this little outing with Emily. In general she seems happier than I've known her for a long time. Last night at dinner we danced together for the first time in nearly twenty years!

We are certainly looking forward to your getting up to the Lake next Tuesday.

No more now.

Devotedly,

Trigant

11 a.m. Off to Ottawa.

To Dr. Charles B. Thompson(10)   Lifwynn Camp, Merrill, N. Y.
New York   July 26, 1932

Dear Dr. Thompson:

Better bring your Greek dictionary and also a medical one. I was just saying to Mr. Shields there is no argument like a pat and snappy term. An apt medical usage in our formulations would be worth pages of description. It convinces reflexly, as it were. When I was at the University of Virginia, fresh from a scholastic Jesuit college, I had compiled quite an ambitious lexicon of prefixes and suffixes, both Greek and Latin. It was all sorts a help as you can imagine in medicine. As I recall it, there was nothing which these appendages did not take care of.

Now to our own applications. This symbolic short circuiting, this doubling on itself as it were, of the afferent and efferent arc

(10) An associate.

through a restricted zone that does not permit of the inclusion of the total reaction of the organism has its description in some definitely established Greek prefix or suffix. Take the Latin 'dislocation,' there must be the Greek for this. I was thinking of the word 'anastomosis'; now a difficulty (dus) or obstruction(?) or even a shunting of a process or function will have its Greek equivalent in medical usage. With these hints I should think we should be able to construct a quite snappy Greek medical word. Dr. Syz is particularly resourceful in philology. Might talk it over with him. But I think you get my trend.

Sincerely yours,

Trigant Burrow

To Dr. Havelock Ellis   Lifwynn Camp, Merrill, N. Y.
London   September 15, 1932

Dear Dr. Ellis:

It is gratifying to know that the view expressed in my paper, 'Psychoanalysis in Theory and in Life,' seems to you sound. In regard to your inquiry, the fact is that in the intervening years of practical observation and experimentation with actual groups which has been the daily routine of my associates and myself since the time of writing that paper, the conviction expressed at that time has grown and deepened with me—the conviction that the social consensus we call normality, with its mentally right and wrong basis of human conduct, is throughout pathological.

I do not know exactly what to say in reply to your comment that our position seems to you sociological rather than medical. Perhaps this is the more correct view. If bacteriology, physiological chemistry, such sciences as serology, immunology and kindred inquiries are the less medical because of the broader biological principles upon which they are based, certainly this would be the interpretation also of our investigations in phylopathology. But I can myself hardly concede this position. Medicine and the laboratory are, it seems to me, essentially sociological. If Pasteur, Koch and Lister introduced into their clinical studies a sociological principle, these investigators are, it seems to me, not less medical but more so. But perhaps, after all, this point of view is dependent merely upon an interpretation of words which it would be idle to argue. In the moment I am trying only to have you sense my own feeling as it bears upon our group investigations of observable human processes.

As I see it, sociology in its preoccupation with social factors is merely dealing with the surface level of things—with images and appearances—and not with the tangible, physiological materials of science. That is why I tend rather to harp upon the structural and medical basis of our much-needed interindividual adjustment.

Surely our schools of public hygiene have developed a most important approach to the problem of physical disease and yet they are not less medical because of the sociological implications of their approach. I think of psychiatry, as it is generally practised today, as comparable to the treatment of the individual tubercular patient in the days before Koch's discovery of the tubercle bacillus. It is, of course, a commonplace how completely the knowledge of pathogenic organisms has revolutionized our attitude toward tuberculosis and other infectious diseases, and yet the advance that has been made is due essentially to the broader sociological and educational factors that have entered into this department of medical research. On the basis of investigations of The Lifwynn Foundation, I foresee a similar trend in the sphere of mental and nervous diseases, if we are to make effective headway against these socially prevalent maladjustments. . . .

I look forward to seeing your manual when it appears. You always put so clearly whatever you have to say. I hope I shall learn to do so too some day, if indeed a facility of this sort is at all to be acquired.

It is always a pleasure to hear from you. What I should best like is the opportunity of talking with you, but that seems now, with things so generally awry with us all in the world today, a very remote possibility.

With my kindest regards,

Sincerely yours,

Trigant Burrow

New York City
February 9, 1933

Dear Dr. Ellis:

I want to thank you for your very good letter and also for your book, *Psychology of Sex*, which reached me a day or two ago from your publishers, Ray Long and R. Smith. I have had time as yet only to glance through it, but look forward with great pleasure to reading this recent work of yours. I have seen many complimentary reviews of it in the American papers.

It was good of you to read my little essay, *The Structure of Insanity*. Why I should be thought of as giving up anything and asking others to do so is not clear—I mean giving up anything in the sense of a renunciation. That I should like to give up physiological behavior patterns that 'cramp my style,' as the vulgar phrase runs here in America; that I dislike the reflex social compulsion that drives my total attentive adjustments into the narrow channel of outlet (and of intake) restricted to the purely mental or symbolic paths of contact with the environment does not mean for me a giving up or a renunciation, but rather a relief from a very burdensome racial habit. The thing I am trying to say really has to do with a race reaction that may be compared to some involuntary tic or faulty postural habit of which one is quite 'unaware' (a reflex facial contraction, let us say, or some automatic shoulder fixation) but yet through which one is nevertheless definitely restricted in feeling and outlook. But there is nothing, I assure you, of the ascetic in me, and it makes me just a little uncomfortable to be interpreted in this light by persons for whom such a quality stands as a distinct recommendation.

I do hope some day to have the privilege of meeting you and talking with you. You could not then think of me, I am sure, as a person with a mission in the sense in which Jesus was dedicated to a mission. It is not abnegation I am after—not by a long shot—but a fuller and broader and deeper sense of the life which I feel myself and my race blindly cheated out of through a sort of miscarriage of function into which we have been inadvertently dragged by some awkward ineptness in our use of the symbol.

I shall try to feel and understand this physiological dilemma more closely and to express more adequately what I have for some years been trying to say. And if I may send you these writings from time to time, perhaps I may be able to make myself clearer to you, or where I am not so clear perhaps you will help me to become so.

With my highest regard and appreciating very much all your interest and kindliness,

Sincerely yours,

Trigant Burrow

To Mrs. Burrow New York City
Baltimore, Maryland February 20, 1933

Dear Brownie:

You must have felt a wreck today. Not more than I, though. Where there exists a fundamental affection between people, where this affection has existed throughout half a life time, the 'false,' the inadvertent sensations or 'ideas,' arising because of a mistaken application of the symbol or *image* of feeling, is most devastating to the organisms which harbor such reversed and mistaken reactions.

Things are really not tragic. The revolution in mind and manners is general. *Our* children are no exception, nor are *we*.

Why can't we for the present, *let things alone*. The apartment in Baltimore is quiet and comfortable. The apartment here in New York of which you have the sole use is also comfortable. You can be here as often as you like. Emily and Jack can go as often as they like to Baltimore. It is only a question of a few months till October, when plans should become clearer and definite.

Throughout the increasing financial difficulties, I have had the great comfort of knowing that at least my wife had the assurance of a home [the Baltimore apartment] which I have bought and paid for and for which the upkeep is only $700.00 annually. This circumstance has been a great solace to me amid the difficulties and exactions of the last years. If the present home you have is not proven to be adequate or practicable in view of the developments to come, we can then make a change, but let us at least act with deliberation.

I did not finish this last night and it is now nearly dinner-time. Had wanted some message to go to you.

Hope you saw Dr. Burnam about the tonsils and will let me hear.

No more now. Hope to hear from you soon.

With love,

Devotedly,

Trigant

To his daughter   Lake Placid Club
New York City   February 27, 1933

Sister!

What's keeping you? No wire yet saying when I may expect you. Boy, Oh Boy, this is the life!

If we could have a week up here together—skating and tramping through the snow of these forests, it might go far toward curing us of our image 'opiates' and setting the course of our lives toward freer, gladder channels. God! the inertia of mental prejudices, of the 'ought' and the 'ought not,' without ever the least suspicion, even in the highest of ranks, of the complete exclusion of individual choice under such an artificial program of action.

I feel so much the need of your sort of understanding and companionship. Far be it from me to wish to encumber youth with anything that is premature or fixed in myself. That *would* be a tragedy. But there are things in my make-up which have been kept more or less fresh and hearty because of the nature of my studies and interests, and when I think of this, it makes me feel that I have something to contribute of understanding and companionship too.

Evening. I got only this far and had to dash to Arena for skating lesson, then lunch, the nap, then skating on Club pond, then bath, dinner and here I am. Paradoxical as it may seem, there is simply no time here for anything but leisure!

I must let this go though now. It is mail closing time.

All kinds of love,

Father

To Dr. A. A. Brill   New York City
New York   March 15, 1933

Dear Brill:

I want to thank you for your very kind note of February 27th. But for my absence from the city from the 24th of February to the 13th of March, it would have received an earlier answer. I value your thoughtfulness in suggesting that I withdraw my application for membership in the New York Psychoanalytic Group and I appreciate the spirit that prompted you to write me as you did. The situation, though, in which I find myself is a little difficult for me as I see things. Let me try to explain.

The Secretary of the American Psychoanalytic Association, of which I have been a member since its inception—of which I was, as you know, a charter member and one of the first group of councillors—sent out a notification stating that, owing to its reorganization, individual members of the association would henceforth hold membership only in the local groups, and requesting that members desiring to continue their affiliation with the American Psychoanalytic Association make application to the regional group.

You, I am sure, will recall something of the zeal with which I espoused the cause of psychoanalysis in the difficult days of its early beginnings here in America, and I am sure you cannot but feel how very natural it is for me to cherish a certain personal sentiment toward a movement with which I have so long been associated. I dislike to intrude my personal feelings in the situation, but it is only fair to you that I try to make clear as best I can the position in which I am placed. I think you know that I would not on any account wish to urge the acceptance of my name for membership in your group if it is unacceptable to the members generally. Nevertheless I would like to have you know how completely false a gesture it would be on my part, if, in response to the request of the secretary that I give indication of my wish to continue my membership in the association, I should remain silent. For me this would be equivalent to saying that I do not wish to be identified any longer with the Psychoanalytic organization. I feel sure no one can understand better than you how such a course would go against the grain with me. Naturally I want to continue my association with the American Psychoanalytic Association and that is why, in response to the secretary's instructions to its members, I made application for membership in the New York Group.

In view of the circumstances I hope you understand the sentiment that quite precludes an act on my part which I should feel to be disloyal to psychoanalysis and false to myself.

May I suggest that, in view of what I have written, you kindly concede to my feeling that my application should stand. I realize it is not to be expected that my sentiment in the situation should be understood by members whose association does not date back as far as mine. But the local group, I also realize, is entirely within its rights in rejecting my application, and I hope you understand I should not for a moment think of questioning its prerogative in the circumstances.

I owe it to myself to say, however, that I do not feel that the discrimination toward me is merited. For years I have striven earnestly to make solid a principle of biology that would give social extension to the unconscious and crystallize man's automatic wish-symbolism as a racial manifestation. Such an undertaking I regard as being quite as legitimate as any other direction of investigation that has developed from the impetus of Freud's teaching.

I am sorry to have written you at this length and I hope you will pardon this intrusion upon your time. I wanted only to make my personal position clear to you as you were good enough to write me personally in your kind consideration of me.

I earnestly hope that the position to which I feel obligated by the circumstances does not create a situation of difficulty for you. It should not, I assure you, as I am quite prepared to accept the adverse decision of your group toward my application without resentment or reservation.(11)

Thanking you again none the less for your kindly intermediation in the matter and with my high personal regards,

Sincerely yours,

Trigant Burrow

(11) Dr. Burrow's application for membership in the New York Psychoanalytic Group was rejected. The reason given was that 'Since the early days of your interest in psychoanalysis, this science has been developed in certain ways that accentuate the divergence which now exists between its present status and your present views.'

To Sherwood Anderson   New York City
Marion, Virginia   April 11, 1933

Dear Sherwood:

You were always more than patient with my gropings years ago,
though for what, it was in those days not yet half clear to myself,
and I have many times thought of your encouraging sympathy
toward that all too cumbersome first tome of mine.

You wrote me once, I remember, that what I was trying to get
at would probably get itself better said through the medium of
poetry. I think you were quite right—I think in a way that what
I have been for so long trying to express and have as yet so
fumbled, is the thing which you have put into terms of poetry,
throughout your writings, whether in verse or prose.

The other day I read in the Times that you and somebody are
collaborating on the dramatization of *Winesburg, Ohio* to be
produced by the Guild Theatre. I know I shall enjoy seeing it and
I shall enjoy seeing it all the more if, in the process of remodeling,
your story does not lose that certain poetic quality that runs
through all your things.

But none of this is what I set out to write you of. What I wanted
to say was that I have asked William Galt to send you a copy of
his book, *Phyloanalysis*.(12) This study by one of the younger
students seems to describe very simply and clearly the principles
that underlie our group efforts of social reconstruction. Anyhow,
your name was among the first of those who, I thought, would
find interest in this study.

(12) *Phyloanalysis—A Study in the Group or Phyletic Method of Behavior
Analysis*, Psyche Miniatures, London, Kegan Paul, Trench, Trubner, 1933, 151 pp.

It would be nice to have more direct news of you and to know how the world goes with you these days. Once a year when summer comes, Miss Bentley always has some word of you for me, pleasantly spiced with some nice naughty anecdote. But from year to year is a long time to wait for word of you. How good used to be those long leisure days of summer on Lake Chateaugay years ago!

Love and good wishes,

Sincerely yours,

Trigant

To his son   Lifwynn Camp, Merrill, N. Y.
Paris   July 7, 1933

Dear Jack:

It was 'mighty' nice to have your letter yesterday, written just as you were getting Emily off for Milan. Your guess was not far off—that we would be up in camp by the time your letter reached us. Your letter arrived with us—yesterday morning.

In a sense it contains for me only one sentence—your thoughtful expression of the wish to be of help to me here in camp. I certainly do appreciate that. It has always seemed to me that with the development of the work in which I am so interested, your assistance would be second to no one's. I have always counted on that. That thought has been a greater comfort to me than I can say during times of particular stress or difficulty. I would not though under any circumstances have you curtail your trip abroad because of any temporary service your presence in camp might mean to me. Your and Emily's trip to Europe is a greater delight to Mother and to me than either of you can perhaps fully realize. And it is not the momentary delight that I think of primarily; not by any means. But rather of its more permanent significance for you both, coming, as it does, just at this transitional moment in the lives of us all.

Perhaps my letters have misled you. I am sorry if that is so. I did not speak of the matters I mentioned without full reflection. I thought, after all, my difficulties are your difficulties, and it would be artificial and, in the last analysis, unfair to you both to withhold from you facts which, in a true sense, belong equally to you as to me. But I would not wish on any account to mislead you. Whatever momentary difficulties there have been they have not been anything unhandleable. It is only a circumstance which would get wholly out of hand that I would at all dread. That I frankly do dread. But there has been nothing like that. I wish you would realize that. I wish you and Emily would realize that, barring the accidents of illness, the conditions in my life grow steadily quieter, simpler, and that this alteration marks something fundamental. I am not unaware—not wholly unaware—that in this greater ease there is also a certain subtle and beguiling tendency toward compromise, but in so basic a drive, so to speak, as ours there apparently have to be these periods of greater easement, else the organism couldn't withstand the strain. Maybe it's part of nature's way and one is often granted a respite in order to build up the needed 'tissue' for the ultimate goal. I just don't know. What I wanted to say to you, though, is that things are not just now at all difficult....

So to come back to the point. Don't think of altering your plans because of conditions here. I wrote you frankly of them merely that you should not be denied what belongs to you as well as to me. But I had no idea of burdening you unnecessarily. There is no occasion for that. If I ever needed you or Emily, you both know that I would not hesitate to call on you. But what I most want now is that you both make the utmost of this opportunity to enjoy Europe—the travel, new scenes, friends, music, and art— together, as well as enjoying the companionship of one another. . . .

You are, according to schedule, probably with Emily now in Venice or Florence. I like to think of your having joined forces again. You, and Emily, will not find what you are seeking in Europe, or in any place or circumstance or person outside of yourself. The answer is, I insist, within yourself. But I am a poor one to be offering prescriptions to others when I have been so reluctant to apply them to my own need!

No more. The weather is cooler, and my fire feels very grateful today. It will be good to have further word and to hear your impressions of Munich and of Innsbruck.

With love to Emily and to you,

Your devoted

Father

To Dr. Havelock Ellis   Lifwynn Camp, Merrill, N. Y.
London   July 19, 1933

Dear Dr. Ellis:

I want to tell you how much I appreciate the very thoughtful article you were good enough to write for the *New York American*. Having this recognition from you is a distinction I deeply value.

As the *New York American* belongs to a syndicated organization, your article cannot fail to have a wide circulation in this country, and in this way will do much to draw attention to the trend of my associates and myself in the field of mental and nervous disorders.

Thank you most heartily for this very generous gesture on your part.

Sincerely yours,

Trigant Burrow

To Dr. Gregory Stragnell   New York City
New York   January 2, 1934

Dear Gregory Stragnell:

I want to thank you for your thoughtful card of Christmas greeting and for your very kind note. It is good of you to want to have my photograph for your office. It will go to you very soon and I appreciate your interest in having it.

Today I am sending you the reprint of a paper which I should much value your running through. It is called 'Crime and the Social Reaction of Right and Wrong' and was published in the *Journal of Criminal Law and Criminology*. Its trend may seem rather far afield for any one of my background but after all medicine is today finding contact-points with so many different fields that perhaps this discussion does not represent a too venturesome excursion on my part.

With my very cordial greetings for the New Year to you and yours,

Always sincerely yours,

Trigant Burrow

To Sherwood Anderson New York City
Marion, Virginia January 2, 1934

Dear Sherwood:

That was such a very nice note you sent me last May. I have thought of it many times and wondered how your 'group' experiment is panning out in the hills of Virginia.

I too shall get me to the hills some day! There is a stubborn, perhaps quite irrational insistence with me, though, to get things rounded up here in a good deal neater shape than they are now before setting out. What a mess it all is! But now that the scope of man's insanity is widening there is some brighter outlook perhaps for getting conditions more clearly before us, for seeing the whole social sweep of it and not focusing upon the mentally sick individual here and there. In this way maybe we'll come to see the situation the world over as an emotional disturbance that involves ourselves as well.

But this is not what I meant to say. I wanted to let you know that I am sending you today a paper, 'Crime and the Social Reaction of Right and Wrong.' I hope you will feel as I do that we have in it a common ground of interest.

I should really like some time to get at this whole business of crime from a rigidly biological angle. Like insanity, it has first to be shorn of rhetoric, superstition and 'psychology' before we can really get down to it and handle it as a definite medical problem.

With all good wishes for the New Year and all good luck to your group endeavor,

Sincerely yours,

Trigant

To a former patient

New York City
January 4, 1934

Dear Miss F.:

It has been so long since I have heard from you, and we used once to have such earnest talks together. I remember them so well. As I look back, though, I think it would be difficult to say to whom they had meant most, which had derived most lasting benefit from them, the patient or the physician. You were a wise teacher, and with you there was no effort, you had no thought of teaching. But I tried so hard to, and I wonder now if I ever did, if certainty of one's knowing and trying to impart it ever really conveys anything.

The years that have intervened have laid open their stores very generously to me. The years teach so much, because they are full of wisdom and do not try to teach.

I cannot recall where we were when we left off! Probably the first rumblings of 'group-analysis' were just making themselves felt. It has been a long and arduous research since then but I have had, throughout, such steadfast companionship in the determined purpose my co-workers have brought to our common endeavor.

I don't know whether your own preoccupations these days quite preclude your being interested in what seem to me the biological aspects of man's disordered life socially and economically. What we have called the depression is, I believe, a quite superficial symptom. Man is sick in body and soul and not knowing his own ailment, he has stumbled and fallen. Of course he has been bruised and shaken as a result. But his falling and the injuries incident to it are not his illness. This is due to conditions internal to him. That he has missed his step and fallen upon evil days and is depressed is the result of his disorder, not the cause. That is deeper-seated. ...

This takes to you my affectionate remembrance always, and with my hearty New Year's greeting to you and to your family, far and near,

Sincerely yours,

Trigant Burrow

To Henry L. Mencken   New York City
Baltimore, Maryland   January 12, 1934

Dear Mr. Mencken:

It is so seldom that the recipient of a 'reprint' acknowledges more than his promise to read it that I am deeply appreciative of your interest in my discussion, even though you take exception to it. (13)

Yes, I know Hobbes' work, that is, in general (or I did during my course in philosophy at Hopkins), and I suppose that just as the story of Genesis and that of the evolutionists are really the same in that they both set forth theories of the origin of species, so in this sense the work of my associates and myself and that of Hobbes may be likened to one another.

I am inclined to feel, however, that carefully controlled observations of the organism's behavioral reaction as a physiological unit make my position somewhat different from that of the philosophers, just as the observations upon which the teachings of Darwin and his school rest would seem to me to place the work of the evolutionists in a very different category from that of the

(13) 'Crime and the Social Reaction of Right and Wrong.'

writers of the Scriptures. But if you have in mind only the matter of literary description and interpretation, perhaps you are right.

Thank you very much for your letter.

Sincerely yours,

Trigant Burrow

To Professor Julian S. Huxley   New York City
London   January 31, 1934

Dear Dr. Huxley:

Perhaps a reprint I am sending you today, 'The Morphology of Insanity as a Racial Process,' will somewhat meet your question regarding the paper on 'Right and Wrong.' At least it may serve to reduce needless divergences in meaning.

I thought I had dwelt rather fully on the problem of guilt, trying to set forth the illusory basis of this reaction and show that, in the organism's adaptation within the social plexus, it is a matter of indifference whether the individual manifests the positive reaction of self-assessment and feels that he is 'good,' or whether he assesses himself at a negative rating and feels that he is 'bad.'

Anyhow I hope that the study I am sending you may make plain my effort to shift the whole problem of human conduct from the field of individual psychology to that of the more basic behavioral causations that affect both the individual and the community as a whole.

Appreciating your interest,

Sincerely yours,

Trigant Burrow

Dear Hanford:

First I want to thank you for all your painstaking reading of my pamphlet on right and wrong and for your detailed notes. You possess the rare gift of knowing how to be a good enemy as well as a good friend. Most people are bad enemies, but you can be a good and gentle enemy where there is need to be. To be a graceful enemy is not easy, and I have again to congratulate myself, as I so often do, as I think of you and of your limitless hospitality.

Now about your recalcitrance regarding Dr. Palmer's instructions .... I can understand, and I feel sure that Dr. Palmer can understand, a patient's preferring a more diversified and interesting life to a long one if it means too great restriction and self-watchfulness. But is there not a mid way? Instead of going all day, as is your present program, why not break the day with a rest and in other ways not too irksome try to accord more nearly with your physician's idea. Even I insist on a rest some time during the day. It is true that my average night is not more than five and a half or six hours, but this midday rest is simply a godsend. So now with your usual moderation and wisdom won't you try to be a better man and without thinking too much about it arrange a more temperate program for your days. ... I am afraid I sound very disagreeable and dictatorial. You must not think me so. Fundamentally I am heartily in sympathy with you. ...

Brownie has gone to camp. I am following tomorrow, and as Jack is not very well and his physician has ordered him to the country for some months, he will be with us this summer at camp. He has had severe attacks of grippe with sinus complications and now the lungs show indication of the need of prompt care and change of climate.

I shall be writing again when we get settled. I have a lot of work on hand as usual. Perhaps you are right about the seriousness of the outlook for this country. I certainly feel gravely apprehensive but my hope is that it bodes a firmer and surer grasp on every side. Man seems to be passing through some sort of growing pains. I cannot believe it is all mere financial depression.

Does Jimmie know the story of the little boy who turned to the Lord in his great need, saying 'Oh Lord, I pray thee to give me *strength* to clean my teeth. But Lord if thou canst not, I *pray* thee to give me *strength* not to go round worryin' about it.' And of course you know Billy Hunt's up to date appendix. Having concluded his petition to his Heavenly Father, he added quietly, 'Billy Hunt speaking.'

Guess it is the heat that is making me more than usually frivolous.

All greetings to you and the Menefers.

Affectionately,

Trigant

To Leo Stein   Lifwynn Camp, Merrill, N. Y.
Florence, Italy   June 18, 1934

My dear Stein:

Of course it hasn't been grippe that has kept me all this while from writing you. It has been more a chronic ineptness in adjusting myself in general to the outer demands of space and time. I could as easily have written you weeks ago as now but for this sheer ineptness. In the meantime you may have been thinking me quite unappreciative of your two good letters—and most justly. I was rereading them last night and thinking of you very gratefully for having written them, the first containing a well merited rebuke for a remissness I was already only too well aware of, the second all apprehension that being momentarily down and out from illness I might be unduly pained by the directness of your reproach. Not for a moment. In the first place what you said was most true, and then there was no mistaking the generous spirit in which you spoke. Not every one can act with unreserved severity and with entire gentleness too.

There is much to say. So many times in the last years I have in fancy gone over it all with you but always very inadequately, as I fear it will be now. This is the case; I don't really go with you in your self-analysis. I never have. Of course I am not so dull as not to recognize that your work is in many important respects far in advance of any other method of analysis with which I am acquainted. So that it wouldn't be true to say that I have not appreciated the keenness of your perceptions nor the subtle shadings of interpretation in which they abound. What you have written me from time to time has been of immense interest and profit to me apart from the fascination of your art of seeing things as they are and of expressing them as you do. But I just don't go with you. I am fully convinced as the result of investigations that have been forced upon me wholly against my will—my *self*—that a mental analysis of mental me by mental me (or any surrogate that 'I' might call in) is wholly fantastic, that the 'I' always reserves to itself a certain fine residue of unanalyzed material and that this residual element is invariably the kernel of the neurosis. We can and will, under pressure, let it all go except this—the one thing that needs to go if the personality is to be freed from the socially conditioned reflex that calls itself 'I' and that never for a moment suspects or has the slightest notion of suspecting that this vaunted 'I' is completely conditioned socially.

This is one reason why I have not been more gracious in answering or even acknowledging your letters 'every word of which,' I still insist, 'is interesting to me' and, I may add, of the greatest value. But their interest and value lie in their analytic art, their literary charm and in their gracious human warmth. I do not think of them as expressions of significant biological realities. The analysis of the 'I' by the 'I'—of any 'I' by any 'I' (whether the same or some other)—simply has no longer any place with me as a physician primarily interested in the health of man as a biological organism, individual and social. It just does not have any longer a part in the domain of my processes of feeling and thinking as a social organism or as a student attempting to explain to himself the social organism that he himself, along with others, constantly embodies.

You do see my dilemma, I am sure. I do not go with you for a moment and yet if I could help it I would not go without you for the world. There I am. That I might have been more graceful about it is most evident now. I guess I am not awfully apt, after all, at dissembling, but like the girl who was glad she didn't like spinach ('because if she liked spinach she would eat spinach') I am glad I am not too adept at dissembling. It means, I think, at least in the present case, a fundamental confidence where confidence is due, though I am sure you will be thinking I've been a trifle tardy in recognizing or acknowledging it!

You are quite mistaken in thinking I am interested in the paleontology of the neurosis. A history of consciousness or of tendencies of reaction possesses interest for me only as it throws light upon the reaction in the immediate moment. How could you of all people so far have missed my meaning! The total reaction-process —the systemic or integral function as contrasted with the partitive or symbolic function—is as completely intact and operates as efficiently and as persistently today as in the days of our earliest prevertebral meanderings. Coghill in his work on the Salamander or Amblystoma has come to a position that is biologically identical with mine in working with the reactions of the human organism.

Of course Coghill was working from the outside in his observations of Amblystoma, whereas my associates and I in our study of human reactions occurring in groups were working primarily from within, with only what assistance might be afforded from the outside by way of analogy. Maybe a paper I read two weeks ago at the 'Psychopathological' will help make clearer to you my position in its immediate, practical implications. (14) As soon as I can, I'll have a copy of it made and send it to you. I don't wonder you are not sympathetic to what you have conceived to be a sort of Neanderthaloid psychology!

On the other hand I earnestly hope I do not seem unappreciative of the psychological work that you and others are doing. It seems fundamental and important to me, but for me, as a physician interested in biological processes and their pathological deterrents, it does not seem, except in its outer indications or symptomatology, to come within my proper sphere of inquiry. Following my experience of the last few years in the immediate observation of physiological reactions occurring within the organism as a total pattern of response, I simply feel out of my element in any other field. I really thought I made it all plain enough in my short essay, *The Structure of Insanity*, and in the article that followed it— 'The Morphology of Insanity as a Racial Process.' Plain enough, I mean, for you. I didn't expect it to be for the average reader, medical or lay.

We came up here to camp a week ago and I am hoping to get no end of work cleared away during the summer. I wish you were here. Do you know the country about here at all? I could not imagine a more ideal spot (or a more congenial life), unless perhaps a villa in Florence....

America seems rather uncertain these days. I guess you've heard. Nobody appears to know just what is ahead but there is a good spirit among us in general and an abiding confidence in the

(14) 'Behavior Mechanisms and their Phylopathology,' *The Psychoanalytic Review*, 1935, vol. XXII, pp. 169–81.

ability and sincerity of the President. It is the situation the world over of which there seems uncertainty and distrust.

I hope you will write me again very soon and say the worst! And do be publishing some of your material before long and let me know.

Always sincerely,

Trigant Burrow

To Dr. Hanford Henderson   Lifwynn Camp, Merrill, N. Y.
Tryon, North Carolina   July 25, 1934

Dear Hanford:

Your letter made me very happy. I had been thinking of you from day to day and wondering how you were. That you should be thinking of Brownie and me as you do, and planning so delightfully for us, when you have been so ill and are not yet by any means fully yourself again—I was very deeply touched by your affectionate thought of us.

We should like nothing so much as to spend a few days with you at Menefer this autumn. What talks we shall have! But we shall make very sure that having even us about won't be too much for you. So if your invitation bears your doctor's endorsement, we should love to come to you. . . .

About my paper anent Crime. I thought your criticism very patient and just, considering what you read, and you could only have read what I wrote! Fundamentally we are in complete accord, I feel. . . .

If a boy should dearly love his mother and show her always only the tenderest consideration, it would seem to you and to me only a quite natural, joyous, beautiful expression on the boy's part—like the joy of looking at a lake beneath the moon, or listening to the laughter of little children, or the joy of seeing flowers 'that sway through sunny hours.' If on the contrary a boy's love and tenderness toward his mother were something he felt he ought to show her because it would look well or be 'right,' dutiful and the worthy expression of a son, or if the loveliness of moon light, or children or flowers reached him in this ulterior way, you and I would feel such an attitude most unfortunate, most unbeautiful. This is the extreme case, I know.

Now in the measure in which precept has, in the process of man's evolution, come to displace or to impinge upon and sully spontaneous, unpremeditated sentiment, the circumstance seems to me one of those tendencies to *faux pas* in man's growth that seem deplorable. It is, in so far, like the premeditated love of a boy for his mother. If this replacement of the spontaneous by the ulterior is traceable to a miscarriage in the processes of man's biology—to a quite alterable mishap in our growth that is accessible to objective observation and adjustment—it would seem worth while to set about locating the difficulty and applying the appropriate remedy. That's all my paper attempted to say. Its fault was that it did not say it. It is with its fault—with what it did not say—that you do not agree, and neither do I! So may the Lord love us. We aren't lacking in accord after all and life smiles again.

It is this conception—this idea of muddying, through calculated effect, the clear stream of unity and integration that underlies man's basic feeling and of which the harmonious functioning of his own organism is the biological prototype—that runs through and is the basic thesis of my work. Throughout my medical and psychological studies, nothing has so impressed me as the primary unity of life—of all living processes. The close physiological union between the organism of the mother and the infant and the organism's intolerance to its interruption psychologically—its wholesome biological intolerance to a separation in feeling and thought —are all part of an inquiry that has meant very much to me over many years. I want to go on with this and learn to express it more clearly.

This must be going on its way, though, now. Keep me in touch with you and your thoughts. They are a greater guide and support to me than you know. Brownie and I can't wait for autumn to come! We shall have so much to talk of and to learn.

With our love,

As always,

Trigant

To Dr. G. E. Coghill   Lifwynn Camp, Merrill, N. Y.
The Wistar Institute, Philadelphia   August 20, 1934

Dear Dr. Coghill:

For some weeks I have had in mind writing you. First I have wanted to have you know how disappointed I was not to see you at the Psychopathological meeting held in June at Atlantic City. You would, I think, have found the meeting in many ways congenial. Its general tone bore no suggestion of the fiasco in Washington a year ago. There was a vitally interesting paper by Hoskins, and interesting papers also by Kempf, Syz, Schilder and by Gantt of Johns Hopkins. Dr. Syz, in his paper, 'Biological Principles in Relation to the Neurosis'(15), laid special emphasis upon your work. My own paper practically took as its text your thesis of the primacy of the total action pattern as the organism's

(15) Unpublished.

central principle of motivation. I should have liked so much to have your reaction to this attempt of mine to correlate the work of my associates and myself in the domain of human biology with the basic principles you have established through your observation of neural growth in Amblystoma. Because of the very divergent field of my observations my angle of approach is necessarily different from yours, so that I could well understand its seeming to you that I have somewhat overstrained the analogy between our separate positions. . . .

But you are probably having your vacation just now and are momentarily of no mind to be bothering with the bio-physics either of Amblystoma or of man. . . .

Speaking of the Psychopathological, I still think it is the group to look to for what possibilities there may be of bringing biological studies and principles into some practical alignment with daily human behavior. While it seemed to me that your paper of two years ago did not at once receive the full appreciation it merited, I feel nevertheless that it was a definite stimulus toward more objective aims among us. If the meeting in Washington showed a lamentable lapse from these biological principles, certainly this last meeting gave evidence of a definite tendency to recover its footing once more. Personally it seemed to me—and I know I am voicing also the feeling of my associate, Dr. Syz—that the meeting bore evidence throughout of the impetus given it through the work you have been reporting over the years.

I am hoping to complete this summer a book I have been occupied with off and on for a good many months. It will include the papers I have just alluded to, and I shall probably call it 'The Biological Basis of Conflict, Individual and Social.' (16) I hope to have this book express the importance for the human species of its reaffirmation in terms of daily behavior of what you have called the 'sovereignty of the total action pattern' in contrast to behavior interpolations that possess a mere symbolic authority and which,

(16) Published under the title, 'The Biology of Human Conflict,' see note 9, p. 42.

as I see it, are for the most part expressions of partial patterns of action attempting to supersede the primacy of the organism's total basis of motivation. It is a large order, though, and tends to cover too wide an area. However I am hoping to bring it within bounds very soon and have done.

I am always interested to have reprints of your studies when you have them at hand. I enjoyed so much your paper on 'The Neuro-Embryologic Study of Behavior' read before the American Association of Anatomists.

Sincerely yours,

Trigant Burrow

To Karl Howenstein New York City
Los Angeles, California January 13, 1935

My dear Mr. Howenstein:

...Your paper seems earnest and its theme clearly stated. 'Findings,' though, is strong language to students accustomed to the objective criteria of the laboratory, and its use invites serious challenge. Communication *is* life undoubtedly. But communication may also be deception, and it remains with oneself to determine in how far the semblances of the former are subordinated to the service of the latter.

The habit of deception—more accurately self-deception—has always been the stumbling block to my own efforts of readjustment as it has been to the efforts of my associates. Indeed I do not know of any better stenographic cipher than 'self-deception' for describing 'the delinquency which is in all of us.' It is this element, I think, that accounts for the highly virtuous, exhortatory note you tend to sustain throughout your paper. In your zeal to have us follow a better life you are straining your voice, and to no avail. In response to the driving demands of self-interest socially current among us, such over-stimulated behavior-reactions are not unusual. I have come upon them time and again in myself. But whenever any of us has recourse to exhortation, it is invariably prompted by self-deception or a secret admiration of one's own image. So that with the assistance of my co-workers I have been attempting to let go more and more the formulations one arrives at merely through the ingenuity of the intellect and have depended rather upon the wisdom one attains through his organism as a unitary expression....

I hope the New Year holds much happiness and interest for you and yours.

Sincerely,

Trigant Burrow

To Dr. Albert E. Wiggam   New York City
New York   March 7, 1935

Dear Dr. Wiggam:

Thank you for your letter of February 28. It is a pleasure to know that my paper in *Human Biology* was of interest to you.... (17)

(17) 'Neuropathology and the Internal Environment—A Study of the Neuro-muscular Factors in Attention and their Bearing upon Man's Disorders of Adaptation,' *Human Biology*, 1935, vol. 7, pp. 74–94.

Perhaps I am not striking a note that is altogether unfamiliar to you when I say that the idea of popularizing my scientific formulations is one toward which I incline to feel very chary. I must not be thought for a moment unappreciative of the work you are doing in this field. Your association with Professor Pearl, Dr. Barker and Dr. Tilney is, of course, sufficient earnest of your qualification for an undertaking of this sort. Nor am I so insensitive to social values as not to recognize that there is perhaps no function of greater importance than that of a judicious presentation to the general community of the more technical medical developments in clear popular language.

And yet I know you will understand if I say that personally I cannot refrain from a certain misgiving. I think perhaps it has to do not so much with the mere task of paraphrasing in simple terms a process based upon intricate experimental tests. I think it is rather the peculiar nature of the work which, together with my associates, I have for the past years been attempting to do—a work whose essential aims require that the observer somehow bring to observation the material of which he is himself an intrinsic biological part—that the subject become object as well as subject—and that he do this through a process of feeling his way back again into his own basic reactions under conditions of consensual objective control.

You can see from this, I fear, that I do not myself put it any too well! Is it any wonder then that I tremble for the outlook of the colleague or student who would attempt to reduce formulae of mine to simpler denominators?

However, I should be much interested to talk with you some time and to have you talk also with my associate, Dr. Syz. It might be that we should all three find much common interest in the project you have in mind. I take for granted that you, no less than my co-workers in the Foundation, would wish to make very sure that any material you might write would be subject to the supervision and control of our scientific staff. In any event I want to thank you for your interest and to assure you that it meant very much to me to have had this gracious word from you in response to my article.

With regard to the article on 'The Physiology of Happiness' of which you spoke, your ideas on the subject would, I suspect, undergo marked alteration should you become acquainted at all sympathetically with the trend of our investigations. People so commonly associate 'happiness' with merriment or gladness and leave quite out of account its more thoughtful, constructive and even *pains*-taking aspects. But of this more anon.

Looking forward to the pleasure of seeing you some time and to discussing with you personally the matters of common interest suggested by your letter,

Sincerely yours,

Trigant Burrow

To Leta Bentley
Williamsville, New York

New York City
March 11, 1935

Dear Leta:

How are you these days anyhow? Though my writing you at the moment is not prompted by purely clinical interest. What I am mainly interested in besides hearing how you are and how things are going with you generally is to ask you if you can tell me of a good and not too unimaginative mason in the vicinity of Merrill. In driving along last summer past the camps that border on the road beside the Narrows, I noticed what seemed to me some awfully well built stone chimneys. The cabins themselves appeared simple and inexpensive enough, and so I inferred that the chimneys must be also. We still hanker for an open fire-place in the dining-room at camp. But it has always seemed so frightfully expensive that we have been chary of undertaking it.

It is not a fair question to ask you, but you know so much in general and so much about hearth and home in particular that, as vague and indefinite as your acquaintance with my particular problem must be (with the setting, the height of the chimney, the roof and all), I thought maybe you might have some notion of what it would cost and whom I might get to do it. For the carpentry we'd be wanting to bank on Mr. Bellows. But I don't believe he boasts any special prowess in the modeling of artistic chimneys. Maybe Miss Lawton would have some ideas on the subject, even some practical ideas through her own actual acquaintance with chimney building. While we should greatly like to have this added charm for the camp we have very much to consider expense these days. But it goes without saying, I suppose, that financially things aren't as they once were with me. Where formerly I used to find the running smooth, now I am brought up against one hurdle after another and fear with each succeeding one that at the next I'll come a cropper. But who in his financial outlook these days does not feel himself to be a steeple-chaser astride a very uncertain mount!

Do tell me your news.... Do you know that Miss Deming is offering her lovely camp with its very complete equipment for the absurd sum of $15,000? And probably the sum could be made absurder still if offered promptly. It would be such an ideal spot for you. No cow bells, no automobiles roaring across your front porch, no engines puffing enterprise across your serene meadows. We'd so love to have you for a neighbor and I promise we'd be awfully nice to you. It has always seemed a sort of irony that Clarence and I should be on one side of the Lake and you on the other. So here's the solution. Be a sport, Leta, and come join forces with us on our side of the Lake.

Maybe Clarence and I will be getting to camp this summer before even you are on the ground. When do you plan to be there?

No more now or there will just be no end!

As always,

Trigant Burrow

To Dr. Daniel B. Kirby   New York City
New York City   March 31, 1935

Dear Dr. Kirby:

Thank you for your note.

This word from you is a reminder of a matter of which I have for some time wanted to write you. The complete story is a long one, and I shall not attempt to go into it fully. Briefly, it has to do with a problem in connection with my experiments of recent years in individual reactions and with the evident relation of certain psychopathological changes to important visual alterations or, perhaps I should say, to alterations connected with the neuro-muscular function of vision—with accommodation, eye-movements, etc.

In general the approach to which I have been led in dealing with so-called nervous disorders and insanity bears upon certain basic conflicts in the organism's internal reaction-patterns. Apparently there exist primary patterns of adjustment which relate the organism as a whole to the outer environment, but in addition there exist certain restricted patterns of reaction through which the organism apprehends the objects of the environment only by means of symbolic perception, that is, through the visual and auditory images that are linked up with the laryngeal system or with phonation.

From the investigations of my associates and myself there is increasing evidence that man's more primary feelings and sensations have become confused in their expression because of a confusion between these two different physiological patterns of response. In relation to these two types of internal pattern, the part played by the position of the eye seems to me of no little significance and it is this coincident function about which I should like to confer with you sometime. I am wondering in particular whether you could devise some sort of lens through the use of which a subject could be trained to maintain the eyes in definite positions—in a state of convergence, for example, or fixed upon infinity—during the period of the reaction-tests.

Mr. Galt has been working with me and if we can arrange an adequate setup he will probably take over the major part of the experimentation in connection with his Ph.D. thesis at Columbia. But needless to say my ideas will have to be largely subordinated to the conditions which may be secured with the optical aids I have in mind.

If through experimentation a means might be provided for shortening in some measure the procedure required to bring about a natural balance of adjustment in the disorders we call, for want of a more intelligent term, 'nervous and mental diseases,' I am sure you realize how very valuable your assistance would be in our efforts to find some means of controlling the position and ultimately perhaps even the finer movements of the eye involved in mentation.

Naturally, it has occurred to me that the experiment may result in practical aid in the field of optics. But you will probably feel that in this regard it is too early to speak with any definiteness. I earnestly hope, though, that an inquiry into the possibility of maintaining the eye in a fixed position does not appear to you from your experience to be wholly impractical.

My general trend has not yet been fully described in published form, but two recent papers which will be included as chapters in a larger thesis on which I am working will, I think, go far toward orienting you as to the general direction of my inquiry. I am sending copies of these to you within a very few days. Do you know, I wonder, of the work of Edmund Jacobson. A paper you would probably find of considerable interest is his 'Electrophysiology of Mental Activities,' *American Journal of Psychology*, 1932, Vol. LXIV, pp. 677-694.

I know how very busy you are and of course I do not want to trespass unduly upon your time, especially as I realize the quite problematic nature of this experimental adjunct to my researches. But if at your leisure I might sometime later go over with you certain aspects of the problem I have in mind I should greatly appreciate it.

May I take this occasion to acknowledge the reprints, which you kindly sent me and for which I have not yet thanked you.

With my kind regards,

Sincerely yours,

Trigant Burrow

To Dr. G. E. Coghill   New York City
The Wistar Institute, Philadelphia   April 12, 1935

Dear Dr. Coghill:

I have allowed too long a time to pass since your very kind letter of last November. It is only today, though, that I received reprints of the paper you were good enough to wish to see—'Behavior Mechanisms and their Phylopathology.'. . . .

The book which you kindly expressed an interest to see is unfortunately not yet completed.(18) It should be finished, I think, by the fall, but the investigations upon which it rests have taken me further afield than I had any idea of, and in consequence the material has piled up beyond all reckoning. So that it will really take the utmost industry to bring my notes into shape by the end of the summer.

Your expression of interest in the trend of the studies I have tried to carry forward along with my associates means more to me than I can easily express. It gives me very special pleasure to hear of the gratification to you in knowing of the analogy between our approach to human behavior-maladjustments and the very fundamental biological principles which you have formulated in your studies of lower organisms.

I am sure you know how much I regret the circumstance of your having been ill for so long. I earnestly hope there has been marked improvement since the time you wrote me and that we may look forward to seeing you at the meeting of the Psychopathological Association in Washington next month.

With my kind regards and very deep esteem,

Sincerely yours,

Trigant Burrow

To Professor Sigmund Freud
Vienna

New York City
May 9, 1935

Dear Professor Freud:

It has been long since there has been any interchange of letters between us, but in recent years my interests have been engaged in

(18) *The Biology of Human Conflict.*

a direction of inquiry that has rather cut me off during this time from wider contacts.

Today I am taking the liberty of sending you reprints of three recent papers. Their trend is the outgrowth of experiments in 'group-analysis' first entered upon by my associates and myself several years ago. In its inception group-analysis owed very much to the principles I had early learned from you, so that I am hoping the subsequent conceptions indicated in these papers may be of interest to you. . . .

Long ago it was your discovery that in the neurotic patient there was to be found an invariable amalgamation between affect and symbol and you pointed out that in this unconscious liaison there were to be traced the infinite elaborations of conflict and distortion in the feeling-life of these personalities. However audacious it may have seemed to many of the more literal followers of psychoanalysis, I have at no time retreated from the position, held by me from the outset, that the investigations of my associates and myself have represented the consistent development of principles first established by you.

It must remain for the future to decide whether in carrying the central principles of your teaching into the field of the behavior of the organism as a whole with all its socio-physiological implications, both phylogenetic and ontogenetic, my application of your original concepts constitutes intrinsically a less faithful transcript of those concepts than the position of the many adherents of psychoanalysis whose allegiance is commonly regarded as the more strictly orthodox interpretation of you.

I should not, of course, wish to urge upon you any affiliation between us that might seem at all unwelcome to you. In speaking as I do in bringing to your notice papers representative of the recent work of my associates and myself in the sphere of human behavior, I want only to record my own feeling of the inherent continuity between what you have given us in the field of psychopathology and what I have attempted to show are the concomitant causal elements in a world neurosis.

With my kind regards and very deep esteem, I am,

Sincerely yours,

Trigant Burrow

CHAPTER 10

CONTINUING WORK WITH
TENSIONAL PATTERNS

As time went on, the arduous pace of their studies and the confinement of city life began to tell on the health of both Dr. Burrow and Mr. Shields, and in 1936 they spent the first of four winters in Clearwater, Florida. Accompanied by one or more of their associates and, at various times by Mrs. Burrow, Emily, or Jack, they set up housekeeping and office facilities at the Florida base. The letters written from the small sun-drenched house at 2 Peach Street attest Dr. Burrow's joy in the days of work and relaxation there.

Meanwhile he continued work on the manuscript later published as *The Biology of Human Conflict*. Its purpose was to serve the function of a series of laboratory exercises in which the reader was to become a participant. 'In presenting the intrinsic work of our organization,' Dr. Burrow wrote in the Preface, 'I think very especially of Mr. Clarence Shields without whose assistance from the earliest inception of my investigation the field of observation reported here would have remained unrecorded.' As president of The Lifwynn Foundation, Mr. Shields supplied the Foreword to *The Biology of Human Conflict*. Along with the papers of this period the book indicates Burrow's increasing concentration on what he calls 'the anatomy of behavior.'

To Mrs. Burrow   The Mayflower, Washington, D. C.
New York   Friday night, May 17, 1935

Dear Brownie:

Rudy Vallee sings or croons something about 'your time' and 'my time.' Well, here *my* time is 10:30, and your time is eleven thirty, but it feels like 12:30 and decidedly bed-time. So don't expect anything adequate tonight.

Meeting satisfactory but small attendance. However, I begin to be content with the signs of improvement in my own work and aims so that I've nothing to complain of. . . .

Love,

As always,

Trigant

To Mrs. W. F. Dummer   New York City
Chicago   October 23, 1935

Dear Mrs. Dummer:

Do you by any chance know rather closely some one of the Law School faculty of Chicago University? I am asking you this on the possibility that through this avenue there may be found some assistance for a young man who wrote me last summer of his great desire to complete his studies (a matter of just one more year, I believe) but who is desperately handicapped by lack of funds. He tries to piece out things by writing for magazines and doing night work, to say nothing of his rigid restriction upon himself in the matter of food. If he is as deserving as he appears from his letters to me and the impression Dr. Syz had of him in an interview with him, it seems too bad that any one with so much gift and earnestness should be as curtailed as he is.

Your heart, I know, is large and you must not let me trouble you too much with a personal problem like this. I realize that it is just one individual in the midst of countless similar cases. But for some reason this young man's difficulty made rather an appeal to me and just on the chance of your happening to know the right person at the university who might intervene in his behalf I am taking the liberty of writing you about Mr. S. If there is anyone to whom you could direct him I know it would mean everything to him.

I did so appreciate your and your daughter's visit and have thought back on it many times. The moment was so brief and so many things had to remain unsaid. But you will have sensed this void, I know, and in your own intuition will more than have filled it. Thank you for your letter too. I always enjoy hearing from you and having this touch with the wide range of your thought and interests.

Do you happen to know two small brochures by a childhood friend of mine, Margaret Prescott Montague? (To think that she is now almost totally blind and deaf!) The first, which I know you would like for its gentle wit and tenderness, has the delightful title *Home to Him's Muvver* and relates a quaint little episode dealing, as I remember it, with one of her institutional children. The other, *Twenty Minutes of Reality*, discusses an experience of her own and analogous occurrences in the experience of others. This, I know, would find much delight in but you no doubt know of both these reminiscences. If you are not acquainted with them, though, you will find them a somewhat refreshing change from your more weighty program of reading.

I believe too—striking into quite a different vein—that your thought would find much peace as well as reënforcement in Swinburne's 'Hertha.' This poem I am myself very fond of, but you probably know it already by heart!

Please remember me to Mrs. Fisher.

With my kind regards,

Always sincerely,

Trigant Burrow

In reviewing Dr. Burrow's correspondence, the editors have been impressed by the continuity of his personal relationships over the years. Frequently he reached far back into the past to renew those meaningful acquaintances which one often allows to lapse through inertia. The following letter—continuing a contact dating from the days of his doctoral studies—is an example.

To Professor Knight Dunlap   New York City
The Johns Hopkins University   October 26, 1935

Dear Dunlap:

I hope that a paper I am sending you today, 'Fallacies of the Senses' (1), may seem to you to indicate a worth-while trend. To my chagrin the editors were unable to include the many notes and references I had added to the important work of others. This lack of recognition will, however, be taken care of in a book I am now at work on in which this discussion will be included.

I have not seen you for so long. How are you these days anyhow? You never write a fellow any more and if reports be true you will soon be putting yourself so far out of reach as the Pacific seacoast. I do want you to know though that I look forward to meeting you

(1) 'Fallacies of the Senses—A Brief for the Internal Study of Man's Organism as a Total Process,' *Scientia*, 1935, vol. LVII, pp. 354–65, 431–41.

in Heaven. Indeed it is largely this prospect that gives piquancy to my hope of ultimate exaltation to this limpid state.

Always sincerely,

Trigant Burrow

To Dr. Hans Syz, Secretary-Treasurer of   New York City
The Lifwynn Foundation   November 17, 1935

Dear Dr. Syz:

I am transmitting to you the enclosed check of $1500.00 as a gift to The Lifwynn Foundation. Needless to say, this contribution goes to you with the heartiest feelings of interest and sympathy in the economic handicap with which the Foundation is faced. But you will, I feel sure, understand my expressing to you my deep regret that substantial donations have not been procured from representatives of the wider community which the Foundation is serving so ably, rather than from those whose work and time and strength go constantly toward promoting the Foundation's aims and who are at the same time seriously restricted in their own financial holdings.

We are students in common of common ineptitudes in behavior, both individual and social; and it will doubtless be of assistance among our members if I may indicate that this inadequacy on our part, in failing to inspire such a reciprocity from the community as would express itself in practical economic terms, marks a defect and inadequacy in our own subjective social processes.

Perhaps it will not be amiss if I take this occasion to emphasize the very special and unique nature of our work—how radical a departure it marks from the usual mental, theoretical, speculative accounts of behavior-disorders conceived, as they necessarily are from this mental premise, only as mental disorders. In considering this radical departure in our approach you will recall that I was led years ago to establish an experimental setup which required that I lay aside all interpretations that had hitherto prevailed with me not only in the entire field of mental and nervous disorders but also in respect to modes of adaptation commonly regarded as normal. You will recall that leaving my habitual associations—the customary circle of family, friends and professional associates—I came to place myself under such daily living conditions as would further to the utmost my abrogation of those premises which had always stood as a bulwark to me in my social and economic relationships. You will further recall that in our zeal to exact of ourselves the completest divestiture in these regards Mr. Shields and I decided that we would each forego even the commodity of a private purse. The outcome for us, as you know, has been a subjective insight into the organism's processes in their primary equipment such as may rest only upon more clearly appreciable biological premises. This discovery on the part of Mr. Shields and myself, which was given sharper, more palpable definition through my experiments of many years in the discrimination of eye-tensions according as they are associated with the organism's total or with its partial patterns of adaptation, has disclosed the existence of a sharp line of demarcation between the function of the not-organism-as-a-whole and that of the organism-as-a-whole that is registered in terms of definitely perceptible physiological alterations. It is this finding that warrants the recognition of the researches sponsored by The Lifwynn Foundation as the expression of an internal socio-biological thesis.

The deep significance of this discovery in the field of human biology has, I think, not been at all clearly sensed on the part of my colleagues of the Foundation. I realize that the lack of due appraisement of this very vital step—a step which has permitted the reclamation of human powers from dissipation in mere theories of mental interrelations and the application of these powers to practical laboratory research in the field of internal behavior-reactions —has been in no sense intentional. It has not for a moment been occasioned by any indisposition on the part of my associates to give credit and support to the principle of investigation on which I found myself launched from the outset of my association with Mr. Shields. Rather, as I see it, the lack is due to an inadequacy on the part of the members of our organization to recognize among themselves both as individuals and as a social community the presence *within themselves* of the same social and economic impediments to the organism's function that I was impelled to relinquish as a prerequisite to closer contact with the biological foundations of human behavior.

This is not in any sense a criticism. I think I do not have to tell you this. Indeed it would be most ungracious of me if I did not promptly add to this statement my very deep and cordial appreciation of the years of sympathetic helpfulness and coöperation that have been accorded me at all times by my associates of The Lifwynn Foundation. If at the moment I seem to be laying undue emphasis upon what appears an inadequacy in collaboration toward our common ends, it is because of the circumstance that just at the moment my attention has been strongly focused upon the urgent need for definite measures that will enable the organization's Scientific Staff to attain internally an appreciation of the needed biological basis for adjusting precisely those alterations which now stand in violation of that internal premise.

Indeed the moment is, I feel, a socially acute and critical one. On all sides there are the earnest, if inarticulate, signs of the community's urgent demand for such a controlled criterion as will serve it as a dependable principle in the organization and regulation of human behavior, both individual and social. I cannot but feel that the years we have devoted in our efforts to bring to light the needed remedy in man's social impasse, as evidenced everywhere in symptoms of conflict, both individual and social, have been too earnest and too far-reaching for me to neglect calling to your attention whatever may still insinuate itself as an unseen obstacle to our ultimate accomplishment.

Sincerely yours,

Trigant Burrow

To Dr. Walter B. Cannon New York City
Harvard Medical School November 20, 1935

Dear Dr. Cannon:

I greatly appreciated your letter of October 25 and the spirit that prompted your speaking of the difficulty you found with my use of the word 'cerebral.' I read at once your paper on 'The Significance of Emotional Levels,' but I have only today got round to rereading my own article.(2)

From the customary neurological standpoint there is no question of the correctness of your objection. Indeed I can well understand how inevitably this would be the reaction of my colleagues generally and how anything that appeared as a lack of recognition of the clear demarcation between specific brain areas would seem particularly inappropriate to you. And yet I find myself no little perplexed in the face of problems that appear to me far less simple.

On rereading the passages to which you refer I realize that, had I been speaking of recognized brain divisions, the word 'cortical' rather than 'cerebral' would have been the natural and correct usage in consistency with our neurological knowledge of these areas. But the situation with which my thesis attempts to deal is not that of specific brain areas and their functions. As I put it recently: 'While there are undoubtedly these circumscribed zones

(2) 'Fallacies of the Senses.'

and the functions specific to them, my attempt has been to indicate the overlapping and consequent confusion in function that have arisen in respect to these originally distinct neurological areas. My studies relate precisely to the neural complicity that has been artificially set up between the cortical system with its projective, symbolic resultants and the thalamo-splanchnic system—between the brain and its external world on the one hand and the brain and its internal world on the other—the physiological complicity and conflict which has been represented in metaphysical terminology as "the unconscious".' So that I cannot but feel that my use of the more comprehensive term 'cerebral' rather than 'cortical,' with its more restricted anatomical connotations, fits more nearly the particular thesis I am trying to set forth.

In saying this I do not mean that there is not a lack of clarity that needs definitely to be taken care of as evidenced in the difficulty you had with such passages. But if my position is correct, 'the brain areas involved in the mechanism of affect-projection (a mechanism expressed chiefly in connection with man's word-conditioned reflexes) include something more than the cortex and the special external senses related to speech. Because of the affect-element in these social responses I cannot but assume some sort of partial, secondary involvement of the older cerebral ganglia—the deeper thalamo-splanchnic system.' Otherwise how explain the transposition of empathic or total-feeling reactions into those symbolic projections we commonly experience as a psychic sensation or affect, my 'mentally' emoted irritation for example, at some one's 'mentally' emoted repudiation of me?

I hope I do not appear arbitrary. I am really no neurologist—not in the sense in which you are—but at the same time I am, as you are, wholly out of sympathy with prevailing 'psychic' accounts of the organism's disorders of behavior. The outer signs and symptoms of man's psychic life, however specific and conditioned, do not seem to me merely cortical, because, if my idea of what constitutes the specific function of the cortex is correct, it fails to explain the distorted empathic element in those hallucinatory processes, those grandiose prerogatives (whether 'normal' or pathological) we find associated with the symbolic or projective system. If functionally there is a dovetailing or an overlapping between the splanchnic (autonomic) and the projective zones (between the cerebro-projective and the cerebro-splanchnic systems as I would prefer to call them), with the result that our meaning-sensations (our affective verbal symbols) are carried into the autonomic or visceral zone and our autonomic or visceral sensations into the zone of our meanings or verbal images, would not 'cortical' (which, if I am not mistaken, leaves out the implication of any direct visceral connection) be a too restricted usage?

It is not so much the 'break' between the newly acquired cortex and the older archipallium that seems to me to constitute man's quandary or neurosis but rather the circumstance that in its symbolic motivation the activity of the cortex tends to throw off the authority of man's deeper autonomic system, even attempting to assume symbolically—one might almost say histrionically—the supremacy of the total organism's primary motivation and integrity. You probably know Coghill very thoroughly. I find his thesis of the supremacy of the total action pattern of no little support in my own thesis, bearing as it does upon the supremacy of man's organism as a total pattern of behavior and in respect to which the symbolic segment, though an integral part of the total organism is fundamentally, for all its upstart pretensions, but a secondary outgrowth. . . .

If in this letter I am making a plea for a terminology that will meet my specific conception, I hope you understand that I have no illusions as to the inadequacy of many of my writings. So that should you still feel there are aspects of my formulations for which you would like to suggest alterations, whether in matters of terminology or what-not, I should much appreciate having your ideas.

Sincerely yours,

Trigant Burrow

To Lawrence K. Frank   New York City
New York   December 3, 1935

Dear Mr. Frank:

I have kept your copy of Alexander's book longer than I had meant
to.(3) The truth is I had expected to have time only to touch the
high spots but on once getting into it I did not put the book aside
until I had read it from cover to cover. Thanks for this introduction to a very refreshing viewpoint in practical orthopedics. I am
returning Mr. Alexander's book to you by mail today.

I cannot tell you how much I enjoyed our talk the other evening.
In spite of all we managed to thrash through, though, I find myself still far in arrears with respect to topics still not touched upon.
We shall have to have you with us again sometime when you can
spare an evening. Incidentally, I forgot to ask you if you had the
reprint for Leo Stein. I have written him that I am hoping you will
be able to send a copy to him.

Will you not be good enough also to send a copy of [your papers]
'Physiological Tensions and Social Structure' and 'Structure,
Function and Growth'—at least those two—to Mrs. W. F. Dummer. . . . Maybe you know her. Anyhow I have written her of
how very much I think it would mean to you both to have an opportunity of knowing each other, and I took the liberty of expressing the hope that you might have the opportunity of meeting her
sometime when you are in Chicago. Apart from a certain mystical
strain, Mrs. Dummer really has done a great deal toward coördina-
ting the several interests of investigators in different fields, and her
house is very much a rendezvous for serious exchange among
students generally. . . .

(3) *The Use of the Self* by F. Matthias Alexander, New York, E. P. Dutton
& Co., 1932, 143 pp.

This is one of the many items I neglected to speak of the other evening. Another is a short paper by Piotrowski, 'Racial Differences in Linear Perspective.' While it is rather obvious that the basis of psychology is too restricted to interpret the field of art, which after all, like poetry and music, is basically a field that has to do with man's feeling, I do sense a deep interest on the author's part in art as well as an underlying feeling for the deeper motives of living. I thought this study might align itself in a certain way with the experimental interests of your group at Yale. I am asking Dr. Piotrowski to send a copy of it to you and I wonder if you would not be good enough to send reprints of your own studies to him. . . .

With my kind regards,

Sincerely yours,

Trigant Burrow

To Dr. Hiram K. Johnson   New York City
Rockland State Hospital, Orangeburg, N. Y.   December 3, 1935

Dear Dr. Johnson:

I was glad to know you found the papers of interest and it was a real comfort to know that you did not understand them. Where there is this tentative attitude of the student there is always the possibility of reaching a common ground. It is the unhesitating assurance of the layman so frequent today in professional circles that quite excludes the reconcilement of divergent methods and aims. . . .

With my kind regards,

Sincerely yours,

Trigant Burrow

To Mrs. William F. Dummer   New York City
Chicago   December 19, 1935

Dear Mrs. Dummer:

It is evident that your study and zeal are carrying you far in respect to the important behavior problems you are engaged with in your campaign of inquiry and instruction among America's teaching staff. I am deeply interested and if you don't mind I am going to interrupt a paper I am at work upon and write you in regard to an aspect of my trend that may, I believe, assist you. Or rather I am going to direct the trend of my paper, as it were, toward you momentarily rather than toward the wider audience to which it is addressed.

Because of the subjectively altered frame of reference that my thesis presupposes, it is difficult for me as yet not to be often misleading. I really don't mean to be misleading, as has sometimes been said. . . . I am so glad you felt there was wisdom in my analogy between Pavlov's differential conditioning of the animal and man's verbal conditioning of himself, with the common result in both of a blocking of immediate function, or a neurosis. The point, I fear, has not been any too generally grasped. But this is in no small measure precisely because people are too prone to grasp only at what appears to offer the more immediate rewards—again our conditioned response to habitual verbal stimuli or social images. It all goes back, as I see it, to the inevitable gap in the continuity of our processes in the absence of an altered frame of reference *from which to observe* the data of observation that are common and internal to us all.

This brings me to the trend I want to speak of. Beginning further back and taking my cue from the paper in hand at the moment I want to speak of the trend that was preliminary to the phylobiological process of experimentation entered upon by my associates and myself some twelve years or more ago.

In the midst of my psychoanalytic work I suddenly came upon what appeared to me a phase of organic sensation and awareness that antedated the infant's earliest objective appreciation of its surroundings. (I remember so well the moment, and the patient—a teacher, by the way, and a highly subjective woman.) I called it the organism's *primary subjective phase* and spoke of the infant's *primary identification with the mother*. This was the inception of a direction of thought and investigation with me of which all my later work has been the fuller development. There was no doubt with me that there existed between the infant and maternal organism a *tensional* rapport (I did not call it that at the time)—a total physiological continuity in sensation and reaction that underlay the entire developmental life of the organism and that was quite different from the tensional modifications brought about with the infant's adaptation to its environment *and to its mother* through the process of outer objective awareness (the employment of the symbol).

I wrote at that time a paper which I called 'The Preconscious or The Nest Instinct' and read it at the meeting in Boston of The American Psychoanalytic Association in 1917. A few years later I developed the thesis into book form but set it aside. Something was incomplete. It did not satisfy me. I regretted this too, because I felt there was much material here of real interest to the investigator in the field of behavior. Still I waited. Then came the group investigation and the quite definite appreciation of the tensional continuity that underlies not alone the processes of the individual in relation to its primary origin in the maternal organism, but that underlies also the processes of all individuals on the basis of their common physiological race origins. It is hard to put it clearly in a brief word like this, but you will sense what I have in mind.

There were other papers about that time in similar trend, among them 'The Origin of the Incest-Awe.' In that paper I find this statement:

The relation between the mother and the suckling infant is primary and biological. It is unitary, harmonious, homogeneous. For the infant the relationship is an essentially subjective one. It exists simply, without conscious arrangement or adaptation. It is the one single instance of inherent biological union—the one perfect, complete phase of conjugation. It exists simply and of itself, being exclusive of choice, of calculation. It is spontaneous, disinterested. Existing without object, it is, so to speak, one with life, like the course of the planets or the growth of trees.

Then in 'The Genesis and Meaning of Homosexuality' there is this:

The infant's organic consciousness is, at its biological source within the maternal envelope, so harmoniously adapted to its environment as to constitute a perfect continuum with it.

There were other papers at that time, 'Character and the Neuroses' for example, which tend toward this same underlying scheme as the basis of the organism's mental and social development.

But then, as I say, came the conception of the continuity of man's processes as a phylum, and the book on which I am now working(4) contains a chapter I called 'The Preconscious' that attempts to bridge the interval between the ontogenetic relation between infant and maternal organism on the one hand and the race of man and his organic race origins on the other. In this book I have tried to relate the organism as a whole to man's conscious processes in such a way that we may gain a practical and concrete awareness of those processes which have interfered with the natural functioning of the total organism.

To come back to your letter, though, and to the diagram you have drawn up in your effort to relate the work of different students in the behavior field, as I see the implications of my own work in relation to that of these investigators, I fear that in view of my earlier background as the starting point in my inquiries I am hardly entitled to a place among your categorical foci. I have tried to see man's problem as an *essentially subjective one* that demands, however, an objective envisagement of it. Certain investigators

(4) *The Biology of Human Conflict.*

have found it very interesting and valuable to adopt an objective viewpoint and an objective technique in artificially inducing a neurosis in a dog or a sheep or a child. But in these experiments we are dealing with objective material—material in front of us— namely, the animal experimented upon. Man's neurosis, on the other hand, is a subjective experience and he will not reach and contemplate this subjective process residing within himself except as he applies this same objective method to his own subjective processes. This is the crux of my whole endeavor. It has not to do with the other man's behavior, not with the behavior of some other race or animal. It has to do with *my* behavior as representing an element in a continuous stream of processes and tensions affecting my race as a whole—processes, however, not appreciable by looking at the processes of others through my trained cerebral segment and believing that I can 'see' such subjective modifications, but by the internal sensing of my own tensions as these tensions are a subjectively continuous process with the individual whom I presume I 'see.' It is this emphasis that hardly permits my fitting into your category of prevailing schools. I know you will understand this and not think me ungracious, but I'd rather await the assignments of the 'new era.' It seems at times so close at hand!

I must not be writing at so great length. You are already too busy with your own many activities. I shall be going off in a day or two to Florida for a few weeks' recess and I shall hope to get in some quiet work on my book. There is need of considerable meditating upon it at this point.

I hope you found a clear response from the teachers' group in Los Angeles. I must thank you for the delightful card of Christmas greetings you were thoughtful enough to send me. Its sentiment is most inspiriting.

With my good wishes to you and to Mrs. Fisher for a very happy Christmas and New Year,

Sincerely yours,

Trigant Burrow

To Morley Roberts   New York City
London   December 19, 1935

Dear Professor Roberts:

I want to thank you for your very gracious note. I do appreciate all its kindliness and interest more than I can say, and your thoughtfulness deserves a fuller answer than I can at the moment offer you. I am just about to leave for a brief holiday recess in the south but I must not let your good letter remain another day unanswered. Perhaps you will let me just briefly paraphrase a letter I recently sent a colleague who wrote me from the same spirit of interest and cordiality that you did, asking that I tell him more about the 'actual case.' I said that it was the most natural question in the world and that from my own clinical traditions I could readily understand how inevitably this question must appear as the specific test 'not only of the workability of a method but of the authenticity of the principle upon which the method rests' . . .

. . . I have observed but *one condition*—a condition that is internal to my organism, to the patient's organism, internal to the organism of the race or phylum—and individual 'episodes' are purely symptomatic, semiotic, epiphenomenal aspects of this one process. These outer manifestations, whether manifest or deeply latent in the 'unconscious,' are not the essential disorder. Restricting oneself to these externalized phenomena only leads away from the essential disorder and from the possibility of discovering and eliminating its cause. What Mr. X. or Mr. Y. or Mrs. W. says, is what everybody says. It is what you and I necessarily say in our dissociated epiphenomenal role of the 'I.' But it can be demonstrated that what everybody says doesn't count. For all they say, their words still leave them mute. It is what they don't say, and what, for lack of an organic articulation internal to themselves, they can't say, that counts. And this goes for you and me. I know you will understand the spirit in which I say this and

I know that you will make allowance for the many ineptitudes in a statement which is necessarily as brief as this.

About evolution in the field of man's behavior being a morbid process, perhaps so. I really don't know. And I believe I really don't care, since disordered behavior or function, however widespread or long established socially, is subject to alteration. Besides, I do feel that a constructiveness, an integral trend, a tendency toward greater coördination is the dominant note in the evolutionary scheme of things behavioral. As regards your thesis, of course you know I am not taking a position opposite you. On the contrary it is simply that my interest in behavior lies in the direction of establishing a larger frame of reference in respect to its disorders. All this image business I lay so much stress upon and to which I unhesitatingly attribute the meaning of man's behavior-disorders throughout the world, whether he's bombing villages in which there are women and children in vindication of his 'honor,' or whether he's praying to the God of his own egoistic image, imploring help in the manner in which *his* opinion would dictate help to mankind—however it may be, it would seem to me from my angle of observation that the deeper processes affecting the behavior of man's organism move on toward greater unity, clarity and harmony.

It was nice to know of the recognition recently shown you and your work, and I am gratified to know this testimony was of meaning to you. I myself, if you will forgive me, feel that the significance of it lay chiefly in your own modesty and that your work is such that no encomiums could add to its essential significance. The pleasure, though, that it must have been to your friends to have extended this gesture of appreciation to you I can well understand, and I should like to add here my own thanks for all that you have done over the years in behalf of science and a clearer outlook. It has been such a help!

Sincerely yours,

Trigant Burrow

To Dr. Hanford Henderson   Clearwater, Florida
Tryon, North Carolina   February 4, 1936

Dear Hanford:

My hearty thanks for *The Charioteer!* Your conception of the Self
and its tripartite functions is a brilliant one and you have, as is your
way, sustained it brilliantly throughout your book. There are so
many viewpoints one accepts and rejoices in, some one questions
and would challenge. But all so simply and modestly and beautifully told. What you say of the individual's relation to the family
and its significance to him naturally interested me in a very special
sense, and here your viewpoint threw a certain fresh illumination
upon my own that I am glad to acknowledge. And yet I have not
half read your book, not really. It isn't the sort of book one 'reads'
that way. I shall have it by me, though, and during leisure evenings
shall turn to it again and again for the sheer loveliness as well as for
the truth that it contains.

The other morning I awakened early and as I lay 'thinking things
over' quietly I began thinking how much I'd like to have you see
a paper I finished just before leaving New York. (I don't seem able
to lay off you, do I? You seem somehow so inviting a victim. I fear
I never shall.) I called it—already I can feel you shuddering—'Altering Frames of Reference in Relation to Man's Behavior and its
Disorders.'(5) Then I bethought me of its technicalities and how
my clumsy language would offend your finer sensibilities for the
fitter word and the nicer choice of phrase. But then I thought to
myself, waxing argumentative toward you, how different are our

(5) 'Altering Frames of Reference in the Sphere of Human Behavior,' *Journal
of Social Philosophy*, 1937, vol. 2, pp. 118–41.

respective media (suppose I should be saying 'our two mediums' right now), the nature of the subject that occupies our interest when we come to communicate it (say it!) to others. Of course I'm all awkwardness in trying to put things into English, the most debased form of it—Latin and Greek awkwardness. But isn't the chemist, the anatomist, the physiologist and the mathematician equally awkward in *his* atavisms? Aren't these dead languages the accepted tools of the scientist, and isn't that why they just won't be interred? 'Isosceles triangle'—'Extensor brevis metacarpi minimi digiti'—'Hexylresorcinol'—'phagocytosis'—these, I concede, aren't pretty words. They are hardly expressions one would care to use in the drawingroom. But they have at least the merit of consistency. What they say, they stick to, whether a hundred years past or a hundred years to come, whether in Tokyo or Topeka, in the Soudan or in Sicily, in Little America or in Big. Their catholicism, like the liturgy of the Roman Church, is surely *something*. And on I went (it being not yet dawn and having the floor to myself, my ideas could have garbed themselves in Sanscrit and not been liable to arrest) but, like all accomplished debaters, reserving the really overwhelming, incontrovertible argument to the last and 'Anyhow,' I said, confronting you squarely, 'do you suppose—in the wildest flights of your imagination is it conceivable to you that anyone of average intelligence and not dispossessed of his reason who *could* write like you *would* write like me?' This seemed to take me over the top. It *got* you, as the Anglo-Saxon pith puts it. I seemed to see you go down in a heap. And I arose that day feeling uncommonly refreshed. And so I do now in reviewing your book. Who that could write that way wouldn't do so? I can't. I am a dull, routine laboratory student who delves habitually into elements and processes in which the fire of rhetoric has no part. But if you'll forgive my brusque untutored language, I'll make bold ere long to ask you to suffer with me the throes of another scientific dissertation.

Emily left me. She returned a week ago to New York to my great regret. Perhaps though I shall concentrate the more earnestly on my book, which with Mr. Shields' help (being himself far from well, he is here with me) I hope to make material progress on in the next few weeks.

Hailing once more—if only from afar—the Charioteer and with all good wishes,

Always gratefully and affectionately,

Trigant

To Mrs. H. A. Sill   New York City
New York   June 2, 1936

Dear Mrs. Sill:

Whatever is decided, the spirit of your letter this morning means very much to me. When I say this, I believe I am prompted by more than the usual implications. The attitude of your letter is to me an earnest of the significance and constructiveness of the Foundation.

It is this equivocalness of which you write that is so very trying, that I myself have found so extremely trying over the years. So many times quite important decisions have had to be made when there really was not the background for making them. But one cannot hold up a lease pending one's 'phylobiological integration'! And so it has been. There is no question but that these issues and the forced decisions have grown clearer and simpler with the re-centring of tensions and strains which through the organism's ineptness have become exaggerated and displaced from childhood on.

I think the line you draw between domestic and professional interests is, as you suggest, a sharp one and one not to be lightly com-
promised. All this I feel with you completely. I think where we
are most in arrears is in the absence of wider community coöperation. That will come. It is coming. There are the signs of this
growing interest on every hand.

But all this, as far as I can see, is merely cheering us on, and cheer
of this sort has its partitive liabilities too. 'Oh cursed spite, etc.'

What shall I say then, after all, unless I make a U turn (or is it
merely an 'I' turn again) and end doxologically by reverting to
the paragraph with which I began?

Sincerely yours,

Trigant Burrow

To Morley Roberts   Lifwynn Camp, Merrill, N. Y.
London   August 31, 1936

My dear Mr. Roberts:

I heartily enjoyed your kind letter to me of June 29. You were
very kind to write me, only I feel a little discomforted that you
should have felt any obligation to send me so thoughtful a letter
when your health is so far from robust and when you are at the
same time so busily occupied in preparation of your own manuscript. I really appreciate your kindliness more than I can express.

It is a great satisfaction to know of the parallels and agreements
between our scientific positions, however different our fields or
however wide the differences between us in technical approach.
I am taking special pleasure at the moment in quoting in a book I

am just now completing a passage from your *Malignancy and Evolution*. It is this:

> There is no denying that the gradual encroachment of the forebrain and the growth of the pyramidal tract, though essential parts of a gradual adaptation to the stimuli of an increasingly complex environment, are largely at the expense of the instincts, and therefore at the expense of the endocrines which dominate ancient nerve tracts and reflexly make up what we call instincts. The relevance of these considerations to modern civilization, over-rapid social evolution, and therefore to malignancy, may be doubtful to some and not to others. I am content if they merely suggest real reasons for what we are accustomed to look on as moral, religious and psychic struggles. The body lives with the brain and often protests. For as the earlier migrants and invaders conquered the muscles, so the forebrain endeavours to dominate the man.(6)

By the way, your title, *Bio-Politics*, greatly appeals to me. It says so much and links in very welcome fashion elements too commonly thought to possess no common structure.

I am glad that my work seems to you to have a biological meaning. For me, if it has not this, it is quite lacking in meaning altogether. For I am sick at heart with what is called 'psychology.' Your paraphrase of our respective positions in regard to the neurosis of man (or of men) cannot, I think, better sum up my position. And with your leave I shall probably take the liberty of making reference in my book to this very apt passage in your letter.

It is not to be wondered at that I should have addressed you as 'Professor.' For if you lack its insignia you still have all that the highest academic opportunity brings.

Assuring you of my deep appreciation of your kind letter,

Very sincerely yours,

Trigant Burrow

(6) Roberts, Morley, *Malignancy and Evolution*, London, Eveleigh Nash & Grayson, 1926, 255 pp.

To a patient   Lifwynn Camp, Merrill, N. Y.
                                      September 16, 1936

Dear Miss K.:

Your letter came just as I had at last finished my book. Indeed the ink had not yet dried on my pen, and it was very welcome to have this word of interest from you regarding it.

I wondered what had become of you, but it is a comfort at least to know that you did not pass us by. I feared you had gone to Montreal and returned without having found time to stop and see us.

The correct thing, I know, to say to anyone who writes me that he is unaccountably disturbed is to reply with some word of sympathy or regret, to say that it is too bad, and to add some word of well wishing or of comfort. Why must I do so, though, when I really don't feel this way about it? Disturbed states of mind, it seems to me, if rightly understood and handled, can so readily open the way to larger vistas and broader opportunities. And if I have read the signs aright there is no other pathway to the fuller life. It seems really too tragic that as a community people should be in the welter and confusion they are and suspect nothing—feel no qualms, sense no underlying disturbance within themselves. The situation is painful for you, I know, but I should be inclined to say that the cause of the pain, the real disturbance, has been there all along and that it is only now showing its head. I do not believe you will resent my position in this or think me lacking in feeling. What is called feeling can be so shallow and given only to coddling oneself and others in the sick effort to silence pain rather than to give heed to its voice and understand it.

Please do not be for a moment concerned about your obligation to me. I quite understand and shall not be the least inconvenienced by the delay.

We shall remain here, if it is at all possible, until at least October 1. But Miss Bredow will let you know, if you phone, just when I shall be back, and I shall be glad to see you as soon as a time can be arranged.

Sincerely yours,

Trigant Burrow

To Dr. Hans Syz   Lifwynn Camp, Merrill, N. Y.
New York   September 27, 1936
              A grey Sunday morning at 8.30

Dear Dr. Syz:

I love to write to you. We have so many things in common and there is always so much to say, but so often, as now, there is the pressure of less flexible interests or of definite obligations and I cannot write you as I'd like.

You asked me about Stevenson. You should have on your desk (it may be in the house or at the apartment—I'm sure I have his *Life and Letters* too—) *Virginibus Puerisque*, *Across the Plains*, and another volume I cannot now recall, but it contains his 'Lantern Bearers.' Then you should look up a book of essays of William James' for one called 'On a Certain Blindness in Human Nature' (title may not be exact) in which he speaks of this essay of Stevenson's on 'Lantern Bearers.'

But this is what I wanted to mention. There is at 27 a book of
Stevenson's verses. Among them is one: 'It is not Yours, O Mother,
to Complain.' I was thinking of *your* mother, and re-read it last
night in the thought that you might care to send it to her. Then I
want you to read some time a poem of Stevenson's I deeply love.
Laura Portor first read it to me, when we were young things, and
finding life good one summer afternoon on a river in Virginia. It
is called 'If this were Faith.' Call me sentimental or religious, if
you must. Even so I think this poem remains a brave and beautiful
thing.

And there is his poem 'The Celestial Surgeon,' if I can recall it
from memory:

> If I have faltered more or less
> In my great task of happiness,
> If I have moved among my race
> And shown no glorious morning face;
> If beams from happy human eyes
> Have moved me not: if morning skies,
> Books and my food and summer rain
> Knocked on my sullen heart in vain;
> Lord, Thy most pointed pleasure take
> And stab my spirit broad awake,
> Or, Lord, if too obdurate I,
> Choose Thou, before that spirit die,
> A piercing pain, a killing sin,
> And to my dead heart run them in!

'Sentimental?' 'Religious?' 'Partitive?' Aye, undoubtedly. And if
I should be debauching youth and you, it is unseemly of me. Part
devotion can only turn us away from a devotion that is whole. But
if in the part there may lurk that intimation of an element that is
organically whole, the germ of something integrant and unitary,
we may not turn too deaf an ear to this 'wee small voice.' That's
why I've read Prof. Palmer's life of his wife, Alice Freeman Palmer.
Every American educator (this means *you*) should read it. And
now to work.

In this interval I've cleaned up right considerable correspondence. Hope this afternoon to get considerable packing done (love to pack) if it rains; if not, Mrs. Burrow, William Galt and I will hie to the woods behind camp in quest of small pine trees. William is busy path-building. The path out to Woods Hole lends itself to a very easy and delectable bit of engineering. The path up to Emily's cabin is a delight. William has also done some extensive and very artistic planting on the west bank of the croquet ground.

Monday, 11 a.m.

I had expected to get back to you before this. Rain yesterday afternoon and night, clearing early this morning with a shift of wind to West and North. So I think we should have dry weather, though the sky is grey. It is well that we are here for this chimney construction. I have to intercept no end of mistakes from the point of view of symmetry and design, and not seldom from the viewpoint of mechanics too. I hope the weather will not interrupt things.

I think the volume of Stevenson I had in mind is called *Across the Plains and Other Essays,* and that the Lantern Bearer story is among the other essays.

If Miss Bredow could mail me the list of the editors of *Philosophy of Science* (Malisoff), I'd be glad.

Feel sort o' anchored here with this chimney. These men can't be trusted out of sight and it would be too bad to have them construct an unbeautiful thing, when it might be satisfactory. The mason is nearly eighty, is stone deaf, has poor vision, is incomprehensible because of speech defect and an inveterate alcoholic! So it takes some integrative resourcefulness to handle the situation, believe you me!

This must go now. Have probably omitted several important items.

Sincerely,

Trigant Burrow

To Laura Spencer Portor New York City
Garrison-on-Hudson, New York January 23, 1937

Dear Laura:

Your distress, I know, is very deep, and you have been much in my thoughts since I read in yesterday's paper of William's death. (7)

What can I say? What can anyone say in a moment like this? And such moments multiply, and lengthen too, I suppose, with the years. But I suppose that out of the need and the necessity we contrive somehow to fashion within us some measure of renewed resistance or defense, and so we go on—or else we do not.

I think of you among those who find a way—who do not bow. And when I say that I know your distress is very great, I know at the same time the strength with which you will meet this hard circumstance. So that I do not link any thought of frailty with your distress. It is the deep distress itself—the relentless sense of loss not only for yourself but for his wife and children that I think of.

(7) William Portor, close relative of Mrs. Pope.

Brownie will have written you already, else she would send her love and sympathy with mine.

Always affectionately,

Trigant

To the parents of William E. Galt
Selma, Alabama

New York City
February 4, 1937

My dear Mr. and Mrs. Galt:

I received both your very kind letters mentioning your pleasure at William's having this trip to Florida. I hope it may mean very much to William, and to judge from the letter I had from him yesterday he seems to be profiting greatly, and I am sure he is using every effort to acquire the utmost benefit from this recess in the sunshine of Florida.

While I do not have to say how much I appreciate the spirit of your letters, it always makes me feel somewhat embarrassed to have you emphasize the significance of what I do for William. I wish I could have you both realize as fully as I do all that William is constantly doing for me. His thoughtfulness, his industry, his untiring zeal and interest in assisting my work, and above all, the way William has stood by me in my effort to bring a new concept of human life to human beings—these are services for which I could never repay him, and I would be glad if you would feel how great is my indebtedness to William and how much he has contributed to my work through the character and intelligence he has brought to it. So that if this trip means anything to William, you may feel sure that it is only due him that he have this opportunity for complete restoration.

The proofs continue to pour in day after day, and we are quite submerged beneath this added work.(8) However, Macmillan has handled the material very ably and there are few corrections. I hope when this book is off my hands to be able to give much continuous and consistent thought to William's thesis. As soon as he is ready for it, that, I feel, should become the central point of concentration in the work of the Foundation. But I assure you William will not be pushed in any way. Indeed he will not need to be. He is really keenly interested in this experimental project, and my efforts for a while will have to be directed chiefly toward holding him in check.

I must not keep you longer now, but want again to express my appreciation of your very kind and always appreciative letters.

With my kindest regards to you both and to Edward also,

Sincerely yours,

Trigant Burrow

To Professor Read Bain
Miami University

New York City
February 10, 1937

Dear Professor Bain:

I appreciate very much this thoughtful letter I have just had from you. . . .

Of course you will be most welcome at the laboratory at any time. My associates and I would be only too glad of the opportunity to talk with you and make our position as plain as we can. Maybe

(8) See note 4, p. 313.

much of the difficulty among our colleagues is just this matter of our 'position' which, as far as one's normal overconfidence and security have permitted, has been consistently that of patients inquiring into a common disorder of adaptation rather than that of the professionally competent physician or teacher who looks on, diagnoses and prescribes.

It would seem that with sufficient looking *in*, the need of diagnosis and treatment is automatically eliminated. This is really not said in any spirit of affectation. I do not think man is merely theoretically sick. I think he is actually so. I have not seen any exceptions. Certainly I am no exception. This is all so commonplace, I know, and I don't want to bore you with what must seem to you very trite. I have in mind that if you should at any time care to come in you will not be discouraged to do so through the mistaken belief that we are some sort of remote and knowing physicians of humanity or something equally tiresome, when all we are attempting to do is to give practical recognition to certain tensional discrepancies in man's feeling which I happened to come upon in the incidental affect frustrations of my earlier work with social groups. . . .

As I see it, or *sense* it, if you will permit me to say so, the disturbance in man's internal posture or physique, his tensional imbalance, is relatively quite slight and lends itself very readily to adjustment when he himself sets about adjusting this disorder within himself. But this disorder in internal neuromuscular tensions (like certain defects of vision, however slight) does greatly distort our outlooks and lead to marked discrepancies of behavior among us.

But we will consider these things some time together, and I am very glad to know that you are to be within closer range and that there may be the opportunity of seeing you here in New York.

With appreciation and my kind regards,

Sincerely yours,

Trigant Burrow

To Dr. Carl G. Jung   Lifwynn Camp, Merrill, N. Y.
Küsnacht, Switzerland   June 24, 1937

My dear Jung:

I have had in mind to send you a letter for many months. Indeed I seem often to have had you in mind, remembering my early tutelage with you in psychiatry and the lasting inspiration that I drew from your teaching and from the broad insights that underlay it. The special reason why for months I have wanted to write you is that it happened that when you were in this country last summer to lecture at the Harvard Tercentenary and later in New York I missed the opportunity of seeing you, as I should have liked to do, had I not been absent from the city and very closely occupied with the summer's chore of experimental work.

I was the more sorry not to have been in New York when you were there because of the very pleasant things I heard from many people who attended your lectures. You certainly gathered to you a distinguished group of people and they were most deeply appreciative of your trend. With you, as with so many other leaders in various domains of thought, it has seemed to me that your 'followers' have not by any means always sensed the true flavor of your teaching. In many cases they have rather distorted than illuminated it, and in not a few instances I have felt occasion to resent their over-zealous interpretations. So that to have had from personal friends of mine this sensitive response to your conceptions was the more welcome.

It has been good news to hear that you will occupy a chair at Yale this coming year. I hope that the winter will bring you occasionally to New York and that I may see you there. This would mean very much not only to me but to my associates as well. Perhaps you know that I am fortunate enough to have with me as my assistant Dr. Hans Syz—a true Züricher. You no doubt know his family there. Dr. Syz is very alert and able, and he possesses at the same time a certain quality of conservatism which is far too rare, I regret to say, among American psychiatrists. Indeed his reticent assents have been a far more welcome assistance to me and to our group than the all-too-ready conformities of the proverbial 'disciple.' Dr. Syz, I know, would enjoy meeting you, and because of the wisdom and originality of his insight as well as his outlook I feel sure you would enjoy knowing him.

As for the course of my own formulations, I hardly dare to hope that it will wholly recommend itself to you. The least I can say is that it has followed a direction which I could not in my wildest flights of fancy have dimly predicted at the outset of my studies with you. So that I fear that in the light of earlier precepts common to us both, you can only look upon me as a sort of thankless renegade. A renegade perhaps, but not thankless. Indeed of the many indebtednesses I owe to Adolf Meyer's thoughtfulness I have at no time failed to recognize that my greatest debt to him was my meeting you. For it was he, you will recall, who, at a period of very great indecisiveness with me, directed me to you and to your very vital seminars in Küsnacht. As for my subsequent divarications it is no little comfort to realize that whatever my digressions have been—however divergent from earlier traditions—you will not be critical of them in any narrow or ungenerous sense.

Perhaps by way of furthering your plans preliminary to a winter in this country you will be coming over to America some time in the summer. If so, and if you can spare the leisure for a visit to us here at Lifwynn Camp, I should be so very glad to have you motor over to see me. Life here does not abound in modern appointments, but you would, I think, not mind adapting yourself for a few days to the crudities of camp life. Anyhow it would be a very great pleasure to Mrs. Burrow and me, as well as to the rest of us here, if we might have the privilege of a visit from you.

In the meantime I hope I am not intruding unwelcomely upon you in asking you to accept—despite its shortcomings, and, I fear, its too obvious recreancies—a copy of a book I have recently published, *The Biology of Human Conflict*. It goes to you, as this does, with my very cordial greetings and ever warm regards.

Sincerely yours,

Trigant Burrow

To Dr. Hugh H. Young   Lifwynn Camp, Merrill, N. Y.
Baltimore, Maryland   July 2, 1937

Dear Hugh Young:

Your paper, 'Transurethral Resection of the Prostate,' came a few days ago, and I have read it with great interest—I only wish I could say, with equal comprehension. But my very limited acquaintance with the science of surgery quite precludes as adequate an understanding of your essay as I should wish. I think I may say, though, that I have read it with sufficient intelligence to realize how thoughtful and important a study this is. Of course it is just one of the many significant contributions that have marked your distinguished career in the field of surgery. Did I ever tell you that my first acquaintance with your work and its wide import was at a lecture you gave to the anatomy class at the University of Virginia in the year 1896? Incidentally I think I was never more thrilled in my life than at that demonstration of yours, and it may amuse you to know that in those days I was misguided enough actually to have believed that I was by nature cut out to be a surgeon!

But I have recently been interested to learn that, for all my surgical ineptness, our supposedly disparate fields of endeavor, strange as it may seem, are not without their lines of contact. Unless I have heard incorrectly, you are at the present time engaged in writing a book that describes your investigations of bi-sexual malformation, as well as your technique of surgical intervention in these cases. As you doubtless know, so much of my early work in psychoanalysis necessarily brought me face to face with the problem of psycho-sexual hermaphroditism ('psychic bi-sexuality') in the neurotic personality. The fact that there exists normally an anatomical homology between the organs of the two sexes suggests a substrate of bi-sexualism that is hardly insignificant in any truly biological scheme of personality adjustment. But as far as the 'personality' is concerned I incline to see the problem of human behavior as one involving bio-physical factors that rest upon a broader phylogenetic basis than students of mental disorders have commonly assumed.

Anyhow in my later work I have emphasized the organic foundations of personality and in the title of a book I have just published I have made bold to use the terms 'biology' and 'anatomy.' In the thought that this recent study may also lie within the field of your own wide interests I have wanted you to have a copy of it. I hope it may not seem a burden to you, though I realize that in its objective basis and method my thesis deviates no little from prevailing psychiatric trends. There are, however, problems in human adjustment which I think call definitely not only for a direct biological approach but also for a social expansion of accustomed points of departure in this field of science. In any event it is a great pleasure to ask you to accept a copy of this recent book of mine, *The Biology of Human Conflict*. It goes to you with grateful recognition and my very high personal regard. . . .

With my good wishes for a pleasant summer,

Sincerely yours,

Trigant Burrow

To a former patient   Lifwynn Camp, Merrill, N. Y.
                                                    July 5, 1937

Dear Mrs. T.:

Your good letter reached me a few days ago, and whether it 'merits' an answer or not it is a real pleasure to write you. There is something queer anyhow about people's attitude toward writing letters (if I may venture an aside). It seems to me so much easier to devote a few minutes to writing a letter than to devote months to not doing so. I suppose it depends upon whether in one's daily jaunting one likes better the rub of the traces or of the breeching.

I think it is very earnest of you—I think it shows a real consistency of purpose that you should labor to read my book(9) In saying 'labor to read it' I am speaking not less earnestly. It is really a study and, in a sense, I suppose a difficult study. I meant it to be so—anything but that type of journalistic treatise on 'psychology' that so readily lends itself to the popularization that is mere vulgarization.

But if this essay has not gusto, it has, I think, a certain definiteness and objectivity that will not be unwelcome to the student of human behavior in these undoubtedly troublous and disturbed times. It is a pleasure too to know that Mr. T. was instrumental in your having the book. It has been a relief to get this task off my hands. Writing a book of this sort, even with the very able assistance I have always at hand, is no light undertaking.

You may not *know* biology, but I doubt that my book requires much biological knowledge. Like the rest of us, interiorly you *are*

(9) See note 4, p. 313.

biological. You could not eat or walk or breathe except as you are a biological organism. Breathing, it is true, like many physiological functions, is purely automatic, but so many other functions including even walking call for very complicated and very delicate muscular adjustments that must be definitely learned by the individual in the process of his growth. This learning, this *knowing*, is dependent upon an internal balance of adjustment that demands correct internal *feeling*. It is the biology of internal feeling that interests me in this book and that can interest and appeal to you no less.

I can well understand the interest, and the exactions too, that you and Mr. T. have in those four sensitive and alert youngsters about you, with all their intense and restless and, as things are, necessarily unsatisfying activities. I think you are both fortunate in the fact that the community mind is far more thoughtful today, and that it is increasingly challenging the intelligence of the young, as it was not and as it did not do a few years ago. The social trend of those times with all the recalcitrance of thought and feeling they brought have left their mark upon the two generations, the young and the old, that were involved in them. In no small degree you escaped all that because, as it happened, that moment of confused and distorted views fell just midway between your own youth and the youth of your children. . . .

You will be interested to know that according to reports my book is being very widely read by the more thoughtful students in the field of behavior, and I have just heard from the publishers that it is to be brought out in England. Only a few reviews have come in so far, but these have all been favorable, and Macmillan tells me they do not look for the fuller response to a book of this kind for several months. But I mustn't be bragging any further at the moment or I shall be taxing even your loyal sympathies.

The days are lovely here, as you will remember. The summer's program of work with us is an ambitious one, but an environment like this greatly furthers the days' accomplishments.

Thanks again for your letter, and my ever warm remembrances at home,

Sincerely yours,

Trigant Burrow

Lifwynn Camp, Merrill, N. Y.
July 24, 1937

My dear Mr. L.:

Your letter (undated) was forwarded to me here at the Foundation's Summer Research Station. I am sorry you felt any hesitation to phone Dr. Syz with a view to calling on him during your recent visit to New York. Perhaps in a personal interview Dr. Syz could more readily have made clear to you our feeling about what has seemed to us your too sanguine espousal of our work and aims in the absence of a more solid basis for its acceptance.

I appreciate your interest in what my associates and I are attempting to do, and I appreciate what seems to me your natural intuitions toward our thesis. But I think you will not be impatient with me or think me unduly dissuasive if I say to you frankly how shy I am of even the most resolute interest or intuition, and of the over-enthusiasm they tend to beget, where there is lacking the opportunity of definitive laboratory acquaintance with one's own all too illusory 'I'-mindedness. This implies no disparagement of you whatsoever. This 'I'-mindedness marks an inadvertence in adjustment that is race-wide.

Your idea of coming to New York to intercede with outstanding journalists and, through them, with the wider community is generous of you, but again I fear your plan savors more of fervor than of fundamentals. Such a course would necessarily remove you from your accustomed social and economic environment. So complete an uprooting from your habitual soil would, I fear, entail serious mental and economic hazards for you. In view of my recently published outline of our position, it would seem to me the clearer policy for me to await the community's spontaneous reaction to it. But I do appreciate your sympathetic response to our endeavors and your kindly interest to promote their wider acquaintance.

Very sincerely yours,

Trigant Burrow

To Dr. Hanford Henderson   Lifwynn Camp, Merrill, N. Y.
Tryon, North Carolina   August 25, 1937

Dear Hanford:

I cannot tell you how pleased I am to hear that you have turned again to your writing. I am pleased not only on my own account and your readers generally, but because I do not see how it is possible for you to be in the fullest health as long as this form of expression so inherent and spontaneous with you is denied you. So that if you find yourself now in sufficient physical trim to turn to your desk once more, I shall look for yet greater health than you have known for a long time.

I am very curious to know what sort of writing you will in the main devote yourself to. I wish it might be about you and your experiences throughout your various contacts and travels. Anyone who is the natural born raconteur that you are should, I should think, excel chiefly as an essayist. But these are things in which I am little versed. I guess I shall have to leave to you both the theme and the manner of it! Do you dictate or do you write in longhand? I imagine that penmanship comes very easily to you—your writing is so legible. My own pen could never start a sentence till I had finished it—so retarded a penman am I. That is why I write you in type this way, though I really know better and feel no little guilty with each offense.

I shall never forget having once sent a letter to my dear mother that had been copied in type. It *al*most estranged us! The affront was only equalled by my older brother when he suggested to her that she discard her horses and purchase an automobile like the rest of our neighbors. You may be sure that no one in the family had the temerity to broach the subject again. The Burrows continued to ride or drive of an afternoon in the park. Such in our household was the disparity between the ideas of the passing generation and the suddenly speeded-up pace of us oncomers. I do so wish you had known my mother. You would have found instant sympathy and understanding in each other's essential feeling, notwithstanding your greater tolerance and flexibility toward much that is coming to pass in these turbulent years.

Dr. Syz, Emily and I returned a week ago from a very delightful trip to Harvard. Dr. Syz and I wanted to gather together some instruments we had had constructed there for our use in our improvised laboratory here. I am much interested in securing some graphs with which perhaps to differentiate between the lesser or 'partitive' patterns of adaptation and the patterns that belong to man's more primary behavior as an organic whole. Nothing may come of this experimental effort to discriminate these two physiological patterns, but at least the preliminary tests are proving of interest even if nothing significant results from them.

On our trip we went from here straight to the coast. This brought us to Portsmouth, and on for the night to Rye (set down in your address book The Farragut Hotel). The next morning we motored down to Boston. While in that part of the country I felt I had to see Cape Cod. So out we sped along the concave edge of the hook to its very tip at Provincetown, and back again the next day along the convex arc to the south. It was great fun. The heat was merciless throughout the drive, and I didn't learn until my return that all one has to do to temper the air when motoring on a hot day is to place in the ventilator a few cents' worth of dry ice. They tell me it lasts several hours and provides you with an air-conditioned car. I pass this on to you and Peggy and Jimmy.

Of course I'd love to have that long letter after you read my book, and I do feel so honored that you are giving to it the careful reading that you are. If it should stir you to write me, I don't have to say how deeply I would value your wise criticism and, I hope, suggestions.

Today there is a tinge of fall in the air. As a tinge it is very welcome, but as a prodromal of fall I could well spare its premature crispness.

Brownie sends you her love as always with mine.

Affectionately,

Trigant

To Laura Spencer Portor   Lifwynn Camp, Merrill, N. Y.
Garrison-on-Hudson, New York   September 23, 1937

Dear Laura:

Your letters yesterday to Brownie and me were a comforting reassurance. With our firmly rooted medical traditions both of us had begun to build up a sense of apprehension that was not a little disconcerting. But I gather that with your accustomed resilience ('come-back' in Manhattanese) you have really done awfully well since the operation. The 'scampering' of the children and your undiminished joy in it amply warrant, I believe, this clinical view!

Brownie and I are enjoying camp just now with especial gusto, as is usual with us this time of year. There are few of us here and there are so many things we like to do about the place. This year we are quite eager over the building of a badminton court. Just why our eagerness over a badminton court in our arthritic old age, you probably ask yourself with no little wonder—perhaps even misgiving. I seem to hear you say: 'I have it—second child-hood!' Perhaps this is the correct diagnosis. On the other hand, I have a hunch (it may prove a mere defense-reaction) that we are building—foolishly building a dream play-ground for the grand-children of our dreams. We haven't spoken a word of it to each other—we just couldn't give voice to such folly, seeing that neither of our children is married or, as far as we know, has any immediate inclination to be. But secretly, silently, I believe this—or something close kin to it—is what we are furtively up to, and yet I do not see why this may not be true and your diagnosis still correct—senility with regression!

But with your and Francis' delight in your own country place and in all that it means to your *actual* grandchildren, you will not be unsympathetic to Brownie and me (whatever lurking pathology it may disclose) in building play-grounds for the unborn children of our dreams as for the children of others.

We shall be staying on here and giving form to our phantasies until October the first. Then New Yorkward. As you say, I hope we'll see each other soon. . . .

With a great deal of love from Brownie and me,

Affectionately,

Trigant

To Jessie Sampter   Merrill, Clinton County, N. Y.
Palestine   September 30, 1937

Dear Miss Sampter:

After hearing Miss Guggenheimer read your interesting letter to
her I could not refrain from asking her to let me say something to
you also when she should be writing you. What I wanted to say
is this: First, how deeply grateful I feel for all your interest and
sympathy in what I have, with a few co-workers, been attempting
to do. I haven't put things awfully well. The truth is that the
essence of the matter isn't easily put well. I should hate to mislead
anyone. I should hate to mislead you. But with the inevitable disparity of background among people, to mislead at times seems
equally inevitable. I think, if I were you, I would not be too confident that Krishnamurti and I are of the same trend. He has the
words perhaps, but not the music. Or, if you like (most people
would like, no doubt) he has the music and not the words. My point
is only that he hasn't both— he hasn't coördinated the organism's in-
tero- with its extero-ceptive function. I heard Krishnamurti lecture.
I read a book of his. He is fascinating. He is exquisitely facile
mentally. I love all that sort of thing but, like so many things I
love, participation in it is sheer voluptuous indulgence with me.
It lacks the robustness of actuality, of direct contact with the raw
materials of reality. But here are words again and not music or,
as I said before, vice versa. It isn't the total organism functioning
in coördination with its kind in their common relation to the
environment. That's a physiological problem. That it is internal
makes it not less but more physiological. It is physiology not

looked at or worded over, so to speak. We are—all of us—such picture people and all our pictorial productions resting upon the wide and limitless canvas of 'I'. Something must be done. Something will be done. Something is, I devoutly believe, at this moment *being done*. It is this process which in a way we of this Foundation seem trying to articulate—not in words or in music or in any external combination of the two, but through their intrinsic coördination in actual communal (not communistic—that's the image again—but physiological) living. Your head and my head won't reach our goal, no more will your heart or mine, however ardent our attack. The problem is biological, and it is internal, and I know of nothing so baffling. For, try as I will, it is with head or heart, with words or music, that I vainly reach for it.

There is a clue though, just a faint glimmer of a clue. This summer, Dr. Syz and I and the rest of us here worked with some apparatus we had had constructed at the Harvard Psychological Laboratory. These experiments give the actual support of objective tracings to my internal experimentation over the years. But even these scientific tracings, the responses of this multiple kymograph [in recording respiratory movements] concomitant to certain internally observable eye-postures (postures which quite exclude the symbolic function), can decoy us too. They too, in spite of their objectivity, indeed *because* of their objectivity, can lead us wholly astray. They can lead to an entire misplacing of emphasis upon the exteroceptive and external. And so it would seem that our quest is beset with snare and delusion on every hand. We can only pursue the clue, hold steadfastly to its indications, and if we falter in these, return again and again to our basic physiological clue, however infinitesimally small. This, I take it, is of the essence of research, and it is I believe amid the paths of research that man's course lies. For research relates the internal organism to the external environment and so establishes finally the balance that is the essential law of life.

I had not meant to intrude at such length upon you and Miss Guggenheimer. I just felt I wanted to say something in response to your very gracious and interesting letter to her in regard to an undertaking which in our separate ways we pursue together toward a common purpose.

Sincerely yours,

Trigant Burrow

To Mrs. Burrow   'Margie's' [Merrill House, Merrill, N. Y.]
New York   October 1, 1937, Friday 2.15 p.m.

Dear Brownie:

Just a note. I'd meant to write last night after you left. But Miss Flora, Mr. Shields and I examined 'lists' for a half hour, and then I dictated a paragraph or two to be included in Miss Flora's letter to Miss Sampter (Palestine), and the paragraphs became quite an essay.

But the real occasion of my writing is to try to give at least a feeble expression of my appreciation of what you were to us all this summer. I realize the enormous amount of work it entailed, the loss of rest, the innumerable items of concern, the wise management, the constant thought, and with it all the unfailing graciousness. It was a rare achievement and only the rare person that you are could have half way accomplished it all.

With love,

Devotedly,

Trigant

To Blanch Pattison(10)   New York City
Chevy Chase, Maryland   November 14, 1937

Dear Cousin Blanch:

For over a year I have watched the succeeding numbers of *The Atlantic Monthly* in the hope of discovering among its pages Uncle Dick's unique description of that fatal evening in Ford's Theatre when Mr. Lincoln was shot. But so far I have watched in vain. When lately I saw among the articles in *The Atlantic* a newly discovered essay of Washington Irving's and felt the interest of this hitherto unpublished record, I was reminded again of the story of Uncle Dick that lies unseen amid other remnants of the past in the chest in your garret—a story that I feel sure is told in all the direct, honest simplicity of its simple and sincere narrator.

Can I not persuade you to part with its message for my sake and for the sake of so many other readers of a generation that is now rapidly passing?

The editor of *The Atlantic*—Mr. Ellery Sedgwick—is the kindliest and most approachable of men. My own personal acquaintance with him is but the meagerest. But from mutual friends I have heard only what is most appreciative of him. Then there is Virginia Watson of Harpers. I am sure she would be equally gracious in response to your sending Uncle Dick's essay to her. I should think you'd want to get it off if for no other reason than that you wouldn't any longer be receiving these tiresome importunities from me! The reason of my persistence is my feeling that here is probably a really valuable and interesting document and that it would contribute in no small way to the historic interest of America as well as to the memory of the gentle and noble spirit that was 'Uncle Dick.'

(10) A cousin of Mrs. Burrow's.

And what of Florida? When are you going down? Unless my own plans go amiss I shall certainly number among those who are rejoining Clearwater's winter colony this year.

Love to you and Miss Jeanie in which Brownie joins me.

As always,

Trigant Burrow

To Dr. E. S. Kilgore   New York City
San Francisco   November 23, 1937

Dear Dr. Kilgore:

I have received your letter of November 11 with which you enclosed the statement drawn up by your committee in reference to the question of governmental participation in medical service. It is hardly necessary to say that this communication was of great interest to me as it must be to physicians generally.

In replying I should like to enlarge somewhat upon the statement of mine published by The American Foundation.(11) Naturally this statement was written from the background of the research work in the field of behavior-disorders I have carried on for a number of years under the sponsorship of The Lifwynn Foundation.

I should like to say at the outset that the lack of properly distributed medical care throughout the community, of which there is no question, seems to me *only one expression* of our widespread social inadequacy, and that there is needed above everything else a clear understanding of all the underlying conditions responsible for our present quite general social disorganization. The specific researches of my associates and myself have necessarily centred

(11) *American Medicine—Expert Testimony Out of Court*, New York, The American Foundation, 1937, 2 vols., pp. LXXIV, 1435.

upon the deeper-seated psychophysiological manifestations of behavior-disorders as these are inevitably reflected in man's outer social symptomatology. Accordingly the question of the social aspects of medical research and practice is from the standpoint of our investigations quite inseparable from these deeper biological implications.

In considering the difficulties and possible dangers involved in the socialization of medicine we fail to realize that medicine *is* socialized and that it is becoming more and more so through a natural process of social evolution. We have to discriminate, though, between the socialization of medicine as research and its socialization as practice. Preventive medicine and research are of their nature community-wide, while medicine as practice seems to me to come under a different category. Moreover, the whole question of socialization from the point of view of practice is much obscured by personal and economic considerations quite irrelevant to the essential issue.

In the field of physical disease the bacteriologists were the outstanding socializers of medicine. They removed disease from the individual by first removing it from the community in which the individual is an integral element. The findings of the bacteriologists have thus greatly contributed to the efficiency and dependability of the physician from the point of view of practice where it is question of the treatment of infectious disorders. The position of my associates and myself of The Lifwynn Foundation, like that of investigators in the field of bacteriology, is precisely that nervous disorders are a community condition. They arise primarily from certain broadly existing ineptitudes in behavior-adjustment which are incidental to the adaptations of civilization generally and which therefore affect the race of man at large. Naturally, then, the socialization of medicine—of medical psychiatry, for instance—is hardly to the point.

Despite the apprehension of the practitioners of four or five decades ago lest bacteriology should encroach upon their usefulness and curtail their economic security in the community, there has been no conflict whatever between the recognition and encouragement of efforts toward the socialization of medicine in the field of infectious disorders from the standpoint of research, and the practice of the physician in his private function. Quite the contrary. Likewise with such community disorders as nervous and mental disease. For when physicians shall have abandoned their tendency to maintain mere arbitrary *ideas about* nervous disorders and insanity (their psycho-this, psycho-that and psycho-the other thing) and shall consistently direct their efforts toward discovering the objective, physiological conditions determining the intrinsic health of both physician and patient as integral elements in a common community disorder (crime, war, social and economic conflicts), we need have no fear of undermining the status of the physician in his private relation to the individual patient. On the contrary, the effect will be greatly to increase the physician's practical usefulness in his special function of physician or repairer in respect to the specific disorder of this or that individual. Neither, it seems to me, will there be any question of a patient's lacking proper medical care. These two considerations—that of the physician and his remuneration and that of the patient and his treatment —will be mutually conserved within this larger compass.

I hope this statement may not appear to your committee to lie entirely outside the field of your inquiry. In view of the years my associates and I have devoted to social experimentation in the biophysical maladjustments of man's organism, it seems to me necessary to emphasize the need for a scientific approach to these deep-seated behavioral tendencies and their disorganizing influence upon the community rather than attempt to develop plans for dealing with specific social problems, however crying a need they may represent symptomatically, in the absence of a consideration of these more objectively observable maladaptations.

Very sincerely yours,

Trigant Burrow

CHAPTER 11

EMPHASIS ON INSTRUMENTAL RECORDINGS

As has been said, Burrow's group investigations stemmed from his mutual analysis with Clarence Shields. From the beginning the association of the two men constituted the core of the phyloanalytic work, and resulted in Burrow's demarcation of contrasting patterns of tension. For many years their studies demanded uninterrupted collaboration, and the letters exchanged during their infrequent separations were not kept. The reader, therefore, has had little opportunity for a direct acquaintance with this important relationship of Burrow's. In order to fill the gap the editors are including at this point excerpts from Mr. Shields' presidential report for 1946–47, The Lifwynn Foundation's twentieth year.

To be accurate and at the same time brief, the present research began when Dr. Burrow and I first met and shortly thereafter realized our common behavioral interests. This interest in human motivation had been outstanding in the lives of both of us long before we had met. And for both of us it had been a powerful interest. With me, this interest took the commonplace, insignificant form of persistent search without knowing what I was searching for. If I read books, for example, it was solely in order to find the answer without even knowing the question. But the interest, the drive was none-the-less imperative. With Dr. Burrow, this same overpowering interest took such orderly form as culminated in those of his early, brilliant papers that were based upon his 'principle of primary identification' thesis.

If, then, in meeting Dr. Burrow, if during the early years of association with him that followed, I considered myself most fortunate, it is hardly likely that anyone else would have had a less grateful reaction in the same situation . . .

In the association of Dr. Burrow and myself, the common behavioral interest, and the study it provoked, consistently topped every other interest. From the very beginning we were committed to a program of mutual analysis. And this study, this research did not at any time present easy going—not even in the very early days. Innately, both of us were fully prepared for a heavy assignment, though at first the prospect lay only within the bounds of Dr. Burrow's psychoanalytic practice. But, when we came actually to work together in the same office, then little by little, as was inevitable in a program of mutual analysis, the unexpected began to happen. Briefly, the 'I'-persona—to use the term Dr. Burrow coined later—the 'I'-persona of each intruded upon the scene. Neither could brook the observations of the other. Our relation became strained. The tempo of the strain increased and turned to mutual pain. There was now rudely thrust upon us a hitherto unsuspected behavioral element. The indomitable 'rightness' of each had obtruded itself and we were wholly unprepared to meet it. To say the least, we were both chagrined. Grave questioning arose between us. But we held on. We had a job to do. And so we stood by.

While Dr. Burrow and I were drawn together by a common behavioral interest—the same interest that, fundamentally, still binds us; the same interest that, fundamentally, binds the rest of the group, as it binds all mankind—we soon began to learn that we, like all mankind, were, after all, merely seeking an ideal, a mental solution, in our approach to human behavior and to each other. We learned this not through intellectual speculation but through actual experience in our relation to one another. Accordingly, we paid a severe penalty. Both of us mutually paid this penalty. There were the unavoidable reactions of disagreement, irritation, resentment, blame and anger. And in time, we began to sense the tendency toward a rift—the behavioral rift that inevitably follows in the wake of the activities of the 'I'-persona—the same rift one may see enacted throughout the interrelational behavior of man anywhere, any time. And this turn of events was, for Dr. Burrow and me, most disheartening. In the beginning it was merely a surprise, later it was a downright shock.

... There was, too, the increasing, the impelling desire to withdraw, to flee. And yet, through it all we managed somehow to stand by. Unlike the interrelational scene on all sides, where a rift inevitably means separation or else tricky compromise, we stood by. The impulse to flee, though, became overpowering. This overpowering drive to quit and flee was as painful as the persistently recurring irritation and anger. Everything within us and around us charged us to quit. But we went on. We stood by.

It was this standing by in face of behavioral disaster that constituted the core of our early association. Nothing more, just this going ahead, this standing by on the part of two individuals. And it happened just this way

—rather unobtrusively and unnoticed in the midst of behavioral affect and pain. It was this very early relationship—a relationship that should have cracked up but did not—that embodied the core of both the insurmountable problem and the consistent achievement.

Needless to say, the behavioral conflict continued, but we also continued to stand by and the study went forward. But it was not Dr. Burrow's study; it was not my study. It was not Dr. Burrow's study of me or my study of Dr. Burrow. It was not a study of the behavior of two individuals by two individuals. It was a circumstance—a nuclear circumstance. It was a nuclear, social behavioral circumstance. And this nuclear circumstance was characterized not by the interest of one but of two organisms. It could have been any two organisms. There was, for instance, the study undertaken by Miss Hölljes and myself. But the number was immaterial. The sole innovation, the sole requirement was that the two, the three or the thirty-three stand by, when the hell of their own—of man's—affect-behavior was laid bare and each was overpoweringly impelled to withdraw.

This nuclear circumstance was not planned. It was not sought after. It was thrust upon us. We hardly knew what was happening. All we knew was that, expecting a congenial relationship in the pursuance of a congenial task in a congenial field, we were suddenly and rudely confronted with a dark, forbidding behavioral dilemma that erased all mental aspiration and left us stranded with the unseemly, with the virulent material of our affect-antagonisms. Here was truly the stuff of behavioral tragedy. But we went on. The study went forward. For in this standing by on the part of two organisms when, by all the rules of accustomed behavior, they should have fled each other, lay the rudiment of an altered pattern of behavior—an altered frame of reference that not only commanded a new and fresh outlook upon, but that also made possible an objective approach to, the subjective phenomena of interrelational behavior.

It was, then, the standing by on the part of two organisms, and the nuclear behavioral circumstance it represented, that formed the background for all of Dr. Burrow's later discoveries and constituted the mainstay of the development we now know as phylobiology. But in the meantime the interrelational dilemma still held sway. The going was hard. There was no precedent. There was no reward in the offing. There was no offing, no horizon. And, too, no trail of endeavor had ever been so thickly pockmarked with failures. Each was on his own. Neither could help the other. There was only one thing we could do, and that we did. We stood by. We had a job to do and we held to this job. When all that we had counted real lay shattered at our feet—both the hidden bad and the seeming good, both the subversive wrong and the universally accepted 'normal' right, one's own and that of others—we stood by, not idly and yet not knowingly, not blindly and yet not sensing wholly. For, in these early days we did not know that the nuclear circumstance of this impersonal standing by on the part of two organisms—each standing alone the while both stood by—constituted the rich soil out of which there later grew Dr. Burrow's clear, physiological distinction between ditention and cotention, between that which belongs to the neurosis, crime and war, and that which belongs to the total, organismic central constant of the phylum, man. And so, standing by, we went on.

In this nuclear event, the behavior of each was equal and common. The opposing rightness of each, the opposing wrongness of each, was equal and common. In this equality and commonness lay the essence of wholeness and health, the foundation of growth, the reassertion of man as a living organism. But it was only a beginning. Organismic man was and still is confronted with the 'I'-persona. This is the real situation. This is the problem.

Dr. Burrow and Mr. Shields returned to Clearwater in December 1937 for their second winter. By this time they had become intensely interested in determining whether instrumentally measurable differences in physiological functioning accompanied the two attentional modes demarcated in their studies. Preliminary results were first obtained using the equipment of other laboratories. Later the Foundation itself established an instrumental laboratory containing apparatus for measuring respiration, for recording eye-movements both electrically and photographically, and for studying brain-wave patterns. Dr. Burrow worked intensively on these experiments, and began to publish results in 1941.(1) A complete summary of the findings is included in the appendix to *The Neurosis of Man* and to *Science and Man's Behavior*.

In 1938 Dr. Burrow's physicians advised a less intensive program of work. The following year he and Mrs. Burrow moved to an attractive house which they called 'Summer Hill' in the Greens Farms section of Westport, Connecticut, although he continued to spend part of each week at his laboratory in New York. Both his son and daughter were married in 1939, Jack to Helen Stapleton of New York City, and Emily to her father's long-time associate, Hans Syz. Their marriages brought much happiness to Dr. and Mrs. Burrow.

(1) 'Kymograph Records of Neuromuscular (Respiratory) Patterns in Relation to Behavior Disorders,' *Psychosomatic Medicine*, 1941, vol. III, pp. 174–86.

To Mrs. Burrow
New York

Clearwater, Florida
December 5, 1937
Sunday morning
Im grünen Winkel

Dear Brownie:

Well, I never felt greater need for you than on the afternoon of our arrival here! As I look back now, our extremity was largely a matter of fatigue from a five days' journey. But anyhow everything seemed suddenly hopeless. The evening was cold and windy, the house unaccustomed, the servant strange, and altogether we could see little to live for! To have to unpack bags and order the next day's food seemed an undertaking too overwhelming to be contemplated and yet retain one's sanity. I told myself that you would turn to without a moment's hesitation and even joyously and that you would adjust the whole scheme of things in no time. It did no good. In fact it made matters worse, for you were at a distance of precisely thirteen hundred miles. It was hell!

As a matter of fact the house is very attractive and comfortable and the servant, 'Becky,' really seems the proverbial 'treasure.' Furthermore the Tilleys show every indication of wanting us to be adequately provided for in every way. I suppose it was just the combination of fatigue, nightfall, three men and their bags! Somehow they seemed to weigh on us so that we haven't unpacked them yet! Your initial menus were a God-send. They simply saved the day, because it was when we went into the kitchen that our suicidal trend reached its crisis. I can smile now, but really it was ghastly on that anthracite Friday of our arrival!

But now to brighter things. Jack has shown himself the world's champion companion. He certainly has been capable and resourceful in every way, as well as most thoughtful of us both.

I hope you know that there was no real, objective ground whatever for our mood of despondency when we first got here. The reaction was wholly subjective, I assure you.

When do you plan coming down? I want you to come, of course, when *you* want to. I was just wondering when that would be.

Jack is quite in love with Clearwater incidentally. I know you will be—and that it will be mutual.

Love from us all,

Devotedly,

Trigant

To William E. Galt   Clearwater, Florida
New York   December 11, 1937
                                 Saturday evening at 6.00

Dear William:

...As to 'the depression—or whatever it is.' It is this clause in apposition that interests me: 'whatever it is.' For this unknown phenomenon I can discuss. It is precisely this X of human experience subjectively that has so captured my curiosity objectively. This unknown quantity—this objective riddle I have 'known'— that is, felt all my life subjectively—felt and been dominated by. It is only in recent years, as you know, that I have attempted to de-label it and, setting out anew, tried to give it objective meaning and subordinate it to a larger principle of behavior more in keeping with the total motivation of my organism. 'From a subjective point of view' to quote from your letter 'things have been very difficult for me' too. It might have been 'depression' with me. It has often been. But of late it was not. It doesn't matter. It is of one cloth with what is known as depression in that both states presume for the 'I' a denied privilege or right or happiness *for itself*. This state has troubled and weighed upon me and interrupted my efficiency and accomplishment in the last week or so. It is always ready at hand to lay hold on me. This X, or unknown factor, is associated in some not yet clearly determined manner with the symbol, with convergence and with some sort of internal (visceral?) change that has gotten hooked up with it. This is the objective side and the only scientific side of the *unknown*, whether external or internal to the organism. With this I begin to work—with this I *hate* to work or rather *I* hate to work. Naturally! It is I that is at stake. The subjective be-all and end-all. Here's a man's job in contrast to the monkey's. But this man must rudely interrupt himself if he is to take this to the P.O. for the 9 o'clock mail tonight. And so 'no more now.' Will go on in a very early installment with this and other mutually congenial and mutually applicable themes.

Yours,

Trigant Burrow

To William E. Galt Clearwater, Florida
New York December 15, 1937

Dear William:

. . . But to return once more to the place I was when I prematurely concluded my last letter to you—for once I don't have to ask you, 'what was I talking about?'—I was saying that 'whatever it is' (to quote your phrase), the unknown factor, the objective X in the sphere of man's subjective feeling, is common, and that this awareness and acceptance is two-thirds of the battle in our effort toward a clear, objective recognition of its structure and function in the organism's economy. It is Emily's, it is Jack's, it is Dr. Thompson's, it is Mr. Shields', it is mine. I was thinking in the night of the aspects of man's neurosis expressed in the primitive manifestation of anthropomorphism—of his abject terror in face of these images of his own creating. It was even then a form of semiomorphism—an arbitrary investment of the symbol with substance and power—identical in mechanism with the semiotic reactions we know today in the 'normal' affects with which we invest ourselves and others. We think early man very primitive indeed but are we less undeveloped, less immature, less primitive in the subordination of our internal feeling and thinking to the mercy of images that possess no more reality than the superstitious projections of 'early' man. Man is still early—too early to know how early he is. But more images cannot outcountenance the images we already cherish. As I have for some years studied this distortion in man's behavior with a fair degree of objective consistency and consensual control—thanks to you and others of our unit—I see no recourse—however faint as yet its intimations—but the internal effort we have of late been directing toward regaining possession of the symbolic (or that element in the symbolic) mechanism that centres chiefly in the visual-mental (psychovisual) or partitive segment of it. Philosophy (that is, morality when it suits me, immorality when it doesn't), religion, character (as ordinarily motivated) and psychology of the psychiatric or psychoanalytic type will, as we know, not avail man. It is cotention, integration, co-centration, dub it what we will, that has given us the first definite physiological hint of the objective nature, as of the objective remedy, for our race disorder of adaptation. Because of its retroactive affect or partitive repercussion man's mentally convergent focus is throughout fallacious. As some George Bernard Shaw of a hundred years hence (or tomorrow) may put it: 'Symbolic mentation is the squintessence of human maladaptation.'

I think we are coming through *physiologically* in spite of our images. I think there are now the definite signs of it. There is still a period—a relatively brief period of frustration and pain to be gone through perhaps, but believe me 'the morning of manhood is risen' and with it the old partitive cry of separateness and egoistic isolationism among us, 'I am I, thou art thou, I am low, thou art high' becomes but a faint and distant memory. . . .

'But now no more'

Sincerely,

Trigant Burrow

To Mrs. Burrow
New York

Clearwater, Florida
Sunday morning at 11.45
December 19, 1937

Dear Brownie:

I hope Emily has adequate recommendations and guarantees from her old lady tenants. Old ladies are usually just a little more immoral—a little more craven than any other variety of the species. That is why I so earnestly hope you and Emily will never become old ladies despite the prevalent tendency to do so. I recommend watching these two old girls, if Emily wants to assure her ninety-five dollars monthly.

I am so glad you are looking forward to your coming down to Florida. I think you will be coming under rather auspicious circumstances. Everything is running so smoothly here. I am not doing *one thing*, for example, in preparation for Mrs. Wallace—except to close my collar and put on a tie! That's the extent of our Clearwater formalities.

. . . It's a little too warm in the sun for comfort.

Love to Jack, Emily and William,

Devotedly,

Trigant

To Mrs. H. A. Sill   Clearwater, Florida
New York   January 9, 1938

Dear Mrs. Sill:

Your letter is still unanswered and now I have had a note from
your brother also. It seems likely that he will come to Florida
and he is good enough to say that if he does come and should be
in this section he will not fail to look us up. I certainly hope we
shall see him.

But your letter: What shall we say to each other? Some day some
one acquainted with literature and folk-lore must gather the many
passages that record intuitively our early physiological wisdom
and that say in song and poetry out of the body's natural coördination what we are now in our maturer sophistication trying to
give expression to in the more cultural patterns of biology and the
laboratory. 'Be still and know that I am God' expresses the very
keynote of this basic intuitive wisdom of man as a race. But our
letters are not still—yours and mine. What we say to each other is,
as you put it, full of concern 'for me.' It is not still. We have
discovered the clue to our restlessness—the restlessness of 'me'—
but apparently we are all too restless now to make use of it. The
habit of *me* is stronger than the clue.

And so with Alfreda,(2) so with your brother, so with us all. The
deeper wisdom will prevail, I think though, in spite of us and our
sophistication. So what does it matter that Alfreda makes *her*
way, and you *yours* and I *mine?* What need for concern?

We are having the right conditions here, I would say, and our
work goes on with us here as there. The closeness to the out-of-
doors of which we take ready advantage means very much to
Mr. Shields as to me.

(2) Mrs. Sill's daughter, later Mrs. William E. Galt.

Alfreda seems to be sailing with the right wind more and more. This new job ought to prove very congenial and productive. She should go ahead now. I hear, by the way, that she has her eye on the governorship!

Remember me to Alfreda and let me know how the new essay is coming on.

Sincerely,

Trigant Burrow

To William E. Galt Clearwater, Florida
New York January 25, 1938
Tuesday, 8.15

Dear William:

Your good and welcome letter came this morning. I was, as always, so glad to have this full account of you. If it was the response to a cumulative stimulus, it was worth many letters of mine to have this thoughtful word from you.

As it happened your letter reached me at an especially welcome moment. I had been troubled about you—I guess I always am when you are troubled. In fact I had been wakened in the night out of a troubled sleep—you were preoccupied and depressed and at the same time trying to carry on. There were features of the dream that readily led back to my thoughts of the preceding day and to the thought of your conflict in particular—the obligations of work and the preoccupations of phantasy. Can I 'help'? Not as others can 'help,' not as I used to believe I could help. I can offer you wholeheartedly the assurance that you are not alone in your conflict, that I am with you in it—and more than that I am here to acknowledge that this conflict that is seemingly yours and mine and other peoples' is of a nature that quite excludes the division into parts we have been taught to designate as yours and mine and other one's, that it is a thing of one substance, one tissue, as you and I and others are of one tissue, of one substance.

It is strange how insulated we have come to feel toward one another. We could not possibly doubt—not any of us—the oneness and continuity of the social structure that unites us symbolically as people of a common language and meaning. We accept without question the common tie of 'meaning.' But beneath meaning and before meaning ever was, there was the structure out of which all our meaning has been fashioned—the common bodily structure and function that have given us the building-material of all our symbols, all our common implements of understanding and social contact.

In a sense there isn't depression, there isn't even conflict. Where tissues are torn apart, there is pain—inevitably pain. We just haven't yet thought of *man's* unity and continuity in terms of organically inseparable tissues and functions. In our restriction to the lens of the personal and partitive we know division only of *the* man—the man that is I, or that through some process of inner identification may be felt as if I (love, sympathy, possession, etc.). And we have not sensed that this lens that has led to our false perceptions, and to feelings that are correspondingly false, has been fashioned within and *of* our own common tissue, that we must return to this common tissue within us if we are to correct our common error of vision and of feeling. This is the philosophy of *integration*. The philosophy. But integration isn't philosophy. Not any more than a surgical operation is philosophy. Like surgery, integration is the reuniting of tissues that have been torn apart. If the process is not accomplished with sutures, it is nevertheless a process of suturing. It is the restoration of an organismic commissure that has been artificially severed.

Your pain, *my* pain, then, is the way each of us artificially looks at the pain of man through the division that is precisely you and me. A manner of healing, though, is definitely in process among us, and therefore, being organismic, among the race of man. We have gone far. We shall go farther, finding heart in what has been done to do more. What we have had the vision to see, we must gradually teach our bodies to conform to. After all, we shall only be restoring a wisdom we have ourselves robbed them of. That, or something closely kin to it, is the story of man's growth.

9.15 Wednesday morning

I must begin this morning with a confession: It is raining and cold (temperature 50); and, boy, was the wind blowing a gale and the sea whipping our shores as I sat before these cheerful logs and wrote you last night! However, I like it. Wind and sea are dramatic, and besides, it makes a welcome change after the long succession of warm, benign days.

But to return now to ourselves: I think we have not yet approached our thesis from a sufficiently broad, organismic (internal) frame of reference. Our approach to a partitive deviation is itself partitive. We still attempt to negotiate an adjustment that is non-partitive, the while we maintain a basis that is partitive, psychic, imaginal—socio-imaginal, of course. It won't work. It is self-preclusive. 'Integration' is precisely the indispensable bridge from the insular position man has artificially adopted to the mainland of his organism as a whole. The bridge is exceedingly narrow, but it is also exceedingly short. To cross it calls for delicate balance apparently, but it must be crossed and by a route that is physiological. With constant, careful and delicate probing you'll inevitably come upon the tiny fasciculus of 'reference' that will more and more firmly conduct you to the mainland of feeling and motivation that was the birthplace of man. It is not proceeding in the direction of the organism's mainland to seek a partitive mitigation of a partitive disorder, such as we do when we revert from the seemingly per-

sonal insulation of 'depression' to the merely socially anaesthetiz-
ing sense of continuity we have in 'elation.' That is to miss the inter-
connecting causeway to the mainland—the commissure or connecting fasciculus between the 'psychic' and the organismic.

The clue undoubtedly lies in the sensation of the eyes themselves
rather than in the habitual sensation of the images 'projected' by
the eyes. Reflexes and habituations are the physiological substrate
of the operation we know or rather experience as wishes. The
wish will not be gainsaid by wishing. That, as I said, is self-preclusive. The steadied eye, however, makes connection, albeit an in-
finitesimal connection, with a pattern that affords a basis of contrast with the wishful (the psychic or reflexly habitual) mode of
adaptation, and this nuance of contrast provides the organism with
the requisite fulcrum for overthrowing the wishfully superim-
posed dominance of the socially insular *I*. But this is the sort of
thing that sets Leo Stein to screaming and I guess I'd better lay
off. It's probably awfully simple. The difficulty is probably in
very large measure my lumbering way of putting it, 'and that is a
strain too,' not alone for Leo but for me as well. Maybe more
probing, more physiological effort to ferret out the commissural
path necessary to regain the organism's fatherland is the only
remedy for *my* neurotic vocabulary and *our* vocabular neurosis....

Yours,

Trigant Burrow

To Dr. Charles B. Thompson   Clearwater, Florida
New York   February 26, 1938

Dear Dr. Thompson:

. . . I like the titles for your lecture, preferring perhaps 'Creative
Interest.' Then I thought of 'The Organic Basis of Interest'! This

I rather like. It is rounder and has a nice rhythm. But your titles are quite as acceptable. It is odd (unless great minds really do move in lock-step), but a few hours before your letter came I was saying to Mr. Shields that the word 'interest' suggested a possible etymological ancestry of significance—that I thought it must stem from the Latin 'inter' and 'est' (*esse*, to be), but my silly little dictionary afforded my speculations no support. Maybe the more ample lexicon in my room will prove more communicative. What I was thinking was that this 'between-being' or 'being-between' had a certain phylobiological import, that it refers to the *inter* factor uniting organism and environment, or else it indicates the secondary *inter*ruption in the continuity between organism and environment due to the transference or the *inter*position of the personal and social element in the primary organism-environment situation, in contrast to the organism's original *intra*-est. I was just thinking, when your letter came with its suggested title of 'interest'! But don't let these errant speculations *inter*fere with your paper and its central idea! . . .

Sincerely yours,

Trigant Burrow

To his son
New York

Atlantic City, New Jersey
Tuesday night, May 3, 1938

Dear Jack:

You were much in my thought throughout the trip this afternoon. Perhaps I was not less with you. For at heart I know that there are no closer pals in all the world than you and I. It will always be so.

I was not very coherent in that hurried last moment as the train was leaving. I had wanted to talk more fully to you but there was just not the opportunity. Perhaps we may talk together when I return. In the meantime let me say only that there is a place for you—definitely a place for you in this confused world as there is a place for me. Those who 'know' much are not the only ones. There is a place too for those who *feel*. It is that place for which, I believe, you and I, in our own confused and limited way, are looking. . . .

So good night and good cheer and my love always,

Father

To Susan P. Burnham(3)   New York City
New York   May 16, 1938

Dear Miss Burnham:

I had not seen the lovely letter you wrote us at Christmas time until my return to New York from Florida several weeks ago. As I went through the various cards and messages of remembrance from different friends I found it especially pleasant to recall with you the many memories of those early days in Norfolk with their many tender associations.

To me too New York has not a great deal of meaning beyond the rich things it holds in store in the way of music, and the drama too of which I am still foolishly fond.

Just the other afternoon I saw 'Susan and God.' Recalling that it was written by Rachel Crothers, I thought of Mrs. Cabell and of you. She must be a delightful person. The play is very bright indeed and capitally performed. I think I especially liked it—and not a little maliciously, I fear—because of its merciless take-off of that silliest of pseudo-religious movements—Buchmanism.

(3) Miss Burnham taught Dr. Burrow during his childhood.

As to what it offers in music, New York is indeed wonderful, though the music I hear comes to me chiefly here in my study through the radio.

We are looking forward to your promised visit to us. Gramercy Park is very lovely these spring days. Brownie and I too plan to stop by at your bailiwick one of these days and see how things go with you there. At the moment, though, I'm preparing to leave for San Francisco where I'm giving a paper at the Psychiatric Meetings to be held there.(4) We'll be seeing you before too long though. In the meantime let us send our love and good wishes.

Always affectionately,

Trigant Burrow

To Professor Joseph Jastrow   New York City
New York   May 20, 1938

My dear Professor Jastrow:

The story of Professor Münsterberg is doubtless an old one to you—how on receiving a telegram from a colleague telling him he had discovered an undoubtedly authentic medium Münsterberg would rush from his class in order not to miss this *bona fide* instance of clairvoyance or what not; and how, later, he would pack his bag but await the second telegram saying that the seance had not proven *bona fide* after all; and how, finally he would not pack his bag!

I received your letter and the questionnaire, and naturally I want to meet your inquiry as adequately and as acceptably as I can. If I may ask your indulgence I shall go about it quite at random, let-

(4) 'Kymograph Records of Neuromuscular (Respiratory) Patterns.'

ting you judge from this somewhat vagrant word how undependable in general my reactions are to the matter in question. And in this way you will perhaps get a fairly good notion of my unsatisfactoriness because of my own personal prejudice.

Rightly or wrongly, I have always been very much against wonders. For some time it has seemed to me that man's own very limited expression of his true and natural powers is answerable for his impatient recourse to powers he calls supernatural in his effort to account for manifestations in the phenomenal world.

For me, extra sensory perception is synonymous with supernatural experience, and at the outset I bristle. From this you can see how unfair I am toward the proposition at Duke University. I do not know Professor Rhine, but, if I am correctly informed, his background discloses lines of interest in which we find wishful trends dominant. I have in mind his rather marked religious tendency. I am going along, you see, in quite haphazard fashion, and from my actual response you can, as I said, the better judge my unfitness to present a trustworthy reaction to your inquiry.

As for the experiment itself, I have really not made any thoughtful study of Rhine's method or controls. I am not qualified to judge the relative influence of chance in the responses obtained. So that on technical grounds I fear my testimony has to be ruled out. A point, though, on which I am especially inclined to discredit the whole procedure is the undoubted prejudice with which Rhine and his co-workers have approached their problem. They *want* to establish the existence of extra sensory perception. No one knows better than you the menace of such a bias. There is no element that you would be at greater pains to eliminate in your psychological laboratory than a factor which anteriorly prejudices the attitude of the experimenter and experimentee toward the outcome of the experiment.

I am not unaware that there coexist in certain individuals an undoubted scientific attainment and a powerful undercurrent of emotional bias. But doubtless you are already discerning in what

I am saying a counter-bias that is no less untrustworthy. This is precisely what I want to have you see. This is why in the interest of your questionnaire I want to write you in this quite spontaneous, if rambling, way.

Carrel comes forcibly to my mind and his alleged observation of the spontaneous healing under his very eyes of a tissue alteration definitely diagnosed as malignant—a process which he ascribed to an act of God. According to his statement, The New York Academy of Medicine has deemed it worth while to send an emissary to France in order to study the properties alleged to inhere in the waters of Lourdes, these properties being supposedly miraculous. Here again, when I hear that a scientific committee has sent an investigator across the ocean to devote two years to inquiring about a spring which, according to an obscure country girl many years ago, spontaneously appeared out of the earth simultaneously with the apparition of the Virgin Mary, it is easier for me to think that the scientific committee is nervous and wishful or reflexly conditioned emotionally than that the water of Lourdes possesses the miraculous qualities imputed to it.

I ought, though, to say this to you too, that it happens that in the course of my life I have never seen anything extraordinary—I mean by that, anything of the sort that people explain through invoking some mystical immanence. All of my experiences have been wholly of the quite ordinary sort. Also I do not happen to know any people who are extraordinary. Again I mean people who possess gifts that set them apart from others of us whose achievements are the expression of purely natural gifts.

While this is not the answer in a strict sense to your questionnaire, I hope nevertheless it will in some measure assist the inquiry in which you are interested.

Your last question, I see, I have not covered. I would say, in general, that a psychologist who goes to the public for confirmation or for corroboration and interest in what he believes to be his findings, is adopting a procedure that is definitely damaging to him. It justly lays him open to suspicion. One naturally asks why did he not go first to his colleagues whose training and equipment would qualify them to assess the merits of his undertaking. The whole thing does not seem to me to warrant the hullabaloo it has seemed to create. As far as I remember, there have always been these periodical paroxysms recurring in the community in which the fundamental motive is the effort to find by hook or crook, or both, an act of God where there exists a perfectly simple phenomenon for which there has not yet been provided adequate knowledge for its correct appraisal.

I believe this about covers both my answer to your questionnaire and my confession of incompetence due to my unworthy prepossessions. So that this may all be of little use to you. But I have enjoyed writing you and letting myself feel in doing so that I could be entirely frank and at ease with you.

With my high regards and cordial greetings,

Sincerely yours,

Trigant Burrow

In the spring of 1938, Dr. Burrow took advantage of one of his many engagements at professional meetings—this one, of The American Psychiatric Association in San Francisco—to make a trip through the West with Dr. Syz. An enthusiastic sight-seer, Dr. Burrow reported on the progress of their journey in the following telegrams to Mr. Shields:

Grand Canyon, May 26, 1938

Grand is the word. Grand also the weather. Greetings to the staff and the distaff.

Los Angeles, May 27, 1938

Arrived on time. Delightful trip. Weather perfect. Both well. Off for afternoon Hollywood.

Yosemite, June 3, 1938

Telegram received. Perfect day. Next message from San Francisco. Both extraordinarily well. Best greetings to all.

San Francisco, June 6, 1938

All mail received. Our sincere appreciation. Delightfully situated here. As usual both well. Writing later.

To Dr. Charles B. Thompson   Fairmont Hotel, San Francisco
New York   June 9, 1938, Thursday night—10.30

Dear Dr. Thompson:

Dr. Syz and I have just returned from China Town, where we dined at Shanghai Low.

We're off tomorrow at 5 p.m., I believe. It has been a splendid trip throughout. Of course I received and enjoyed your letter. It has not been easy to write. But you've understood.

We have both so appreciated the thoroughness and the thoughtfulness with which everything has been attended to at that end—the shipment of graphs, the provision for their return, the letters, etc., etc.

But I mustn't write at this late hour. There's packing still ahead before retiring.

It will seem good when we have all gathered once more at camp. I'm not satisfied with my Ottawa paper. (5) It's probably the most auspicious opportunity. I do not feel I have met it. Dr. Syz and I have in mind to consider the paper anew. We cannot let down at this stage.

But I mustn't write on. There is so much. There will be no end, if I do not come to a peremptory halt. Be seein' you soon.

As always,

Trigant Burrow

To his daughter   Lifwynn Camp, Merrill, N. Y.
New York   August 3, 1938

Dear Emily:

This is the fairest of mornings—the sort you so love to inhale with me. I wish you were here.

There is much to be done, but it all has to be mined out of the depths of a certain bio-physical brain centre that appears to co-ördinate and control the organism's functions as a unitary whole— a physiological constant that is central for the race of man as well as for the individual. It is difficult of access—this basic regulator of our common processes—but I fumble along, hoping ardently that soon we shall reach again this touch-stone of balance and repose with which man has for so long been out of touch.

Believe me, my dear, there is in this world of *man's making* nothing quite equal to the cultivation of a finished technique in whatsoever

(5) 'Secondary (Neurotic) versus Primary (Healthy) Behavior Reactions, with Illustrative Graphs,' unpublished.

field one finds himself. Language and a technique of language undoubtedly have their place and I salute them, but there is a technique of life that is spontaneous, automatic, and if I at all sense the drift of things it is the re-discovery of this deeper technique, this more fundamental finesse that is our common job.

With love,

Father

To his daughter
New York

Lifwynn Camp, Merrill, N. Y.
Evening—8 o'clock
Monday, August 15, 1938

Dear Emily:

Ah cert'ney have miss mah honey chile! Three weeks seems so long. It must have been a warm reception that New York gave you today. Here the thermometer registered 90° at noon.

At the moment, believe it or not, I'm sitting in one of my cane seat chairs, tilted back against the midmost of the birches on my terrace, clad only in white shirt and trousers and am as comfortable as though it were Florida. There's a soft south breeze from the Lake, and the twilight is so quiet except for the note of the peewees and the chirp of the crickets, that I miss you more than ever.

Do you know—I discovered it only yesterday, but you probably do know—I am a wee bit shy of you. For so long I raked so ruthlessly through my feelings, turning up often such unsavory material and sensing so much else of pettiness and immaturity in myself that I find myself at times a bit timid and uncertain even with you who are so close to me in sympathy and understanding— with you who are my very own. This will never do. We'll have to look into this. I must quickly bring my eyes to a stand-still and sense the common organism I share with you and that we share with the world at large. But the twilight is growing too 'dim and doubting,' so as we say 'no more at the moment.'

Gute Nacht
Father

To a former patient   Lifwynn Camp, Merrill, N. Y.
August 23, 1938

Dear Mr. A.:

Your good letter of some weeks ago sounded so much like your old self, the real self. It was reassuring to have it—reassuring, I mean, in respect to the broader social problems that are our common interest and obligation.

Of course I wrote you 'in a large way,' the only way that would adequately measure to your own proportions, to your old, your real self. . . . In a sense it's silly to talk about this or that 'nervous patient' when the whole social order is nervous and perplexed, when it is utterly at a loss to discover its own basic need or a technique for embodying its recognition of it in activities consistent with the capacities of man.

Today there are signs of a broadening outlook among us—signs that the more thoughtful psychiatrists are coming increasingly to see the larger discord, the wider social maladaptation underlying and answerable for the disorders of their patients. While they recognize, of course, the special need momentarily of the individual who has been thrown out of commission by the sick social forces about him, they are not unmindful of the presence within the social body of fundamentally discordant processes or of the relation of these processes to their own obligation as students of behavior. . . .

The summer has not lacked its usual interest and refreshment. The setting here at the Lake always affords a bountiful measure of both. I think I can say that with my associates and myself there has been this year a more than usually consistent emphasis upon technique, or a facilitation of internal adjustments, rather than upon preoccupation with the psychological aspects of our investigation. This has meant much. Where one really enters upon a consistent technique of behavior, even very little means much. Because, apparently, a consistent technique is fundamentally of the organism, and, where it appears, the organism seems to welcome it heartily, to reclaim it, so to speak, as its very own. I suppose that basically this is what people the world over mean (or mean to mean!) when they speak of truth and give their ardent support to the cause of truth. But our 'truth' as yet is only verbal, sentimental, self-reflexive. For the most part we seem unable to say it without the tears and the bleatings and the pathetic mien that are merely the earmarks of our self-admiration. But for all this piffle about 'truth,' there is a technique, an order, a symmetry and an organic equity of behavior that sets the organism free of its pious self-images and makes it one and indivisible with its kind. Talked sentiments, talked nobilities, talked equities—all these symbolic entertainments that make us the charming and undependable people that we are—only obscure, only make sport of this deeper, more organic and inwoven sense of truth we embody racially as elements in a unitary, functioning whole. But I am growing voluminous which is to say that I am myself once again falling into the precise error or untruth I am supposedly disavowing. And so less talk and more technique to us!

I hope you and Mrs. A. are enjoying this particularly gracious season of the year. Write me ere long and write again in your *own* large script.

Always sincerely,
Trigant Burrow

Yellow Taxi Driver No. 1398   Lifwynn Camp, Merrill, N. Y.
Chicago   September 19, 1938

Dear Sir:

Contrary to appearances I really have not forgotten your alluding
to your speech disorder the day you drove Dr. Syz and me about
Chicago on that very interesting tour of the sights of special interest to us. I meant of course to write you earlier, but medical meetings here and there, and finding myself launched in the writing of
a new book momentarily intercepted my better intentions. I hope
you will forgive me.

The physician in this country who, in my judgment, does the most
outstanding work in disorders of speech is Dr. James S. Greene,
126 East 30 Street, New York City. I know his work from actual
results and from my own personal acquaintance with him. He is a
frank, honest, whole-souled, unaffected person and that of itself,
it seems to me, is of tremendous assistance in the treatment of
speech (or as I would say, tensional) impediments.

I ought to explain to you that my own work, while dealing with all
forms of neurotic disharmonies, approaches problems of behavior-
disorder from the broader basis of community research. While I
should be glad to give you what assistance I could, were you in
New York, I do not think you could do better than to see Dr.
Greene for the relief of the immediate condition. I have written
him and when I hear from him as to whether he has an auxiliary
institute of any sort in Chicago, my secretary will let you know.

In the meantime my good wishes, and many thanks again for a most
interesting sight-seeing drive.

Cordially yours,

Trigant Burrow

To Dr. Charles B. Thompson
New York

Clearwater, Florida
January 14, 1939

Dear Dr. Thompson:

Just a few casual thoughts that drift across the azure of my phyletic consciousness, as clouds (silver-lined, of course) across a summer sky.

I was speaking to Jack in a letter to him this morning of the lack of any succinct definition of phylobiology, phyloanalysis and group-analysis such as would be suitable to the purposes of a dictionary or encyclopedic definition.

... Among the memoranda relative to this item, I would suggest including the editorial comment published some time ago in Malisoff's Journal—*Philosophy of Science*—in which he calls for an article describing clearly the meaning of Phylobiology. Also data should be gathered regarding the specific dictionaries or encyclopedias in which we would have the definition of phylobiology etc. included, and we should ascertain prospective dates for the editing of new editions of these publications.

Mr. Shields believes that these publications include their definitions without solicitation. I had not in mind an obvious solicitation or any overtures that might seem amiss or in any way an affront to these editors. I had in mind a dignified allusion to our work when the opportunity presented itself, or could be found, for contact with them. Anyhow I think it should be on hand and ready for prompt delivery to any proper inquirer.(6) ...

(6) At the request of Dr. Hinsie, Burrow supplied forty-one phylobiological terms and their definitions which were included in the *Psychiatric Dictionary*, edited by Leland E. Hinsie and Jacob Shatzky, New York, Oxford University Press, 1940. Twelve of Burrow's terms appeared in *Vocabulaire de la psychologie*, edited by Henri Piéron, Paris, Presses universitaires de France, 1951.

I'm thinking specifically in the moment of my suggestion, I think in a letter to you, of your using the first opportunity to mention my prior authorship of the term group-analysis, and the infringement entailed in the use of this term in a wholly different meaning. You remember you wrote of having spoken to Bromberg of the presumption on Schilder's part when he used the term *social neurosis* in a sense other than that already established or standardized (can't think of the word. Not 'patented,' but in that vein) by us. The dictionary definition would contribute to block this type of trespass.

No more.

Yours,

Trigant Burrow

To Dr. Hans Syz   Clearwater, Florida
New York   January 27, 1939

Dear Dr. Syz:

Yesterday Mr. Shields and I (the 'and I' is mostly literary euphemism) spent our first real session at the laboratory. (7) The result —Mr. Shields got the instrument set up. It was a preliminary setting-up only, but a robust beginning. We are going over in a moment for further adjustments. I shall leave Mr. Shields there, as yesterday, and return here and to your recent letters. Was much assured by this word this morning 'everything here going along well.' Take it your cold was short-lived, and am much relieved.

And now Connecticut and a word in recognition of the time and

(7) A room had been made available for Dr. Burrow's experimentation at the Morton F. Plant Hospital in Clearwater.

care you have given to the problem.(8) Not in vain, though, it seems to me. . . .

The neighborhood seems most desirable and the country attractive both as to arability (high ground) and rural charm. Then socially it appears pleasant. The description of the 23 acres appealed to me as to developmental possibilities. I think I ought to try now to be more specific as to my central idea—specific as far as I can be.

To me everything is The Lifwynn Foundation—that is, the organismic *foundation* of the life of man, its autonomic primacy, and the social, economic and cultural development that will ensue from the practical recognition and application phylobiologically of such a foundation. A place in the country means literally the soil of such a foundation. A home for me and my family would in such a setting have the status that a professor's home has on a college or university campus. The main interest would be a laboratory of psycho-physiological experimentation. I picture a development on a more substantial scale of the general features of Lifwynn Camp. I have come to, not necessarily the age but to the circumstance perhaps, where, I realize, 'not in my life-time' has to be appended to most future provisions. But I'm thinking of a modest beginning. It is not easy to express all that I have in mind. Your own very receptive feeling will have to supplement much for which I have no language. Mr. Shields needs a shop, materials and tools. It is an organic need with him. You and I need it too, but we don't know it yet. (See with what vague outlines I am trying to fill in the picture.) Re-establishing the primary centre of motivation in the behavior of man requires an environment. The environment requires quiet without isolation. Such a basis of motivation is continuous with the organic environment of man at large. A new science of government is needed. How desperately it is needed a tragically divided Europe is about to inform us in no uncertain terms. This is disease. Disease and its causation is studied in the retirement of the experimental laboratory. How different *our*

(8) A search for property in Connecticut to serve as a home for Dr. and Mrs. Burrow, and as a base for The Lifwynn Foundation.

laboratory, though, in its approach. We are the patient too. We sit before our instruments, we measure and record, while the fever and waste of the disease we study is raging within our own organisms. The professor in the college or university *goes* from his home *to* his laboratory. We *are* our laboratory—the professor, his family and his home. How can we go from one to the other. In our case the interval between the two is but the creation of our own sick phantasy—the very phantasy our laboratory provides instruments of precision to study and to remedy.

In our quest of a farm with which to make the beginning of the development of more healthful human relations, let us keep in mind our basic dedication to the laboratory of human behavior and our need for the beautiful surroundings that will best nurture its development.

Sincerely,

Trigant Burrow

To Dr. Hans Syz   Clearwater, Florida
New York   January 31, 1939

Dear Dr. Syz:

We are momentarily expecting Sue and Marion for dinner. I want though to begin at least a letter to you in answer to yours of Sunday afternoon. I shall start at random, filling in the omitted items later.

Your picture of the effort with us and of the ever-recurring failures, frustrations and unfulfillments is not alien to me. I think you know that. Perhaps you do not know, though, that I was thinking (not disconsolately at all, but just summing up) along precisely the same lines as you were, and at just about the same time—over the same period of days. And then a white-clear resolution seemed to come. Not an answer, not a solution by any means, but the clear indicator of the needed direction. It seems to me that things will not go much further forward in their present impetus or aim. We can hold our own (which is much) and record even a measure of gain here and there, and this is much too considering the scope and urgency of our endeavor. But we have come to an impasse, I believe—a wholesome impasse. We have, of ourselves, assisted ourselves extraordinarily as organisms. We have challenged and re-challenged day in and day out, hour in and hour out, a false mode of behavior-adaptation. I think there was never before this challenge of behavior on the social plane upon which we have conducted it. The partitive, socially congeneric or socio-cortical reaction-system prevailing throughout the species man has acquired a bio-physical definition among us in terms of neuromuscular patterns of response which we have placed in the category of the scientifically objective and isolable. The importance of this achievement cannot be adequately estimated. We ourselves do not begin to appreciate all that this means biologically and culturally. But I think a new and indispensable need has now to be recognized. I think another step has now to be taken and for us the final step— the step to which all our efforts thus far have been slowly leading.

As I say the picture you draw is not alien to me. It is the replica of a similar drawing of my own. I have come to feel that in the absence of a further step the picture we have presented will continue to stand as now. For I find it quite unthinkable that a challenge among us of the partitive by the partitive will, of itself, ever lead us out of the mode of activation that is partitive. I cannot conceive of a system of verbally, symbolically conditioned reflexes that has now become dominant and all-embracing throughout the species turning about and effectively remedying *itself*. Upon what axis shall it turn but upon its own? It is the fallacy again of tugging at one's own boot-straps in order to lift oneself.

If we will consider it, scientific progress is synonymous with instrumentation. In medicine our advance has been marked by the mediation of the objective instrument, whether pill, probe, X-ray, the lens or the laparotomy. We approach the thing to be affected *with* something that is not *of* the thing itself. This something is introduced from without and applied *to* the condition to be affected. The instrument furnishes the new term or factor with which to approach a condition with the external grasp or hold that is needed. It is the application of the objective within the vicious circle of all pure subjectivity.

It was an extraordinary and epoch-making clue to the needed instrument, that was given us with the observation of the physiological connection (never mind how vaguely sensed) between eye-tensions and respiratory rhythm, between the factor of convergence, in association with the symbol, and the shortened respiratory function in the production of the symbol. When I place a weak prismatic lens before my eyes and there is automatically induced in me a slowed respiratory rhythm together with an absence of the anxious affect type of sensation and self-conscious concern we associate with bionomic insecurity or the neurosis, we are given a clue (never mind how faint and ill-correlated) to the type of instrumentation required to mediate between man and his neurosis or instability. It is the first step toward introducing into man's needed rehabilitation—into the relation of himself to himself—the external agent or new term requisite to *objective operation* by the subject upon himself. It is the needed lever for the effective application of force where *change* is needed.

Don't misunderstand. I'm not derogating what we have accomplished in our futile socio-cortical challenge of the socio-cortical, nor am I derogating the impasse it marks phylobiologically. The futility and the impasse, as I said, are wholesome. The awareness of them—their affront to the autonomous 'I'—has been an extraordinary accomplishment. Realizing this, we need stoutly to hold our own, to ply our technique as heretofore, recognizing that it will lead inevitably, that it inevitably has led to the instrument. . . .

I wish very much that the five students of behavior who represent the Scientific Staff of The Lifwynn Foundation—and each of them possesses his own particular sort of mechanical ingenuity—could as a unit present an organismic front to the task of devising the needed instrumentation required to aid us in restoring the neuro-muscular balance and coördination to the disturbance of which we have been able to trace the neurosis and insecurity of the indi-vidual and the group.

We fear the instrument, we fear experimentation where it in-fringes upon the traditional province of God, namely, the behavior of man from the basis of an imaginal good or bad alternative. Who does not? Until man grasps the instrument of his own constructing and applies it in the service of his own need, he can only fear and gainsay the uses of the instrument in the adjustment of his own processes. The kymograph is not the end. It is only the means (the instrument) to the end.

But no more, because it's mail time. Long letter from Cooney—very friendly.

Must meet Mr. Shields now at laboratory, continuing later.

Yours,

Trigant Burrow

To Dr. W. H. Marshall Carrington
London

Clearwater, Florida
March 2, 1939

My dear Dr. Carrington:

I appreciated very much your letter of January 12, and still more the spirit in which you wrote me!

What you feel to be the parallel between my approach and that of F. Matthias Alexander is interesting. One cannot fail to recognize in reading his book, *The Use of the Self*, that Alexander has done much in getting at certain physiological reactions, and I was greatly impressed with the originality of his method and the very thorough and precise procedure he developed in the observation of his own behavior. May I say, however, that there is a fundamental difference between Alexander's technique and that developed by my associates and myself in the laboratory of phylopathology.

I cannot help believing that Professor Dewey must have felt this difference between Alexander's work and my own. I say this because in two notes I have had from him acknowledging material I had sent him, he made no mention of Mr. Alexander or of the parallel you speak of. My own feeling is that Alexander is a unique, creative genius and that his work, expressive of an innate scientific endowment, needs no endorsement beyond the objective evidence upon which it is based. To me his patient, painstaking and carefully controlled self-observations represent an amazing achievement in the field of human behavior. I myself . . . have not worked at all in the field of consciously controlled reflexes. What my associates and I have done is to challenge among us a social system of reflexes over which we found to our chagrin that conscious control by the individual was wholly excluded. Briefly, our technique was one of definite challenge and obstruction of a system of habitual (normal) social reflexes. By slow stages, our studies and experiments indicated that human conflict resided not in our interindividual system of symbolic interchange but in the organismic physiology of man as a species, and that back of this conflict lay the primacy of the organism of man in its functionally balanced motivation. Naturally, this finding was followed by consistent research into the nature of the organism's basic behavioral processes and the reconstruction of the primacy of man's autonomic solidarity as a phylum.

I should indeed be sorry to have seemed to you ungracious—still more to have seemed ungenerous—in not having given recognition to Alexander through my failure to align the work of my laboratory with his personal researches. Such a connection did not occur to me. Alexander's contribution to the field of behavior is, as you mentioned in your letter, a half century old. His thesis has indeed become a 'commonplace.' My work, on the other hand, is only in its beginning. Though it is twenty years since I gave up my private practice in psychoanalysis to devote my time to research, and while there were always for me the indications of basic biological and physiological factors underlying human behavior, it is only recently that I have arrived at a position that gives promise of objective demonstration. This present stage of my investigations, with its emphasis upon definite internal physiological tensions, has opened up an entirely new field to me. . . .

I sympathize with your request for clearer physiological definition. It is indeed very important, as you say; and I am sure you will be interested to know that the practical demonstration of the internal physiological motivation of man's interrelational conflict is fundamentally our major trend. . . .

May I say again how very gratifying it is to have your expression of interest in the investigations we are carrying on.

With my kind regards,

Sincerely yours,

Trigant Burrow

To his son　　　　　　　　　　　　　　　　　Clearwater, Florida
New York　　　　　　　　　　　　　　　　　　March 7, 1939

Dear Jack:

For some days I have wanted to write you about the house at Westport and tell you of the welcome that waits you there—you and Emily—whenever you can come out to us. There is hardly need of saying this, but I wanted to say it anyway for the pleasure it gives me to do so.

And now I have your letter of yesterday in which you speak of you and Helen(9) and of your wish to marry.

Let me say first that I think you need have no doubt of my being with you. I should like to say too that from what I have seen of Helen you are quite justified in holding her in the high regard in which you do hold her. She is a lovely, modest, wholesome girl, and besides, she possesses resourcefulness and independence. I feel sure you will not wish to deprive her of her capacity to work and bear her part in the economic scheme of things and that you have been completely frank with her in regard to the limitations financially of yourself and your family.

It is one of the tragedies of this world that the union of two young people should bear any relation to a circumstance so extraneous to mating and reproduction as finances. But in the present system of things *it does*, and one is not only shortsighted but most unjust to his partner in life if he fails to look this stubborn fact squarely in the face.

And so while I want to be heartily with you and Helen I feel sure that you and Helen want no less heartily to be with me, and with me to recognize that in a wholesome union one enters into an economic partnership as well as a partnership of love. In saying this I am voicing Mother's feeling as well as my own. But of course you know this.

I think I need not write more beyond the expression of my feeling that in your and Helen's plans there need be no barrier to our complete sympathy and interest in you both.

There is perhaps just one thing that I would like to add. We have of course had at heart your happiness and we have spoken of

(9) Helen M. Stapleton who was married to Mr. Burrow the following November.

Helen's qualifications for making *you* happy. I would so much rather that we thought what your qualifications—what our qualifications are for making Helen happy. I would certainly regret to see ourselves outdone by her in her thoughtfulness and concern not for herself but for you. But I believe that in this too you and I understand each other.

But I must be leaving now for the Hospital and a session at the laboratory.

With love,

Devotedly,
Father

To James P. Cooney (10)
Woodstock, New York

Clearwater, Florida
March 10, 1939

My dear Mr. Cooney:

My not having written you long before this has not meant that I did not appreciate your letter, and still more the generous spirit in which you wrote me. Letters are really a very great pleasure to me and yours was especially welcome in its wholeheartedness and warmth. While I appreciated it and the quite frank account you gave me of your earlier efforts and disappointments, and all the struggle they have entailed, your suggestion that I contribute a paper to *The Phoenix* made me feel somewhat abashed. Gifted and generous people seem always inclined to credit others with

(10) Editor of *The Phoenix*.

equal gifts, not realizing that they are quite undeserving of so much confidence. . . .

I think you are very much to be congratulated upon your periodical. What appeals to me most about *The Phoenix* is the ardor and genuineness with which you and your wife have gone ahead with it. I like your fearlessness in setting forth so heartily the things you believe in. But here again I find myself feeling diffident and as a stranger among you. To confess the simple truth, I haven't a belief to my name or any special ardor, not one. . . .

This dearth of belief with me or of inspiration must sound to you iconoclastic and cynical, I fear. I don't really think it is that. But what it is, I find difficult to explain. It is all bound up with my studies in human behavior. The experiments of my associates and myself over the past twenty years have resulted in a very different outlook upon human problems and human ways. They have given us an altered frame of reference, personally and socially toward the field of human behavior and its motivations. Much of our story is told in a book of mine, published by Macmillan two years ago, *The Biology of Human Conflict*. It isn't gratifying reading and is difficult but it represents the last published statement of any length regarding my position. . . .

This brings me to your own plans toward a solution of your very pressing and oppressing problems of social adjustment and to your question as to 'what I think of it all.' You were speaking, you remember, chiefly of your plan, and that of your associates, to establish a remote colony somewhere and so 'extricate yourselves from the deathly débris of this crumbling civilization.' I do not at all see how you can withdraw this way from the sick muddle of things and not take me with you—me and the other millions of people that make up the common run of us. Unless you feel that our pain and confusion are less than yours or that we are less sensitive to it than you are, but I do not believe for a moment that this is your attitude. I could not imagine you, of all people, differentiating yourself from others in any such fashion. And yet your program of isolation for yourself and your group has definitely in it this element of discrimination, of setting yourselves apart. That is why I liked the letter of H. Gaylord Collins. Colonization seems a form of escape—a sort of running away. I'd rather stand and take it. It seems healthier. And what is more I think you would. I think you'd rather stand with the rest of us, for all our stupidity and inadequacies of feeling and motivation, than move apart from us. I just think you are that sort. And so, since you ask me, I'd weigh carefully this idea of a colony of place and opportunity and security. I'd think rather of the possibilities of a colony of *thought* and *feeling* within the very midst of the confused social community in which you and I find ourselves. I think you might find restriction and curtailment in any other course. I think you might find your genuinely deep, human sympathies denied their full expression in any setting other than the immediate need and confusion of our common humanity.

Then too, there is this. For all one's gifts, for all one's earnestness, one does not know how young one is at twenty-eight, and that the views which at that age he maintains with certainty and even finality he may have none of at thirty-eight.

I hope I am not presuming in speaking this way—that I am not speaking with more frankness than your letter invited.

In any event and whatever the outcome, I want you to know that you have my very hearty sympathy and good wishes. . . .

Thank you for your interest and thank you for the copies of *The Phoenix* you so kindly sent me. All the success to it that it merits, however alien to its fine purpose my own direction of investigation and interest may be.

Success and happiness to you too, and, may I add to your wife and to Deirdre—very especially to Deirdre. . . .

Sincerely yours,
Trigant Burrow

To Lawrence K. Frank   New York City
New York   May 11, 1939

Dear Mr. Frank:

Your letter was forwarded to me at Clearwater as I was just making preparations for leaving. I am glad you wrote me as you did. Your letter seems to me to contain a very timely as well as significant challenge.

I do heartily concede the necessity for the social patterning of which you speak. That the 'prohibitions, compulsions and values' you mention are a part of man's cultural development and equipment I do not for a moment question. But I do question—all my experimental work in phylopathology very seriously questions whether these cultural values have not represented a merely transitional stage in man's social evolution; whether there may not be found in human behavior a cultural adaptation that is more widely integrative socially and that may with advantage be made to replace the ethical values that have hitherto formed the basis of man's cultural life.

Let me be quite concrete. Take ourselves, for instance. Suppose I want to take from you something that is yours. Let us assume that I want to steal something from you—whether your purse, your good name, or your academic ideas, isn't important. In this circumstance I find it handy, and socially valuable, to employ a mechanism of prohibition or restraint, and thus avoid trespass upon your person or your personality. On our (man's) present interpersonal basis of relationship this device isn't bad. It has become automatic in the course of my training, and works every time. But I would hold a type of cultural development to be far more efficient which quite precluded my entertaining *any desire* to take from you what is rightly yours. My ethical values would appear to me far more sound if they rested upon a basic inability to wish any advantage for myself which would entail a disadvantage to you....

With my good wishes,

Sincerely yours,

Trigant Burrow

After Dr. and Mrs. Burrow moved to Connecticut, there was a more frequent exchange of letters with Mr. Shields, of which the following is the first to appear. It illustrates Dr. Burrow's way of using the process of communication to work out significant material he later developed in his writings. For instance, the analogy of the tennis player presented in this letter appears in *The Neurosis of Man* (pp. 250–253). In addition, this letter contains the first suggestion of Dr. Burrow's search for a word to substitute for 'attention' as he used it in contrast to cotention. Burrow finally adopted the word *ditention* to designate the attentional mode characterizing so-called normal interrelational behavior. In this mode attention reverts back upon the image of the self and its private gain, and fails to mediate directly between organism and environment.

To Clarence Shields   Greens Farms, Connecticut
New York   June 16, 1939

Dear Clarence:

... I see nothing for it but direct environmental mediation or 'instrumentation.' Let me ramble on. If the technique of my tennis stroke is faulty I do not 'know it,' until I have achieved a physiological (stereognostic) sense of its inadequacy through the direct experience (physiologically) of a *correct* stroke. We've been over this, of course.

If not *attention*, but a species of partitive interest or *bi*-tention characterizes my relation to the environment (because of my loss of touch with man's basic cotentive interest), I shall not 'know' the inadequacy of my organism-environment relationship except as I experience a cotentive or physiologically correct experience of the environment.

The tennis expert, I believe, analyzes a player's stroke. Knowing the elements that make up a correct stroke he can do this. He can dissect out, as it were, and expose the faulty elements and demonstrate their relation to the elements that enter into a correct stroke. The instructor has not only an internal experience of the correct stroke but he has also an acquaintance with the separate details of which it is composed. ...

Where there is the possibility of analyzing the elements that enter respectively into cotention and bi-tention (partitive attention), there would seem the possibilty of a student's acquiring a physiological experience of the organism's cotentive as well as of its bitentive adaptation to the environment and thus his recognizing physiologically and distinguishing stereognostically the difference between a faulty technique and a correct technique in man's organism-environment relationship.

This is why I want to assemble whatever elements it may be possible to assemble or to 'dissect out' in the mechanism of bitention on the one hand and of cotention on the other. If the organism may be shown to react differently in its various mechanisms according as its response is bi- or co-tentive, and if this difference may be shown to be consistent in the organism's different physiological spheres of behavior—pupillary reaction, eye-movements, convergence reactions, electrocardiographic, electroencephalographic, respiratory, metabolic, etc., etc., there is established through an analysis of its elements the nature of cotention and the nature of bitention in clear objective terms, and with this difference *before* him, the student may now attempt to learn to discriminate, as in the case of the tennis-player, between a correct and a faulty technique of adaptation to the environment through his own internal or physiological experience of the two different modes of adaptation.

In any other course our efforts toward correcting faulty behavior appear to me mental, symbolic, socio-cortical or inter-personal, as contrasted with intra-organismic.

It seems to me that the Director and the Scientific Staff of The Lifwynn Foundation must get at demonstrable, possibly measurable, experimental data with a view to their physiological appreciation of the difference between healthy (correct) technique and neurotic (faulty) technique in their adaptation to the environment. Like the tennis expert once more, we shall have an internal experience of the correct behavior-reaction, because we shall have an acquaintance with the separate details of which it is composed. In short, through an analysis of the elements, we shall attain an organismic synthesis of them and hence a balanced organism-environment relationship. . . .

I think of the early part of this letter—the real purpose of it. I hope it may be of some assistance to us both in pointing to more and more concrete experimentation with the elements contributive to the organism-environment relationship and in inciting us all to active efforts to this end.

Sincerely,

Trigant

To a friend   Lifwynn Camp, Merrill, N. Y.
Sue de Lorenzi   August 23, 1939
Merrill, New York

Dear Sue:

It has been a disappointment to me not to have seen you and Leta(11) in all these weeks or to have had you both come over. I've been the more disappointed to hear that you have not been feeling quite up to the mark this summer. I hope you will be feeling more your usual self in a short time and that we may have a visit from you.

Brownie and I, as you now know, have lately been secretly entertaining a very great happiness.(12) It had been my plan, after she went down to New York, to go over to Merrill and have you and Leta share it with us. Emily would have wanted you to. Unfortunately, though, it happened that I had a slight attack of summer

(11) Leta Bentley.

(12) The forthcoming marriage of Emily Burrow and Hans Syz, which took place August 12, 1939.

grippe the very day after Brownie left and I wasn't able to be about with comfort until the very day I had to leave for New York and the wedding. So that I was denied what would have been for me the very welcome inclusion of you both in our confidence and happiness. But Brownie and I know how completely you are with us these days, even if we didn't reach you as soon as we would have liked with our news.

I certainly am glad to hear that Leta is to be with you for a while in Clearwater next winter. The inner circle will be complete! Why don't we persuade Leta to open a school in Clearwater? It is nice to know that Dr. Austin is with you. I'm sure you'll be a better woman for her presence.

I hope you have good news of Helen and of Marion. Remember me to them.

Here's hoping to see you soon.

Affectionately,

Trigant Burrow

To Alfred L. Loomis   Lifwynn Camp, Merrill, N. Y.
Tuxedo Park, New York   September 6, 1939

Dear Mr. Loomis:

I am writing you on the chance that you are still working with the electroencephalograph and that it may be possible for Dr.

Galt and me to have your assistance in a problem of special interest to us. The day we spent at your laboratory some years ago I may have spoken to you of our experimentation with a phenomenon I have called cotention—a reaction induced in part at least through the suspension of mental images or of the usual process of attention.

As I may have mentioned, we have found with this reaction a marked slowing of the respiratory rhythm. Recently my son-in-law, Dr. Syz, and I have had tests made with basal metabolism and also with the electrocardiograph, both of which gave indications of alterations during the cotentive reaction. We were particularly interested in tests which we made with Professor G. T. Buswell of the Department of Education of The University of Chicago with the very precise instruments he invented for the photographic recording of eye-movements. With these instruments we found the reaction of cotention to be attended by marked visual convergence as well as by pupillary contraction.

These different clues to physiological alterations in response to the arrest of mental images or of attention have led us to wonder what indications might be shown through tests with the electro-encephalograph. One or two very casual tests with this instrument have already indicated the existence of certain modifications, but we have in mind a more extensive series of experiments with a view to establishing with definiteness whether there is a difference in the type of brain wave shown according as the subject passes from the state of attention to that of cotention.

I regret that Dr. Syz is not in this country at the moment to take part in these tests. He and my daughter are at present in Switzerland. But it would mean a great deal to Dr. Galt and myself in our work in relation to behavior, especially in relation to disordered processes, if on our return to New York we might ask the privilege of having some records made in your laboratory. Of course I shall expect to meet whatever expense would be involved in the making of the records.

As I am leaving tomorrow for my home in Westport, Connecticut, and shall be in my office in New York the first of next week, may I ask you to address your reply to me at 27 East 37th Street.

Very sincerely yours,

Trigant Burrow

To Mrs. Burrow   Clearwater, Florida
Greens Farms, Connecticut   Saturday night, December 23, 1939

Dear Brownie:

It was good to get your air-special this afternoon and to hear of the Christmas preparations—entrance decorations—at Summer Hill.

Yes, it does mean a great deal that you think of me—the more so as circumstances have and still make me one of the most unpleasant of companions. But it has not been my 'work.' It has been only my incapacity in relation to it. So it is sweet indeed to know that in spite of all you find it pleasant to think of me and include me on the day of all the year that is fullest of cheer and happy re-membrances.

This must go in a moment, as the mail is closing. I think two other letters are on their way to you. Maybe one has already reached you.

My love to you all. Can't wait to hear all the news of the day. How good it is to have added Hans and Helen to the home circle. Truly our cup runneth over.

My love to them all and to you dear, and a Merry Christmas all 'round.

Devotedly,

Trigant

To Dr. Hans Syz   Clearwater, Florida
New York   December 31, 1939

Dear Hans:

. . . Psychiatric practice: I understand and fully share your feeling. I think we have to discriminate between an attitude of compromise and one of palliation, so to speak. Compromise is a course pursued in deference to our own weakness—our own lack of conviction—whereas palliation seems to me a quite justifiable policy resorted to out of a quite thoughtful regard for a patient's weakness. A surgeon who is quite definite in his diagnosis of a condition and whose unalterable course is a specific operation can well afford to indulge the patient's quite primitive and sentimental view of his own condition in so far as the office interview is concerned. So with ourselves, when our conviction is unhesitating and unanimous as to the phylopathological substrate of so-called mental disorders and we are accordingly bent upon applying measures of correction consistent with our position, it seems to me we are quite warranted in lending a tentative ear to the patient and his primitively sentimental viewpoint. This, it seems to me, is the course of palliation and is entirely in order medically under certain circumstances. Compromise enters where we are not on sure ground ourselves and are unconsciously led into assuming that the patient's position is *bona fide*. Under these circumstances professional integrity and scientific stability are thrown to the winds and we enter into the artificial systems of beliefs and superstitions which the mores common to the patient's and our own social traditions force, all unawares, upon him and upon ourselves.

Let us rather strengthen and secure our own conviction through an intensification of the program of internal observation and adjustment as it is obtainable within ourselves, and so be in a position to apply a procedure that is frankly, technically, palliative without entailing the least shade of compromise or double-dealing on our part. This awkward statement may assist us both some little in arriving at the undoubtedly needed adjustment on our part. . . .

Devotedly,
Father

To Flora A. Guggenheimer (13)   Clearwater, Florida
New York   January 5, 1940

Dear Miss Flora:

All my Christmas letters have been written long ago, but you remain unanswered still. It is inevitable that you should be last. It is the place you yourself always choose. But though I know there's a catch in it—that in this human-all-too-human world of private enterprises it could not be otherwise—I invariably assign to you the place to which your secret egotisms like best to be allotted.

However belated the acknowledgment, the Christmas box was and *is* a joy. I don't have to tell you how much thought we know went into it and how much it even exceeded in our appreciation the many good things you sent us.

Later 7:30 p.m.

Dr. Galt and I, after concluding the morning's work, had such a pleasant afternoon at the Dixie Tennis Games in Tampa. I was so

(13) See pages 116-17.

greatly impressed with Bobbie Riggs, the world's foremost champion. Every other player was straining every nerve and virtually tearing himself to pieces, but not Mr. Riggs. He was utterly nonchalant, the perfection of grace, making no unnecessary movements, yet carrying everything before him without once interrupting his complete relax. It was quite delightful.

But before I was interrupted this morning, I was about to tell you how much your Christmas box had contributed to the success of the party we gave to The Inner Circle Wednesday evening. The wafers, the salted almonds, the delicious stuffed dates were the chief units of our generously filled table. It was really a very nice evening.

I can think of little else now, though, than my book. I earnestly hope it may go well. It ought to, considering all that has been contributed to its material in the work and self-exactions of the members of our organization.

But Dr. Galt is taking this to the night post. You should see the comfort 'the little doctor' (as our laundress calls him) is to the household and so particularly to me. He did the 'honors at the party' as the house manager and was most efficient and graceful in presiding. But no more tonight. Greetings to you and to all and do write soon of you *all*.

Yours sincerely and gratefully,

Trigant Burrow

To Mrs. John D. Burrow
New York

Clearwater, Florida
January 24, 1940

Dear Nemmie:

What's all this I hear about you and Jack being worried and concerned in a moment that should be the happiest of your young lives! Of course when one feels as below par physically as you do just now, it inevitably dulls the brightest outlook. But the discomfort and indisposition you are experiencing in the present weeks is not unusual, as you know. However trying, it should soon pass now.

As for your having to relinquish your work at Columbia, I know what a real regret that is to you, but, after all, this is an emergency measure, a precaution you are taking at your physician's orders. The financial aspect of it really must not trouble you. After all, a problem that is yours and Jack's is Brownie's and mine also. If we can be of assistance at a difficult moment like this, I'm sure I need not tell you the privilege it is for us and how happy we feel in it. So that I am glad Jack wrote me as he did and let me know definitely of the assistance he would need. You may feel assured it was a real pleasure to respond to his request. I know how proud and independent you are and I would not have you different. But the situation is exceptional. Conditions like these, conditions of undue economic stress, arise in the lives of all of us. You must feel it is our common problem and let us share it together. I know, Nemmie dear, that in the circumstances you will let pride and your cherished sense of self-reliance give way to the more generous view and let us feel our part in your and Jack's temporary discomfiture.

It was good to hear of your feeling well enough the other day to go down to Emily's apartment for a while. And Jack wrote that you and he were to have dinner Monday night at 27 and that he would go over to the armory later for badminton. This sounds more like it! Why, you too will be going out for a routine of more active exercise before long. I want to hear increasingly good news of you from now on. I'm sure I shall.

With affectionate thought always, dear,

Devotedly,

Father

To his daughter   Clearwater, Florida
New York   Wednesday, March 13, 1940

Dear Emily:

You are much in my mind following the latest report of the anemia, the low blood pressure and the indications of some irritation of the eyelid. You were deploring your unfamiliarity with the anatomy and physiology of your own body and of the general dearth of knowledge in this regard. You spoke of it when you were here.

I guess you do know roughly the relationship between respiration and the supply of oxygen to the blood—how the red blood corpuscles are driven at regular periods into the capillaries, or the very tiny blood-vessels surrounding the air-cells of the lungs, and there pick up the oxygen necessary for the nutrition of the body, as the blood conveys it to all parts of the organism.

There is no greater handicap in life with its manifold handicaps than impaired health or invalidism. Anemia is a particularly tenacious and obstinate malady when once it has reached a certain point. You have been earnestly counseled by two physicians independently to take into serious account your habit of substituting, over periods of varying length, the heavy impure chemistry of tobacco-laden air for the natural chemistry of air not so tainted. Your intelligent acceptance of their warning has come to be a matter of vital importance to your health, your life and your working efficiency.

The notion that it is hard to give up smoking is greatly exaggerated, if not wholly fallacious. People with the 'habit' of jumping off roofs would find it exceedingly hard to give up, but for the fact that the first indulgence in this pastime usually ends fatally. The habit stops itself. I suppose all of us have the impulse or urge to jump from roofs, but it is so obviously impractical that the great majority of us refuse to entertain the thought for a single instant.

To persist in a habit which one's physicians point out as being, in a particular case, extremely hazardous, is likewise most impractical. The impracticality of such a course has evidently escaped your clear recognition, or else, like the impulse to leap from a roof, you would likewise not entertain the thought for a single instant. A habit hard to give up? Nonsense. No more than the habit of wanting to jump from the roof by way of 'relief.' What is hard, if it can be called that with a person of your intelligence and clear-seeing, is the one, quiet clear act of intelligent recognition that, for you, smoking is burdening your life with a serious and permanent handicap. Under the circumstances and knowing you I cannot believe that you will for a single instant refuse to look the clear facts clearly in the face.

It will assist the one single moment of clear recognition the circumstance requires, if you will consider with Hans and me our deep and urgent need of you by our side. I haven't words to tell you how much your assistance and your coöperation mean to us. We have a difficult and exacting piece of work in process. We need our utmost health and vigor to sustain ourselves and one another. 'A word to the wise.' (14)

Your ever devoted

Father

Clearwater, Florida
March 19, 1940

Dear Emily:

Your good long letter reached me yesterday, and I am hastening to send you this word in order to offset any misgivings you may

(14) Emily stopped smoking!

have as to my reaction to it. There was at first, like Mother, the not unexpected, though mild, jar to cherished sensibilities that anyone could suppose for an instant that the living-room at Summer Hill could possibly be improved upon. But my better council straightway recovered itself and I thought, 'of course your feeling for the more up to date taste in decoration is sharper, more alert than ours,' whereupon I began to see your point. As you say, that heavy mahogany bookcase is no museum piece. It is not even a period piece—unless the early Pullman—and could well be spared in the interest of modern decoration. Personally I *love* open book shelves (very plain) in a room of that type. Could not one be placed at each side between the sofa and the French doors? But what's the matter with the sofa on the left of the fireplace? Couldn't that go between the French doors? I'm thinking of economy. And as to rug, I had been thinking that Hans and I (this was prior to your yesterday's letter) might readily spare the larger rug in the office (my mother's) and put it in the living-room at Summer Hill. Mother (*your* mother) has never cared for the rug now in the living-room because of its conflict with the draperies. Here again, there'd be an economy in not buying another rug. But maybe you have your heart set on the plain rug. I'm sure that the greatest happiness in the world to Mother, as to me, is your personal interest in and love for our home—your feeling that it is *your* home, as it most certainly is. And basically I know Mother, like myself, is deeply happy in your interest in assisting us with suggestions as to improvements in decoration of the house. The upturned table that Aunt Nora painted I always liked, but I should think it would go beautifully in the northwest corner of the dining-room. So, feeling as strongly and as gladly as I do that 'my house is your house' and that your share in it with us will be doubly real to you to the extent in which you share in the thought and care and responsibility that go into its making, I am in spirit wholly in sympathy with your letter and its suggestion. As for the changes I believe you will not find me uneducable. Already I begin to get a very congenial feel for the general scheme you outline, and believe the alterations will, as you say, go far toward enhancing the distinction of a room that is, in my feeling, already notably distinctive.

Let me say a word again in regard to 'social prestige.' I have no quarrel whatever with 'social prestige' in so far as it is the community recognition of something for which I really stand by reason of my work, my intelligence, my gifts, my accomplishments and what-not. My only criticism of 'social prestige' is leveled at the sort of thing that *substitutes* for real achievement the distinction that comes of the pretense, the 'laborious pretense' of being something or representing something that one doesn't represent. In short, fake prestige for fake accomplishment or no accomplishment at all. But I think we understand each other in this regard.

So glad the wrist has healed. Hope the shoulder will follow suit. So glad too that you and Hans saw Debussy's Pelléas et Mélisande, and that you enjoyed it so completely. You are a real opera lover. I regret that I don't really know this Opera. But I can say now that I know I wouldn't get a really deep appreciation of it from a first hearing. I just don't, if music is worthwhile.

But no more now. A dog gone nap and then on deck again.

Love to you and Hans,

Devotedly,

Father

To Dr. Hans Syz   Clearwater, Florida
New York   April 15, 1940, Monday, 1 p.m.

Dear Hans:

Your welcome letter came this morning. I do not wonder at your great distress of mind over the situation in Europe nor at your serious apprehension of still worse ahead. You have been held on the rack for so many months I don't see how your outlook could be other than the darkest. I cannot help feeling, though, that the developments of the last weeks place Switzerland in a far more favorable position. The battleground has been shifted so many thousands of miles from her borders. And as for England, unless *I* am only half awake, she is by no means as sleepy as may have appeared. I feel the Allies are proceeding with great foresight, wise organization and careful precision. They seem to feel there can be no mistake this time. I only wish I knew that America was as fully awakened as England. I only wish I felt that the reproaches we are increasingly bringing upon ourselves through our quite callous attitude were unmerited. Anyhow, if you can forgive me, I see or think I see a decidedly positive, constructive aspect in this strange war—this strange world-war. There is a progressive urge and a challenge of the old order that inevitably confronts the partitive system in man's adaptation in the ultimate analysis. I wish we could align our sympathies and our hopes with this undoubted world trend.

I did so value your letter to Dr. X. This consistent disregard of me has its interesting, its intriguing side. It just isn't the ordinary community reaction against a new position. The thing has its insane (unconscious) roots and we should be able to lift them out of the soil and expose the disease that is attacking them, not in any spirit of acerbity but in a clear objective interest in a behavior process.

It is good to know of the completion of the respiration literature. I know you've done a good job. I wish I could say as much for my part in the writing of the new book. It hasn't gone well. We've just not been up to it. With its breadth of concept and plan I am more or less content. But it isn't on paper. There are random passages. The outline lacks coherence. I lack something. Maybe you and I can bring something into shape together.

I shall try (as you suggest) to get what sun and warmth I can in the remaining time. It will be good to see you all again. There will be many things to attend to in the next ten days, many things to attend to on our return. I'm glad there have been 'somewhat fewer interruptions lately' and that there is the better opportunity for looking into some of the other things you have listed—attention, etc.

To go back a moment. Don't you think that this war is to be a real world-war, that we in America are already on our way into it? The basic occasion of it—the universal sense of economic insecurity on our present universally partitive level—seems to admit of no alternative but a general war. America maintains still for the most part its elated phase in this socially partitive dislocation, but so have the other nations passed through this social episode of gaiety. I can only see in it all, though, a deeply (phyletically) constructive urge toward man's phyloörganismic basis of motivation.

But no more tonight. My love to your dear, sweet wife and my precious daughter.

Devotedly,

Father

To a friend   New York City
Henry Parr   July 8, 1940
Ozona, Florida

Dear Mr. Parr:

I was just saying the other day in a letter to Dr. Whitford how remiss I had been in not having written you in all this time. On returning to New York I had thought that our laboratory staff would be plunging into an intensive program of kymographic recordings of respiratory movements. I should have known better. As soon as I got back it was evident that the important thing was the preparation of a report on experiments already done, including some of those carried out last winter in Clearwater. This got me in deeper than I had expected. So that I have been busy in the preparation of this material ever since my return and I only finished the report a week ago. The paper is a very brief outline of the more important data to be included in the book I have been at work on for some months. This larger work, if the experiments justify it, should include data on brain waves, so that we have spent some time working in the laboratory of Dr. Rheinberger at the Jewish Hospital in Brooklyn. These experiments already show evidence of a difference in the electrical potentials according as the subject is in attention or 'cotention.' But the results have to have considerable treatment yet which means, of course, a lengthy analysis by Dr. Rheinberger. We shall not hear from this until the last of July.

Another thing that has interested us somewhat is the possibility of discovering some drug whose effect upon the brain will aid the process of cotention. Of course any drug that would dull the sensibilities—a drug like opium, for example—is necessarily ruled out, as naturally the subject must be in the fullest possession of his faculties in the cotentive period. There is, however, a drug which has much the effect upon the brain centres as opium, but without the detrimental results of that drug. This is nothing other than cobra venom. I don't know whether Dr. Whitford has used this drug at all. Its effects on cancer patients are quite remarkable. It relieves pain in these chronic cases more effectually than opium and, instead of dulling the patient's senses, has quite the contrary result. Furthermore it has no habit-forming consequences, and the influence lasts much longer. As yet the drug is very little in use, but I learned of it through a colleague, Dr. David I. Macht, formerly of the pharmacological department of Johns Hopkins, and now director of the pharmacological research laboratory of Hynson, Westcott & Dunning of Baltimore. Dr. Macht, to whom Dr. Syz wrote describing our problem, thought perhaps the cobra venom might offer some assistance in our researches, and so we are planning some tests with it in ordinary attention [ditention] and in cotention with a view to discovering, if possible, whether there is any marked influence on the latter reaction.

Another trend has been occupying us of late, and that is the tabulating of the results gotten with the spirometer or the basal metabolism apparatus. It seemed well in writing up my report to include the minute-volume of air, the tidal air and the oxygen utilization. The gathering of these data has necessitated considerable study and computation. But this will give you an idea of the extent to which the kymograph has temporarily gone by the board, and it is very much a question whether we will be able to carry on any experimentation with it during the summer. This will explain, I hope, why we have not had the opportunity of forming a maturer impression of the modification you were good enough to make on the kymograph record—the horizontal lines you devised for us as an adjunct and 'control' of the tracings. But I hope to be able to tell you later on of their bearing upon our continued experimentation. I can only say now that both with Dr. Thompson and with Dr. Syz, their first reaction was one of great satisfaction in having this further control in the taking of the kymograph tracings.

As I wrote Dr. Whitford, Jack and William are quite encouraged over the prospects of a satisfactory camp season.(15) Unfortunately there has been a great deal of rain with cold weather, but the last news brought word of clearing skies. So we are hoping for the best. For those of us who have been at work here in the laboratory and in working up material for my report, the cool weather has been most welcome. Today has been really the first warm day but, with the immediate experiments and the paper off my hands, we can submit more or less gracefully to some hot weather. Besides, we'll be getting off to camp very soon now. Mr. Shields and I hope to go away Wednesday, and two or three others at the end of the week. It is quite a question with me just how those of us who have for years been accustomed to the quiet studious sur-

(15) Dr. Galt and Mr. Burrow opened a camp for boys and girls at Lifwynn Camp in 1940. After two successful seasons the project was given up because Dr. Galt entered the Army and Mr. Burrow took a position in defense work.

roundings of Lifwynn Camp are going to adjust ourselves to the necessarily altered atmosphere created by the children. From one angle I have rather dreaded it, but in the last days it has occurred to me that it will probably do me and the whole bunch of us old people a world of good. I suppose, of course, it is going to be an anxious summer for us all, with the ghastly uncertainties of Europe and now of England and maybe even of ourselves in the not too remote future. Certainly it would seem that man has fallen upon evil days, and the outcome defies prediction.

I hope life is being kind to you these summer days. If the weather is proportionately cool as with us, Clearwater should have been very delightful these past weeks.

We are looking forward to seeing Dr. Whitford in camp on the 15th. Weather and children should be settling into favorable routine by then, and we should have some interesting weeks there at the Lake. I begin to see your point of view about the chilliness of the Adirondacks, but I still insist we have many days in camp that are as lovely as the days we know and love in Florida.

You must not bother to leave your sailing or fishing or your tinkering to answer this too-long letter. It is itself a too-long delayed answer to all your interest and painstaking workmanship in my behalf.

My own and Mr. Shields' warm remembrances to you and Dr. Whitford.

Sincerely yours,

Trigant Burrow

P.S. By minute-volume is meant, of course, the amount of air inspired per minute. And I should have explained that tidal air means the average volume of air per respiratory movement.

CHAPTER 12

A DEVELOPING TECHNIQUE

To Sue de Lorenzi   Lifwynn Camp, Merrill, N. Y.
Chicago   August 31, 1940

Dear Sue:

As I am momentarily in expectation of becoming a grandfather—
even now William may be returning with a telegram—you won't
expect a coherent letter from me or a letter half worthy of the
delightful word I had from you some weeks ago. I so enjoyed your
news and was heartily regaled to know of the wonderful apartment you had found with its exceptional outlook, and of the fine
opportunity you so love for the execution of your various domestic
enterprises.

But today I am writing only to tell you how happy Brownie and
I were made through the rumor that we may count on a week-end
from you at Summer Hill this autumn. We shall do what we can,
believe me Sue, to transmute rumor into reality.

How restless I am these days, you can imagine. I have been big
with grandchild ever since last winter, as my Clearwater physician, who had me under observation, can testify! Helen and Jack

and the baby are to be with us when she leaves the hospital, and you know the joy that will mean to Brownie and to me. The way we have been multiplying in the last year is nothing short of phenomenal. For thirty years we had but two children, and here we are with four, and a fifth momentarily awaited.

These last days in camp are, as usual, a great delight to all of us. It always means some additional construction. This year, if you please, it is a 'ball-park.' What was on Monday a forest is already a terrain rich in promise of a fine play-field for the children. Carl, son of Albert Perry, Carmen (so named because his head is as red as the eternal fires), the son of Harry Merrill, Bernard, the son of Westcott Moore (it sounds like the Book of Genesis, doesn't it?) and Albert Furniss, of course, at the plough with Cash Bellows' sturdy little horse, Prince, are all contributing their doughtiest part toward making the new emprise of Lifwynn Camp all that it should be. As you read all these familiar names you must feel that you are right in the heart of Merrill. And I haven't mentioned the redoubtable work of Dr. Thompson or William, or the rare generalship of my own self in the role of foreman. . . .

Did I tell you of the delightful visit we had at Miss Farrar's one afternoon just before coming up to camp? She was, as you would know, her ever charming and gracious self. I think no one was ever a more graceful hostess than Geraldine Farrar. Her interest to keep, or perhaps I should say renew, the common touch is in my feeling the surest witness of her graciousness. After such triumphs as hers, it is really very beautiful to see her complete participation in the homely interests of her simple rural surroundings. We are certainly looking forward to having her over at Summer Hill when you are with us.

. . . Thank you again for your good letter, Sue, and with my love to you and Marion,

Always affectionately,

Trigant Burrow

Penelope Sherwood Burrow was born on September 4, 1940, and her cousin, John Devereux Syz, the following year. 'The grandchildren of their dreams' had become a reality for Dr. and Mrs. Burrow. Within the next two years their happiness increased still more when both their son and daughter moved to homes in the immediate neighborhood of 'Summer Hill.' During the war years, Jack was engaged in defense work in Bridgeport, Connecticut.

Burrow's papers, during the period of the present chapter, deal increasingly with the instrumental recording of physiological mechanisms under conditions of ditention and cotention. This experimentation depended, of course, upon the ability of the subjects to shift from the ditentive to the cotentive mode. Several of the letters in this chapter refer to the procedure followed by Burrow to arrest the constant flow of mental images associated with one's prestige (ditention) so that the organism's primary tensional pattern (cotention) is forced into recognition and into 'conscious directive efficiency.' This procedure is touched upon in his letter to Adolf Meyer, October 1941, and at the close of his long communication to his friend John, May 1942. Another description of the 'cotentive technique' appears in the next chapter in a letter to William Galt during his service as an Aviation Psychologist in the Army Air Forces.

To Dr. William E. Galt   New York City
Selma, Alabama   February 5, 1941

Dear William:

This is just a word. There is really not enough news to warrant even a word. But speaking of 'words,' for your phylo-etymological thesis, I want to suggest the word 'care,' because of its possible phylobiological implications. 'Care' equals 'burden,' 'responsibility,' and it carries the implication of pain. Then there is the expression, 'to care for a person,' so that there seems to be a certain identity between affection and distress or pain. Affection doesn't bring freedom and joy and gladness such as would be the natural biological reaction, but unhappiness and fear and worry. (Cf. 'The course of true love never runs smooth,' etc.) This could hardly be true affection. It must be obstructed, partitive, decentred, for a thoroughly true feeling of kinship or 'of one kind' with others as a primary biological emotion could not be anything but joyous and fulfilling. Incidentally we have spoken of the apparent connection between 'affection,' and 'affectation,' between 'affect' and 'affected' (artificial). By way of illustration of this conflict Miss Aimée(1) suggests in lighter vein Mrs. Ulman's story. You remember, Mrs. Ulman asked her colored maid if she did not think she'd like to get married, and she answered, 'No ma'am,' she never 'spected to get married. ' 'Cause ef you marry a man, you get to care for him, en you know, Mrs. Ulman, that's a strain too.' A little touch of levity to enliven your ponderous tome would not be amiss.

I have been thinking again, though, about your article and the possibility of concentrating all your work on its larger development into a book. Condensing so extensive a thesis within the small compass of a paper is going to entail a great deal of work, and I was wondering whether that work might not be given from the outset to the book. But we can talk this over when you come back.

Hope everything is going well in Selma and that Anne has definitely signed up for camp. I know how much you are enjoying being home again. Remember me to all.

Sincerely,

Trigant Burrow

(1) Aimée Guggenheimer, a student and volunteer office secretary of The Lifwynn Foundation whose editorial assistance was greatly valued by Dr. Burrow over the years.

To his daughter   Greens Farms, Connecticut
North Conway, New Hampshire   March [1941]

Dearest Emily:

The prospect of a whole week without seeing you is not a cheerful
one. I shall try to make it a busy week. I shall try to formulate
something that will be clear and worthwhile and ultimately perhaps bring a little enlightenment and relief to this sorely afflicted
world.

It has been a lovely day. After lunch Mother and I walked to the
post office. It is nearly dinner-time now and Elmer Davis is doing
his bit on the radio. And to what purpose after all? But there will
be the symphony tonight and that always brings a certain healing.

I do hope you will enjoy your trip, that it will help build you up.
These colds always deplete you more than you realize. That's
why your shoulders tend to sag so, following these attacks. Try to
think of your posture while you are away. Perhaps at Conway
there will be someone who gives certain helpful physical exercises.

As I thought of our talk last night about cultivated English and
accurate grammar, etc., I thought how trivial these elegancies of
language are (valuable as I concede them to be in their proper
place and relation) compared with the cultural need in whose
persistent, if slow, development you have from childhood been a
participant. Broad, inclusive, healthful feeling is the primary prerequisite to any culture. Without it, what is called culture is false
and idle. We know this—you and I—and in spite of the difficulties
and distractions, we shall slowly but surely make this organic principle our very own. This organic code will form the unfailing

background of whatever culture we may aspire to along lines of social and educational self-improvement.

Devotedly,

Father

To Kenneth Pride   Greens Farms, Connecticut
London   April 19, 1941

Dear Mr. Pride:

Your letter—I haven't it out here in the country with me—reached me Thursday morning, following the frightful raid on London the night before. Everyone in America was filled with horror at the thought of what England had gone through. I hope you, yourself, did not fare ill.

I was glad to have your letter and to have you recall the very kind letters Lawrence once wrote me. It meant no little to me also to know that you found *The Social Basis of Consciousness* of interest. That early essay seems distant history to me now. Much water has flowed under the bridge since those days of my first struggles with group-analysis—phyloanalysis, as I came later to call it, because of the wide alterations those first formulations had undergone. I often wondered what Lawrence's reaction would have been to the more biological modifications in viewpoint and in behavior the later developments brought about—whether he would have been sympathetic or antagonistic. And as I read your very kind letter reminiscent of my early gropings into human motivations, I wondered what would be your reaction to me now— whether you would be as sympathetic to my trend today as in those early group-analytic years. . . .

You do not tell me anything of yourself. I'd like to know your own interests and background. I'd be better guided in looking up reprints to send to you. Lacking this orientation you must forgive me if I send you papers that are little to your liking or interest.

My office address is 27 East 37th Street, New York City. I come out to my home here only once or twice a week. What a contrast from the peace of these hills to the desperate days you are living through. Be assured that all our thought is of England.

Sincerely,

Trigant Burrow

To Geraldine Farrar
Ridgefield, Connecticut

New York City
May 23, 1941

Dear Miss Farrar:

It has been so long ago now perhaps you will have forgotten that you were good enough to say I might send you a reprint of a brief essay dealing with a thesis of mine that I have deeply cherished over many years.(2) It goes to you today with my very cordial greetings.

I hope you and Mrs. Gilmour had a delightful trip throughout. Sue passed on to us one incident that was especially heartening— your accompanying Miss Telva's singing of Schubert's Ave Maria amid the quiet of that mellow church interior with its traditions of a bygone civilization. In these grim and desperate days such moments of remembered loveliness are all the more treasured.

Mrs. Burrow and I have thought of you and Mrs. Gilmour many times and of the happy gathering we had together before you went away.

(2) 'The Human Equation,' *Mental Hygiene*, 1941, vol. xxv, pp. 210–20.

With kindest remembrances from us both,

Sincerely,

Trigant Burrow

To Dr. Kurt Goldstein   New York City
Boston   May 24, 1941

Dear Dr. Goldstein:

I am very pleased that you should wish to have a reprint of 'The Human Equation.' I had already set aside a copy for you, believing that it expresses something of the outlooks we share in common.

Indeed I have not forgotten you. Your note at Christmas time to Mrs. Burrow and me meant very much to us both. Although I have not yet told you so, we greatly appreciated this word from you and Mrs. Goldstein. It is pleasant to find so close a kinship as yours with one's own deepest sentiments.

Sincerely yours,

Trigant Burrow

To Richard Connell   Greens Farms, Connecticut
Beverly Hills, California   June 1, 1941

Dear Mr. Connell:

Some weeks ago I had the pleasure of seeing your recent Cinema, 'Meet John Doe,' and I want to tell you what a splendid job I think you've done. While I cannot qualify as a movie fan, I had heard very much about this picture. And knowing that its author was my predecessor in the occupancy of this delightful house in these friendly New England hills, I am taking the liberty of writing you.

What I especially liked was the underlying idea of your story. It is, I believe, *the story of the future*. That interested me deeply. Incidentally I thought it flawlessly acted throughout. But it was your theme that impressed me, especially its breadth of sympathy and kindliness.

My own interest has for years centred in what I call man's social neurosis. My thesis is that the life of man is primarily unitary and integrated. ('Know ye not that ye are all one body?') As a physician interested in mental and nervous disorders (I was among the earliest of the American psychoanalysts) I soon came to the position that the real conflict in these disorders of behavior—and there is always the element of conflict in these conditions—is a basic, if deeply latent, sense of this originally unitary structure and function and *feeling* common to us all, and that the real pain is due to the organism's separation from this primarily unified principle. We don't *want* to be greedy and competitive and self-centred. It is due to an inadvertent *faux pas* in our evolution.

I remember years ago, in the very beginning of my psychoanalytic work, having written a play, 'The Dream Interpreter,' that dealt more or less with this underlying concept. Mrs. Burrow and I used to work at it in the evenings. I recall that we were immensely pleased over Prof. George Baker's criticism of it. But practice became pressing, and later came research and writing, so that our play was crowded aside. Perhaps we will some day return to it, having found heart again in your delightful screen play. . . .

Should you be in the East any time, I hope you will come to see us. It should not be difficult to make you feel at home here in your own Basque house. . . .

Thanking you again for a very pleasant evening and a very heartening experience, I am,

Yours cordially,

Trigant Burrow

To Virginia Watson
New York

New York City
June 27, 1941

Dear Virginia:

You are very good to ask me to have tea with you at the Cosmopolitan Club. I have been hoping for some letup in the unusual stress of things with me sometime between now and the 15th of July when I was to go to camp (my office and work go along with me.) But I have been suddenly obliged to advance the time of leaving to the 8th, and this quite shatters my hopes of being able to see you before leaving, and talk over old Atlantic days. (3) As for my juvenile escapades, I think I am still the most amazed of listeners when I hear them recounted. They tell me they are still a breath-taking legend in Norfolk—that I am a sort of tradition not unlike Max and Moritz, and that to this day mothers cannot conjure a severer reproach to their young hopefuls than to say to them, 'Upon my word, you are almost as bad as Trigant Burrow!'

Do let's get together in the fall, and do tell me of some of the episodes for which you have, like many of my friends, so extraordinary a memory.

I hope your own summer will go well, and I am so glad you were sympathetic to my little essay. Remember me please to Eugene.

Very sincerely,

Trigant Burrow

(3) See page 87.

To Leo Stein   Merrill, Clinton County, N. Y.
Florence, Italy   July 26, 1941

Dear Stein:

You used to say I had a way of writing you that I had just received
a letter from you and would answer it at a more fortunate moment,
and that the fortunate moment never came. So I want at least to
make a beginning of breaking up a bad habit by not letting a real
interval pass this time without following up my sanguine assurances of an early comeback when I wrote you just as I was leaving
New York for camp.

I have been here now for nearly three weeks, but have been asleep
most of the time, and in what few waking hours there were I just
didn't give a damn. This behavior I would have you to know bodes
real progress with me. One of the main reasons why I give so poor
an account of myself has been my inability throughout the years
to let down.

To go back to your letter and the paper of which you speak, there
has been in the last year or two an ebullition of writing that marks
in a sense a new phase with me. There will be other such in the
next months, I hope, and there is the possibility still of their pre-
humous publication. The present trend might be called 'psychosomatic.' This really doesn't cover my meaning, but just to keep
sweet I'll let it go at that. 'Phylosomatic' would be the better term
if I dared as yet to put into currency a coinage so alien to prevailing
behavioral premises. But people everywhere—all of us—are going
to let go of a lot of graven images in the long aftermath of recon-

struction that will undoubtedly follow the present clash of inter-individual or psychogenetic self-interests. Undoubtedly individuals and nations will more and more be forced toward the mental recognition of their conflict through a somatic acceptance of the internal (physiological) basis of it. I feel sure that as nations and peoples we will come at last to appreciate as *intra*-tensional those discrepancies of behavior we now project, and have projected *per omnia saecula saeculorum*, as *inter*-psychic.

No amount of prating on this theme by an isolated group of research workers is going to yield the slightest concession from individual or community in their present subjectively ensconced security—a security that has mere images of self-interest (whatever the form) to support their wholly moralistic (really narcissistic) claims. The soma (the phylosoma) is from a considered evolutionary point of view undoubtedly in the ascendant, and the knell of man's image-begotten interrelations and dependencies has already tolled.... The whole grand illusion with which the partitive segment has symbolized life will suddenly pass, and the actuality of life will enter into its indigenous and universal own.

Perhaps in so short a time as a hundred years hence (maybe even fifty) we will wonder why all the rumpus. We will ask how it has been possible that men with whole brains have allowed themselves to be pulled around through all these ages by their nosy part-brain or prosencephalon. ...

I am glad your painting goes well. It is too bad that this prolific output of yours has come at a time when there must be so poor a market for all creative forms of expression. Perhaps the great aftermath will be the answer. In the meantime it must be very awkward to find yourself marooned on the continent of Europe as you are. But at least you are more fortunate than those who have stood for months on the docks at Lisbon and been unable to board so much as a raft bound for America. My sympathies are yours. And yet, loving Italy as you do (and how we all have loved Italy!) there may be compensation even in the midst of the general disorganization of things throughout the world—a disorganization of which, as you know, we here in America are already experiencing the distressing prodromals.

Sincerely yours,

Trigant Burrow

To Margaret Prescott Montague   Lifwynn Camp, Merrill, N. Y.
White Sulphur Springs, West Virginia   August 15, 1941

Dear Margaret:

Of course it's Margaret and Trigant. The 'Dr. Burrow' gave me quite a shock. And after all these years!

It was good to hear from you and from 'Oakhurst Orchards.' I remember it so well, and its delightful setting among the mountains. It must be lovelier still now, with its trees grown larger and sturdier. I like to think of you there—of your returning there with the renewing of each year, or as you once put it in *Home to Him's Muvver*, 'when May swings into her perfumed place among the months.'

I appreciate so much your writing me as you did about 'The Human Equation,' and your difficulties with it. And 'Spider Self' I fairly dote on. Your phrase, 'the ephemera of self,' is especially delightful. I remember that apt word from William James. Some day I know I shall be quoting this poem of yours by way of adding the more graceful touch to what must often seem a very staid thesis with me. If it has been published, I should be glad, for the convenience of the reader, to know where.

As to what you say of religion, I am afraid I cannot go with you, and I like so to go with people of your sort. I have thought a good deal of these aspects of man's subjective experience, but only in a desultory sort of way. If, as I see it, religion is just another name for devotion, I can't quite bear 'thinking' about it—objectivating it. Devotion to science is different. This is objective devotion. It is devotion to things as they are. With science, there can't be too great awareness. Objective observation is synonymous with science. But it does seem to me that with religion, as with love or peace, contentment or health, once we look at it, there is nothing there. It is like trying to juxtapose self-consciousness and spontaneity. They simply do not mix. (You remember Emerson's Eros?—

> They put their finger to their lip,
>   The Powers above:
> The seas their islands clip,
> The moons in ocean dip,
> They love, but name not love.)

I hope that in disavowing these dissident admixtures I do not appear to be growing coy. Coyness and senescence would, I am sure, seem to you an equally inept combination! . . .

You ask, 'How are we going to cure a disease which you apparently feel afflicts the whole of humanity?' Freud once asked the same question, 'Does Burrow think he is going to cure the world?' But after all, why not? Of what earthly use is science if it serves the need of anything short of the whole world? Where, pray, would we be today if the early bacteriologists had taken the position that infectious diseases must be eradicated from, let us say, the families of Pasteur and Koch, or that only the communities embraced by the Latin Quarter or the Canary Isles must be rendered immune to infection? Think what has happened with tuberculosis in the mere flash of a momentary fifty years! And there is no disease more communicable than nervous disorders.

Yes, Margaret, let's cure the world. It's so much easier than attempting to cure you or me, or any other Tom, Dick or Harry in the midst of our sick and soul-infected human species. I hope God will forgive me, but I'm all out for the world at large. Anything less than the race of man seems partisan to me, and I'm sure that your own hope envisages no less a quarry. All that is needed, all that has ever been needed is that man know clearly, demonstrably what the matter is—what structure and what mechanism is disordered or impaired. Once the real focus of a disorder is clearly established, man pursues the remedy indefatigably. Nothing stands in his path. It will be this way increasingly with man's attitude toward his own disorders of behavior—his insanity, his greed, his competitiveness, his cheats, his wars, his sentimental dependencies, in short, his subjective devotion to things as he would like to see them rather than his objective devotion to things as they are. You will see. . . .

I am in hearty accord with your proposal that we talk together of these things sometime. And, if ever I'm so fortunate as to get out Greenbrier way again, I'd love to see you. In the interim of the years I've heard such fine things of Cary's work as well as your own, and I should be so interested to hear more of you both.

Sincerely yours,

Trigant

To a former student   Lifwynn Camp, Merrill, N. Y.
            August 21, 1941

Dear Dr. M.:

It certainly was a pleasure to have your letter. I'd begun to think you had quite forgotten us. I did so enjoy having the news of you and your interests and also the word about R.(4) I know how reassuring it must be to you and Mr. M. that he is making his way.

I still think it quite outrageous that you are not making yours. Competent, socially minded, exceptionally educated, fine medical training, wide experience in the field of missionary medicine, a real feeling for service, liked by everyone, and admired by everyone except me, yet with all this you sit dawdling up there on some hill in the conventional thickets of your parochial Yorktown!

Things have gone so very well with us. I don't know how we have managed without you, but you will be pained to know that we somehow pulled through and that the outlook was never brighter in respect of our scientific endeavors.

It would be mighty nice to see you sometime. We lunch at one and dine at 6:30, and your place is always set and awaiting you at 27.

It was splendid to hear of your selection for the chairmanship of the organization for Chinese relief. I know they could not have appointed you to a more congenial piece of work. That you were so successful goes without saying. My salutations to you and your committee. It is nice too to know that you have at last squirmed yourself into high society, and are now moving with New York's upper bracketeers. It is only a step now to Newport. If only you do not entirely forget that you once knew us.

You may not have heard, or it may have gone in one ear and out of the other, that Jack and William have taken over Lifwynn Camp as a summer camp for small boys and girls. You might keep this in mind. They are looking for the right sort of children with the right sort of background and recommendations. And you might pass it on to some of your socially minded friends with whom your work brings you into contact. I feel sure Jack and William sent you a copy of their prospectus.

(4) Her son.

As I say, all that you wrote about R. interested me immensely. I would love to see him sometime. It is good that he makes friends as he does and has developed, or rather shall I say, has released such broad human sympathies as he goes his industrious way. . . . It is amusing about his taking up Chinese. I'll wager his inclining this way was not uninfluenced by the early affiliations with China of his immediate antecedents.

I hope you will let me know of your change of base. I should be interested in it and what it may bring forth. I do hope it is the beginning of your too-long belated career in individual and social medicine. It is just unpardonable that you aren't with us in our common field.

All this, and I haven't said a word about the most important item of news—our adorable granddaughter, Penelope Sherwood Burrow. She is really the loveliest, sweetest, healthiest and happiest infant you can possibly imagine, and the sturdiest camper among us all. And Emily and Hans are very happy in the expectation of the Christmas gift to which they are now looking forward. Emily has been so well throughout her pregnancy. She and Dr. Syz have been playing tennis, taking motor trips and long walks about the woods here, and in general have thoroughly enjoyed this month of his vacation here in camp. . . .

When you can find the leisure I hope you will read 'The Human Equation' which I so kindly sent you some months ago. It might even do you good.

My warmest remembrances to you and to Mr. M. and to R. when you write him. This goes equally for Mr. Shields and all of us.

As I said, lunch at one, dinner at 6:30.

Auf Wiedersehen,

Sincerely,

Trigant Burrow

To Dr. Adolf Meyer   New York City
The Johns Hopkins Hospital   October 23, 1941

Dear Dr. Meyer:

It happened that just the evening before you came in, the Foundation held its annual meeting. Following the meeting Mr. Shields suggested that you might be interested to see my report when you came in the next day. The next day, though, there was so much of mutual interest that many things had to go by the board. So I am sending you the report with this, believing that its trend will give additional support to what is, I am sure, our common 'meaning.' For your convenience I am enclosing this self-addressed envelope.

Dr. Syz and I, and our associates, were greatly stimulated by your visit. It seemed to set so much in order and to open possibilities of fresh orientation. But I awakened early in the night, my thoughts completely overborne by the happenings of the day. It was not now a quiet, ordered stimulation. The buzzing social segment had me. Thoughts raced helter-skelter. I sought to invoke cotention, but it was not to be decoyed. In my over-alertness I had no heart for cotention. The decentring was too complete with me. There was only a whirling orgy of the day's recollections—a repercussion of the things said and the things unsaid now rapidly formulating themselves in a riotous quest toward a better meaning, a closer commonness. But it was all hurried, obsessive, 'partitive.'

This was at 3.30. The tumult went on. There were efforts to shift the pattern of tension from the eyes and forebrain, but again and again the attempt proved futile. There was lacking the larger basis. There was lacking the central balance for directing thought and feeling upon an inclusive purposive course. . . .

After a while some slight order, some basic direction, began gradually to replace my self-important striving and concern. There came a shift in tensional emphasis from mere abstraction and symbol and concept to something less personal, less insistent, less 'knowing,' and with it the gradual slipping into a mode of behavior or a pattern of tension that was quieter, more determining than determined, more acquiescent, more of one piece—and whole. With this involuntary submission to a direction or purpose that was consonant or cotentive, after an hour I fell asleep again.

In a way this effort of re-articulation in internal patterns, so to speak, goes on throughout the days. But too often I am as little competent, my readjustment is as little efficient as in the hour I have described, during the night. Of course I am never going to help man in the fundamental reconstruction of his own behavior. Nobody is. It is only my long-conditioned habits of abstraction, affectivity and consequent isolation that ever led me to suppose I could. Man must avail himself of the discoveries of science to help himself. I do not doubt, though, that even now man is in his own way assisting himself, that he is somehow getting back to biological base, that all this world revolution—as ghastly, as insane, as destructive as it is—is somehow an expression of man's need to come to himself. My part, your part—the part of the social biologist, as I see it, is to use whatever authority we possess to assist this process of man's re-adaptation. It is to show as far as we can that man himself (and we along with him) is the only authority in matters of his own behavior, that this authority is internal to him, as it is internal to us, and that wherever we presume to *know*, wherever we presume to make an abstraction of this thing that is man's internal motivation (I am writing you just as the thoughts come to me) we are only deceiving ourselves and man. We are only adding to the obstruction, and retarding man's ultimate self-actualization. . . .

I think I was never more confident than now, and it heartens me more than I can say to realize that not in all the years that I have known you, have I felt your own confidence more keenly than at the present time. This is for me not merely an incitement but an omen. That there should be anywhere this surge of assurance in respect to human behavior in the midst of the behavioral chaos we are faced with today is to me the promise of a rehabilitation in man's processes such as the human organism has never before experienced.

I cannot tell you how much your visit to us and your interest meant to me. I earnestly hope it is the harbinger of a fuller, completer understanding of mutual meanings and aims that will make what may have seemed an interruption in our continuity of purpose only the surer evidence of a deeper collaboration between us.

With kindest regards from Dr. Syz and from our unit generally,

Sincerely yours,

Trigant Burrow

To Chester Colson   New York City
Medford, Massachusetts   December 19, 1941

Dear Chester:

Your good letter was very welcome. Letters from you always bring back memories of the very pleasant evening at Pawlet where we first met and where Mr. Shields and I first saw your interesting paintings.

I was much impressed by your questioning of your preparedness as yet for a one-man exhibit. I like this attitude of conservativeness. It speaks for balance and sanity, and a self-objectivation that will, I believe, contribute more toward the sure and steady progress and authority of your work than all the technical improvement in the world in the absence of this balance wheel. You are to be congratulated upon this tentative position in respect to your own work. It will stand you in good stead throughout the years. I am very glad to know, though, that you think of sending the photos of your pictures to Miss Etta Cone for which she asked.

Now as to 'success.' Isn't success too often the urge to 'see' oneself getting ahead—in truth, getting ahead of others? An old teacher of mine many years ago, Sir William Osler, though in those days at Johns Hopkins he was just 'Dr. Osler,' used to say that success was doing what one wanted and getting paid for it. I think I'd rather put it: 'Success is making one's living doing the things one likes.'

Do you know Oscar Wilde's essay, *The Soul of Man under Socialism?* What I have in mind is expressed very beautifully in the spirit of this essay. You probably know his *Ballad of Reading Gaol,* and, I hope, his *De Profundis.* Anyhow I'm sending you a volume of selected writings of Wilde's containing *The Soul of Man* and the *Ballad*—not the volume I wanted to get for you. I find that is out of print. I'm sorry.

As you know, Oscar Wilde's moral rating was not high. His sexual deviations are legendary. But he was a great artist and a superior personality nevertheless. So many outstanding artists—Michael Angelo, Leonardo da Vinci, for example—failed to adhere to a sexual manner of life that was according to Hoyle. They failed to conform to the social norm in these expressions, just as they abandoned the norm in respect to their creative abilities. But until man's 'norm' is more sound—more true to the primary biological type—we may not judge the behavioral deviate except as the expression of an inevitable pathology affecting man as a race or species. What could be more pathological, more insane than this hideous world-war? Yet who of us is not a part of it?

I am at the moment very comforted in the safe arrival two weeks ago of a fine baby boy to my daughter and son-in-law, Dr. Hans Syz. Both mother and son are doing splendidly. They are to be with us at Summer Hill at least for the holidays, and we are very happy in the prospect.

I must tell you that I am giving the more daring of your two canvases to Dr. and Mrs. Syz for Christmas, and to Mr. Shields the more restful of the two. So I shall have them both at hand to enjoy with them. The Old Print Shop did such a fine job in framing the pictures. I am very pleased. So you see we owe much of our happiness this Christmas to you.

My hearty greetings and best wishes for Christmas and the New Year,

Sincerely yours,

Trigant Burrow

To his son   New York City
Westport, Connecticut   Wednesday night at 10, April 1, 1942

Dear Jack:

I fear I seemed very ungracious this afternoon when you took formal leave of us. (5) I didn't realize what was happening. That was why I was not more responsive when you said good-bye. I don't want to say good-bye. I don't want to think of circumstances in that way.

When there was first the possibility of your withdrawing from the Foundation to enter defense work I was not a little saddened at the prospect of your absence. You have contributed something to us that I have deeply valued, something that was peculiarly your own. Recognizing its significance, it has been most welcome, and I am loath to part with it. Then too I have treasured our daily contacts throughout these years of our association—the occasional talks, the passing comment, the little exchanges from time to time,

(5) Mr. Burrow had been on the office staff of The Lifwynn Foundation since 1939.

and always the welcome greeting at the beginning of each day. These things have meant much to me, and then, in the larger view, there has been, as I say, the comfort of your own particular quality. That has been much and that will remain. Because of this there can be no parting between us. The word 'good-bye' is just not in our lexicon. I think we understand each other.

My love to your sweet wife. We share together the comfort of knowing you are just 'on leave.'

I'm hoping to see you for a while at least this week-end. There'll be, as usual, many things to go over. Here's looking forward to it.

And so, dear son, auf Wiedersehen,

Devotedly,

Father

The unusually long letter that follows is an example of Burrow's application of his findings to interpersonal problems. While his essential concern was with research rather than with practice, he was genuinely interested in everyday problems, and his counsel and assistance was always available to those who sought it.

To a friend New York City
May 21, 1942

Dear John:

I am glad you wrote to me as you did, and I need hardly say that I deeply value your confidence in me. May I say that merely to feel there is someone who will understand and appreciate one's problem goes far in itself toward the solving of it.

You must try not to think of yourself and Mary as in any sense isolated in your difficulty of adjustment. It is the common lot, John, and when we take such burdens too personally we only add needless weight to them.

I do not know how helpful I can be beyond assisting you to see your problem as a social problem and not confine it too narrowly to yourselves. So many, many fine young people are 'getting on each other's nerves' these days. These are times of very radical social change. Marriage as your parents and grandparents knew it, with its limited parochial conformities, is not the marriage of men and women today, with our rapidly changing social values.

To take up the items of your letter somewhat at random—you speak of wanting Mary's happiness 'more than anything else in the world.' That is one way of expressing devotion, I know, but I believe we can better it. I have known people to whom another's happiness has meant more than anything in the world to them, but who nevertheless have themselves been the real impediment to this very happiness they wanted above everything to give. Can't we see together that the higher, the more generous devotion would be one which would allow another the utmost freedom to pursue his own happiness as he himself sees it. Somewhere I have read, 'Self-ishness is not living as one wishes to live, it is asking others to live as one wishes to live.' Love is so largely a matter of asking others to live as we wish them to. But this is not the larger, the more generous devotion. Such love lays claims, it takes possession of others, exacts ownership of them. This is not healthy. Health, you know, means *whole*. Love that owns is self-interested, divisive. If you and Mary would each think more of your own happiness—I do not mean the happiness you find in your likes and dislikes, in your approvals or disapprovals, in the corroboration of other people's opinions, in hugging to yourselves your habitual prejudices, in being important to yourselves. But I mean the happiness that would come to each of you through your own fullest development, through your own closer touch with your needs as a developing personality. You and Mary need to be more alone. I mean each of you needs to be more alone. It is only as you may learn how to be alone in yourselves that you may learn how to be alone with one another.

Like so many other dear women, Mary (bless her heart) is too good to be true! Your going to the 'show' in Atlantic City was undoubtedly silly and not at all up to your developmental level, but who of us is not silly? Who doesn't at times step down from his proper plane? As for Mary's not 'forgiving' you, people forgive or do not forgive one another who own one another, that is, who have a right to others and to their way of living and thinking and feeling. This is all wrong. It isn't sound. You and Mary cannot make a go of things on an unsound basis. And you are both too intelligent not to be able to sense the unsoundness of your present premise of feeling and thinking.

Some of this may seem unacceptable to you. You may be pained by it. But I feel sure that were there the opportunity for me to talk with you, you would know that I would on no account pain you intentionally. I think you would know too that I could not speak differently to you than I do in honesty to myself and to my conception of the dignity of human behavior. You see, John, this inept organism that is mankind in the making is only just now awakening to the real meaning of human life. This present world-war, as ghastly, as tragic as it is, will contribute to this awakening through the sacrifices and self-examinations it will demand of us. People's standards have been too external, too *moral*. This may shock you unless you realize the sense in which I mean it and the spirit in which I say it. Morality is the precept we obey at the behest of others, at the demand that lies outside ourselves. In this, morality is no better than immorality. Both are based on emotion and the wish. Real integrity of personality builds from within. It rests upon thought and self-development.

With regard to you and Mary in particular, we must all three see that, after all, Mary is a professional woman. Marriage in its present status tends to narrow her outlook. It cannot do that without undermining her personality, her development. Both of you need larger interests than merely those of the nursery, as vital as I recognize the nursery interest to be. Does Thomasville exclude the possibility of a nursery school for little children? And if there is the right person for such an undertaking, cannot you and Mary give some effort to promoting such an innovation in your little community? Do you and Mary keep abreast with the current of the times? . . . What I am getting at is the importance of you and Mary having a broader ground to meet on than just your own domestic interests.

The plan to have Mary rest for two hours every afternoon is a most excellent one from every angle. But what about you? Don't you return sometimes from work after a day of rather exacting duties with your nerves somewhat on edge, and feeling a bit jaded? Would not a half or, better, three quarters of an hour of rest before the evening meal go far toward clearing the horizon for you too? I certainly should not reduce the pace of my work. The work will never hurt you. It is the worry, and all worry is opposition to work. Do your full measure of work and take a real rest after it is over— the sort of rest you recommend for Mary, even though it cannot be so long, of course.

As for changing your job, this would seem to me quite fatal. Let's dispel any such thought as quite rash. Your difficulty is not outside of you. It is neither the job nor the girl. It is your own reaction to both of them, as it is Mary's reaction to her job and to you. I have always wished that Mary could have some contact with her profession. That is what I was thinking when I mentioned the possibility of the nursery school. Just three or four hours a day of freedom would do wonders for her, or at least open the way for her doing wonders for herself. With her as with you, though, the real difficulty is within. With her as with you and the rest of people, there is too much conformity to external rules of conduct—too much morality in place of the personality's basic integrity.

Of course, with you as with Mary it is inevitable that you project your irritation with yourselves upon each other. But, as I say, this is the common lot. Man must come to himself and begin reckoning with a condition epidemic to him as a community or race. When you and Mary say harsh things to one another, you *do* mean them. Each of you really thinks the other is responsible for his own state of mind. You mean them because, in possessive love, it is inevitable that one 'dislikes' as much as he 'likes.' When one 'likes' oneself, one 'likes' one's mate. When one is at odds with oneself, one's mate is equally unacceptable to him. This is the penalty of morality or of standards of behavior motivated outside of oneself, outside of one's own intrinsic self.

Now as to technique and method. This, I feel, will not seem any more inviting than the rest of my therapy which, in a nutshell, requires that you bring your conflict back to its origin, namely, *in yourself*. There is the physiological basis of what we call ourselves, and this physiological basis is what interests me. And it is the technique of recovering the physiological self that is the distinctive feature of my work. Some years ago, by virtue of the laboratory work my associates and I have for some years undertaken in disorders of behavior, I discovered a method of attention that is now nowhere in use as a conscious effort of adjustment to the world of reality. This form of attention I have called cotention because it is attention with or within, not out or toward, as is the case in ordinary *at*tention.

To induce cotention it is necessary to secure quiet conditions, as for example when you take your three quarters of an hour of rest on returning from work in the afternoon. If with the eyes closed you will let yourself become aware of your eyes as organs in your head, you will close out all the restless images that make of us such mental gadabouts. In the effort to hold the eyes steadfast, in the absence of any point to focus upon, you necessarily develop an increasing awareness of the muscles about the eyes that maintain them in a position of equilibrium. As you first undertake this experiment you will probably become drowsy and will fall asleep, but you have fallen asleep in a healthy posture as far as your eyes are concerned. I don't know whether you know that all thought is accompanied by fine eye-movements or tremors. So that in re-gaining control of the movements of the eyes you automatically eliminate mental images or thought. It is this procedure that brings you back to your own organism, to your basic physiology, to the condition that was native to you as an infant, and native to your race in its infancy.

In first undertaking cotention you will find it difficult, and you will find every excuse for not continuing with it. Thinking, es-pecially emotional thinking, is so much a habit with you now, as with the rest of people, that it is easier to be pushed on by this habit than to let go of it. But it is precisely this restless mental habit prompted by emotion that you need to alter—you and Mary.

If you do not have success with cotention, hold yourself answer-able—yourself and your gadabout mental habits. If in the course of time you do have success, don't congratulate yourself or feel the least cocky. It is nothing to plume oneself upon. You have merely returned to a phase of attention or behavior that is basic and natural to the organism of man as a species. If you swell your chest over it, be sure it is *not* cotention.

As I said in the beginning, I don't know whether I can be of help. I don't know whether what I have written places your problem in any clearer, saner light before you. As I say, if we could talk together sometime it would be simpler. But lacking that oppor-tunity I have tried to do what I can to answer your very earnest appeal for assistance in the understanding of your and Mary's needed adjustment.

My love to you and Mary, and if the 'suggestions' I have tried to give you in response to your need are not clear, do not hesitate to say so. On the other hand, if they seem in any way workable between you, I shall be very happy and interested to know.

Sincerely yours,

Trigant Burrow

To a friend
Elizabeth Dickson   Lifwynn Camp, Merrill, N. Y.
White Sulphur Springs, West Virginia   July 28, 1942

Dear Elizabeth:

. . . When we were young how little thought we gave to the serious, the unhappy side of life. We thought it would always be as then, when never a day was long enough for all the gladness we used to crowd into it. The thought of loss, of the inevitable parting, of the fatal ending of all that made life such a joy was completely alien to the years we used to know when we were young and when Mountain Home was the centre of the life of ourselves and of our families. How changed the scene!

In a sense I suppose we haven't the right to think in this way, to make so much moment of our own personal lot, when the whole world is so desperately unhappy and so greatly in need of some sort of lasting, dependable guidance. I suppose we have no conception of, certainly no adequate feeling for or realization of the widespread suffering in Europe. It is all on too gigantic a scale for us to be able to appreciate. But the slow agony from day to day of the subjugated peoples of the smaller nations must be terrible beyond words. I suppose as it draws nearer our own shores—the increasing threats, the hidden, underhand blows, the widening practices of sabotage, the restrictions and sacrifices necessarily imposed by our own government, the steady flow of our young men to the different theatres of war—all these changes in our lives as they come closer to our own experience and our own homes will bring us at last to realize what this vast world revolution actually means. Here in the retirement of these woods it is hard to believe there could be such chaos in the world. It is hard to realize the enormous and the needless loss of life and property this world-conflict entails.

I like to take my thoughts back to Mountain Home and the peaceful retreat it has been to so many of us over the years. You and Sadie can feel very proud in having preserved a home like that with all that it represents. You can feel particularly what it has meant to Geraldine and her children ever since her early widowhood—that home and all that you two devoted women have stood for in your faithful work and service. (6) It must be a great comfort to you both to realize how much you are appreciated by all your family. You have certainly set a high standard for Geraldine's children and they idolize you. I hope the better word of Geraldine will mean still further relief for her.

We've had delightful days in camp so far. It has been quite cool throughout July. This is the time of year when Greenbrier was usually at the height of its summer beauty, but I suppose the war has affected White Sulphur as it has other resorts. I hope 'the boys,' as Elizabeth calls them, haven't found business too dull.

But I must hurry and catch the mail boat, so this must be all.

Love to you and all,

Devotedly,

Trigant

---

(6) Sadie and Geraldine were sisters of Miss Dickson. Geraldine was the widow of Dr. Burrow's brother, Devereux.

To Dr. Alfred E. Emerson   Lifwynn Camp, Merrill, N. Y.
The University of Chicago   July 31, 1942

Dear Dr. Emerson:

When I received your reprints in March I wrote you that after having read them I would write you again. . . .

I need hardly say that I found your papers most interesting. As it happens, the one that appealed most strongly to me was 'Biological Sociology.' I do not mean that this paper was necessarily more outstanding than the others, but I felt it had a closer bearing upon the work of my associates and myself. It is this paper, therefore, for which I want especially to thank you again. Indeed I am grateful that there is a biologist of your interests and perspective.

The 'superorganism' has been slow in taking hold of the biological mind. The tendency of students—certainly of students of human behavior—is to restrict their observations to the overt behavior of the individual, or to adopt a type of theoretical exploration that bears the unmistakable earmarks of the mystical. Your emphasis, therefore, upon the importance of group coöperation and group solidarity strikes a resounding chord within my own pattern of reaction regarding the behavior of man as a species. While my first teaching appointment was in the field of biology, this background of mine is of little avail today in relation to maturer biological concepts. I fear, therefore, that as a student of behavior in the lower animals I am somewhat handicapped.

My interest, after all, is in the study of the human animal, especially in the manner of its performance from within—not intellectual knowledge about the habits and ways of this remarkable phylo-organism, not its behavior as we look at it in the mental way in which we look at everything not ourselves. On the contrary, I am interested in man's need to acquaint himself with his own motivations as these motivations lend themselves to internal observation and internal control by the organism observing. When I say motivations I do not mean ideological motivations, but motivations that are organismic or, as you would say, 'superorganismic,' and that exist entirely apart from the individual as a socially conditioned persona. My associates and I are not concerned with ideas of behavior or with theories of conduct; nor are we interested in political, ethical or economic concepts of man's relation to the environment, but in the direct and immediate sense of the organism's primary unity and activation in respect to its surrounding medium.

Perhaps I am very inept in formulating my ideas, or else there exists in my scientific audience a marked distaste for this type of approach—this sort of self-reckoning. Or perhaps it is both. However this may be, the acquisition of this inner sense of one's own motivation as an integral element within a common species represents my sole interest in the study of human behavior. So that when it comes to a question of the behavior of the lower orders of animals, I can only point to the analogies which such investigators as you have come to know at first hand. . . .

Thanking you again I am, with kind regards,

Sincerely yours,

Trigant Burrow

To Mrs. Burrow   Lifwynn Camp, Merrill, N. Y.
Greens Farms, Connecticut   August 28, 1942, 9:45 a.m.

Dear Brownie:

I have certainly been exemplary this summer as far as obeying the injunctions of my physicians is concerned. Ordinarily I would have forced myself to sit at my desk through the long morning hours of each day and to have returned in the later hours of the afternoon and evening in order to check and amend the results of the morning's dictation. I have done nothing of the sort. There has been some desk work, of course, but so little as to be almost negligible. Except for my meticulous regard for all correspondence, my desk has had little claim upon me throughout the summer. Where I have applied myself without stint has been in the field of biological medicine. With Mr. Shields' assistance I have adhered very consistently to the work of our laboratory of human behavior. The table sessions have proceeded with unabated concentration throughout the summer, augmented, supported by an equally consistent schedule of cotention throughout the many quiet, private hours with myself. I don't know why I'm mentioning this, except to have you know something of my summer's program in its relation to my need to remain away from compelling mental work at my desk. In this I certainly have adhered faithfully to the advice of my physicians.

I'm sorry not to be on hand for Penny's birthday, but, if I do stay on a week or so longer, I shall be devoutly thankful not to be on hand for mine. I have no heart for it. The personal celebration of this sort seems utterly out of keeping with the circumstance of man's universal anguish and confusion today. I appreciate of course your interest in these little home touches and the interest of the family—the commemoration of life's milestones is not without *its* loveliness too—but except for the children, the little children, they seem to me out of order in these grim times and in the yet more grim times that lie ahead. If I remain here, the day will pass unnoticed. Tomorrow Miss Flora and Miss Hölljes leave for New York, on Monday William goes. We will be but a handful and, in William's absence, a very disconsolate handful.(7) In the circumstances, under present world conditions I would rather it were so.

My love,

Devotedly,

Trigant

(7) Dr. Galt was entering the Army.

To Frederick J. Hoffman   New York City
The Ohio State University   October 2, 1942

Dear Mr. Hoffman:

Your letter of September 26 reached me. Your research seems an interesting one, and I wish that in answering your inquiries, I might contribute my mite to it. (8) I fear, though, that my information is purely negative.

When I first knew Anderson many years ago, Freud's ideas were just beginning to reach this country. Yet Anderson was already acknowledged an outstanding novelist. He had written *Winesburg, Ohio* and *Windy MacPherson's Son*, and was well on with *Marching Men* which appeared very soon. *Mid-American Chants* came too about that time.

My feeling is that Sherwood Anderson was, like Freud, a genius in his own right. Anderson was a man of amazing intuitive flashes but again, like Freud, the chief source of his material was his own uncanny insight.

I can say very definitely that Anderson did not read Freud, nor did he draw any material from what he knew of Freud through others. Don't you think that all schools like to lay claim to an apt scholar? I think this largely accounts for the psychoanalysts' quite unwarranted adoption of Anderson. Of Anderson I would say that socially he was one of the healthiest men I have ever known. His counter offensive in 'Seeds' amply testifies to this. Indeed on this score many orthodox psychoanalysts might very profitably take a leaf from his book. Yes, I am the analyst to whom Anderson referred in this story.

With regard to Lawrence there was no 'association' between us, as it happens that I never met him. A student of mine interested him

(8) Mr. Hoffman quoted this letter in his book, *Freudianism and the Literary Mind*, Baton Rouge, Louisiana State University Press, 1945, pp. viii, 346.

in some of my earlier writings, and through them he was prompted
to put out the little volume he called *Psychoanalysis and the Unconscious*. Lawrence was very sympathetic to my trend at that
time and showed an uncommon insight into it. . . .

I regret that I cannot be of more assistance to you.

Very sincerely yours,

Trigant Burrow

To his niece, Elizabeth Burrow   New York City
Lewisburg, West Virginia   November 18, 1942

Dear Elizabeth:

With the occupation of North Africa by the Allies, with the successful Naval operations in the Solomons, and with your taking up
typewriting, I have been lifted to heights hitherto unknown to
me. Incidentally the practice of typing for the period of an hour
is not recommended. It is contrary to the psychological laws bearing upon fatigue. Where exercise is carried to the point of fatigue,
learning ceases, and results become negative. If you cannot practice, as is recommended, three times daily for fifteen minute
periods each—if it must all be done at one time—I strongly recommend that you do not use the typewriter beyond a half hour.
Under the circumstances that period will be far more profitable
to you. . . .

There was such a good letter from William yesterday. He seems
to have buckled right down to Army life and is finding his usual
efficient place in it.

My love to you all.

Devotedly,

Uncle Trigant

To Gretta Palmer　　　　　　　　　　　　New York City
New York　　　　　　　　　　　　　　　January 16, 1943

Dear Miss Palmer:

Word was brought me of your phone call and of your wish to have reprints of my writings on 'Phylobiology.' I much appreciate your interest and I want to respond to it in the way that will meet it most adequately.

So often in the past where I have been asked for material that might assist in the preparation of a popular article on my work, the outcome has not been satisfactory. Perhaps the fault has been largely my own. My writing is technical and in the very nature of the subject my material difficult. After all, the position to which I have been brought calls for a wholly altered basis of thinking and feeling, and this is not easy. It is not easy for the reader and it has not been easy for me.

Please do not misunderstand me. I do not wish to discourage your interest in the work my associates and I are doing. Indeed I appreciate very much your thoughtfulness in wanting to know something of our research and have it reach the wider community. But in your own interest and in mine I am going to suggest that you first come in to see me and let us talk over my essential premises and aims. If then they do not seem to you too staid or formidable for popular presentation, or if you are led to consider writing a more searching article than you now have in mind, I shall be only too glad to be of what assistance I can.

. . . If you should care to see me, will you not call my office the first of next week to arrange a time.

Very sincerely yours,

Trigant Burrow

To Maxwell Nurnberg   New York City
Abraham Lincoln High School, Brooklyn   February 3, 1943

Dear Mr. Nurnberg:

Your book, *What's the Good Word?*, is affording me all manner of entertainment, and I want to thank you for having written anything so delightful. You certainly know how to mix the three elements I hold to be the requisite ingredients of all instruction—interest, humor and the-reason-for. You even succeed in making one's errors exciting. But why are you so gentle with the radio commentators? Here are people shouldering the responsibilty of addressing the English-speaking world and thus setting an example to many millions of people in the use of their language, and yet whose own errors are often quite unpardonable. Take Mr. Roosevelt, for example. I think everyone would concede that his speech is unusually correct, nevertheless the head of our Govern-ment permits himself to say 'Gover'ment.' He also says 'Septemba,' the final syllable being pronounced like the final syllable in 'rumba.' While I believe it is permissible not to pronounce the r in the last syllable of words ending in er, I don't know of any authority for altering the vowel sound. Though one pronounces the pronoun 'her' without the final r, one may hardly change the vowel sound, as the negroes of the South do, and pronounce 'her' as if it were 'huh' (or as the a in 'rumba'). Or am I wrong about this?

As for the pronunciation of the radio speakers in general, consider the following list of words that I gathered quite offhand in a couple of evenings here at my radio:

          Al'-lies for Allies'
          Centen'-ary for cen'-tenary

> Galax'-y for ga'laxy
> Quorrel for quarrel
> Pinchers for pincers
> Prefer'-able for pref'-erable
> Res-pite' for res'-pite
> Formid'-able for for'midable
> Inte'-gral for in'-tegral

and finally the usage

'One reason why . . . is because'

These are just a few, but there are many other errors occurring from time to time that I have not jotted down. And I haven't mentioned Mrs. Roosevelt's habitual 'hospit'-able' instead of 'hos'-pitable.' So that I find you more benevolent than I incline to be when, in speaking of the radio commentators, you say that 'all of them certainly pronounce their words with reasonable care and correctness.' (Page 30)

. . . Under your heading on page 95, 'The Problem of Time,' I missed a reference to the usage, 'Do you have?' for 'Have you?' This form has come to be very general, it seems to me, and I cannot think it is correct. If I should ask a clerk in a store 'Do you have gloves?' I would mean, 'Is it your custom to sell gloves, or to have them in stock?' But I would not ask a friend, 'Do you have a knife?' I would ask, 'Have you a knife?,' because I am not interested in knowing what his custom is in the matter of carrying knives but my question is 'Do you happen to have a knife with you at the moment?' Maybe you will clarify this point in your next edition. And perhaps in a subsequent edition you will also tackle the phrase, 'Aren't I?' I should be interested to know your position toward this growing usage.

These remarks are not offered in a spirit of querulousness. I am sure you recognize that they are prompted only by the most friendly and appreciative criticism. As a matter of fact your amiable, if challenging, study seems to me to fill a long-felt need. At least the need has been long, whether felt or not, and I should think your book would be in a fair way to stand at the top of the list of best sellers.

One of my younger associates, Dr. William Galt (now in the Army), first drew my attention to *What is the Good Word?* He saw an excerpt from it in the *Science Digest* and wrote asking me to send him a copy. You will no doubt be interested in an essay of Dr. Galt's which is scheduled to appear in *The Psychoanalytic Review*—an essay he has called 'Our Mother Tongue or the Etymological Implications of the Social Neurosis.'(9) Dr. Galt's theme deals with a special application of philology to our phylobiological thesis. I think you will find in this study of his a stimulating point of view, and I am putting your name on the reprint list for this article, though it may be a matter of some months before the paper is published. Incidentally Dr. Galt, along with my son, conducts (or they were conducting before the war) a summer camp for a limited number of small boys and girls. As a result of his contact with children he feels there is much educational value even for the younger ones in an acquaintance with the origin and the relationships of words, and that it is possible to inculcate in children quite early a knowledge of the implications of words from the point of view of human behavior.

Thanking you again and with my congratulations upon a fine job,

Sincerely yours,

Trigant Burrow

---

(9) *The Psychoanalytic Review,* 1943, vol. 30, pp. 241–62.

To P/O Charles A. Wondolowski(10) New York City
Sidney, B. C., Canada February 9, 1943

Dear Charlie:

I don't know when I have received so exciting a letter as this last word of yours from Sidney. You certainly have been piling up the thrills since you reached the west coast. I am delighted for you. So is the family and so is everyone here to whom I read passages of your letter. It is so good to know too that on top of it all there was the reassuring word from overseas. I know you rejoice in the prospect of being sent to England, not only for military but for personal reasons too.

That was a very amusing account you gave of your elevation in rank, and finding yourself suddenly consorting with men so much older than yourself and of so much higher rank. I can understand that your situation was no fun at first and that you felt no little ill at ease.

What is the correct address in personal greeting to one of your rank? If a friend is introducing you, what is the proper form? Would he say Lieutenant Wondolowski, or would it be Officer Wondolowski? Was just curious.

I have decided that a batman is what I need. Such personal attentions would be right up my alley! I haven't known them since I left the Old South.

By the way, I am going to take the liberty of correcting your spelling in two instances. I would do so with Jack. Why not with you? I like so to have you observe these little details in spelling, and I am encouraged to do so, knowing your sensitive feeling for the more correct usage in all respects. Watch out for 'nonsense.' You wrote 'nonsence.' And then I have to catch you up on a very

(10) Before beginning his training with the Royal Canadian Air Force, Charles Wondolowski worked as chauffeur and gardener for Dr. Burrow who encouraged his interest in mechanics and aviation. He became a brilliant war pilot and was decorated by the King of England.

frequent error with people generally. In using the noun the spelling is 'advi*c*e,' differing from the verb, which is of course 'to advi*s*e.' But I must say you do not often give one the opportunity to catch you up on spelling.

You certainly are getting plenty of English tea, but I like to think of you in these English surroundings and amid these pleasant social customs; and you always seem so at home in any situation. I am really very proud of you.

It must mean a good deal to you to feel free to go into Victoria and not to have to be too punctilious about getting in at night.

This clipping I am sending you, regarding Eisenhower's sense of discipline, I thought would interest you in view of the lack of discipline you noticed among the soldiers on the street when you were in New York, and the absence of tidiness in dress.

It was wonderful having all that back pay accumulating while you slept. It was good to have been spared the awkwardness of having to go into debt. I am looking forward with eagerness to a photograph of you in the new uniforms. I know they must be smart and that you must look quite tops in them. Yes, Charlie, we'll have to remember always January 14, 1943. That was certainly a red letter day. But you have worked hard to earn it, and all your happiness and success are rightfully due you.

This is a poor letter in return for such a stirring one from you, but you won't look for anything from me comparable in interest and stimulation with your good letter to me.

Thought you might possibly care to see the reprint of a recent paper of mine, though the technique of the EEG is, I fear, somewhat alien to that of the modern aeroplane.

Don't keep me waiting too long for more news of you. Every detail of your work and days is of the greatest interest to me.

All are well here in Connecticut, and the news from Dr. Galt is good.

And now this must be taking wing to you. All my thought and good wishes,

Sincerely,

Trigant Burrow

To a student   New York City
                                                     April 15, 1943

Dear Miss N.:

I have your two petits bleus. The first is supplemented in the second, so that I shall answer only this one. It seems too bad and yet, I know, so inevitable that you should be cudgeling your poor brains over a convulsive outbreak that you believe is your own when, in point of fact, it is but a small part of a world paroxysm. Whether overt or covert, whether in you or me, in the Axis powers or the democracies, the disorder is the same. As long as each of us thinks he is the universe, he will go on cudgeling what he believes to be his universal brains. Our job is to recognize the illness of man, and our own involvement as but a very tiny element in the larger disturbance of the race of man. Neither you nor I is as important as each of us believes himself to be. But we like our importance so we cling to our belief.

There is a way out I think. I think the hunch as to this way out finds its strongest expression in the work of The Lifwynn Foundation, and this work possesses for you as for me greater significance (whatever our personal limitations) than anything else within our experience. For me, knowing this is all. The rest isn't my concern and doesn't trouble me except as my sick habituations within a social neurosis tend to draw me away from this basic chore.

We will work on—inadequately perhaps, but we will work on. What else matters outside of our common job? So never mind the 'efflation.' As a matter of fact, it was very welcome. And incidentally you have given me a new word which I find rolls pleasantly upon the tongue. Too bad it wasn't in 'the book.' But you may be sure I shall not omit it from the next!

I did appreciate more than I can say your ever generous attitude toward what you are gracious enough to think of as my understanding service to you. I only wish I might do more. Perhaps some day I shall. Not I of course, but this common job of ours.

Sincerely,

Trigant Burrow

To Dr. William E. Galt   New York City, Thursday, 8:30 a.m.
San Antonio, Texas   April 29, 1943

Dear William:

I was thinking yesterday—last night to be exact—how much your letters have meant to me throughout the winter. I have probably not expressed the appreciation that I feel, so that I would like to do so now. I do not have to tell you that the winter has not been without its difficulties (not too heavy, any of them, nor apart from the usual run of things of which you are only too aware). So that having your letters that always underscore your unfailing vitality and unfaltering purpose has meant more to me than I know how to say. But perhaps there is no need to—perhaps that is what means most to me after all.

What does 'frame' mean in the etymology of slang? Was it the idea of singling one out, setting him apart, removing him from continuity with his kind, as one frames a picture by demarcating it from every other article of furnishing in the room? We *frame* a mirror; it is not a part of the rest of one's familiar belongings. It is extraneous and only reflects them. And we *frame* a door. It too doesn't quite belong. It is the exit. Like the window and its frame, it 'gives out upon' another environment—upon something different. I wondered whether to 'frame a person' didn't carry this import too.

Then I must look up some time the relationships of the word *miracle* (*Wunder*, and our English *wonder*, *wonderful*), *mirage*— possibly even *mirror*. So many words contain in their common root the germs of our common or phylic neurosis. But I must set to work at yet other aspects of the roots of man, discovering where I can (within myself of course) wherein man's behavior reflects only the superficial derivatives of a common motivation to behavior rather than embodying the original meaning and unity of more basic roots to be traced beneath these superficial behavior aspects. . . .

Yours,

Trigant Burrow

To Aimée Guggenheimer   New York City
Baltimore, Maryland   May 15, 1943

Dear Miss Aimée:

I do not have to offer you any apology for not having written before now—the first available moment since reading my paper yesterday afternoon at the Psychopathological meeting. Dr. Syz and I found the customary audience; considerably bored, somewhat irritated, not a little impressed, distinctly mystified but, as always, unfailingly respectful.

You have spoken many times of the satisfaction it has been to you to have been with Mrs. Ulman at this time. (11) I want to take this opportunity to tell you how very much it has meant to me that you and Miss Flora could be with your sister in these past weeks. As I think you know, to have you with her would have meant much to me under any circumstances and at whatever inconvenience. It just happens (and I wish you would try to have Mrs. Ulman realize this) that I could spare you both at this time without being incommoded by your absence. This last paper of mine was one that called for very sedulous digging in. In this *re*-search I really had to strike at my very roots, and for this, strangely, I felt the need to be quite alone; it seemed to assist in recovering the state of mind—or heart—that better expresses the true and original meaning of this little understood word—*all-one*. To be by one's self is a cinch compared with this inner phylic return. . . .

Sincerely,

Trigant Burrow

To Mrs. Burrow   Lifwynn Camp, Merrill, N. Y.
Greens Farms, Connecticut   August 9, 1943

Dear Brownie:

My cryptic wire probably conveyed my love and commemorative greetings in spite of Western Union's restrictions upon messages of this sort. It could not convey though, nor can this supplementary word half tell you all my love and the treasured memories of the years. But, God be thanked, *we* understand. . . .

(11) Miss Guggenheimer's sister who had just lost her husband.

I was certainly glad to have your long letter of Saturday. A real letter from you—I mean a leisure letter—is a real treat. You usually have so little time for writing. And then the briefer word that followed. I'm so glad the roses were lovely and that you enjoyed them. It seemed so little—anything would! . . .

Yes, dear, of course we'll be dancing at our golden wedding ten years hence without question. Can't wait for the day! . . .

And now to the bungalow for a bit of reading.

Devotedly,

Trigant

To a student   Lifwynn Camp, Merrill, N. Y.
                                               Thursday, August 12, 1943

Dear Mr. Y.:

I would say 'yes,' that you're 'on the right track.' But I'd feel the need to qualify this statement or at least to amplify it. 'You' (as we've said before surely) might be on the right track and your organism very far off of it. You'll be saying: 'Now he's getting rough again.' But surely we have learned to discriminate between *me* and *man*, between what I like or aspire to in my purely partitive (affecto-symbolic) identity and what is fitting to me as a totally integrated organism. There is so much one could say and so many ways of saying it. I hardly know where to begin.

I think you've done good work. I think you are doing good work. You are intelligent and you are earnest. The rest will come of itself with consistent adherence to a very simple, if baffling, technique. You need not bother. We need not be concerned. Our concern is for 'me.' 'Me' has thrust itself into the foreground and interrupted the consistent pursuit of our technique—the technique of cotention. You expressed it well in your letter. 'Yours,' you said in effect, 'is not to reason why, yours is but to do—to cotend.' Have you forgotten? How often we all forget! Do not let it trouble you. All of us apparently still insist upon believing that cotention, or integration, is some sort of stunt, rather than a fixed habit of total phyloörganismic balance. Slowly though, gradually, we seem to be learning. Slowly the organism seems to be inculcating in us what all our philosophies do not yet even begin to suspect. . . .

In feeling that 'mental understanding' of our endeavor is not the answer, your thought comes close to touching bottom. I wager you would under no circumstances have expressed yourself in these terms but for some actual experience with cotention. One cannot *think* clearly or inclusively apart from his ability to *feel* clearly and inclusively. It's amazing when one considers the extent to which we habitually credit this superficial trick of thought without reckoning upon the basis from which all thought arises— the organism's primary feeling or motivation! . . .

I think we do not sufficiently sense the phylic implications of our thesis. We tend to think of me and mine. We argue from the artificial premise of the symbolic 'I'-persona, rather than from a basis that is organismically common and unitary throughout the race. This is what words cannot say, will never say. This is not a mental theory, but a physiological function. Hence cotention, or the physiological adjustment that stresses more and more the prior significance of the phylic organism as a whole—a phylic principle that is no less the individual's than it is the species'—in contrast to the merely socio-symbolic pattern that too commonly serves the private interests of the 'I'-persona.

Your cowardice? It just doesn't exist. *Man* is the coward. You (or I) are merely a symbol—a part-expression of man, the phylum. Being affectively bound up with the symbol that you yourself have come to embody, you falsely identify yourself—your organism—

with this symbol of man—this mere affecto-symbolic 'I'-persona. But again 'you' cannot realize this organismically in the absence of the organismic pattern I've called 'cotention.' You see, all roads lead to this central, primary pattern of behavior. But you have said the same thing—that you cannot reach a (symbolic) 'cowardice' mentally, but only cotentively. I'm sure that only the accidental circumstance that led to the opportunity of group-analysis and group living, with its relentless frustration of habitually comforting social affects, could ever have recovered, have unearthed the phylic elements of man's feeling we are coming to sense practically in cotention. But why do I say all this? It is a familiar theme to you by now. I like to refresh my memory though regarding data that have meant much to me and that may some day become deeply significant to man.

I'm glad you liked Baltimore. I have a very warm place in my heart for it, especially for that section in which you lived and so admired. . . .

Of course I appreciate your interest in seeing my work reach a wider audience. I am confident it will. But I feel it is so important to insist upon soundness, upon scientific verification step by step. This may make for the slower progress, but it makes for the surer growth in the end. But I do value your interest. I'm sure you know that.

I fear that in my enthusiasm for a subject that is all my life I have written you at too great length. It is a weakness of mine you must forgive.

Sincerely yours,

Trigant Burrow

CHAPTER 13

HEADQUARTERS IN CONNECTICUT

In October 1945 The Lifwynn Foundation moved its headquarters to a large house in Westport within a five-minute walk of 'Summer Hill.' Here amid what he loved to call 'the gracious Connecticut country-side,' Dr. Burrow spent some of the most productive years of his life, with wife, children, and grandchildren about him. A year previous another marriage had taken place within the organization when William Galt married Alfreda Sill, the daughter of a long-time student. On Dr. Galt's release from the army the couple joined the group at Westport, living in a small 'annex' on the Foundation property.

But this period brought deep sadness with the death in 1946 of Nelly Hölljes, R.N., Nurse in Charge at the Laboratory. Her capacity for applying the phylobiological technique to her own interpersonal reactions had grown with the years, and in time her work became a vital contribution to the research. Warm-hearted and genial, she met the ordeal of a prolonged illness with unshaken courage and serenity, and her death was a loss to the organization that was keenly felt by all its members.

At the time of the move to Connecticut, Burrow was already at work on *The Neurosis of Man*, the book he regarded as his *magnum opus*. It had been undertaken at the suggestion of the distinguished author and art critic, Mr. Herbert Read, a director of the London publishing house, Routledge and Kegan Paul. The work was to be a complete report of the many years of phylobiological investigation and was in the author's words 'a supreme effort to put into the hands of man what belongs in the hands of man.'

To those accustomed to the usual individual approach to literary composition, Burrow's method of writing was both novel and interesting. All his writing was done in a group setting, from composition, through the development and refinement of his material, to the ultimate polishing and careful checking. Between working sessions it was his habit to jot down words, phrases, sentences or other pertinent notes as they occurred to him. He kept pad and pencil with him wherever he went, and many notes were made at night while working on the differentiation of internal patterns of tension. These brief notes might grow into paragraphs or the major section of a chapter, but their development usually took place in a group including Mr. Shields and at least one other of his co-workers who had facility in shorthand. It was not that Dr. Burrow depended upon the suggestions or advice of his assistants, welcome as they seemed to him, but rather that in this setting he functioned more freely in regard to his material.

To participate in these literary sessions with Dr. Burrow was to participate in a dynamic social analysis. Here in a working group were present the identical division, competitiveness and dependence that had been found to characterize the interrelational behavior of normality everywhere. There was the need to recognize the factor which tends always to distract attention from the business at hand. Burrow was at all times ready to observe in his own immediate behavior and in that of others the presence of 'the social neurosis.' To work with Dr. Burrow meant, then, the opportunity to observe within oneself the operation of socially consolidated habits of ditention.

The final reading of the manuscript of *The Neurosis of Man* took place at Lifwynn Camp in the summer of 1946. A year earlier a new series of experiments with eye-movements in cotention and ditention had been undertaken by means of the Lifwynn Eye-Movement Camera. This special apparatus was built in accordance with Dr. Burrow's requirements by Dr. Henry Roger of the Rolab Laboratories. The new data obtained were included in the Appendix of the book.

To Mrs. Burrow   Lifwynn Camp, Merrill, N. Y.
Greens Farms, Connecticut   August 19, 1943, Thursday morning

Dear Brownie:

. . . Yesterday Miss Hölljes felt better. She has felt such great fatigue. I thought she looked somewhat better yesterday. As far as I am concerned (and Mr. Shields, of course) Miss Hölljes (her health and outlook) is the most important consideration The Lifwynn Foundation has before it at the present time. No one will ever know her value—her devotion to it. . . .

Love to all,

Devotedly,

Trigant

To Lt. William E. Galt   Greens Farms, Connecticut
Miami, Florida   November 20, 1943, Saturday night, 9:30

Dear William:

Last night before going to sleep I took serious counsel with myself regarding the problem of my (man's) incorrect behavior interrelationally. (I know nothing of course about a subjective defect of adaptation in man, except as I know it in myself or subjectively.) I was going over the rationale of the situation—the mechanism of man's tensional deflection (ditention) as it occurs in the symbolic segment. It seemed so baffling, so elusive.

I thought how long and, I think I may say, earnestly I have been working on it without yet establishing cotention as a spontaneous habit—without correcting the reflex habit of reaction as one corrects a verbal error or a faulty muscular coördination. The problem seemed very large and, as I say, baffling. So that I found myself quite caught up—not altogether without value, I think—in the mental or theoretical aspect of the condition. I thought something radical, something consistent must be done. A new and fresh thesis requires a new and fresh adjustment to the problem involved. On and on I thought. Then, but very reluctantly, I began to pull myself away from the fascination of my mere mental preoccupation with it. With difficulty and much resistance I began to remind myself of the feeling (empathic) nature of my (man's) problem, and so little by little to let myself into, yield myself to the tensional or stereognostic (and therefore internal, *non*-mental) character of my (the organism's) task. The mental path was barred, if the organism's basic need was to take its course, and only the path of feeling remained to me. And so the mental problem fell away, and with it the affect and fret concomitant to it. Where the mental stress or pain had been—in the frontal, orbital areas—there was now a physiological, tensional stress that stood out in its place (as 'sensum') against a feel of the organism as a non-mental, non-personal, or phylic whole. The problem was the recognition of the artificial demarcation between organism and symbolic segment and the gradual reabsorption of the digressive element into the total somatic, the total tensional system. All this I write now, I know is purely mental, purely conceptual. I know that when I return to bed tonight, I may not go on in this vein, whatever its theoretical value. I know that no laboratory procedure occupies itself with concept, that its quarry is the recording of objective data, and that one may not escape this canon of the laboratory when the laboratory happens to be one's own organic processes. . . .

As always,

Trigant Burrow

To Alys Bentley
New York

New York City
December 18, 1943

Dear Miss Bentley:

I do not readily forget the brief talk we had on the porch of the Merrill House a few days before leaving the Lake in September. You were speaking a little disconsolately, I remember, and your thoughts were a bit gloomy as to the outlook for future summers at Owlyout. I thought afterwards of how much you had accomplished, how much your life and work have meant to so many people—so many young people whose lives would have been very different and would have held far less of gladness, beauty and achievement but for you. I was wishing I could have you see this, and take from it the comfort, the joy and the deep satisfaction that is very justly yours if you will permit yourself to recall all those young faces that must brighten today and every day because of the thought of you. In these reminiscences I am sure you have occasion for much cheer and much gladness in the days ahead.

My love to you, and my good wishes,

Sincerely yours,

Trigant Burrow

To Clarence Shields   Summer Hill
New York   January 22, 1944, 12:45 p.m.

Dear Clarence:

I'm so much better. *Feel* like writing this. It would have been a cosmic undertaking yesterday.

Yes, I'll go slowly; I'll take care. There's so much ahead.

The matter of the preparation of the description of the Lifwynn Ophthalmograph is on my mind. That should be put in motion. Dr. Roger should be told of our intention to write it up for *Science*, and he should begin his contribution to it—the technical aspects. The article should be signed, though, by Dr. Syz. It should be concise above all.

Should Miss Rukeyser phone in response to reprint, it should be said to her that I had thought she might be interested in it because of the reference to Willard Gibbs. Should she phone for some other reason, she should be asked at close of the talk whether she received (Dr. Shoup just left. Finds me getting along well—chest etc.—and says I may begin sitting up) the reprint and then the 'above' message given her.

7:15

Have had a good day. Mrs. Fournet is so quiet, quick, thoughtful, and efficient. She is a very acceptable presence.(1)

(1) Sybil Fournet, R.N.

Will you thank Miss Flora for her good letter, and Miss Aimée for her daily missives and memoranda.

It is my earnest hope that you will not fall victim to this pernicious flu-germ. Remember one of the cardinal rules?: *Always* go out on clear, bright days, *never* go out on the rainy, dark days. And speaking of the latter, we haven't lacked for rain and drabness this morning—the first though, in many, many weeks.

Was somewhat concerned about Charlie.(2) The interval since his last letter has been rather long. Mrs. Burrow phoned Francis for me last night. He had heard two weeks ago. Charlie has been promoted to 'Flying Officer,' as Mrs. Burrow understood. Charlie's certainly on the up and up!

But I was going to speak of 'our work.' It isn't as clear now what I had to say. I thought of it more fully in the night, but it doesn't come back at the moment. This brings to mind the chemical, the pharmacological phase in man's needed readjustment. *Curare?* Perhaps, or perhaps in combination with some other drug—one of the milder sedatives, it may be. This seems to me an important stone in the gradually ascending series of steps that marks the development of the Laboratory of Neurodynamics otherwise known as The Lifwynn Foundation. In Sollmann's(3) letter, by the way, in speaking of *curare*, he said something about a *metrazol* ingredient which in my fevered retrospection mildly interested me.

I would like to see you, but I would not like to disturb the order of your days when they are so crowded with obligations as it is. As I've said, Mrs. Fournet is such a comfort. Think this is all.

Sincerely,

Trigant

(2) F/Lt. Charles A. Wondolowski.

(3) Dr. Torald H. Sollmann, pharmacologist, Western Reserve University.

To Herbert Read   New York City
London   May 1, 1944

Dear Mr. Read:

Just the other day I received from your publisher, Faber & Faber, a copy of your extremely valuable and very delightful book, *Education Through Art*. As no letter accompanied the book, I do not know whether your publishers sent it to me as a routine matter for my inspection or whether I am indebted to you personally for the courtesy of a copy of this interesting work of yours. In any event I am most grateful to have the opportunity of reading this scholarly treatise. I shall pass it on to my associate and son-in-law, Dr. Hans Syz, because of his interest in behavior generally, and incidentally because of his interest in education and art as they apply momentarily to his small son. I hope that your book will be as well received and as widely read as it merits.

You have been extremely kind in your references to me. I greatly value their understanding quality as well as the sensitiveness of your application of my position to your own thesis. Through what I have read of your book, I only regret what appears your unfamiliarity with my more recent study, *The Biology of Human Conflict*. Perhaps conditions in England incident to the war are answerable for this circumstance. Anyhow I am today sending you with my compliments a copy of this later work of mine. It gives me pleasure to send you at the same time reprints also of recent writings by my associates and myself.

With my very kind regards,

Sincerely yours,

Trigant Burrow

To Clarence Shields   Greens Farms, Connecticut
New York   9:30 p.m. Sunday 1944

Dear Clarence:

I am so grateful that you are, that we have our work still, as
through the years, that we may still go on together. I am so grateful
that at last our work begins to grow, to take on definite meaning
and interest, that there is now the assurance that it will take hold,
that perhaps even in our lives man will come forward to meet it.
You and Nell have been such a rock of strength and understanding.
There could be no going on without you. I am very grateful. . . .

No more now.

Good night, Clarence,

Trigant

To Lt. William E. Galt   New York City
Randolph Field, Texas   June 5, 1944

Dear William: ·

. . . Tuesday, 12:30. I was interested in what you wrote about
pilot-training—the extension of the whole person into the controlling of the plane—or, as we would say here, the extension into the
controls of the basal brain with its total pattern of function. Certainly, the centralizing of the plane in relation to the organism is
consistent throughout with the function of man's total reaction-
pattern in relating him to the environment. My interest would be
in a cotentive pattern that at all times extended the central func-

tion of the basal brain into the subject's organism as a whole—as a *phylic whole*—thus automatically preserving the individual against the artificial segmentation of his processes as now is the case under the sponsorship of the organism's ditentive pattern. What is the rub, that we must reserve the balanced function of cotention only for the stunt of flying? Why come down to earth only to be in the air again or ditentive?

But a truce to the cogitations of the unwelcome man.

I had so hoped to finish my paper at least a week before the day of reading it. Aber behüte mich Gott, es hat nicht sollen sein! I shall be pounding away at it when the gavel raps for order.

But this must be catching the early afternoon plane. So Auf Wiedersehen. To think that it will be but little more than a month before you alight at the Lake—or on the Lake!

As ever,

Trigant Burrow

To Mrs. Burrow   Lifwynn Camp, Merrill, N. Y.
Greens Farms, Connecticut   July 5, 1944, Wednesday night, 9:20

Dear Brownie:

I was so very glad to have your letter at noon today with its news of you and the family and the little social gatherings at Summer Hill and Shadowbrook(4), but most especially of your walk home alone across the fields at evening and your dear thoughts of me. It will be so good to see you in just a week now, but I know of course that you aren't leaving the interest and comfort and love-liness of our home and making this trip up to camp out of any thought of yourself and your pleasure, but solely because I asked

(4) Home of Dr. and Mrs. Syz.

you to come. I hope, though, that the change will not be unfruitful in many ways. The different climate and scenes and interests cannot but react favorably upon you in some measure. And I do so want to see you.

I've been so very well—tired of course, but sleeping a great deal and loafing most of the time as compared with my schedule in New York.

Though it is not yet ten o'clock I'm very ready, as usual, to turn in for the night.

We'll be seeing each other so soon now. I know it's lovely too at Summer Hill tonight.

Goodnight, dear, and my love,

Devotedly,

Trigant

To his son and daughter-in-law   Lifwynn Camp, Merrill, N. Y.
Wilton, Connecticut   August 8, 1944

Dear Jack and Helen:

Both your good letters have lain too long unanswered. I have been in the throes of an address to the World and his Wife, and you both know how absorbing these paroxysmal efforts are once I become enmeshed in them.

You and Jack would have enjoyed the wedding days here. It was really very quaint and festive. William and Alfreda are the world's originals in bride and grooming. They could not get back to Lifwynn Camp soon enough following the wedding and, having gotten back, were straightway off to their out-of-door enterprises, cutting and trimming and planting and hauling and what-not. The landscaping those two doughty craftsmen accomplished in their two brief weeks has completely rejuvenated the grounds. We really were rapidly going to seed.

I know you were glad to see Mother back again and looking so well, and that it meant much to you to know how genuinely she enjoyed every minute of camp. While Mother had every opportunity for the exercise of her interests, she of course had no routine or compelling duties for two weeks. Everybody did so enjoy having her here, and certainly she richly merited this brief recess after nearly fifty years of unbroken domestic servitude. I think it meant a great deal to Mother to see still the grace and charm of the camp—to know that the traditions set by her were being carried on.

Everybody here sends love to you all. I wish you were here this very day. The temperature this morning when I got up at quarter of seven was 47 degrees. It is now at 10:15, 65 degrees, and the lake all amethysts and diamonds. But you know of old.

With my love to the trio of you,

Ever devotedly,

Father

To Lt. William E. Galt
Bryan A.A.F., Texas

Lifwynn Camp, Merrill, N. Y.
Friday morning, Breakfast time
Temp. 47°. At 6, temp. 45°
August 25, 1944

Dear William:

. . . Already the foliage has turned considerably. It should be quite lovely in its autumn tints before we leave. Last night after supper as

Dr. Thompson and I left the dining-room to come via 'the long way'to my cabin, the air was so deliciously cool, the twilight well advanced and the smell of the vegetation so sweet. As we sauntered up the path through 'the Park,' the clear-cut crescent of a moon hung over the trees toward the west across the tennis court. It was so peaceful, so quiet, so exquisite a moment. It seemed to me its mood—its *Stimmung,* as the Germans so beautifully express it— must be of the deeper, inner pattern. It was none of mine, and none of it was mine. It could not be. What need to reach for it, to lay claim to it. Already it filled me through and through. Being within me, it was part of me, as I was part of it. Coming into the cabin Miss Aimée was here before us. The three of us reread the letter to go to England. It was very pleasant working beneath the lamp-light with the fire burning gratefully as the night grew colder. I thought of you. . . .

Ever,

Trigant Burrow

8 p.m. my study

Tonight again the quiet and the twilight, the cold still air, the Park, the sweet scent of the earth, the deserted tennis court and the slender moon. I don't wonder you love this place. And now the fire on the hearth is very welcome. Dr. Thompson has just come in. He said things are getting finished. He and Francis tackled the shop in earnest this afternoon. And now for an evening of reading.

9 o'clock Saturday morning,
Temp. 42 at 7

A lovely clear day. This loveliness of Lifwynn Camp on which I seem to have laid so strong an accent in this letter is certainly warranted. But I detect a decided sentimental note in my feeling. As if all natural beauty weren't equally appealing—or wouldn't be, but for the partitive 'I'-persona with which we interpret it. And now to work. Hope this reaches you at your temporary address.

To Dr. Henry Roger New York City
Sandy Hook, Connecticut January 10, 1945

Dear Dr. Roger:

Following his visits to your laboratory Dr. Syz has given me careful reports regarding your work on the eye-movement camera. It is gratifying to know that its construction is progressing well, and especially that the problem of adequate illumination has been solved after your consultation with Mr. Herbert E. Grier of the Massachusetts Institute of Technology. . . .

As I explained to you at our first interview, the work of our laboratory has to do with the differentiation of internal patterns of behavior, particularly with the determination of those impediments in physiological function we find to be associated with nervous disturbances and with disorders of motivation generally. We are engaged not only in the investigation of nervous disorders in the restricted medical sense, but also in the investigation of those disorders so widely expressed today in social conflict and international chaos. For in our study of so-called normal groups or communities we find the presence of essentially the same internally distorted patterns as exist in the frankly neurotic personality. And so, if our researches are carried to a stage of practical application, they should prove timely in throwing light upon the deeper causations that underlie the community's general health and welfare.

As I believe I mentioned to you in our first talk, the definition and discrimination of an organism's tensional patterns bears a direct relation to its underlying impetus or motivation socially. And hence the experimental determination of these physiological concomitants is of great importance to us. In the past we have established specific records both in regard to respiration and in regard to electrical brain waves. But the systematic clarification of our observations respecting alterations in the neuromuscular reaction of the eyes remains to be added to our findings in order to complete this phase of our investigations.

In view of what I have said you will understand, I am sure, how urgent we feel it is that the eye-camera be completed at the earliest possible moment. In addition, my English publisher asked me several months ago to complete for early publication a book I have under way and which in a previously published statement of mine I had promised to prepare. I am giving all my time to the preparation of this manuscript, but in the chapter that deals with physiological aspects I shall have to include records of the behavior of the eyes in both *cotention* and *ditention* in order to complete the report of our findings. Naturally I shall be unable to do this until we can make the crucial experiments with your camera. So you will appreciate that I am somewhat concerned lest any obstacle to these experiments delay the appearance of my thesis.

I am putting the situation quite frankly before you as I feel confident that in doing so you will not think me impatient or unmindful of the great technical difficulties our problem has presented to you. Dr. Syz and I have often spoken of this, and we have counted ourselves extremely fortunate in having secured your assistance in this feature of our experimental work. We realize that our opportunity has been a unique one. So that I think I need not tell you how much we appreciate your patience and your resourceful inventiveness in confronting the various difficulties and mastering the many complexities that have arisen during the development and construction of the apparatus.

It is my earnest hope that we may look forward to beginning the experiments with the new instrument before long now, and I shall much value an early word from you letting me know of your feeling as to the outlook.

Sincerely yours,

Trigant Burrow

To F/Lt. Charles A. Wondolowski
Royal Canadian Air Force, Overseas

New York City
January 20, 1945

Dear Charlie:

Your good long letter written the night of December 27 reached me just a few days ago. Only a few days earlier I had posted a letter to you, thanking you for your thoughtful card of Christmas greeting. We all appreciated your thinking of us. From your letter of the 27th it appears that I may not have been far wrong in sensing from the writing on your Xmas card that all was not too well with you. I well understand the depressed mood in which you found yourself the night you wrote me. I wish you were here that I might talk of it and of you very fully. Of course, Charlie, the immediate conditions gave you ample ground for feeling blue. To be denied participation in activities with which you have been so long identified, and to see all your comrades carrying on without you—flying off to their targets and returning each day so full of the exciting events of their flight—must indeed have been a trying experience for you. (5) But not even this quite accounts for your depressed mood. It goes deeper than that. External

(5) F/Lt. Wondolowski had been temporarily assigned to administrative duties.

circumstances may contribute to one's sense of gloom, but they are not the whole story. This war has caused the disruption of so many personal, so many conventional ties. But its vast unitary purpose has brought the realization of far deeper, far more elemental bonds. It has made men feel their common blood, their common need, their identity as one great human organism. Together they have known incessant hardship, and grim, unremitting struggle. Together they have faced danger and death, and in all this they have found—they have rediscovered—a primary bond. Many of these boys have returned to this country wounded, some badly wounded. They are given every care and attention and all that medicine affords or surgery can apply. But as these soldiers rest in the security and comfort of their convalescence, as they are attended by the thoughtful nurses and know again the luxury of clean, smooth sheets and days on end of rest and easement, their thoughts are not of their personal good fortune; they do not reflect 'how lucky *I* am!' Not at all. They are haunted by thoughts of the buddies they left in the fox-holes and in the forward trenches, buddies with whom they suffered and fought *as one organism*, and their one desire is to return and fight again beside these men with whom they've shared life as common pals in a common need. This instinct of our oneness as a people, as a race is, I believe, the most powerful, the most deeply motivating principle in human life. It is in times of war, when men are again thrown back upon their elemental unity, that all the petty personal ties, the vain striving for one's own self-interest—one's wealth or success or distinction—become an empty mockery. I think that from this background your depression and loneliness are readily understandable, Charlie. I think it is understandable that your sense of desolation is most poignant precisely at the moment when your own distinction and success are at their height and when one would expect your personal happiness to be at its peak. You have known what it is to be one with your kind in a desperate struggle for life, and in this you've sensed comradeship in its deepest meaning and found that nothing personal can ever take its place. I think I understand your mood. It is, I believe, a forerunner of the needed social adjustment in the world reconstruction that lies ahead.

No more tonight.

Sincerely,

Trigant Burrow

To F/Lt. Charles A. Wondolowski   New York City
Royal Canadian Air Force, Overseas   January 21, 1945

Dear Charlie:

Last night I wrote you a V-mail letter. It was in answer to your fine long letter of December 27. I wrote you in longhand as I wanted to speak to you of the more personal passage in your letter—in that letter written late at night two days after Christmas. But this morning Miss Hölljes comes in to my room in much excitement to tell me of having heard over the radio late last night (WEAF) an announcement concerning 'Charles Wondolowski of Bridgeport, Connecticut, and his wonderful citation.' And this morning we find this news comment is given a top-line notice in *The New York Times*. Of course it is an Associated Press item and will appear in all the papers. (I am enclosing the clipping with this.) How delighted all your family will be. And are *we* proud of you! You have certainly made a wonderful record, Charlie.

But, as I said to you last night, I believe I understand how much more the opportunity of working, of risking all and of sacrificing all, if need be, in the close union of a common cause with your fellow airmen means to you—how much more it means to you than all the personal distinction and acclaim your own alertness and courage and daring may bring you.

To go back to your letter for a moment, it occurs to me that there is really no occasion for fret or impatience that you have been temporarily withdrawn from combat duty. Such an order cannot have been made without full consideration, and it seems to me it may well indicate that there is something very special in store for you with the development of this great process of which you are an integral part. Try to be patient until your turn comes for further activity in the air.

By the way, I must tell you that your white birch is still doughty and thriving. Only the upper third was cut off and it has flourished and become a very lovely tree in its newly fashioned foliage. So you see, your tree surgery was all to the good. . . .

Sincerely yours,

Trigant Burrow

To Mrs. William E. Galt   New York City
Dallas, Texas(6)   February 7, 1945

Dear Alfreda:

I must not let another day pass without getting some sort of word to you, however brief and inadequate. Not that there is any hot-off-the-griddle news to pass on to you. Rather the contrary. Judged from all accepted external standards, our days are as like as dominoes. But if one can speak of the old and the primary and the basic in the same breath with what we ordinarily know as 'news,' there is much, much to report. The ancient and basic principle underlying the activity of living forms—the principle we know in the sphere of human interrelations as cotention and that is the major interest of The Lifwynn Laboratory—becomes of increas-

(6) Mrs. Galt was on a business trip.

ingly vital, insistent significance within our small group. And with this deepening of the sense of our laboratory values, human and scientific, the major report of our organization—my so-called book —takes on ever broadening meaning. . . .

Ever affectionately,

Trigant Burrow

To the Reverend Terence J. Boyle, S. J.   New York City
Fordham University   February 20, 1945

Dear Terry:

Many years ago I went to Cardinal Gibbons and asked his Eminence if he would not be so good as to order my aunt, the Reverend Mother Mary Antonia, at that time Superior of the Convent of the Sisters of Mercy at Vicksburg, Mississippi, to Norfolk, Virginia, for a visit to my mother who was quite unwell at the time. His Eminence was his usual gentle and benevolent self, and our family had the great pleasure of having my aunt reunited once more to us for a few weeks. I prefaced my request by reminding the Cardinal that I had come to him once before seeking a favor, and I feared that in approaching him a second time I must seem to be taking advantage of his great kindness to me on the earlier occasion. With the twinkle in his eye so characteristic of him, he said, 'Well, you know, Trigant, gratitude has been aptly defined as a keen desire for renewed favors.'

You were good enough to come to my assistance several years ago when it was a matter of some information that I wanted. It had to do, you may recall, with the correct form of an old Latin usage. So I am reminded, you see, of the Cardinal when I come trotting back to you today asking for further enlightenment from you.

This time again it is a question of Latin usage, and I hope you won't mind my troubling you once more.

My brother Alan was very fond of quoting a saying that occurs in Cicero's *De Officiis*. The passage, as Alan repeated it, ran 'Nunquam minus solus quam solus,' and I have always delighted in the sentiment expressed. I have no doubt that one *is* really never less alone than when alone. But as I come to look up the reference I find the wording quite different from this. Furthermore, it is in indirect discourse. The author is quoting from Cato who in turn cites this phrase as being Scipio's. As you probably remember, Cicero's precise statement, at the beginning of *Liber Tertius*, is 'nunquam se minus otiosum esse, quam cum otiosus, nec minus solum, quam cum solus esset.' But it occurred to me that the laconic form in which Alan quoted it might probably be a terse paraphrase of one of the Jesuit Fathers. Anyhow my ear has become keenly attuned to the shorter form, and if it would be permissible Latin to quote it thus in a book I am writing I should be glad to do so. On the other hand, I should not care to go on record as wantonly misquoting this renowned Roman orator of whom we read so much in good old Fordham days. I would much appreciate it if you could set me in the path of grammatical accuracy.

Can you tell me too what news there is of John O'Rourke. I have wondered whether he is still in Rome or whether he had been transferred back to America before the outbreak of the war. He has often been in my thoughts.

I hope things go well with you. At least we can all be deeply grateful that this hideous and, as I believe, utterly useless and insane war is approaching an end—not a true end perhaps, as far as men's hearts are concerned, but at least an end of this particularly blatant expression of human bestiality.

The other day I read of the death of Dan Kiernan. I always ranked him among the pure in heart. He must have made a splendid priest. It would be good to hear news of you again, and news of others of our class whom you know of.

What strides Fordham has made in the world of education and letters since our early days on its campus!

With my kind regards,

Sincerely yours,

Trigant

P.S. I assume that you are still at Fordham and are still holding the chair of Apologetics. It all sounds very profound.

To Herbert Read
London

New York City
March 9, 1945

Dear Mr. Read:

I have many things to acknowledge and thank you for—*The Peckham Experiment*, your own pamphlet *The Education of Free Men*, and the good letter from you of January 25 that followed in a week or so. We are all greatly interested in the medico-social experiment sponsored by Scott Williamson. His ideas are most stimulating. I took the book out to the country with me the week-end that it came and was much intrigued with his plan and, as it seems to me, his very sane research into a program of social health. I had no idea that there existed anywhere an experiment of this kind. I am glad to have your pamphlet too and to rekindle my earlier acquaintance with you and your *Education Through Art*. Thank you so much.

Just a few weeks earlier we had seen the notice from the Holliday Bookshop of your new book of poems, *A World Within a War*. Needless to say, I ordered a copy forthwith. I took it out to my home and greatly enjoyed being with it in the quiet of a week-end there. I am sorely in need of education in the newer manner and form of poetry, but I am not so illiterate in the current idiom that I do not have moments of very deep thrill.

I am enclosing the translation by Malcolm Cowley of a poem by Henri Michaux that appeared in Bruce Bliven's *The New Republic*. This poem too appealed to me no little. I hope you will care for it also. But you probably know it in the original.

I had not known that you were the editor of an art journal. I happened to hear of it indirectly through Dr. Lionello Venturi who spoke of your journal's having made its own way, a circumstance unique in the financial history of art journalism.

As a writer you are blessed with a simple and clear name. My own has to take a beating from almost everyone who does not know me or my family, the first name being French and the second name (originally French also) having the accent on the second syllable. It is not a matter of much moment, I suppose, how one is pronounced except that among one's friends one likes to believe that his name is as familiar to them as his home. . . .

Of course I lost no time in passing on to Dr. Galt your gratifying comment about his essay on 'Cooperation.' (7) He would be very pleased, I know, should Mr. Woodcock care to publish the paper in his magazine.

As for my book (8), it is not getting into shape as rapidly as I had hoped, but I must say I am no little pleased at what seem to be the possibilities in its development. It gathers momentum, though, and I am hoping soon to reach the point where its construction will progress more rapidly. There is no lack of behavior-material or incentive in these tragic times, and I do not see the outlook growing less tragic, but more so. Despite their benign intentions, the United Nations are necessarily planning their world reconstruction upon a purely partitive basis. However provident and farseeing from the standpoint of statesmanship, their inciting motives are still unilateral.

(7) 'The Principle of Cooperation in Behavior,' *Quarterly Review of Biology*, 1940, vol. 15, pp. 401–10.

(8) *The Neurosis of Man.*

I cannot say often enough how much your interest in my work and in furthering a wider acquaintance with it means to me and to my associates. My thesis, as I think I have told you, is not popular. But I believe it can be. I am convinced that just as there is nothing on the instinctual level that is more 'popular,' more welcome organismically than the feel of mutuality and common kinship, so a thesis that attempts to expound the biological basis of this instinctual trend should become equally acceptable within the community. Certainly I know of no behavioral impetus that cries out for emphasis more strongly than this basic unity and integration inhering in the human organism—if only I can stimulate, as I know you would wish me to, a conscious recognition of this common bond among us.

I have really no ground for complaint that there has not been a wider recognition of my aims among my colleagues in America. The fault or rather the ineptitude has been largely my own. My work set out awkwardly. It was unavoidable that it should, because of the inevitable circumstance of my own partitive limitations. As I look back upon it, that first book of mine—*The Social Basis of Consciousness*—gives evidence in plenty of my own involvement in 'the social neurosis' with its unilateralism and its sick dichotomy of 'you' versus 'me.' And so, of course my colleagues were resentful. Our research work was necessarily a progressive adventure in the observation of human behavior, and what I lacked then in my intellectual aloofness was the profounder phyloanalysis and challenge of my own 'I'-persona—a goal that our investigations had not yet reached.

Your interest in 'The Autonomy of the "I" ' pleases me very much. When I read that paper in Cincinnati many years ago, it was received by some with stony silence and by others with undisguised antagonism. But the essay which more than any other got me into hot water was 'The Heroic Role—An Historical Retrospect.' Indeed there was such an outcry against it that I could never bring myself to send out reprints of it. I felt that because of the resentment it would arouse it might cause more pain than understanding.

I am sending a copy of it to you today along with other papers written about that time, thinking you may care to look through these earlier studies of mine sometime.

With my kindest regards,

Sincerely yours,

Trigant Burrow

To Mrs. William E. Galt   New York City
Dallas, Texas   March 12, 1945

Dear Alfreda:

You will be feeling a bit lonely these days, and I don't wonder, with this further interruption of your 'long honeymoon.'

I too have felt that cotention was very much in the background with you and with William. But here again I don't see how it could have been otherwise. The pattern—the internal pattern of our adaptation—is not personal, not individual. It is social, and no individual can possibly control it. It would be like expecting a muscle of the forearm to govern the tone or tensional pattern of the body's muscular system as a whole. It is of course the other way round. It is the total pattern that governs the behavior of the individual element or part. One does have, it seems to me, the opportunity, or one can make the opportunity when one is alone—between switching out one's light at night and the moment of the day's return in the morning—to sense one's partitive confusion and to insist on maintaining the sense of one's perturbed and agitated state, however impotent one may be to do anything about it *beyond the mere sensing of it*. But damn it, we don't do that. We keep right on too often in our abject, externally dictated or socially conditioned whirl. It is instinctive that with distress there is the organism's attention to the distressed part or organ. The very animals seek protection and quiet and a period of rehabilitation. But with this dislocation in man's adaptation to realities he is too distorted, his attention is too led away by the false interests of suggestion and habit and social tradition for him to know, to have any realizing sense of his distorted condition as an organism. That is the problem. That is the task—somehow holding still against the agitations of our external, superficial and purely fanciful excitements. As far as my own experience goes, this exercise in self-collectedness, however incomplete, however ineffectual—this passive restoration of total sensation and the physical awareness of the stress and conflict that one's agitation imposes physiologically —does seem essential toward inculcating an appreciation of our opportunity as a laboratory of consensual observers. This does seem to me a very significant part of our research task. But we always have to have 'results,' immediate results. I mean that mentally we are spoiled and impatient. We are not willing to bring the same research patience to the observation of our own wheeling, gyrating tendencies of feeling and thinking that we demand of ourselves in any other field of objective investigation.

Of course our efforts are defeated again and again. But what does one expect of research? Why must we look for child's play where there is question of an extremely serious problem in subjectively deflected reactions? But no, the baby has got to be entertained. Tootsy Wootsy has always been taken up and bounced when his or her little moments of impatience have vented themselves in whimpering and complaint. But after all, can we not as adults take our childishness in hand, not with the usual recourses or from the usual mental or moralistic background, but as a disturbance in the organism's balance, in the organismic balance subjectively of myself or yourself or whoever's self? How stupid we are not to grapple with our problem, but to be always disheartened by repeated defeat.

I was interested in what you wrote of your and William's silence where there might be the possibility of discussing phylobiology with others. You don't know sufficient about phylobiology within yourselves, and you are embarrassed, as the rest of us here are, where it comes to speaking—to giving 'evidence of the faith that is in you.' The faith is not in you—the faith that comes of practical and controlled and consistent objective observation of one's own internal reactions.

I am very happy in the thought of your mother having the little cottage beside 'The Trees' (9) and the rather pleasant setting it will offer for receiving her friends, and most particularly her children and grandchildren. Naturally I think of all the grand-children, and of course not least of the grandchildren you and William will bring to us. Already so many things come to my mind of practical meaning to John, and therefore to Emily and Hans, in the saner upbringing of this youngster of 'ours.'

I am glad you feel as you do, that you share this sense of 'ours' with us, but indeed without cotention, or common tension, there will not be this sharing. There will be conflict and competitiveness, and jealousy and all the old, tedious dichotomies that necessarily go along with man's repudiation of his unitary basis of motivation and of life.

Yes, I still feel the importance of not crowding one another as all the newly and not newly weds the world over insist on doing, to the inevitable destruction of their union. Of course your visits to one another 'count,' and there is no reason why it should not be this way always. But a permanent group feel as a background, I am convinced, is essential to this sanity of adjustment between any two people, whether married or not married.

I don't think you have anything to reproach yourself for in the prospect of losing out on your job because of your interest in Wil-liam. I think you have done a splendid job so far in both your relationships—home and work—and I don't see that you have per-mitted any major conflict to come between them. Of course there are the inevitable inattentions and of course they do mean funda-mentally the organism's uncoördinated function. But they, as I

(9) Name of the property later occupied by the Foundation.

say, must await the coördination of the group as an organismic whole. The real group, of course, is the species man, nothing less. But I see no reason why the spirit of this larger group may not be embodied in some small unit of it. That, it seems to me, is our job— yours and mine, William's and the rest of us.

But no more now. This is just a letter of greeting and of momentary solace, perhaps, during these days of your readjustment to your new surroundings.

With my love,

Ever,

Trigant Burrow

To Aimée Guggenheimer   New York City
Baltimore, Maryland   May 19, 1945

Dear Miss Aimée:

This is just a word—who was it said, 'A word to the wise is sufficient'? But who is wise? Wisdom is primarily of the body—of the body's autonomic system. But who is in touch with this basic system of man's motivation? Whose head any longer concedes the priority of this all-wise source of the organism's balance. And so what avails 'the word'—the word that the head picks up and casts off for its own private unilateral ends.

You think, for instance, of your getting back to your work. That's the head. But the manner of your getting back—your fitness, your need—the need for the gradual restoring of your normal adequacy or the matter of the body's wisdom in respect to its task—this does not concern you.

Until one is wise, what avails the word.

Sincerely yours,

Trigant Burrow

To his niece, Elizabeth Burrow
Virginia Beach, Virginia

Lifwynn Camp, Merrill, N. Y.
August 22, 1945

Dear Elizabeth:

... I was sorry to hear of the break with Mr. M., and I quite understood your feeling of disappointment in him. You are going to meet that situation, I fear, more than once, Elizabeth, in your career as a business woman. More than once you will come up against situations in which your employer will hold his interest at so much higher price than yours—in which he will not hold to the terms of his agreement with you. I admire your forthrightness and I sympathize with your spirit in not countenancing Mr. M.'s behavior. If he promised you a job for the summer, of course he should have lived up to the letter of your common understanding.

I do want to say this though. I want to say it to you, especially because it is something I learned only after many years of disappointments of this sort. And that is that it is wise to learn early that this world is for the most part not a fair or just world—that the truly fair or just person is a rare exception, and the reason is that people do not see things in their true light. A personal bias disguises actual facts. Now I don't want to destroy your ideals. Your father proceeded always in the same forthright and uncompromising way, and I always admired him for it. Were he living today, though, I am sure I would say to him what I am saying to you now—that the actual world, the world with which we have to deal in daily contact with it—*is a world that is not capable of clear thinking and feeling* and that there are times when it is wise to put aside one's resentment and deal with a circumstance in a quite dispassionate, objective way. There are not many people to whom I would say this. It could easily lead to a violation of principle. Of course you know I would not direct you to any such course. What I am trying to indicate is that you are going to have dealings many times with people of whom you cannot expect thoughtful, balanced behavior—people who have not had your background but who might learn much from you if there were the opportunity to come into closer relationship with you. . . . I could tell you what I have in mind much better than I can write it. So if I have not made myself clear, don't let it trouble you. I believe I can do so sometime when we are together. Maybe this fall. . . .

Devotedly,

Uncle Trigant

To Flora A. Guggenheimer(10) Lifwynn Camp, Merrill, N. Y.
New York

August 24, 1945
Friday morning at 10
Temperature 55
At six o'clock 42

Dear Miss Flora:

Your letter was an unmitigated joy. It came at a most timely moment—a moment in which as it happened we had set the book aside and were mourning and wailing vociferously over you and your unhappy fate—no servants, no mountain breezes, a lame knee, no companionship, etc., etc.—when, lo!—in the very midst of our ditentive luxury, came your blithe letter. It shifted the scene completely, as you can imagine. We wanted straightway to take Julia and Hester into our tender embraces. It all seemed too good to be true, and of course our desolation was transformed into keen delight.

6:15 p.m. Mrs. Sill read to us at dinner your letter to her, and at noon William got your telegram. He and Alfreda went over

(10) Volunteer house manager of the Foundation.

to Merrill after dinner to spend the afternoon. William was to wire you immediately. We were extremely amused at the description of you and your knee shuttling miserably between '27' and Tudor City each day, but in submissive elegance.(11)

Had such a good letter from Emily today and one from Mrs. Burrow. Emily is all concern about my trip down. Guess our best bet is to motor to Saratoga.

We love these cold days with their preview of autumn. The work goes well. Dr. Thompson and William are hard at it, as are Mrs. Sill, Alfreda and Florence.

It was good to hear that meals will be served at '27' so soon. You really have accomplished wonders.

But the 'second bell' will be ringing in a moment. I must hurry down and see what progress Dr. Thompson has made in repairing the breach in the wall of the front lawn.

Everybody well. We closed the book temporarily yesterday. I feel like a schoolboy at vacation time! No more. The bell. Be seeing you soon.

Sincerely,

Trigant Burrow

To Dr. Grace Whitford   Westport, Connecticut
Ozona, Florida   December 3, 1945

Dear Dr. Whitford:

I certainly enjoyed having your letter, except for the uncomfortable feeling that I did not at all deserve it. I do appreciate your

(11) Dr. Burrow had insisted that while reopening the New York headquarters Miss Guggenheimer should use taxis to take her to her temporary quarters.

having written me again on your return to Clearwater, especially as I failed to answer the good letter you sent me as you were about to take off for Chicago. . . .

The card you received will tell our story. We are really here in Westport (Greens Farms). The move is actually a *fait accompli*. The undertaking had appeared to us all something super-colossal. You can imagine the accumulations there were in that very large house at 27—accumulations of nearly twenty years. And then the absence of our usual staff of servants in these difficult times, of course, added greatly to the job.

But we are here, and Oh! it has been such a worth-while move. The house is well adapted to our needs and I cannot tell you what it means to us all to be able in a moment to step out into the sunshine of this lovely country. . . .

The actual move started October 8. I discreetly left the house with my effects on the 5th and was rolled out here in my car. The packing of the vans started Monday morning, and with a huge van-load each day, the moving was completed at midnight of the 11th. But I should say now, though, that the real chore began then. But, as I say, it is just a joy to be here, and everything is so very comfortable. Hans has not left a stone unturned in providing the necessary alterations and adjustments for receiving an incorporated scientific organization into what was a private home. . . .

The place is not five minutes' walk from my house, so that it is very handy in this way. Of the three rooms across the south side (the side looking toward Summer Hill) the centre and smallest room is my study, with its fire-place and unusually large bay window extending nearly across the room. At the moment I am sitting in a flood of sunshine looking out across the snowy hills and on the sound this marvelously bright day. The temperature is actually 20 degrees, but one would think it hardly lower than 40, the air is so very dry and still. . . .

I could write on and on, but I must not. My book goes well at last. There is still much work ahead on it, but its course in general is clear now. So that, with many chapters completed, the rest is relatively easy sailing. . . .

But here I go 'on and on' anyhow, and there are endless matters crying for attention. . . .

My warm remembrances to you and Mr. Parr, in which family and group join me.

Affectionately,

Trigant Burrow

To Dr. Louis K. Anspacher   Westport, Connecticut
Purchase, New York   December 3, 1945

Dear Louis:

Your gracious word of salutation upon my coming out here into this pleasant countryside is very heartening to me. It is like a breath of this lovely countryside itself. It was good of you, and like you, to write me in so generous a spirit. After all, what is there in life more precious than friends who remember?

Brownie and I are more grateful for your thought of us than we can half express. You know, Louis, you have always been one of our very special prides. Just knowing you has meant so much.

Thanks for the leaflet and the glimpse of the welcome inset of you. It is a delight to see that that noble head grows no less lovely with the years.

I cannot tell you how I am enjoying having my life and work out here in these Connecticut hills. It seems almost too good to be true. I could not ask for more congenial surroundings in which to work on the book I am hoping ere long to complete. It is the more welcome now that there is at least a momentary surcease of this terrible world-war. But if only we *do* something about it. If only, having beaten our swords into ploughshares, we can resolutely turn this good earth to sane and constructive purposes. It is the time, if ever, when we must all pull together. I look forward eagerly to your part in the new effort toward the real reconstruction.

Brownie, who to my regret is momentarily confined to bed with an obstinate bronchitis, sends you her love with mine. We cherish your proposal that we four meet again when the moment is available and talk the heads off of us. We do so want to meet your lovely wife of whom we have heard so much.

As ever yours,

Trigant

To two young friends, Florence
and Margaret Weatherly
Mamaroneck, New York

Westport, Connecticut
December 31, 1945

Dear Florence and Margaret:

Mr. Shields and I were so pleased with your delightful gifts to us, and no less pleased that you should have been so gracious as to think of us. Your picture, Margaret, is lovely, and I shall enjoy it and think of you. And Florence, I cannot wait to get to your story. It is about a horse, and that is enough for me to know how thoroughly I shall be interested in it. I had to peep at the first page even though I was scheduled to begin work at once, and these early lines of your sketch have intrigued me greatly.

One of these days you both will no doubt read *Lorna Doone*, and about the wonderful horse that Richard Blackmore describes in this novel of his. You have probably read *Black Beauty*, but that is a bit fantastical and, I believe, was written more in the spirit of propaganda for the S.P.C.A. than from any artistic inspiration.

You have no doubt read also Hawthorne's description of the fascinating mythological fable of Pegasus and Bellerophon.

There have been some wonderful horses in more recent times too. Do you happen to know of Heatherbloom whose record for going over a hurdle was nearly twice the height of any other horse? When I was a youngster not much older than you, Margaret—I guess—I used to hear much about Maud S. and J. I. C. and St. Julian. They trotted respectively in what was then the remarkable time of 2.08, 2.10 and 2.12. Maud S. was, I think, owned by Commodore Vanderbilt. But the extraordinary thing is that J.I.C., after having made such an outstanding record in the trotting races, was some years later taken from the track and after two years' training returned to the turf and established the world's record for pacing!

But I can talk horse forever, so I must not let myself go on this way. I hope you will be able to spend a week-end with us very soon. I was sorry not to see you on Saturday. Thanks again to you both, and to you both and to your mother and father hearty New Year greetings from Mr. Shields and me. I hope we'll see you all out here ere long.

Sincerely yours,

Trigant Burrow

To Karl Howenstein   Westport, Connecticut
South Pasadena, California   January 22, 1946

Dear Mr. Howenstein:

I want to thank you for your very kind message of Christmas greeting and for your renewed expression of interest in what you conceive to be the work of The Lifwynn Foundation. That last phrase sounds a bit rough, I fear. It is not meant that way—I think you know that. But I do say quite pointedly, quite without reservation 'what you conceive to be' the work that my associates and I are attempting to do. People so generally fail to sense—and necessarily this applies no less to you—the quite organismic basis of our endeavors. They do not get the pragmatic, the essentially biological nature of our laboratory undertaking, or realize that it has entailed a definite *physiological* wrench from all the nice mental and social habits of man's feeling and thinking.

So often friends write me (I know that they write me only in the kindness of their heart) of how 'interested' they are in my thesis. Frankly it has never interested me for a moment. Neither has it interested for a moment the handful of students who have really settled down with me to the task of synthesizing our commonly dissociated, however 'normal,' processes of behavior. Tuberculosis, cancer, arthritis, and the measures employed for their relief, may appear very 'interesting' to the physician or the clinical pathologist, but unless he is a completely unbalanced personality, you will not find the patient taking that view of the case. To the patient (from *pati*, to suffer, you remember) for whom the condition is internal, and unremitting, his disease is sheer pain and discomfort.

So with patients, 'normal' and neurotic, who appreciate the internal physiology of their (man's) behavior-disorders. To the research student who commits himself to a serious inquiry into neurotic impediments of function as they are appreciable *within* himself, these pathological reactions too are sheer pain and discomfort. Such a student is not gaily interested in the process from which he suffers. Where the interest is gay and debonair, it is invariably traceable to the circumstance that the student is not really a patient or sufferer, that he is one of those cheery 'normals' or neurotics whose affect-dissociation has permitted them only a symbolic, only a mental or metaphoric approach that is equally dissociated. They are but naïve and innocent onlookers at their own unsuspected pathology.

I really hadn't meant to write you all this. I fear it may seem to you unappreciative of your unfailing graciousness. I do value deeply your kindness, but I feel so earnestly the internal biological significance of our work and the misapprehension on the part of my colleagues in regard to it. So perhaps you will pardon my frankness in writing you in this way of my personal feeling.

After all, maybe the fault is in large measure my own. It may be that I haven't yet clarified my thesis as fully as I should, and that a book I am now at work on will offer suitable amends in this regard. . . .

. . . With my very good wishes,

Sincerely yours,

Trigant Burrow

To Mrs. John B. Reilly(12)   Westport, Connecticut
Los Angeles   February 14, 1946

Dear Margie:

One is reluctant to write when one has sad tidings to impart.

After the most gallant fight I have ever known anyone to make and sustain through years, Miss Hölljes was taken to the Presbyterian Hospital last Friday, where she died Monday afternoon. No words can describe the loss the passing of this valiant nurse means to me, to Mr. Shields and to her associates of this organization. I shall always revere the picture of her in these last months—the first one in the office each morning, with her immaculate white uniform, eagerly busy at her desk arranging for the day's items and activities. But it was the spirit with which she approached her work and her contacts, whether among ourselves or in the wider community, that lives most vividly in my memory of her. I don't think I have to tell you how much she admired you, or how deeply she appreciated all your thoughtfulness for the members of Lifwynn Camp, as indeed for everyone about you. . . .

(12) Proprietor of the Merrill House at Merrill, New York, whose friendly spirit had greatly endeared her to Dr. and Mrs. Burrow.

I hear from Clare quite regularly. He is very good about writing, and today I am sending off a letter to him in the same mail letting him know also of the clouds that have hung over our days during the last weeks.

You will be glad to know that William is back with us again and is his precisely same old self—busy, helpful, happy and profoundly interested in his work. At the moment he is especially occupied in the preparation of an address he has been asked to give before the New York Academy of Sciences in New York City next week.

Everyone sends their cordial greetings to you, and hopes that you and Mr. Reilly are both well.

With kind regards,

Always sincerely yours,

Trigant Burrow

To Marie C. Byron, R.N., Superintendent   Westport, Connecticut
Neurological Institute, New York   February 15, 1946

Dear Miss Byron:

The members of this organization and particularly Mr. Shields and I feel deeply the very close bond that has been wrought between you and your associates and ourselves. Realizing what you meant to Miss Hölljes (13) means very much to us. Of all the physicians and nurses of the Neurological no one, I am sure, was more devoted to the ideals of your hospital than Nelly Hölljes. And need I say that in her association with us of this laboratory there has been throughout the years this same devotion, this same loyalty to the aims for which The Lifwynn Foundation stands.

(13) For many years Nelly Hölljes had served as registrar at the Neurological Institute.

These are things I need hardly say to you. I know how much past associations mean to you, as they do to me, but I feel sure that in our thought of this valiant nurse and of the bond of feeling she has forged among us all, we shall wish to keep pace with her and look always, as she did, to the future.

I hope we may keep in touch with you, that you and Nell's other friends at the hospital will feel that The Lifwynn Foundation holds a close welcome for you always in her name.

With very cordial regards from all of us here,

Sincerely yours,

Trigant Burrow

To Soheil Afnan(14)   Westport, Connecticut
Haifa, Palestine   March 28, 1946

Dear Soheil:

I know you will pardon my addressing you in this informal manner. But we are old friends and you so much the younger.

It was a great pleasure to have your good letter of January 25. But naturally I was no little distressed to hear of the cruel pangs of fortune you have suffered since I last heard from you. I can imagine the terrible blow the sudden death of your youthful brother must have been to you. One senses in the valiant occasion of his death something of the nobility of his young life. You have my very deepest sympathy. . . .

What you wrote me of your attitude toward Man—of your dual or seemingly contradictory feeling in regard to mankind generally —interests me deeply. It interests me because of its close coinci-

(14) A young Persian whom Dr. Burrow happened to meet while walking in the Swiss Alps in the summer of 1925. This brief contact led to a correspondence that, off and on, continued for more than twenty years.

dence with the position of my associates and myself toward our common race. I too have 'lost faith,' or rather I have quite deliberately relinquished faith in the dependableness of our current manifestations of human relationships, that is to say, in the generally accepted expression of social adaptation commonly regarded as 'normality.' On the other hand, the systematic questioning by my associates and myself of the validity of man's prevailing standards of behavior has by the same token immeasurably strengthened my interest and sympathy in the fundamental integrity of man as a biological organism. In this sense your position is not different essentially from ours—nor, I am sure, any less consistent at heart. Man on the surface is one thing (and what we know of him in the 'normal' purview is all that we do know of him), and man—the primary biological organism—is quite another. It is this organic phase of the life and motivation of man with which human beings currently have no contact. It is on the premise of this contrast between what man *is* and what he *appears to be* that the whole structure of our phylobiological thesis rests. You will understand then, I am sure, how sympathetic I am to you in your criticism of human society and how heartily I accord with what might appear superficially to be an inconsistency in your feeling toward our human kind. Your attitude seems to me a most natural and indeed inevitable one.

As to man though, let me explain. Following our group investigations of many years, there remains no doubt that man is a dual personality. As I say, there is on the one hand the organism of man in its native, spontaneous interests and activations, and on the other there is sophisticated man—man who has been tutored from infancy in self-consciousness, in conforming to laws that are not intrinsic to his organism but that relate solely to his external appearance and to his own advantage. In his spontaneous behavior, man's processes are as ordered and harmonious as the course of the stars. But in the process of his 'civilization' reactions have arisen that are throughout artificial and subversive of the basic health of man.

This situation seems to me tremendously important. It seems to me to entail very heavy and unescapable responsibilities for us all. But I think we have to see it as a common indictment in which we are all equally involved. Not a moral indictment, of course, but a social indictment of man in his evolution as a conscious species. But I mustn't bore you in this way with my thesis.

My book should be published ere long. In the last few days I have been rather heartened to have Mr. Herbert Read of England here with us as he is momentarily giving a course of lectures on the Fine Arts at Yale University. It was really at his instance that I undertook the writing of this new book of mine. Mr. Read is one of the directors of the London publishers, Kegan Paul, and is himself a prolific writer and poet.

I think you would enjoy seeing some of his books—*The Meaning of Art, Education Through Art,* and his last book of poems, *A World Within a War.* It is extraordinary what insight this writer has gleaned through his acquaintance with psychoanalysis and, what to me is still more extraordinary, is his grasp of the principles of phylobiology, the method of behavior-adjustment initiated by my associates and myself. This is especially evident in his book, *Education Through Art.* . . .

My very good wishes to you,

Sincerely yours,

Trigant Burrow

To Wiley Hitchcock   Westport, Connecticut
Westport, Connecticut   July 9, 1946

Dear Mr. Hitchcock:

. . . I was much intrigued by your question as to whether in our view the economic disparities throughout the world and the prob-

lems they present are secondary to the problems of human understanding with which the researches of my associates and myself are
concerned. I wish we might talk of this. I wish we might together
find the answer. It is, I believe, really quite simple. At least from
our point of view it is simple.

Would the physician who treats a patient for an infective illness,
with its many and complex symptoms—the grilling headache, the
prostrating fever, the rapid and intermitting heartbeat, the labored
respiration, the pain, the restlessness, the apprehension—would he
regard these aspects of a patient's suffering as secondary in the
sense that they are not worthy of his special thought or attention?
Would he do this just because he happens to know that the illness—
that all these distressing symptoms are due to the invasion of the
organism by a definite, if unseen, germ whose virulent effects are
the *real* menace to the patient's health and life, and therefore the
essential condition to be eradicated or overcome? I know how
fully, how completely together we are when I answer your question in this way. And it is precisely in this way that the group of
co-workers of The Lifwynn Laboratory have put before them
the question of man's individual and social disorders of behavior,
man's inhumanity to man.

For us the political and economic aspects of man's behavior are
painful and tragic and heartbreaking. And they are of the deepest
concern to us. But we regard these interrelational expressions as
symptoms of a deeper-lying disorder within the organism of man
as a race or species. It is to this deeper-lying lesion that we have
addressed our investigations with a view to removing what we feel
is the essential cause of man's symptoms.

In this sense perhaps, but only in this sense, can we possibly speak
of the devastating symptoms existing throughout man's world today as secondary. Indeed, I should say that the chief stumbling
block to our investigations throughout the years has been our
inability to look away from these tragic social conditions in which
we are all common participants. They seem so immediate, so pressing, so close to the disease itself that we find it all but impossible

to take our minds off these distressing conditions with sufficient resoluteness to pursue, as behooves us, our quite objective study of the physiological tensions and strains which our researches show to be the primary cause of man's outer social symptomatology.

I really hadn't meant to thrust all this upon you. But you will forgive my answering your question at such length. It is a question that I am sure you realize lies very close to my heart.

With my very kind regards,

Sincerely yours,

Trigant Burrow

To Dr. Hans Syz   Lifwynn Camp, Merrill, N. Y.
Greens Farms, Connecticut   July 25, 1946

Dear Hans:

. . . It has cheered me more than I can say to hear of Emily's forward-looking interest and happiness. She is a true soldier. I think of her so much. I always have: but still more so in recent weeks. I think of her in connection with myself and the work—the vitally searching work in which I find myself engaged. Emily, of course, is immersed in the same habituations, inured to the same mood-conditionings as I. And, of course, like myself, she has tended to submerge, to escape her discrepancies of mood or feeling with purely mental, interpretive rationalizations—the world-old phylic trick of phylic man to escape with external projections the pain of a disorder that is internal to him, internal to his mood or motivation, internal to what is now his very identity, his own *self*. Yet, withal, Emily strangely has not been wholly out of touch—as an organism she has not been wholly unacquainted with this alien mood of man or with the deeper feeling-principle lying beneath it. Like myself, she has been completely helpless to do anything about a mood that reflected a neurosis within man as a species. How could she? But Emily has been somehow very patient, very forbearing, very understanding toward conditions within and about her—conditions involving disorder and conflict which to one who *feels* their pain and pathology are almost beyond human endurance. These are the things for which I think of Emily, for which I have always thought of her. It is these things that make her and that will always make her very precious to me. It is because of them that, without word or sign, Emily and I have somehow always understood each other.

Early this morning I felt I wanted to write you. I did not know why: I had written you only a few days ago. I know now. I know now that for a long time I have wanted to write just this to you.

Devotedly,

Father

To Mrs. William E. Galt
Doctors Hospital, New York

Westport, Connecticut
February 9, 1947

Dear Mummy:

The news is too good for words. We are all more happy than we can say. Of course Grandmother is unendurable. Such overbearing airs I have never seen. And as for life with Father, I don't know how I can face it!

Can't wait to see George Egleston. Understand he is a thing of beauty and abounding health.

My love to you both.

Affectionately,

Trigant Burrow

CHAPTER 14

A PLEA TO SCIENTISTS

What Burrow called the most stimulating experience of his scientific career grew out of a delay in the appearance of *The Neurosis of Man*. Owing to industrial dislocations in post-war England the book could not be published until 1949, two years after its completion. However, Burrow felt too keenly the urgency of man's global crisis to permit his findings regarding the social neurosis to lie unread. He sent advance chapters to many outstanding scientists in the United States and abroad, and invited their comments on the altered orientation embodied in phylobiology. It was the resulting exchange of views which the author found so stimulating. Later this correspondence formed the nucleus of *Science and Man's Behavior*, the book on which Dr. Burrow was at work before the onset of his fatal illness.

This broadening of contacts with the scientific world was a significant step. Heretofore, the audience addressed by Burrow represented for the most part the behavioral and social sciences. However, his correspondence about the advance chapters of *The Neurosis of Man* cut an interdisciplinary path, as it included scholars in the biological and physical sciences as well. Burrow felt that it was primarily the scientist, with his training in subordinating personal prejudice to objective data, who would concern himself with a research procedure that challenged prevailing preconceptions regarding human behavior.

Many of the comments of his colleagues on the advance chapters, and their requests for clarification of certain points, appear in *Science and Man's Behavior*. But other letters incidental to the exchange are included in this chapter and the next.

An important outcome of this correspondence was an invitation to address the Second International Symposium on Feelings and Emotions, held at Mooseheart, Illinois, and The University of Chicago in October 1948. It was while working on his paper for this gathering(1)

(1) 'Emotion and the Social Crisis—A Problem in Phylobiology,' published in *Feelings and Emotions—The Mooseheart Symposium*, edited by Martin L. Reymert, New York, McGraw-Hill, 1950, pp. 465–86.

that Dr. Burrow, then at Lifwynn Camp, suffered the heaviest blow of his life. His son Jack, though only 43 and apparently in perfect health, died suddenly in Westport of coronary thrombosis. While Dr. Burrow met this ordeal with characteristic stamina and courage, it left its permanent mark. Only his letters can tell in some measure the story of his heartbreak.

To Herbert Read   Westport, Connecticut
London   April 28, 1947

Dear Mr. Read:

It is not possible to tell you how overjoyed I am to have you write me so appreciatively of my book. My delight is the keener, knowing your exceptional qualifications as a critic. I am really most grateful to you for your kind letter. . . .

Your speaking of the fuel shortage and its effect on printing is just a further reminder of the terrific condition to which England has been subjected during and since the war. I have thought of it so much and with no little embarrassment, considering the fabulous opulence of our own country. We should be sharing in the sacrifices that Britain is making. By imposing appropriate rationing upon ourselves, we could so easily make a gift to England of a billion or so and be the richer for it. Within one's own family of people this would seem so slight a gesture after all. But again it is the 'I'-persona, and there is no arguing with a dislocation that is anthropological. Had Mr. Roosevelt lived, I think he would have been more gracious toward our English cousins. This is not meant as a slur upon Mr. Truman. As a matter of fact, he seems to be doing very well, and we must not forget that he stepped into shoes it would not have been easy for any man to fill. . . .

With my good wishes,

Sincerely yours,

Trigant Burrow

To Dr. Hans Syz
Zürich, Switzerland

Greens Farms, Connecticut
June 6, 1947

Dear Hans:

John(2) dropped in after school yesterday for a session with Mr. Shields and me, and will be back today. Indeed, I hope this will be a daily habit with him. The seminars are informal. Yesterday he and I devoted the time to explorations in the garret. Our gatherings, though, rest upon a phylobiological background. Yesterday, for example, à propos of something I do not recall, I said that we were all one large family, that all men were the same—same eyes and hands, same lungs and hearts and stomachs, that men were just one organism—but he promptly interjected 'and ladies too?' He evidently had in mind that Mummy was not to be excluded from the confederacy. . . .

Love,

Father

To his son
Westport, Connecticut

Westport, Connecticut
July 13, 1947

Dear Jack:

It seems absurd to be writing you when you live—praise God— just over the hill. But it is so good to have you back again, and I so enjoyed seeing you yesterday afternoon—the only drawback was Helen's absence—and there were so many things I would have liked to talk of with you and have heard from you that I must just drop you this line to let you know of the happiness it is to have you here again.(3)

(2) John Syz, aged 5.

(3) Mr. Burrow had accepted a position with the Fairfield News Company. He and his family had returned to Westport from Burlington, Vermont, where they had been living for about a year and a half.

I thought the evening so pleasant, not the least of which were the voices all about us of the children at play. It was heavenly.

Do come in soon and let us take stock of new developments. I was most interested in the contact with Mr. Hollister, and I am sure, had there been time, I would have been feasted with many more such items. It all seems too good to be true.

Be seeing you,

Devotedly,

Father

To Mary L. Murfitt, R.N.   Westport, Connecticut
Boston   July 26, 1947

Dear Old Darling:

What's this I hear about your having to slow up a while and catch your breath? I know how this goes against the grain with you, against the spirit of you—and there never was a spirit more daunt-less than yours—but indeed this ultimatum is not too bad by any means. It is a timely reminder. You know perfectly well we all have to put on the brakes a bit in the later years. And you know that your counsellor in this knows what he is talking about. . . .

I think I know in part what the trouble is. People of spirit, people like *you* have to learn that there are two great and important phases of the human spirit, two phases that are precisely opposite one an-other, and that call for a totally different technique of approach. You see, there is the phase that is all activity, all energy and ex-penditure, all enterprise. But then there is the phase that is equally strong, equally necessary, equally important in the world's work. And that is the phase that accepts and is patient, the phase of quietude and conservation. . . . You must exercise the spiritual technique of patience and so prepare yourself for the years to which we must all look forward, the years of reduced activity, the years when your presence and your counsel must serve us while those willing feet are given fewer hours in the line of duty. Why, any baby would be lucky—he would be guaranteed a fuller, healthier, saner life just to breathe the same air that you breathe.

But you understand all this. You probably understand it better than I do. You are a woman, and women understand everything better than men do. And such children as you have brought forth. My lord, Muffie, just to sit under an elm and think of Penny and John and George and the rest of your children and grandchildren should give you joy and comfort and all that your valiant spirit can desire.

So here's cheers aplenty for our beloved Muffie and for the years ahead of her and ahead of us all.

As ever,

Trigant Burrow

P.S. I am just reminded of Goethe's lines. They ought to do both of us good.

> Rest is not quitting
> The busy career,
> Rest is the fitting
> Of self to its sphere.

To Mrs. Burrow   Lifwynn Camp, Merrill, N. Y.
Greens Farms, Connecticut   July 31, 1947, 6 p.m.

Dear Brownie:

As I write before supper, it is much colder, and I'm digging in for a cold Adirondack night. I hope you are feeling better, that is, quieter, more collected. The confusion is general. The neurosis is man's. There is need of turning aside from moral nonsense and accepting a program, a technique of biological—of phylobiological research. We cling to habit, to conditioning, to unthinking, emotional conditioning. We *like* our emotional conditioning. We prefer it to intelligence, to balanced thought and feeling. Man's got a job! . . .

Devotedly,

Trigant

To Dr. Hans Syz   Lifwynn Camp, Merrill, N. Y.
Greens Farms, Connecticut   August 2, 1947

Dear Hans:

You of the low country must be enjoying a very welcome change in the weather. This morning again at six the temperature was 38. It is a lovely, clear, still day.

Your little son is precious. Yesterday morning we had a long session together here in my cabin. 'Bill Galt,' as he calls him, came in for the mail. John said, 'When you bring Florence and Margaret over to camp, (they came with Miss Aimée yesterday) tell them not to look for me anywhere near the lake because I won't be there. Tell them to look for me in the hills or in the valleys.' He meant that the lake shore was forbidden territory. . . .

He was much interested in Dannemora prison and its high walls for people who 'did not keep the rules,' as he put it, following my explanation. This will form my text when there is the opportunity for a few comments on phylobiology or the behavior of Man. When there is the cue, I believe I can address myself quite simply to Florence, Margaret and John—sometime at the table.

Miss Flora was greatly pleased—she was really very much touched —at John's having asked her each evening to come over and say goodnight to him after he gets into bed.

I am enjoying my furlough very much. We seem to be a congenial and coöperative group, and things thus far run along smoothly and pleasantly.

Yesterday, John said something to me about 'getting gold and, with the gold, getting a lot of money.' This, need I say, will be another cue. In our common neurosis we are not slow to induct childhood into the reversed pattern of *owner*ship, *property*, and of *getting* for the sake of getting. It is too bad. And we work so hard, early and late, to defeat in children the native gift of life, as this gift was in our early childhood defeated in us. I am so glad for this opportunity to be with my grandson and to try, if it may be, to lift his mind and my own above the sordid things with which we are all early imbued. The trouble with the neurotic—to put it in a nutshell—is that he has no soul, and the trouble with us all is that we are all neurotics—or gay, glib, fatuous 'normals.'

I thought of you especially yesterday and I think of you today (there are not many yesterdays or todays that I do not think very specially of you and yours) and I send you my heartiest birthday greetings and my love.

Ever devotedly,

Father

To Mrs. Leo Stein
Florence, Italy

Lifwynn Camp, Merrill, N. Y.
September 4, 1947

Dear Mrs. Stein:

I was so very shocked in reading in *The New York Times* a few weeks ago of the death of your gifted husband. Only five days earlier I had sent an airmail letter to him but doubt whether this word ever reached him.

I have thought of him so much in recent weeks, of his humor, his courage, his wide interests, his gaiety and his charm. I had just seen an announcement of his new book, *Appreciation*, when I wrote him of mine. I wanted him to know how pleased I was at the favorable reviews of it. There is certainly no evidence in these essays of any failure in the familiar spirit that was Leo's.

You have my deep sympathy in your loss, and I do want you to know of my thought of you.

Sincerely yours,

Trigant Burrow

To Herbert Read   Westport, Connecticut
London   October 9, 1947

Dear Mr. Read:

I was very glad to have your letter of September 19. . . .

You have commented on the surprising dearth of interest in my writings here in America and this has certainly been the case. In very recent years, though, there has been far more interest, though for the most part unacknowledged, in the trend of my work. Furthermore there has been among American writers lately a marked interest in the social aspects of behavior and all this has tended to highlight the thesis of my associates and myself. . . .

As it happened, I finished the detailed reading of *The Innocent Eye* the very day your letter reached me. There were in it many passages that I hope sometime to come back to with you. They were a reminder of my favorite theme—that of the 'preconscious,' as I call it. I have in mind a preconscious mode that is phylic or racial. There is this, for example (p. 115): 'Deep down in my consciousness is the consciousness of a collective life, a life of which I am a part and to which I contribute a minute but unique extension.' And again (p. 198): 'The sun was warm and seemed to cast a golden peace on the scene. A feeling of unity with the men about me suddenly suffused my mind.' And then more significant still for me in the light of the preconscious, you say in speaking of the period after youth passes out of the mode of the innocent eye of childhood (pp. 64–65): 'It is a callow and confused phase, in which the mind is unconsciously acquiring its social armor of habits and inhibitions. It is the stage at which the sensibility of most children is irretrievably destroyed. The sense of sin or guilt is imposed on the innocent impulses, and actions lose their animal playfulness. Relations with other people become conscious instead of instinctive; the child has to begin to plot its way through a maze of regulated paths.' (4) This penetrates far, it seems to me, into the primordial stage of the organism's unity and quietude. I have no end of notes on this preconscious phase of the organism's development and may some day return to them for what value they may have in a clinical appraisement of socio-symbolic man.

I am so glad to know the reviews were of interest to you. I feared I was sending coals to Newcastle. Here is still another, and I must tell you that a day or two ago the Westport Library announced in the local paper that a copy of *The Innocent Eye* was now on their shelves and would be available to readers. Mrs. Sill went down immediately to get it but was told it was already out. I don't believe Henry Holt need worry about the sales!

I suppose you revisited The Grange during your recess this summer in Yorkshire. I can imagine that returning again to the old familiar scenes inevitably brought its own nostalgic pain. I recall so well from college days some lines from Cowper's poem 'My Mother's Portrait': 'Children not thine have trod my nursery floor,' etc. It all came back very vividly as I thought what your feelings must have been on returning this summer to your childhood home. If you have kept to schedule you are leaving today for Athens. I do hope this lecture tour is going to bring you plenty of interest and renewal. I have no doubt that these occasional trips and their contacts are quite congenial to you. . . .

(4) Read, Herbert, *The Innocent Eye*, New York, Henry Holt, 1947.

With best wishes in which Mrs. Burrow, Hans and Emily cordially join me,

Sincerely yours,

Trigant Burrow

To a student

Westport, Connecticut
November 1, 1947

Dear Miss N.:

There are your recent letters to Miss Aimée that I have just read. I hope you know how much assistance it is to us to have your interest in running down items of news, or references that are of significance in our work.

Then there are your letters to me of the 26th and your note of this moment. How you are driven and tormented by personal worries or nagging queries as to the meaning of this or that, in you or in others; and how you must be ever trying to understand and adjust these infinite occasions of conflict and perturbation! It seems too bad, as I feel there is no answer to this type of personal rumination. With myself, the more I see these mental preoccupations as expressions of a common lot, the less my own personal problems possess meaning or validity for me. I am holding down a fairly worth-while job and doing so fairly consistently. As it happens, it is a job that aims at the alleviation of human conflict and ignorance and pain. I really feel this is enough—that I have no need to trouble myself with doubts of this, suspicions of that, or with too deep a sense of my own inadequacies.

So it is, it seems to me, with you. You have a worth-while job. You stick to it through thick and thin. This job of yours has as its aim helpfulness, relief, a clearer, cleaner, saner life for the community in which and for which you work unflaggingly through day after day. So, unless you must, why all the pother? In saying this, I don't mean in any sense to single you out. There is this eternal pother to greater or less degree in everyone. But, as I told you before, I think man is on the way to getting hold of himself— to getting at the cause of this universal community affliction. . . . Here again, you, like myself, have your part. It has been a helpful and steadfast and devoted part. And, as I have said or tried to say many times, I am grateful to you for your many services on behalf of The Lifwynn Foundation and the behavior reconstruction for which it stands. In the midst of this unhappy world I wish you could share with me a certain solace in having, with me and with others, contributed your devoted part.

Sincerely,

Trigant Burrow

To Sadie Dickson   Westport, Connecticut
White Sulphur Springs, West Virginia   December 23, 1947

Dear Sadie:

This is a clear, cold winter morning. The sun has not been long up. The outlook over these Connecticut hills is very beautiful.

I have been thinking of you so much ever since I heard you had been ill and that you had to go to the hospital for a check-up.(5) Brownie and I were very distressed on first receiving Elizabeth's (Burrow's) letter but were soon reassured on learning that the doctor expected to let you return home in a few days. I do hope you have made a speedy recovery and that you are feeling quite yourself again by now.

Somehow we seem not to grow any younger as the years go by. I don't know what can be done about it but it is certainly very inconvenient. It is difficult to believe that Christmas is here again. It was here only yesterday, it seems to me. But these are the days of young people's parties, of lighted evergreens and Christmas carols. I've just been listening to the early Christmas music on the

(5) Dr. Burrow knew that Miss Dickson was suffering from a fatal illness.

radio. How did we ever contrive to get through the days without the radio? It is such a source of entertainment and interest. To people living close to New York, Station WQXR is a special delight. It is devoted almost exclusively to music—to classical music. Last night I was listening to the strains of Sibelius' lovely 'Valse Triste.' You used to play it so beautifully. I hope you still do. The sound of it always takes me back to Mountain Home, and the big parlor and the nightly dancing—especially to recollections of the special feature Elizabeth and I would offer with 'Dancing in the Barn,' vying with each other in our efforts to 'cut a dash' for the benefit of the assembled Robinsons and Davises and MacCombes, not to mention the unseen audience of colored servants who watched surreptitiously through the windows of the dining-room, the while our mothers sat on a corner sofa and viewed the scene with somewhat mixed emotions, not wholly approving my rakish unrestraint and being particularly critical of the ambitious high-kicking of your fair sister. Aye, those were the days! There just haven't been any more since then. Everybody these days seems so staid compared to the like of us in the old times. I still cling to the hope of at least one more turn at the Virginia reel in the old parlor, with you at the piano and Elizabeth doing her stunt, though with somewhat more restricted excursions of the right heel.

I know you are all going to have a wonderful family gathering at Christmas. Hope Devereux is still with you and that Elizabeth can get home too at least for the day. (6) I certainly would love to drop in and say 'hello' and a 'Merry Christmas' to all of you. You'll have to accept the written word, but it certainly takes to you and all the heartiest of greetings. I hope to hear that you are quite yourself again and fully enjoyed as usual all the day's festivities.

With love to you and Elizabeth, and cordial greetings to the household, one and all,

As always,

Trigant

(6) Nieces of both Dr. Burrow and Miss Dickson.

To Dr. Stanley Pargellis, Librarian   Westport, Connecticut
The Newberry Library, Chicago   January 22, 1948

Dear Dr. Pargellis:

Your letter of January 16, which was forwarded to me here from the Foundation's former address in New York, reached me yesterday.

It will give me much pleasure to hand over to your library the letters of Sherwood Anderson you requested. I greatly value these mementos of him and so shall want to have photostat copies of them made before sending them to you. I shall also want to make sure that there are no personal references which might be embarrassing to Sherwood, to myself or to others. So there may be some delay in getting the letters to you.

There are twenty-one of Anderson's letters. Most of the early ones are undated, but I have established the dates roughly for all except one. They were evidently written between 1919 and 1937.

Sincerely yours,

Trigant Burrow

To Mrs. Samuel W. Lippincott(7)   Westport, Connecticut
Baltimore, Maryland   February 19, 1948

Dear Helen:

You should be with us more. Brownie and I haven't been the same since you went away.

The snow is melting rapidly and in just a few weeks, with the good earth coming to life again, there are going to be gala times in these

(7) Long-time friend of Dr. and Mrs. Burrow.

hills. So come soon. Bring Wallace and Mr. Chipps, and bring the red paper curtains (I am authoritatively informed they are a knockout), and if the man in the third floor back is inconsolable, bring him too. We'd love to have him, and I am sure you and Brownie can put him to good use. But come.

Then there's that trip abroad to be taken up in detail. There are many things to be gone over in connection with it. It is so important for you to get the utmost out of an experience like that, and Brownie, you know, is a born cicerone. Her reputation is international. In addition, there are books you should be reading about the Holland scene. Then there's the new terrace (your own inspiration), and Brownie is really regal in your new coiffure! So do come soon and bring everybody.

Lots of love from us both and from the children,

Yours affectionately,

Trigant Burrow

To Count Alfred Korzybski   Westport, Connecticut
Lakeville, Connecticut   March 10, 1948

Dear Korzybski:

I want to thank you for sending me the summary of your recent luncheon address on 'The Understanding of Human Potentialities' enclosed in Miss Kendig's very kind letter of February 23.

You must have found a very hearty response to this timely address of yours. I should like to have been among those who were privileged to hear this talk. It seems to me man will be forced to adopt a larger premise than has been his custom and that his feeling will eventually expand in respect to his own behavior in somewhat the same way that his mental outlooks have broadened in respect to phenomena lying outside of him.

Appreciating your thought in having the folder sent me, and with my best wishes,

Sincerely yours,

Trigant Burrow

To Herbert Read
London

Westport, Connecticut
March 16, 1948

Dear Mr. Read:

You are probably giving much time these days to the thought of the lecture or lectures you are giving at Johns Hopkins next month. I have been wondering whether it is the Percy Turnbull series that you are delivering this year. They have always been very well attended and were a delightful feature of our Hopkins circle years ago. . . .

I hope the concept of the preconscious and of cotention does not appear too intangible as I have presented it. Your life and works seem to me so very largely an expression of this basic pattern of motivation. It is a pattern one cannot readily put one's finger on. It is evidenced more in a pervasive mood or tone not easily described in the everyday vernacular. I think it is perhaps the intimation of this nuance of feeling and outlook that was chiefly answerable for your interest in *The Social Basis of Consciousness*. Anything as awkwardly written as that book would, I should think, have repelled you but for the cotentive mood within yourself and the sympathy you found in this trend of my approach. . . .

I would say that the whole thesis of phylobiology has emanated from the preconscious and that it could never have come to expression but for the recognition of this early racial principle. I have tried to get at it with the tools of the objective scientist, but you seem to me to embody it without any tools. Indeed, I think it might easily spoil something if you attempted to approach this phase of man's behavior too studiously. Cotention is probably the 'kingdom of heaven' and, like the latter, is within us.

I recall my son at the age of eleven—it was at the outset of that first world-war—saying very earnestly and spontaneously that he would rather be shot himself than have to shoot anyone. I remember the dramatic gesture with which he threw open his arms to express his greater willingness to receive a missile in his own breast than hurl it at another's. This, I realize, was not Jack, but man and his primordial and unitary preconscious instinct.

Throughout four years of active service in a world-war that was inspired by international hatreds, you were far more conscious of the organic bond that unites men as fellow human beings than of the differences that momentarily separate them as political 'enemies.' Even in the clash of combat, you could not bring yourself wilfully to kill an adversary because his ideological creed happened not to be in accord with your own or with that of your country, preferring that he live, because of your deep sense of the ties that bind men together as members of a common race.

I do not mean that your life has not been surrounded, like my own, with ditentive interests and motives, or that you have not, like myself, been caught up in and largely governed by these deviate incentives. Yet, throughout the chaos of man's separative self-interests, we have, like many others, managed somehow to recognize instinctively this unitary principle of mutuality and common accord among men. . . .

In closing I do want to salute again what seems to me the very exceptional punctuality and efficiency on the part of your publishing house throughout all the interchange we have had with them. It has been such a satisfaction, and I cannot help thinking must represent a quite unusual record. This, I know, is traceable in no small degree to your own thoughtful interest in my book, and once more may I say how grateful I am.

With kind regards from us all, and looking forward to seeing you before long,

Sincerely,

Trigant Burrow

To Kevin Wallace(8)   Westport, Connecticut
San Francisco   May 11, 1948

Dear Mr. Wallace:

I have not yet acknowledged and thanked you for your good letter
of April 26. So earnest, so thoughtful a letter as yours merits a
fitting reply, but I do not feel that I can answer it as adequately as
I would like. For years the work of my associates and myself has
been consistently directed toward disparaging our intellectual
convictions in respect to behavior. For us there has been but one
single problem—the recognition of the complete dissociation of
the personality of man and the concrete task of adjusting this
radically distorted identity as it is made perceptible within one's
own organism.

Naturally you have written me from a mental, intellectual background, and it just happens that my work does not readily lend
itself to a mental approach. I suppose I shall continue to find myself somewhat embarrassed in face of such thoughtful letters as
yours, and that I shall only embarrass you with such replies as this,
until the work of my associates and myself has gotten further on.
In our findings—and this finding has applied equally to ourselves—
man does not live *in* his behavior but talks *about* it, the while he
firmly believes that this *is* behavior. I believe the most important
step in our work today is the publication of my Report, *The
Neurosis of Man*. I do not for a moment mean to say that it is all
I would like it to be. But whatever its shortcomings, it does seem
to me the next step because it is an effort to approach just this
interval between the application of intellectuality to behavior and
the recognition of the distorted internal tensions that are responsible for this mental approach to the behavior of one's self and others.
I think my forthcoming book does deal fairly competently with
this altered frame of reference, with this needed internal readjust-

(8) A journalist.

ment of an identity that is throughout dissociated in its motivation or behavior. . . .

I do thank you again for your letter, and I do wish I were capable of writing you in a way that might offer assistance to your very earnest aims rather than seeming to put you off. As I try to say in the final chapter of my book, behavior really isn't the problem of you or of me—of any 'you' or any 'me.' It is the problem of man, and man, as a phylic organism, has got somehow to shoulder it or we'll be going to war or sending our sons to war, or to asylums, *ad aeternitatem.*

Thank you too for your very generous contribution to the Foundation. You know, I am sure, that the Statement of Aims was not sent you with any thought of solicitation. Your gift is a gesture of supererogation which we much appreciate.

I hope you will feel free to write me any time.

With kind regards,

Sincerely yours,

Trigant Burrow

To Elmer Diggins
Toledo, Ohio

New York City
May 26, 1948

Dear Mr. Diggins:

Your very earnest letter reached me, and I don't want to delay sending you some word, however hurried, in reply to it.

You are, of course, quite right, I do resist mysticism. It is a system of ideas that is undoubtedly right, and I resist it. My friends who are Democrats insist upon how right they are, and so it is with my Republican confrères. Some people I know who are Communists write me that I resist their right system of ideas. My Catholic friends write me in similar vein, and I do recognize how right all these systems are from their point of view. Accordingly, in scientific honesty I must confess that, by the same token, I am all wrong.

It just happens, though, that as I look about the world, and more particularly as I consider the process of study that has for so many years occupied my associates and myself, I have not been impressed with right people or their right systems of ideas (I am being frank too, you see). Rather than embrace a right system of ideas as an escape from my unquestionable wrongness, I would prefer to remain wrong and, from this acknowledged basis, acquire if possible some clearer insight into this world-dichotomy of right and wrong systems and people. My hope has been that in some such process I might ultimately bring assistance to my own 'right' thought and feeling and, just possibly, to the thought and feeling of others. In our group-analysis one thing became unquestionably clear: We were all *right*—incorrigibly right. And I have greatly valued the privilege of this opportunity that group-analysis gave me for sensing how very 'right' we all are—we and our various systems of ideas.

So I do not take issue with you for a moment. I have no wish and no ground for argument. From your background (from my basis I would say 'conditioning') you are right in your mysticism, and from that same background I am of course wrong in my resistance to it. But, as I say, inadequate as my wrongness is, from what I have seen of right people and their right world, I am not inspired to follow their course. Instead of accommodating myself to right systems of ideas, I prefer to go on with my associates, and challenge our own obsessive tendency toward rightness. However mistaken, however misguided my position must appear to you, I prefer to investigate this inveterate rightness, in the hope that our group-analysis may ultimately throw a much needed light upon this tragic dualism in man. In view of the basic disparity between us, may we not let the situation rest here and so preserve ourselves against the futility of further discussion.

I believe you will find much interest in the writings of Herbert Read, if you do not know them already. His most recent book,

The Innocent Eye, is a vitally interesting study or 'biography of the mind,' as he calls it. You will doubtless find much enjoyment too in his many books of poetry. Then there are his penetrating studies, *The Meaning of Art* and *Education Through Art.* Mr. Read is a competent and brilliant scholar in whose books I am sure you will find much congenial companionship.

With my kind regards,

Sincerely yours,

Trigant Burrow

To Dr. Adolf Meyer
Baltimore, Maryland

Westport, Connecticut
May 26, 1948

Dear Dr. Meyer:

In a letter the other day from my friend, Neil Wholey, he told me of his visit to you and of the pleasure it had been to him to see you and to have from you a real account of your condition. This visit of his meant much to me too, as his letter was the first really comprehensive word I have had of your illness.

I have, I know, been a dissenter from all the old established views I once used so to cherish, but I have really never been recreant to old established friendships or to you. Perhaps the distinction is not easily drawn, and I do not doubt that in my somewhat ruthless espousal of newer values I have at times seemed awkward and impatient of accustomed orientations. So that when Dr. Wholey' letter brought me this word of you and spoke of your kind inquiry for me, it meant very much to me. For naturally I have thought of you often and, realizing the bond that has held others of your colleagues so close to you throughout the years, I have hoped that despite my ardent ventures upon uncharted seas, this same bond still preserves between us also the close personal sympathy and understanding of earlier days. Whatever changes time has brought these past ties I really do not forget.

What tragic times these are, and how needless all the conflict and pain and loss and disheartenment on every hand. As Dewey comments in his recent book, *Problems of Men,* 'The scene which the world exhibits to the observer at the present time is obviously one of general instability, insecurity and increasing conflict—both between nations and within them. . . . ' Surely medicine will not much longer withhold its hand in face of a problem that is so definitely a medical as well as a social one. . . .

We like it out here in these gracious Connecticut hills. The surroundings are most congenial for research and writing. The Laboratory is only a stone's throw from my home, and Hans and Emily with their two small sons are just up the road, and Jack and Helen and their little girl are not far distant. We count ourselves very fortunate in having them all so near. . . .

With warm remembrances from us both to both of you,

Sincerely yours,

Trigant Burrow

To Herbert Read   Westport, Connecticut
London   May 30, 1948

Dear Mr. Read:

During the past week or ten days I have been preparing plans to bring the publication of my book to the attention of some of my scientific colleagues and a few men in other learned categories—John Dewey, Ralph Barton Perry and others. Among them are correspondents from whom I have from time to time received appreciative comments on my material, and others whose own writings on world problems indicate that they might be sympathetic to the trend of *The Neurosis of Man.* With the world situation as it is, I feel it wise to make what use I can of the intervening time before the appearance of my book.

I have written a quite comprehensive letter requesting the privilege of following it with certain material from my book, and it now looks as though it will be sent out to thirty or more scientists and other scholars.(9) . . . I am enclosing the letter in case you have time to glance through it. The last paragraph describes the material I have in mind for distribution to the recipients of the letters. . . .

My special reason for writing you now is to ask whether such an approach to American scholars could be adopted also for England and other countries. I have in mind especially men of the calibre of Arthur S. Eddington, and we would indeed welcome your suggestions as to names, since you and your associates are in a better position than we are to select names of the type of scholars we hope to reach. We are including in our list three or four key people in the fields of psychology, philosophy, anthropology, physics, biology, and sociology, as well as a limited number of other students and writers. The letter will be addressed only to men and women in the very top rank of their professions. Einstein, for example, is among them, as he has made strong pleas for better human relations. . . .

With my best regards,

Sincerely yours,

Trigant Burrow

To Max Eastman   Westport, Connecticut
Chilmark, Massachusetts   June 11, 1948

Dear Mr. Eastman:

I have just sent a letter to a few of my colleagues prominent in various fields of science, in which I have attempted to elicit their sympathy in the researches in human behavior conducted by my associates and myself of The Lifwynn Foundation. As I said in

(9) The number was later increased to 165 scientists and scholars.

that letter, for years my analytic quarry has been the state of mind so universally, yet so fallaciously known as 'normality.'

Recently I read your book, *Enjoyment of Living*, having been attracted to it by Orville Prescott's disparaging review in *The New York Times*. I found your story most delightful and, as I read it, thought more than once that you would probably find some interest in the work of our group on behalf of a world that you so love.

If it isn't presuming, I am going to enclose a copy of this circular letter also to you (one of them, by the way, went to your old teacher, John Dewey), thinking that you too may be among the students of our aberrant human ways who might care to see the material I speak of in this letter. I make no bones of wanting terribly whatever interest I can rally for our scientific cause—a cause that would see man, with all his conflicts and ineptnesses, in clear objective perspective and so bring to his aid a process of study sufficiently forthright and unsentimental to reach his tragic disorder of mind.

As to your own book, I take it you are surely not going to dismiss us from your company at the tender age of thirty-four, but that we may expect ere long a sequel to your intriguing biography. In the next of my serial attacks of bronchitis I plan to read your *Enjoyment of Poetry*. Sherwood Anderson told me years ago he felt sure that what I was trying to say could be expressed only in poetry. I was never altogether certain as to just what he meant, but perhaps I shall discover his drift when I read this earlier work of yours.

Max Rosenberg used to speak of you with unreserved enthusiasm when he was studying with me years ago in Baltimore and you happened to be lecturing there. Max's hearty championing of you in those early days, and this courageous book of yours will, I hope, extenuate somewhat my trespassing upon you in this way.

Sincerely yours,

Trigant Burrow

To Professor John Dewey   Westport, Connecticut
New York   June 17, 1948

Dear Dr. Dewey:

I don't wonder you were taken aback by my reference to the species man as 'neurotic.' My title is, I know, an audacious one, but it seems to me warranted by prevailing ideologies which, in face of political and economic conflicts, prompt us to exchange bombs with one another rather than take sober internal counsel *with ourselves*. But I hope that, as you suggest, 'my book will resolve the difficulty you now have.' I do not believe that our positions are, in fact, so far apart. Indeed, as you will see, my book sets out with a quotation from you that more or less aligns man's political and economic patterns with the madness of war. (*Human Nature and Conduct*, p. 115.)

As I have not a complete manuscript available, I thought that these few selected chapters I am sending you today might afford you a sufficient preview of my book as a whole to mitigate the seeming audacity of my thesis and so permit your giving me the benefit of your comment. It would be gratifying if sometime you might care to discuss my material with Dr. Hook(10) who is also among the scholars to whom I have written. Of course the entire book will go to you as soon as copies are received. It is not scheduled to appear before the late summer or early fall.

I much appreciate your good letter to me, and especially the promptness with which you were kind enough to reply.

With my high esteem, believe me,

Sincerely yours,

Trigant Burrow

(10) Dr. Sidney Hook, Professor of Philosophy at New York University.

To Dr. Martin L. Reymert, Director   Westport, Connecticut
The Mooseheart Laboratory for Child Research   June 21, 1948

Dear Dr. Reymert:

Thank you very much for your letter of June 15. It is with pleasure that I write to accept your kind invitation to present a paper at the Second International Symposium on Feelings and Emotions to be held in Mooseheart and at The University of Chicago, October 28, 29 and 30. I note your wish that a 300-word abstract of the paper be in your hands by September 1, and of course I shall have a copy of the complete address for you, as you request.

I was very glad to see the name of Dr. David Katz among the foreign contributors to the Symposium, as I recall knowing him most pleasantly a good many years ago. It is just possible that I shall meet other old acquaintances from abroad with whom there will be opportunity to renew former contacts. If at a time convenient to you, your secretary will be good enough to let me have the names and addresses of the additional contributors to the Symposium, I would much appreciate this courtesy.

In view of the many dislocations in man's feeling and thinking throughout the world today, I should like to express my appreciation of the great importance of the Symposium you have arranged and to extend my hearty wishes for its fullest success.

With my kind regards,

Sincerely yours,

Trigant Burrow

To Donald B. Mason   Westport, Connecticut
Westport, Connecticut   June 25, 1948

Dear Donald:

Need I tell you that you and Hildegarde(11) have been much in

(11) Mr. Mason's wife who had recently died.

our thoughts. I remember so well the first time I met her. It was only a few days after we had come here to live, and Hildegarde came over to bring Mrs. Burrow some flowers out of her garden. She came quite simply across the lawn, emphasizing the friendliness of her gracious gesture. We felt how sincere, how whole-hearted, how real she was. When she had left, we said to one another that if this is typical of Connecticut we have made no mistake.

Hildegarde was always like that. We never shall forget her thoughtfulness of Emily in her trouble. Emily was saying only recently how much Hildegarde's letters had meant to her in those difficult days. Remembering all this, and so much else, I find myself resenting the circumstance that my work and its demands have throughout the years permitted me so little contact with you both.

Come over to us, you and Jerry, whenever you care to. If there is anything we can do, let us know. We shall be thinking of you and wanting to help. Please remember me to Jocelyn.

Sincerely yours,

Trigant Burrow

To Professor Robert M. Yerkes   Westport, Connecticut
Yale University   July 1, 1948

Dear Dr. Yerkes:

I have your letter of June 28, and also the material you returned.(12)

I want to make what headway I can in replying to your letter, but it will hardly be adequate at best, as things are rather rushed with me today in preparation for leaving this evening for my camp in the Adirondacks.

(12) Dr. Burrow had sent the selected chapters of *The Neurosis of Man* to Dr. Yerkes.

Yes, I do recall you at the time of my receiving my doctoral degree at Johns Hopkins and I faintly remember having a passing glimpse of you at some meeting or other at a later time. But aside from this we are not personally known to one another.

Like others of your colleagues, I have naturally been an admirer of your work, in many ways so different from my own. Indeed, I do not wonder that you have not a clear recollection of me, as I can lay claim to nothing comparable to your own distinguished record in the field of psychology.

After taking my Ph.D. degree, I spent the summer with Adolf Meyer at Ward's Island and came upon Freud's *Studien über Hysterie* in the library at the Psychiatric Institute. I was wholly intrigued by this early work of Freud's, and after conferring with Dr. Meyer felt I should go to Europe for a year or so to study psychoanalysis. It happened that Freud and Jung were in New York that summer. I had the pleasure of meeting them and thereupon arranged to participate in Jung's psychoanalytic seminar the coming year. It was a memorable year for me and was made more so through my association there with August Hoch whom I came to know very closely. But for Hoch I think I should have been no little discouraged by what seemed to me then, and still seems to me, the unwarranted extravagance of certain aspects of Freud's psychology.

Following my stay abroad I returned to Baltimore and entered on the practice of psychoanalysis in which I received the unforgettable encouragement and assistance of Dr. Meyer. With the opening of the Phipps Clinic the following year I was given an assistantship there. While I did not at any time undervalue the training I had received under Dr. Stratton in experimental psychology, my time, as you see, was given to very different interests. Neurosis, and neurosis alone, became my absorbing preoccupation on leaving Johns Hopkins.

At least, though, it was some compensation to me when, some years later, I was able to give encouragement to my young associate, Mr.

William Galt, at the time he became interested in animal behavior and in obtaining his degree in experimental psychology. That, I hope, makes some amends for my own lack of contribution to the field, until recent years made possible the experiments with the neuromuscular reactions concomitant to the varying modes of attention I have for some years described as cotention (total attention) and ditention (partitive attention).

But from the beginning of my work in psychoanalysis I was interested in the social implications of the neurosis. I was interested in the social implications of the *self*—my self included, naturally. It seemed to me that analyst and analysand challenged everything but this central core that is one's own socially conditioned identity. This interested me, and this has been the major concern in my group investigations.

It is interesting that you ask the origin of the name, 'Lifwynn,' because, as it happens, I cannot recall having been asked about it before. When Mrs. Burrow and I with our young children went to the country near Baltimore to live, we were quite thrilled at the home we had secured in Ruxton. In looking for a name we decided upon the Anglo-Saxon word, 'Lifwynn,' meaning 'the joy of life.' Later we gave the same name to our camp on Lake Chateaugay—a recreation spot that was also a great delight to us. As the practical group work—that is, a group of people living and working together, with a central research purpose—originated at Lifwynn Camp, when the Foundation was incorporated it was given the name, Lifwynn. It seems a frivolous name to give to a soul-searching research, such as our group-analysis was, with its constant challenge of cherished feelings and associations upon every side.

From what I have said, you will gather that I fully accord with your description of our separate approaches to the field of behavior, my own having leaned far more to the medical side. To turn to your question: No, I am not inclined to say that the neurosis is traceable to erroneous religions or philosophies. I would rather be inclined to say that erroneous religions and philosophies are traceable to the neurosis—to the unconscious but universal instilling into the human offspring of a wishful, non-objective sense of right or fitting behavior rather than a biological and objective sense of discrimination between what is fitting and not fitting. I suppose this is hardly satisfactory and I cannot now elaborate on it as I would like, but I think in the main you will sense my trend. As I said, this is really not the opportune time to be answering your very thoughtful letter. But I want to have this word go to you before plunging into the batch of work that awaits me on settling down in camp.

To reply to your query, I should say that the attitude of the maturer or maternal generation to the immature or infant generation begins to operate in very early infancy and to inculcate a ditentive mode in the species man. By 'ditentive mode' I mean a mode that disposes the child to adopt a wishful criterion of behavior whose aim is merely the personal advantage of conforming to the parental mood or will. Ditention now automatically places differential advantage above considerations of total biological motivation and health.

I was indeed interested to hear of your own manuscript and of its running neck to neck with mine in matter of length! I am very pleased, too, to have you express your feeling that our goals are not unrelated, however different our backgrounds. It must be a keen satisfaction to you, as it certainly has been to me, finally to have gotten through a report of such length and scope.

Let me thank you again most earnestly for your interest and coöperation. It means very much indeed to me, especially when I realize to how great an extent my medical and psychiatric interests have alienated me from scientific fields that are so close to your own heart. You are really very generous, Dr. Yerkes, and I deeply appreciate your kindness.

May I assure you that nothing you have stated in your letter will be quoted unless I have received your permission to do so.

This takes you my best wishes for a good summer.

With kind regards,

Sincerely yours,

Trigant Burrow

To Mrs. Burrow
Greens Farms, Connecticut

Lifwynn Camp, Merrill, N. Y.
August 14, 1948

Dear Brownie:

Emily's haemoglobin is '85'! It is so apparent in every way, too, that Emily is getting right on her feet again. She has been so lovely to me this summer. It's like old times. Guess maybe *I* am improving!

Hope to heaven there'll be a letter from you at noon, saying how you are feeling now.

John is such a joy—Stephan too of course (13), but John is a more prevalent one. He was too funny yesterday. He barged in with my pepsi-cola as usual on the dot of eleven o'clock. Instantly he spied a package of chiclets on my desk. Dashing over and pointing to them, he said in mock surprise: 'You don't say!' He has the keenest sense of humor. To me he is completely captivating.

But no more now. Time presses so. Every minute counts.

With love and hoping to hear,

Devotedly,

Trigant

(13) Dr. and Mrs. Syz' younger son, born September 5, 1947.

To E. O. Haes, Chairman   Lifwynn Camp, Merrill, N. Y.
The Australian Psychology Centre   August 16, 1948
Sydney, N. S. W., Australia

Dear Mr. Haes:

Your letter of July 26 reached me yesterday and was most welcome. It particularly interested me to learn that you and your groups are throughout laymen. While, of course, the principles of phylobiology intermesh with those governing the other biological sciences, physiology, zoölogy, anthropology, etc.,—indeed the whole array of disciplines having to do with the evolution of man— I see no reason why anyone may not be a phylobiologist where it is question of the simple, unaffected relationship of his organism to the environment. I myself did not go to a scientist in my feeling of the need for the realization of this simple, basic rapport between the organism and its surroundings. As I said years ago in *The Social Basis of Consciousness*, and as I say again today in *The Neurosis of Man*, it was a layman(14) who supported me, who supports me still—not so much with knowledge, not with any pride of learning, as scholarly as he is—but through the earnestness of his feeling for the oneness of man, as for the oneness of man's relation to the world of external phenomena.

So you will understand how welcome, how sympathetic your letter to me is, and you will understand how I value the spirit in which you have written me. I am really deeply touched by the sincerity of the work of yourself and your associates. I am greatly appealed to by the unobtrusiveness and simplicity of it.

As for the books of mine you have been good enough to study and, in a measure, live by, I cannot but feel how far short of their real

(14) Clarence Shields.

aim these earlier essays fall. My interest and anticipation lie in the work I am about to publish—*The Neurosis of Man*. This thesis is written from within, as it were. It originates at the core, while by comparison my earlier books seem to me now to have dealt mainly with material not too far beneath the outer covering. One could approach *these* formulations intellectually—not so this latest Report. This study presents an iron curtain to the intellectualist and his vicarious rationalizations with regard to the basic motivations of man.

I have an idea, too, that your group will find considerable interest in a paper that is to appear in the January issue of *Philosophy of Science*.(15) This is a rather careful epitome of the thesis of *The Neurosis of Man*. But the paper that interests me most and which I set most store by as a possible link between the scientific principles of phylobiology and principles which form the basis of other sciences is one that I have just completed, 'Emotion and the Social Crisis—A Problem in Phylobiology.' It is to be an address I look forward to giving at the Second International Symposium on Feelings and Emotions to be held in October at The University of Chicago, under the auspices of the Mooseheart Laboratory for Child Research. If my associates and I are to escape the platitudinous misinterpretations of the sentimentally minded, it is essential that we elicit the understanding of scientists whose interest may incite the creation of a non-sectarian international organization for furthering man's orientation in his relation to his environment and to his kind.

Let me thank you again for your letter and for the very kind expression of your 'strongest feelings' for the work of my associates and myself.

Sincerely yours,

Trigant Burrow

(15) See note 4, p. 246.

To John Syz   Lifwynn Camp, Merrill, N. Y.
Greens Farms, Connecticut   August 23, 1948

Dear John:

We all miss you and Poppy and Mummy. But Dada misses you
most of all. I miss you in the dining-room where you were always
first to enter. I miss you at the 'burning-pile,' where just now
Kenny is burning some evergreens that crackle and hiss as the
thick smoke rises. I miss you on the tennis-court where one evening
I watched you playing with Happy and Margaret and Florence.
And then I miss you at our mid-morning refreshment, when you
would bring Dada his cool drink and watch it bubble over with
glee.

I miss you all the time and everywhere, and I can't wait till I see
you again.

With love to you all and to Stephan too,

                                                Your devoted

                                                        Dada

To his son   Lifwynn Camp, Merrill, N. Y.
Norwalk, Connecticut   August 23, 1948, 9 a.m. Monday

Dear Jack:

All arms around for a great big hug—just the way it used to be
when we were boys! I am so happy for you, son, and for the way
everything has turned out with Helen. How that poor child has
suffered and so uncomplainingly. Well, it's over now and we can
set out anew and renewed.

I know you've been almost beside yourself with worry and anxiety
in the last weeks and that the successful outcome of the operation
and Helen's splendid reaction to it have taken a heavy load off
your mind and heart.

This is a lovely morning. Hans and his family have just left the dock bound for a two-day jaunt to Westport. The camp begins the inevitable process of breaking-up at summer's end. I always regret it.

You no doubt received a cheque of $100.00—a preliminary sum—and some days later $300.00. The former, as I remember, went to Newtown Avenue, the latter to your office—Fairfield News. It was such a happiness to have these remittances go to you in a time of trouble.

My love to you and Helen and Penny—I hear that you are all to be united again in a very short time because of Helen's fine progress and hence her timely release from the hospital.

Ever devotedly,

Father

This letter never reached Dr. Burrow's son who died that day.

To Mrs. John B. Reilly   Westport, Connecticut
Merrill, New York   September 9, 1948

Dear Margie:

I haven't yet written you, but I know that you have understood, as you always do.

My wife and I will never forget all your kindness, all your thought of us in those first hours of our great sorrow. You were like a daughter to us. You have been a daughter to us always, Margie. And we do think of you and we do love you, as Jack did.

We seem to miss him more with each day. There have been some very lovely testimonials of the love and honor in which our boy was held on every side. I cannot resist enclosing to you a letter from Mrs. Brennan, the wife and business associate of the owner and director of the chain of newspapers for which Jack served as advertising manager. This letter will not tell you anything that you do not already know, knowing Jack as closely and as long as you have. But it will mean much to you, as it does to us, that other people—even those who knew him but a short time—held him in the same high regard and affection as we do. I am enclosing also the clipping from the New York Herald Tribune.

You will be glad to know that Helen, who was in the hospital, having ten days earlier undergone a surgical operation, and who had to be brought home two days earlier than planned, to attend her husband's funeral, is gaining strength and doing as well in every way as can be expected, following so great a shock. Penny, too, has been quite wonderful, though the strain of her father's passing has betrayed itself in an undercurrent of extreme tension and nervousness. She idolized her father as he idolized her.

I can write you better another time. We are so unaccustomed to Jack's absence that writing is not easy. I know you understand. As I said, you always do.

With our love, my dear,

As always,

Trigant Burrow

To Dr. A. J. Carlson   Westport, Connecticut
The University of Chicago   September 9, 1948

Dear Dr. Carlson:

About a week ago I mailed to Dr. Reymert a tentative copy of my Symposium paper, 'Emotion and the Social Crisis.' In sending it to him I was naturally reminded of you and of your kindness in wishing to include me among the participants at the Chicago meeting.

As I wrote Dr. Reymert, there are further remarks to be added before the address is completed for publication. Among them I hope to include, if only as a foot-note, a reference to the current demarcation usually described as 'religionist' and 'atheist.' As a student of behavior, I cannot but be concerned with the behavior of 'religionists' as distinguished from 'atheists.' As it now stands, this discrimination conveys a slant I find quite unacceptable.

Personally, I do not believe in any of the current Gods or in the Churches that represent them. But, for that matter, neither do I believe in any of our prevailing forms of government today. Yet it would certainly not be in order for anyone to describe me as an anarchist, when the more positive statement of my view is that there can be a government only of the whole world of man, of the species man—a government that is based upon a recognition of the common needs, interests and affections that fundamentally unite all its members.

I hope I do not seem unduly concerned. After all, the exaltation that religionists commonly reserve for themselves, and the corresponding note of derogation with which they speak of 'non-religionists' is nobody's fault. One cannot point the accusing finger. It is all just part of a general ineptness in man's social evolution. But I do feel that scientists have been altogether too temperate in face of these unmerited affronts. I mention this because I know how sympathetic your own position is with this viewpoint, and because of the reassurance I have found in the reprints you were good enough to send me, particularly in your essays on 'Science and Supernaturalism,' and 'The Science Core in Liberal Education.'

... Needless to say, I look forward with great pleasure to meeting you at the Symposium, yet (and this I suppose I need hardly say either) being myself no Titan in fields of science, I do feel some trepidation as to my ability to align my subjectively tested criteria of behavior with the standards of measure that you have over the years so ably sponsored in fields of external phenomena.

With my kind regards,

Sincerely yours,

Trigant Burrow

To Dr. George M. Stratton(16)   Westport, Connecticut
Berkeley, California   September 30, 1948

Dear Dr. Stratton:

The letter you have written me is so very generous and so heartening. I cannot be grateful enough to you for this splendid response. Indeed no words can express my pleasure in the replies I have received from the various scientists and scholars to whom I wrote and sent the chapters from my book.

I believe, though, it is because you have not had before you my book as a whole that you are led to think I hold the view that primitive man was wholly cotentive. My position is that man as a biological organism possesses all the potentialities for cotentive living, but that coincident with his acquisition of the symbolic function (a function that has, of course, been of incalculable benefit to man in the course of his evolution), he has acquired a false sense of the self and of the behavioral norm which regulates the interactions of the individual with others of his kind.

With regard to the question of conflict among animals, as I said in a letter to another of my colleagues, there is not the slightest question in my mind as to the interindividual antagonism existing at lower evolutionary levels. But the interindividual conflict in man to which I have attempted to draw attention is, in our finding, not in the category with these spontaneous biological antagonisms. My book attempts to show the quite dissociative state of mind out of which the behavior-conflicts in man habitually arise. The point with me is that in man the parental generation has put the younger up to 'rights' or prerogatives for which there is no biological foundation and which are answerable throughout human society for the ideological conflicts existing within and among us. I try

(16) See pages 17–18.

to bring out evidence of the induction in man of an image of the self which is quite fantastic and which, in investing the child with an artificial sense of its personal preëminence (I am referring, of course, to the generic child), automatically sets the stage for competition and conflict throughout the species.

There was so much in your letter I would like to talk of with you if it were possible to do so. But I believe I should profit more from a heart-to-heart talk with you if you had had the opportunity to read my thesis in full (I think I wrote you earlier that I look forward to having a copy of it go to you as soon as it is published). Anyway, such a talk would mean much to me regardless of the book. There are so many joyous associations with you in past days. And to have from you today an expression of your friendship from our earliest acquaintance means more to me than I can at all express. The inspiration of your teaching has never dimmed for me and through the years I have never ceased to have a feeling of unusual understanding and closeness toward you and Mrs. Stratton. I am certainly looking forward to seeing your own book when it is published. I only wish I might have had the benefit of its learning and wisdom before writing my own.

I believe I wrote Mrs. Stratton some time ago of how ideally we are placed here in this congenial New England countryside of Westport, with my laboratory only a stone's throw from my home, and the homes of my children and grandchildren also close by. It has seemed to us greater good fortune than we at all deserved. But, as often happens, it could not last. A heavy blow has fallen upon us since that letter was written. On August 23 our precious son, Jack, died suddenly from a heart attack just after leaving his office. One of our friends wrote of him as 'the boy with the sun in his heart.' He was very close to me in his feeling for my work, and so tender always toward his mother. His passing is very hard for his young wife and little girl.

Thank you again most earnestly for your thoughtful letter. It has meant very much to me.

With my best regards to you and Mrs. Stratton,

Sincerely yours,

Trigant Burrow

To Mrs. Frank Nash(17) Westport, Connecticut
Norfolk, Virginia October 8, 1948

Dear Lucia:

It has been far too long since Brownie and I received your lovely letters to us. I have meant to write you—I have wanted to do so, but it just has not been possible. I felt I wanted to write you in some detail, and particularly of Brownie. And so I have been obliged to postpone writing until there would be the more favorable opportunity.

Brownie has been remarkably brave, but her heart is broken. Jack's passing is almost more than we can bear. I see Brownie down in the garden in the early morning gathering flowers for her son's grave. She is in the car and off to the cemetery the first thing after breakfast. The cemetery or the little country churchyard is very close by, so that it is easy to visit Jack's grave and keep it fresh always.

Helen, too, has been quite wonderful, though she too, young as she is, is utterly brokenhearted. I don't know whether you know that she had been operated on two weeks before and had to be brought from the hospital two days earlier than was planned, to attend Jack's funeral. Of course, on going home she had to return to bed, and this enforced inactivity made her grief all the more poignant. Her one thought is to get to work 'for our little girl,' and to have her develop in the way that she and Jack had planned. They were such close pals, the three of them. Penny is only eight, but she is very mature for her age, not only in her advanced standing in her school curriculum, but also in her sen-

(17) Cousin of Dr. Burrow's, formerly Lucia Smith.

sitive feeling and thought. She is really adorable, and could not be more like her father, both in appearance and in her ways.

Jack was very unusual. I do not know how to express it in words, but his life seemed to hold a message. There was an understanding, a sympathy, a tenderness—and with it all, a selfless joyousness that was very rare. The message of Jack's life is a very beautiful one, and I want my own life and work, in the time that remains to me, to carry on that message, to keep alive the radiant spirit who was my son. When he was not more than six years of age—we were living on St. Paul Street in Baltimore; it was just after our return from the year spent abroad—and as we sat at dinner (I suppose we had been ruminating on the question of life and its meaning) I turned to Jack and in a somewhat playful mood said, 'Jack what do *you* think life is?' And, after looking away somewhat pensively, he turned to me and said, 'Oh, just God and my heart, I guess.' I was startled by so unexpected a reply, and have never ceased to note the consistency of his life with the sentiment expressed at that time. His heart was so much one with his kind. He had Devereux's feeling for others, especially where they were in pain or need. This is so characteristic of Brownie, too. Her response to others in distress is reflex with her.

To me Jack always seemed so like the young English poet, Rupert Brooke. He loved Brooke, and would read him frequently. I was paging through my copy of his poems just the other day, and I was struck by the lines of Wilfrid Gibson that appeared in the brief biography. They remind me so of Jack, and that certain golden glow about him.

> He's gone.
> I do not understand.
> I only know
> That, as he turned to go
> And waved his hand,
> In his young eyes a sudden glory shone,
> And I was dazzled by a sunset glow—
> And he was gone.

. . . I believe I wrote you from the Lake immediately, telling you of the terrible tragedy, and that Brownie was expected at camp in a few hours. She and her close friend, Helen Lippincott, arrived in such gay spirits. You can imagine my distress in knowing the dreadful news I had to break to her. We sat through dinner, and walked about the camp a while, showing Helen the different beauty spots of this congenial mountain home of ours to which we went thirty years ago when our children were so young and where there had been so very many happy memories. Then Brownie and I went to my cabin, and I told her. It was, as you can imagine, a terrible moment for us both. Brownie showed the same incomparable spirit that you and I would expect, knowing her as we do.

I think in the first days of a grief like that, that people are stunned —mercifully—and unable to grasp the reality of it all. . . .

Emily has been so very wonderful to Brownie and me. She and Jack were so very close throughout the years, and her grief is very deep. But her thought is constantly of her mother and me, showing itself in so many gentle attentions, in so much tender thought of us. I don't know what we would do without her. And Hans has been a rock of strength throughout all these weeks.

We were all away at the time. Emily was returning from camp through New Hampshire. Brownie was on the way to camp, and Helen was in the hospital. Hans and Emily were the first to reach Westport, so that all the responsibility of arrangements of every sort fell upon Hans.

Just an hour before Jack's death, on talking on the phone to his mother who was leaving in a few minutes for camp, he was telling her the route he thought she should take, and the hotel at which he thought she should stop overnight. The last thing he said was, 'Be sure to send me a telegram on reaching the hotel, because if I don't hear, I'll worry.' He seemed so very well and so joyous over the prospect of Helen's returning home completely well, in just two days. . . .

It is a terrible thing to lose a son. It is the parents who should first pass on. This would be the natural course of things. I remember so well Mother's anguish at Sister's death, because it seemed so unnatural. As she said, it was contrary to the laws of nature for a child to precede the parent. We can only keep our dead with us in spirit. We are so frail of spirit, all of us—all of mankind. It is only as we recover and hold to the things of the spirit that we may feel the closeness of those who are no more with us.

Man has much to learn. Perhaps in the present horror of a third world-war confronting us all, we shall take ourselves more seriously and seek to discover in the social and political muddle of man's own making the cause of this disorder within man himself. It is a great, but a crying responsibility, and it rests squarely and equally upon us all. . . .

I must not write you more. Already I have imposed too long a letter upon you. Today you and Brownie and I have so much in common. I am sure you understand my writing you as I have.

I want you to have the enclosed material because it helps tell the story of our precious boy. He was so generally loved, and his genuineness so universally *felt.* . . .

With my love, dear Lucia,

Always affectionately,

Trigant

To Dr. Daniel B. Kirby   Westport, Connecticut
New York   October 25, 1948

Dear Dr. Kirby:

I am returning enclosed the paper on which you ask me to comment. I have been over it with interest and am, of course, most sympathetic with the emphasis you place on inculcating in the patient a constructive psychological outlook. It has always seemed to me important that the surgeon be in close touch with the life-situation of the patient rather than in the position of one called in only because of his exceptional skill in excising specific parts of the body tissues. This, I feel, applies particularly to eye-surgery for, in general, patients show especially marked emotional disturbance where it is question of the loss of sight. You are doing a great service to your patients when, in addition to affording them technical operating skill, you take the necessary measures for promoting peace of mind and freedom from nagging problems and worries that can so impair operative success and impede convalescence. I like your pointing out the tendency of surgeons to project the blame for difficult operations on the 'bad patient' when, as a matter of fact, the patient is 'bad' merely because he has been given insufficient psychological preparation, or sedation. This is a point that might profitably be emphasized with physicians in general.

Your reference to the importance of relaxation in eye-operations brings to mind the work of the physiologist, Edmund Jacobson of Chicago. You may be familiar with his writings. Dr. Jacobson has worked out a technique of *progressive relaxation* which he describes in a book by this title. I hardly think his technique would be applicable as a pre-operative measure since it requires considerable training before the subject can attain a completely relaxed condition. Also (in contrast to the situation that holds for curare) Jacobson finds that the eye-muscles are the most difficult of all muscles for the subject to relax through conscious control and that they are the last to relax through his method of progressive relaxation. But I thought you might be interested to know of Dr. Jacobson's work, if you are not already familiar with it. Incidentally, he gave a lecture last week before the Psychology Section of the New York Academy of Sciences.

I am greatly interested in your successful use of curare. Both in this and in your effort to quiet your patient through psychic means I believe you would be greatly assisted by including in your research the too neglected field of *attention* in relation to behavior-disturbances. Were there the time, I would be very interested to undertake some tentative experiments with you in determining the influence of curare on this all-important bionomic function. Deviations in the process of attention are so commonplace today as to have become 'normal' and hence to have escaped completely the recognition of psychologists, not to speak of so-called 'normal' subjects. Perhaps we may talk sometime of this aspect of the organism's adaptation in relation to your problem and to mine. . . .

All success to this comprehensive book of yours on the treatment of cataract.

With best regards,

Sincerely yours,

Trigant Burrow

To Karl Howenstein   Westport, Connecticut
South Pasadena, California   November 30, 1948

Dear Mr. Howenstein:

The Symposium is over. The gathering was a great success. The trip to Chicago—Dr. Thompson, Dr. Syz, Dr. Galt and I—was, as you can imagine, an interesting and stimulating one. We are glad, though, to be back at our desks and the many demands that await us in the coming months. The schedule for each of us is heavy, but a congenial and inviting one.

There has been a surprising dearth of notices in the paper regarding the Symposium, though the press was amply represented at the banquet Friday night. Are they awaiting the lull following yesterday's stormy election? By the way, my paper, I was told on arriving, was with the *Chicago Daily Tribune*. (I'm not sure I caught the name of the paper correctly.) Naturally, I'm more interested in comments from such organs as the *Science News Letter*. But whatever the reaction of the community, another milestone has been passed, and there are others ahead that are no less exciting in interest.

It would be nice to have some word of you and yours. I shall not forget your understanding letter about Jack. I think of it often, as do Mrs. Burrow and Helen and my co-workers. Jack has left us so much. I hope that in some small measure we can live up to it all. My own debt to him is immeasurable. As Dr. Galt said to me the other day, 'Jack always had quite naturally what the rest of us here are striving to attain.' Yes, my dear Karl, you did know Jack.

I'll let you know of any reverberation from the meeting in Chicago.

Ever sincerely,

Trigant Burrow

CHAPTER 15

LOOKING FORWARD

'My associates and I recognize, of course, that in our group approach to the problem of behavior we have made but a beginning, and a very meager beginning,' Dr. Burrow told the scientists assembled at the Second International Symposium on Feelings and Emotions in October 1948. 'We recognize too that even this meager beginning of an understanding of social man must abort in mere futility unless there is the coöperation and participation of scientists the world over in defining and accepting the larger biological pattern of behavior native to man as a social organism. . . .

'Just a few decades ago scientists at last ceased squabbling over their separate ideologies regarding the problem of contagious disease and, as a scientific unit, set out to discover and destroy this common enemy of their kind. . . . In this common battle against a common enemy, scientific investigators the world over were automatically made at peace with one another by virtue of their common and consistent interest in relation to a hostile external environment. Likewise, when men cease wrangling over their separate ideologies with respect to behavior and enter commonly upon the task of combating an internal behavior complex that is equally the common enemy of mankind, they will automatically be at peace with one another in their undivided interest to defeat the enemy within the internal environment of man.

'It is, of course, not within my province to offer suggestions as to ways and means of establishing such a scientific federation of individuals and peoples. But from my experience in group- or phylo-analysis I feel strongly the need for the organization of a generic state based upon inclusive, scientific principles, as contrasted with regional states based upon affective, political differences. There is the need of scientific scholars the world over who will reject prevailing discriminations among individuals and peoples with respect to geographical boundaries or other differences, and who will do so for the very practical reason that, as things stand, individuals and peoples are now destroying themselves. They are ruthlessly destroying both themselves and the natural resources of their environment because of the socially false basis of behavior necessitated under the prevailing sovereignty of a partitive or right-wrong premise of adaptation. There is the need of some such biologically homogeneous state in order to guarantee the very survival of man. We need to establish a world state in which scientists and laymen are organized not to fight one another's affects and prejudices, but to fight the archenemy of all states and all peoples, that is, the spurious, dissociative "I"-persona now besetting the balanced behavior of man as a phyloörganism.

'. . . Phylobiologically, the talk of politicians about "one world" means absolutely nothing. . . . There is need throughout the world for a unification of scientists who will approach the problem of conflict, now dominating human behavior, from the basis of a universal principle that rests upon a universal biological norm. But the reorganization of world behavior begins at home. No scientists in the field of behavior can point to what other people should or should not do. The reconstruction of world behavior must begin with the analysis of our own behavior.

'. . . The lesion from which man suffers is within the organism of man.

'This internal lesion is our problem. It is the problem of the men and women who are here today and whose colleagues are distributed throughout the world—men and women who have proved their competence and authority in varied fields of investigation. It is we who, in respect to man's social behavior, must take over what is ours, namely, the scientific understanding and formulation of the basic cause of man's world-wide disharmonies. It devolves upon us to remove the problem of human behavior from the entire field of tradition and speculation—from religion, as now understood, from morality and other supernatural instrumentalities—and make plain to ourselves and to the community that the understanding and control of disordered behavior-processes is a discipline that lies within the category of the biophysical sciences. We must compass at last the neurodynamic dysfunction embodied in neurosis and war, just as the scientist has compassed the understanding and cure of somatic disturbance in the organism of the single individual.'(1)

The American edition of *The Neurosis of Man* was finally published

(1) 'Emotion and the Social Crisis—A Problem in Phylobiology,' published in *Feelings and Emotions—The Mooseheart Symposium,* edited by Martin L. Reymert, New York, McGraw-Hill, 1950, pp. 482, 484-6.

in August 1949. Among the letters Burrow received was the following from the eminent physiologist, A. J. Carlson:

I have now studied your book, The Neurosis of Man, sufficiently to realize that it is a significant contribution to the understanding of Man. I congratulate you, and I thank you.

In view of Burrow's effort to broaden understanding of his thesis among leaders of thought in diverse branches of science, such comments meant much to him.

The publication of this book concluded a significant phase of Burrow's thirty-year investigation of disordered behavior-processes. Although he was now seventy-four, his questing spirit was so youthful and eager, his sense of man's behavioral impasse so poignant, that many plans for new projects and experimentation were occupying his attention. He further explored the possibility of finding a drug that would facilitate the establishment of the cotentive mode. In the fall of 1949 he completed his last and one of his most telling papers, 'Prescription for Peace,' for a symposium volume edited by Pitirim A. Sorokin.(2) Meanwhile he continued the correspondence concerning the advance chapters of *The Neurosis of Man*.

To Sir Stafford Cripps   Westport, Connecticut
London   December 1, 1948

Dear Sir Stafford:

It was heartening to have your note of November 4 with its kind expression of interest in my book. It will give me much pleasure to have a presentation copy of it go to you on publication.

I wish I could tell you when that will be. *The Neurosis of Man* has been in press with Routledge and Kegan Paul for almost a year now, but owing to the industrial dislocations with which you are only too familiar they are not yet able to set the date of publication. Mr. Herbert Read has done his utmost to hasten the appearance of my book, but from the outset he has repeatedly

(2) See note 4, p. XIX.

warned me of the delays and disappointments for which I must be prepared.

Thank you earnestly for the generous spirit in which you have written me.

With my high esteem,

Sincerely yours,

Trigant Burrow

To Arthur Upham Pope   New York City
New York   December 16, 1948

Dear Mr. Pope:

I greatly appreciated the spirit in which you wrote me and am deeply grateful for your kindness in wishing to help. Realizing how overwhelmed you are with prior commitments and with 'hourly emergencies,' I value all the more your goodness and sympathy toward the endeavors of my associates and myself. While your work in archaeology and your study of Asiatic culture do indeed seem to me to provide a 'great, living social and psychological laboratory,' I fear that, unlike the vital researches of Kinsey, our analysis and—if it may be—our synthesis of man's tensional patterns of reaction in the actual moment (as immediately perceptible within ourselves as observers) hardly makes contact in any direct way with your significant historical researches. Indeed I wish there might be some close link with anyone of your research interest and broad, inclusive spirit. However, you could not have been more hospitable in the expression of your generosity, and I have been heartened by it more than I can say.

I do hope my excerpted material has not imposed too great a burden upon you and your associates. It is debatable whether it was wise of me to presume that such incomplete material could possibly represent my thesis as a whole. It is debatable whether it was thoughtful either of my colleagues or myself. . . . But whatever the inadequacies of the advance chapters, I shall be glad to have your reaction at least to this very fragmentary preview of *The Neurosis of Man*. . . .

Your mention of the financial limitations of your organization strikes a further chord of sympathy in me. Such a handicap is one of the heaviest obstacles under which we have been laboring throughout the course of our researches. But this doubtless is the common lot among students of science, particularly in the fields of pioneer investigation.

This takes you my best wishes, and again my thanks for all your goodness.

Sincerely yours,

Trigant Burrow

To Mrs. Samuel W. Lippincott   Westport. Connecticut
Baltimore, Maryland   January 6, 1949

Dear Helen:

It has been a long time since we have had so comforting a message as your letter to Brownie yesterday brought us. The thought of having you and Muffie(3) with us is a real solace, and we shall certainly welcome you with open arms. Your letter held a twofold pleasure for us. It brought the assurance that Muffie is definitely on the mend. Some weeks ago she would hardly have felt in a mood for even this amount of traveling. Of course she will feel completely at home at Summer Hill, knowing she can do just as she

(3) Mrs. Lippincott's daughter.

pleases—and when! It will mean a great deal to us to have this visit from you and to be able to share with you the satisfaction of helping restore Muffie to her accustomed strong and healthful self. I only wish the season were brighter and more gracious. But there will be the clear, sunny days too as there always are during the winters in Connecticut.

Everyone among us is well, I'm glad to say. The impetus of habit forces us along in its established current. I don't understand, but outwardly the days go on much as usual, and somehow Brownie manages to keep abreast of things. She is pathetic, though—so restless, so harassed, so unhappy. You will have to take her in hand again, Helen dear. But you and Muffie must not think you are coming to a gloomy home. It won't be that way. We are so grateful to have had Jack with us for these forty-three precious years. But we do miss him so. He was so sweet, so understanding, so thoughtful, and withal so gay and gallant a spirit.

Helen is everything to us as she was to Jack. Her devotion to him and her valiant effort to go on and to bring Penny up as he would wish mean more to Brownie and me than I can at all express.

Emily, too, shares with us from day to day the void of Jack's absence. They were so devoted, and in our common loss Emily could not be more tender, more thoughtful of us at all times.

You are a busy woman and I hadn't meant to impose upon you with so long a letter. But I'm taking the day off (or part of it) for a bit of rest, and I wanted to have this too long overdue word go to you.

Having you and Muffie will be such a help to us. I hope it may be some help to Muffie and to you.

With our love to you both,

Affectionately,

Trigant Burrow

To Professor Carl R. Rogers   Westport, Connecticut
The University of Chicago   January 13, 1949

Dear Dr. Rogers:

I have read your paper—'The Implications of Recent Research in Therapy for Personality Theory'—with much interest, and wish to thank you for sending it to me. Your research and your preparation for it follow lines so different from those of our group that I should be presuming to attempt to offer a constructive criticism of it. Its value, of course, is obvious but I especially like your emphasis upon the study of the organization of the self as basic to the understanding of personality. The pervasiveness which you assign to the self in its influence upon human behavior is a generalization with which our results are certainly in close agreement. As I wrote you earlier, my interest was particularly piqued by your finding that the acquisition of a new idea of oneself is the most potent factor in bringing about changes in behavior.

In view of the physiological trend of thinking which you mention in your letter as developing among you and your associates recently, I regret that you have only fragmentary portions of my book in your hands and not my thesis in its entirety. The material I selected for sending out included, for the most part, the more general discussion. I fear that it reported very little of concrete nature in regard to our physiological studies. But the book itself contains chapters that deal in considerable detail with the actual technique employed in our group experimentation—both in the earlier phase of our investigations and also in the later phase of our work in which we dealt with differentiations in internal tensional patterns. These pages contain full information as to the standard laboratory procedure, the techniques and apparatus employed under varying experimental conditions, and the control experiments that were run to rule out extraneous factors. The physiological data are presented in numerous graphs and tables, and standard statistical methods are employed to determine the significance of the differences obtained. . . .

Sincerely yours,

Trigant Burrow

To Kevin Wallace   Westport, Connecticut
San Francisco   January 21, 1949

Dear Mr. Wallace:

I shall certainly *not* let this welcome word from you yesterday go unacknowledged. I don't know when anything has piqued my interest more completely than the keenly understanding trend of this memo you prepared for Mr. McArdle. It was read here at the luncheon table at which my daughter (Mrs. Syz) happened to be present. She said to me later, 'Father, I want to read Mr. Wallace's statement again. I believe I begin to have a really clear idea of what your work is all about.' To which I said, 'I believe it helps me too to sense more clearly what I am driving at!' If, in view of the too common puzzlement of my readers, I should ever need a translator, you are the person I would want to have translate me.

So you see, Mrs. Wallace and your sister do not present a sporadic case. The trouble with us all, I think, is that we cannot rely as we have always done upon the 'old bean.' Recourse to intestinal fortitude is absolutely indispensable.

In all seriousness, I cannot half tell you how impressed my associates and I were on reading this clear and simple résumé of my trend. We are really very grateful to you for all your interest and helpfulness.

I do hope there may be some day the opportunity of our knowing each other. Of course, if you are at any time in New York, you will not fail to come out to see us. . . .

With my kind regards,

Sincerely yours,

Trigant Burrow

To Dr. Ludwig von Bertalanffy   Westport, Connecticut
Vienna   February 1, 1949

Dear Dr. von Bertalanffy:

Your letter of January 16 reached me a few days ago. It has given me much pleasure to write Routledge and Kegan Paul of London requesting them to send a presentation copy of *The Neurosis of Man* to you in care of the Springer Verlag, Vienna. I appreciate more than I can say your plan to review my book for the journal, *Biologia Generalis*.

You will find in my thesis much that may seem to show a singularly radical departure from accepted psychological tenets. As I wrote another of my scientific colleagues: Ordinarily, when students of research hit upon some trend of inquiry, they set their separate *minds* to work, whereas in our study of the basis of human behavior and its motivation, our chief objective was to *set our separate minds aside*—to *set aside our separate aptitudes and attainments*—and, as far as possible, to discount the personal processes of the projective mind of man in its habitual attitude toward behavior. Our group work has consisted solely in the effort to define a *mood* we definitely recognized in the reactions of the individual and of social groups as being arbitrary and unstable, and to challenge this arbitrary mood as a falsely imbued sense of the 'self.' We set out (associates, students and I) to study our *selves*—the *social self* of man and his motivation as a phylum.

This reversal of inquiry upon the inquirer has not been an easy task, and may in part account for much of the awkwardness with which I have reported it. It has entailed many basic readjustments in our habitual outlook. . . .

May I say again how deeply glad I am that you will review my book. This will be of great assistance to me and to my colleagues of The Lifwynn Laboratory.

I know that you are a busy man, but my hope is that the reading of my book will not be without its compensations for you. I say this because I feel very strongly that, in common with other scientists, we are faced with a problem in human behavior whose solution can only be found through recourse to controlled scientific procedures. From our researches, there seems to be evidence of the presence of a fundamental biological impediment in the development of man's behavior as a species—an impediment that appears to be coeval with his acquisition of language. This developmental mishap undoubtedly plays a major role in our social and economic conflicts and dislocations.

I assure you that I reciprocate most heartily your kind expression of the wish that we may sometime meet here in America.

With my renewed thanks for your interest in the work of my associates and myself,

Sincerely yours,

Trigant Burrow

To the Reverend Terence J. Boyle, S.J.   Westport, Connecticut
Fordham University   February 5, 1949

Dear Terry:

I seem to knock on your door at the most unexpected times and upon the least predictable occasions. This one, I fear, is the least expected and the most unpredictable of all!

On page 67 of *The New Yorker* for January 22 of this year, there is a paragraph the first line of which reads: 'Laws, especially of this nature, are . . .' Then, further along, there occurs this extraordinary statement: 'In 1892, the president of Georgetown University, a Jesuit institution, was a Negro.' Can you riddle me this? In the first place, I recall having heard in Fordham days that no Negro could become a Jesuit. (I remember this rule of the Order because I was no little troubled by it, wondering secretly what would happen if God himself should elect to call a Negro to the Jesuit Community, and not having possessed the theological gumption to reason that God would know better than to implant in the heart of anyone a religious vocation to which he was not eligible.) Besides, unless memory fails me, Father Richards was president of Georgetown in 1892.

So that my real question is: Hasn't *The New Yorker* slipped up for once? Do please, enlighten me. That a Negro should in that blithe day and generation have been the president of what was practically a Southern University seems to me quite fantastic. What in the world is the answer? Perhaps you or some other member of the faculty will wish to drop a line to the editor (Mr. Harold Ross) and inquire just where he got his data. (4)

. . . In the midst of all the stress and dislocation of things these days, it is hard to believe we live in the same world we knew in our boyhood.

Best regards and all good wishes,

Sincerely yours,

Trigant

---

(4) According to Father Boyle's reply, *The New Yorker* referred to Father Healy, S. J., Rector of Georgetown in 1892 or thereabouts. Rumor had it that there 'was negro blood somewhere in his ancestry.'

To William L. Phillips   Westport, Connecticut
The University of Chicago   March 4, 1949

Dear Mr. Phillips:

I have a bad conscience at not having answered your letter of February 20 far sooner than this. I hope you will not think my delay has been due to a lack of interest in your letter or in your dissertation on Sherwood Anderson's *Winesburg, Ohio*. I am really much interested in your project and only hope I can offer you some measure of assistance in your quest for information regarding the relationship between Anderson and myself. Unfortunately my memory is not too clear about some of the details of our meeting.

As I recall the circumstances, my wife and I, with our two young children, paid a visit of two weeks at the camp of Miss Alys Bentley on Lake Chateaugay in the summer of 1914. Tennessee Mitchell was also a guest at the camp and our meeting her was one of the outstanding experiences of the summer. We thought her charming, and greatly enjoyed knowing her. She spoke frequently to me of Sherwood and expressed the hope that we should sometime know each other. The following summer (1915) I returned to the Lake, as we had rented a camp on the opposite shore. That summer we used to take our midday meal at Camp Owlyout (Miss Bentley's) and, as Sherwood was also at the Lake and having meals at the Bentley Camp, I saw a good deal of him. Whether Tennessee was there that summer I do not recall. The following summer (1916), having completed the building of a camp of our own (Lifwynn Camp), we again returned to the Lake.

During this summer there were frequent contacts with Sherwood and Tennessee. This was the summer that there was the particular talk with Anderson of which I wrote in my paper in *The Psychoanalytic Review*. He had canoed over in the early morning, probably for breakfast, as he and Tennessee would not infre-

quently come over to us for sausages and waffles, 'Southern style.'
That particular day, I remember, Mrs. Burrow had put up lunch
for us, and Sherwood and I set out on a two and a half mile jaunt
to Rocky Brook. We sat there beside the brook and talked the
livelong day, and our talk was entirely along psychoanalytic lines.
It was a delightful midsummer day and I have thought back upon
it many times. Of course, there were other days and other talks
during this as well as the previous summer, but the talk that
especially stands out in my memory is the day long discussion we
had beside the brook. Sometime in the fall of 1916 Tennessee and
Sherwood visited us at our home outside of Baltimore. At that
time they were married. It must have been in the summer of 1916
that their marriage took place in most informal fashion at Lake
Chateaugay.

I fear that part of what I wrote Mr. Hoffman(5) was quite mistaken. I had not at that time reread, as I have since done, all of
Sherwood's letters to me. I think now that there is no question but
that my acquaintance with Sherwood antedated certain of his
writings which, at the time I wrote Hoffman, I thought were
written before I knew Anderson. So that it would now appear that
Anderson was not uninfluenced by my talks with him on psychoanalysis. I should mention, however, that almost from the outset of
my work in psychoanalysis I became interested in what seemed to
me the social implications of the neurosis and it was this aspect of
our talk that took strong hold with Anderson. I do want to emphasize, moreover, that Sherwood Anderson was an original psychologist in his own right and, if he profited by any insights of mine, I
also profited in no small measure by the exceptional insight of this
literary genius. Of course at no time did Anderson take part in my
researches in group- or phylo-analysis. This phase of my work was
a much later development.

I believe this answers your first four questions. As to the fifth,
Anderson did talk of his writings, and of some short stories, but
my memory is not specific about this.

(5) See letter to Frederick J. Hoffman dated October 2, 1942, p. 442.

By the personal equation I meant, at that time, the unrecognized bias of the individual; by the personal (human) equation I mean today the unrecognized bias that exists within man as a species. I mean the system of affects and prejudices that constitutes the impediment to man's healthy functioning I have described as 'the social neurosis.' That early article referred to the freehand interpretations too often to be traced to the unrecognized complexes of the individual analyst. I did not analyze Anderson. Our relationship rested upon a quite unusual sympathy and understanding of one another that was spontaneous, immediate.

I wish I could be of more help to you—if indeed I have been of any! At least I hope you will feel free to write me further if anything occurs to you that I might assist in clearing up.

All success to the dissertation and to you,

Sincerely yours,

Trigant Burrow

P.S. I have talked again with Mrs. Burrow and our dates are not entirely in agreement. So that I am writing to a friend who was at the Lake during those summers and with whom we have kept in touch over the years. I hope to find that she is better oriented in regard to Sherwood's visits to camp and the other items you mention than we appear to be. As soon as I hear from Miss de Lorenzi, I shall get word to you.

To William L. Phillips
The University of Chicago

Westport, Connecticut
March 10, 1949

Dear Mr. Phillips:

I have heard from Miss de Lorenzi and am hastening to pass on to you the information contained in her letter. Miss de Lorenzi is sure she has the data necessary to establish the dates, but they are under lock and key in her safe deposit box in Chicago and she is at present in Clearwater, Florida. Her memory is, however, that the first summer that Sherwood and Tennessee were at Lake Chateaugay together was in 1916, and that they were married during that summer.

Miss de Lorenzi speaks of Waldo Frank's being at the Lake during that summer of 1916 also, and of Waldo, Sherwood and herself spending almost every afternoon on the beach together. She writes: 'Sherwood had a "name" for me or rather my "type" of personality, and he and Waldo did a bit of "experimenting" on me during those interesting hours on the beach. They read me *unpublished* manuscripts of Sherwood's. One, I remember, they said, *could* NOT *be published*. . . . Would that I had realized then the value of all the words that passed between those two men of outstanding genius! Waldo had a short time before given Sherwood a very fine write-up of appreciation of his talents, and this was their first chance, as I understood it, to have a long time together to *talk* and *talk* and *talk* to their literary heart's content.'

It occurs to me that Mr. Frank may be of assistance to you in placing any dates but more particularly in regard to the influences that shaped Sherwood's writings. I do hope that he can provide you with the specific information you desire regarding the time that the Winesburg stories were written. I only regret that I personally cannot give you more concrete information. I know how important it is to you that your statements be accurate. It would be so easy for the Freudian-minded to see Freud as the inspiration to Anderson's work. But, as over against that, there is my feeling, as I wrote you the other day, that Sherwood possessed insights into behavior, especially with regard to the sexual determinants of it, which arose from his own independent intuition. This original quality may in no small measure have influenced the writing of *Marching Men* and been largely responsible for the broader social conception running through this novel. It was chiefly in works of this character that I thought that any influence of mine showed itself. I do hope that Mr. Frank can be of more assistance to you than I. . . .

Regretting that I still am unable to be definite about the dates in which you are interested,

Sincerely yours,

Trigant Burrow

To Kevin Wallace   Westport, Connecticut
San Francisco   March 12, 1949

Dear Mr. Wallace:

I was glad to have your reference to E. M. Forster's work. Before another day passes, I mean to read his short story, 'The Road to Colonus.'

As for your having early experienced a mood that savored of cotention, this, it seems to me, may well be set down among the many, many intimations of what I used earlier to call the 'preconscious mode,' that is, the pre-symbolic, pre-verbal mode of consciousness. The thing that so grips me today is the phylic sense of cotention—the adult mood that sets at naught the social modalities based upon our current affects and projections. In this phylo-organismic mode (the primary, natural mode of man) I am not under the social compulsion to *like* or *dislike* this person or that. I cannot. Your affective likeableness or mine is purely artifactual. And, incidentally, it is a matter of untold relief to the organism that we are not 'nice' in this spurious sense—that neither of us has any longer to play up to this insufferable social amenity. The comforting sequel, of course, is the realization of a spontaneous mood of common feeling, of a common identity among us, among men and women the world over. To sense even faintly the presence of this basic biological principle is worth, it seems to me, whatever organismic responsibility one must take on in his effort to dispel the ditentive social reflexes now sponsored by man's illusory 'I'-persona.

I am interested in what you say of your early thought of undertaking 'the transformation of the novel.' I am intrigued by the possible phylobiological implications it may hold. But this opens vistas that are too enticing, and I must not write you further today beyond expressing my appreciation that you should say you would 'like to spread the news about my book.' If your generous thought went no further than this, it would be quite sufficient for me that anyone should feel so genuine a sympathy in the trend of my work. I am really very grateful. But I am sure that it *will* go further, that it will do very much to create interest throughout the wider community in the research objectives of my co-workers and myself. . . .

With my kind regards,

Sincerely yours,

Trigant Burrow

To Professor Ludwig von Bertalanffy   Westport, Connecticut
McGill University   March 25, 1949

Dear Dr. von Bertalanffy:

Your very kind note has just reached me. I need not say how keenly interested I am to see your new book *Das biologische Weltbild.* . . .

There is undoubtedly, as you say, a similarity between us to which even this brief statement you enclosed provides ample testimony. 'This world of symbols may be in conflict with biological trends that have become displaced by it, thus generating the forces that cause behavior disorders.' This is a theme on which I have long been harping. And your sentence, 'This symbol world which makes of man a *human* being, at the same time is the social cause for the bloody course of history,' bears further witness to our common thought and language. This mutuality of ideas is indeed most heartening to me.

With my kind regards,

Sincerely yours,

Trigant Burrow

To Kevin Wallace   Westport, Connecticut
San Francisco   April 2, 1949

Dear Mr. Wallace:

. . . You are going to find many inept attempts in the early stages of phylobiological groups. Only some ten days ago a letter I received contained the comments of a leader in group studies, which purportedly are phylobiological. They are unadulterated semanticism. They are mental, verbal, projective. The statement is unquestionably able, but it makes no contact whatever with the basic feeling of the organism. This is not criticism. It really reflects in no small measure an inadequacy in ourselves, in our formulations, and in part it reflects a certain chronic inaccessibility on the part of the wider community because of the very nature of a neurosis that is social and that can always count on the consensual backing of this rigid *status quo*. But I don't believe for a moment that the difficulty is insurmountable. There is yet more work to be done. The clearer account of things, I feel sure, will come, in time. . . .

In the letter before this last one from you, you were speaking of phylobiology in relation to literature. Perhaps we will follow this up sometime. I wish we might talk about it together one of these days. Muriel Rukeyser told me some years ago she felt that American poetry had definitely been influenced by my trend. Certainly Sherwood Anderson, in conversations, and D. H. Lawrence, in his letters to me, expressed very deep sympathy in my psychoanalytic interpretations. You probably know the latter's *Psychoanalysis and the Unconscious*. But all this was long ago. I don't know how far either of these authors would have gone along with me in my later researches. Some people were alienated by my Freudian defections, or what they considered defections. They were really not that. . . .

The passage that particularly impressed Mr. Shields and me in Forster's *Passage to India* was the opening paragraphs of Part II where he describes the Malabar Caves. This does have definite intimations of the primordial mood of the preconscious. I once assembled material for a book on the preconscious, and if the time, the spirit and the opportunity should combine to make it possible, I want to turn back to that material with a view to its publication.

With best regards,

Sincerely yours,

Trigant Burrow

To Dr. Guy Steele   Westport, Connecticut
Cambridge, Maryland   April 25, 1949

Dear Dr. Steele:

Brownie has been quite unable to settle down to her desk and reply to the many letters of condolence received by us. So that it has fallen to me to offer what expression I can of our very deep appreciation of the understanding thought and feeling to which the letters from our many friends attest. I want you to know there was none that meant more to Brownie than yours, with its expression of sympathy to her upon the death of our son. She would wish to write you, I know. I know that she will. I cannot pretend to write you as she would. I only want you to know that your letter has not lain all this while unanswered through any lack of appreciation of it on the part of my dear wife.

There was also that earlier letter from you to Brownie. She did so value it, as did I. It was a very beautiful letter, and it could have been written only by a personality of very rare and sensitive feeling. You spoke of past days, of memories of her girlhood, and of how wonderfully sweet and lovely you always thought her. Brownie was greatly touched by your words and your gracious remembrance of her. Believe me, I was not less touched than she by that wonderful letter with its heartfelt testimonial to her. For, after forty-five years of married life, I can heartily endorse and accent all that you wrote. I did appreciate the generous spirit in which you wrote her, more than words can say.

It would sorely grieve you to see Brownie these days. There is the same spirit, the same charm and loveliness, the same spontaneous outreaching in helpfulness to all about her, but her heart is broken. It is pathetic to see her going out in the early morning to gather the spring flowers from the garden to take to her son's grave. Jack loved them so. She has made the corner of the little country churchyard where our son lies a very beautiful spot. It is a very comely memorial of myrtle and evergreen to our precious boy.

The loss of a son is such a terrible thing. It is an unnatural trauma that penetrates one's very organism. Jack was so handsome, so joyous, so earnest and devoted, so sweet and gallant. We shall not look upon his like again. But we must go on. There is still the obligation to live and work and wait. It is extraordinary how the same life can continue still, when one's heart has turned to ashes. . . .

Thank you again most earnestly for all your thought of us. It is good just to know there are such people in the world as you.

Sincerely yours,

Trigant Burrow

To Dr. Henri Piéron   Westport, Connecticut
The Sorbonne, Paris   May 5, 1949

Dear Dr. Piéron:

Thank you for your kind letter of April 25 which was forwarded to me here at Westport from our New York office. I wish to acknowledge also your courtesy in sending me the reprint of your address before the Edinburgh Congress. I look forward with much interest to reading it.

It is gratifying to my associates and myself to know that you plan to include some of our phylobiological terms in the psychological vocabulary you have in preparation.(6) I hope that you will be assisted by the Glossary in *The Neurosis of Man.* However, if you find yourself troubled in your task of reproducing any of the definitions in French, please do not hesitate to call on me for whatever help I may be able to give you. While no member of my staff is completely at home in the idiom of your language, several of our group have no difficulty in understanding spoken French, and enjoy reading it. When your vocabulary is published, I shall much appreciate your kindness in letting me know of its appearance.

With my best wishes,

Sincerely yours,

Trigant Burrow

To Thomas Sancton(7)   Westport, Connecticut
The Nation, New York   May 21, 1949

Dear Mr. Sancton:

I much appreciated your letter of May 16 with its very kind expression of interest in the trend of my writings. I wish you might know something of the later development of the work of my as-

(6) See note 6, p. 375.

(7) Newspaperman. In two issues of *The Nation* (April 9 and 16, 1949) Mr. Sancton made reference to Burrow's thesis as it bears upon the nature of man's responsibility for warfare.

sociates and myself in the field of human behavior. I think I cannot make a better beginning than to have you see the enclosed copy of a letter I sent out some months ago to colleagues of mine in various fields of science. I am including with it the Table of Contents of my new book, *The Neurosis of Man.*

In this Report I have attempted to present evidence of the presence in man of a biological impediment in the evolution of his behavior as a species—an impediment that appears to be coeval with his acquisition of language. From our investigations, there is evidence that this developmental mishap plays a major role in our social and economic conflicts and dislocations. For many years my co-workers and I have tried consistently to counter our own community habituations by attacking *within ourselves* the affects and prejudices that commonly clutter the 'thinking' of so-called normal man. This research has contributed to alter in no small measure our accustomed frame of reference with respect to the problem of human behavior. 'After all,' as I remarked in a recent paper(8), 'to lock oneself in a house for years with associates and students, with normal and neurotic personalities, all of whom have voluntarily pledged themselves to a schedule of unremitting challenge of their own habitual reactions, personal and social, is an experimental discipline that definitely gives pause to one's customary prepossessions—to one's reflex affects and projections.'

I earnestly hope that my book may serve to awaken a broader, more fundamental biological view of human behavior. In saying this, I have not in mind broader *concepts* of behavior. That would indeed be presumptuous of me in view of the able formulations we already owe to our many distinguished biologists. But I should be glad if I might assist in furthering the internal recognition of the phylic implications of behavior-disorders—if I might assist in making evident the nature of the subjective feelings and motivations that are the incitement to our behaving, as a species, in the way we do behave.

(8) 'Emotion and the Social Crisis,' p. 477. (See note 1, p. 501.)

As I see it, the condition of neurosis is common and generic, and we are faced with a problem in human behavior whose solution can only be found through recourse to controlled scientific procedures. If our difficulty is really the business of the scientist—of the physiologist, the biologist, the anthropologist and kindred students—must not these trained investigators find a way to cooperate in making clear to themselves and to man at large wherein his real difficulty lies? Judging from my own experimentation, it lies in a very different field from what is commonly assumed to be the case. On the basis of our researches, I am sure that ultimately students the world over will rally to a sense of their obligation to investigate the phenomenon of prejudice or biased emotion with the instruments and techniques of the biological laboratory.

It is a gratification to have gotten off my hands at last a report of these years of investigation into the behavior of social groups. Today I want to have you know of the scheduled publication of my book on August 6, and to ask you to accept with my compliments a copy of it as soon as the advance copies are available. On many counts it is not as adequate as I should like it to be. This is inevitable in view of the unprecedented material and objectives with which my associates and I were confronted in undertaking an objective analysis *of* ourselves *by* ourselves. But my hope is that other investigators, with their widely differing background and experience, will find in our modest beginning the scientific incentive for examining man's subjective deviations in behavior as expressions of a bio-physical (neurodynamic) disorder.

You are, I know, very busy, and I should regret to intrude unwelcomely upon you. My excuse must be your own very able description of the unilateral emotions involved in the attempts of our deliberative bodies to handle important affairs of government. It is a pleasure to look forward to a further article from you dealing with aspects of behavior of mutual interest to us. If the direction of my recent investigations may seem to you pertinent to the many pressing problems that confront us today in the political and economic world, I should be glad.

With my kind regards,

Sincerely yours,

Trigant Burrow

To Frederick Hoelzel   Westport, Connecticut
The University of Chicago   May 21, 1949

Dear Mr. Hoelzel:

Your good letter of the 18th reached me yesterday and I want to thank you for it. I appreciate your keen observations on the inconsistency of a hungry scientist. How frail we all are where the inner man comes into conflict with outer habituations! Then, too, as you say, most medical men are not scientists, and this undoubtedly is a large factor in the disappointing reaction your researches have encountered. This whole subject of fasting apparently requires far more controlled experimental inquiry than has as yet been commonly conceded it. Your broad comment to the effect that a nation's diet is a nation's destiny is indeed arresting.

My own approach to the investigations of the inner man—to his unwarranted affects and prejudices expressed by individuals and groups—qualifies me to be especially sympathetic also to the rather lukewarm interest you have found toward your researches in respect to one of the most fixed and adamant of human habituations—man's gastronomic bias.

I am very grateful to you for the two reprints you were good enough to enclose. I have read them with great interest and am looking forward to receiving the other papers on the subject of fasting which you are sending separately. . . .

Sincerely yours,

Trigant Burrow

To A. J. Muste, Secretary   Westport, Connecticut
The Fellowship of Reconciliation   June 9, 1949

Dear Mr. Muste:

I am so glad to have from you this morning your letter to me, the enclosed letter to *The Times*, and your pamphlet on Dictators. I look forward to reading this promptly and with much pleasure as I shall be interested to trace the parallels you speak of in our analysis of social issues.

I am greatly impressed and heartened by the deep sincerity and social courage of your Times letter. This is the sort of integrity that cannot but count. As I see it, it is the sort of spiritual *integrity* that is basically of one cloth with the biological *integration* of man's organism as a species. Such forthrightness is a challenge to us all.

As to your very pertinent question of therapy in connection with our researches in phylobiology; as we know, healthy processes are native to man and of course ever resident within him. This principle is basic with us. I hope to send you in a few days the reprint of a paper by Dr. Syz and myself that has just appeared in *The Journal of Abnormal and Social Psychology*, and that attempts to present this principle in concrete form.(9) As you will see from it, false motivation is artificially inculcated in the younger generation by the older, so that curative measures must be in part at least educational. But I can't help feeling that, as this educational process must reach early and deeply-rooted habits of conditioning internal to the organism, we must look to whatever bio-physical measures may be applicable from the various fields you cite. As I mentioned somewhat casually in my book, the next step in our researches would seem to require experimentation in the field of pharmacology. Even quite offhand, unsystematized tests with certain drugs seem to indicate the possibility of our finding through collaboration with the pharmacologist a drug that will prove of

(9) 'Two Modes of Social Adaptation and their Concomitants in Ocular Movements,' *The Journal of Abnormal and Social Psychology*, 1949, vol. 44, pp. 191-211.

specific assistance to the organism in its effort to reverse man's artificial shift from the primary pattern of cotention to the adventitious mode of ditention. I think especially of the mild drugs that have very recently been used for alleviating those disordered mental states in which an excess of affectivity is the predominant symptom.

As you surmise, some suggestions in regard to the social applications of my thesis are contained in my forthcoming book, chiefly in Chapter xiv. But it seems to me that at this stage the emphasis should be upon the internal factors determining man's relation to man—upon the organismic level underlying our human interrelations. The work of my associates and myself, I realize, is still incomplete. But my hope is that other investigators, with their widely differing background and experience, will find in our modest beginning the scientific incentive for examining man's subjective deviations in behavior as expressions of a bio-physical (neurodynamic) disorder. The discovery in our phylobiological laboratory of the existence in the organism of physiological patterns of tension that are concomitant to discriminable mental states (contrasting modes of attention or interest) leads me to feel that the coördination of the sciences of biochemistry and pharmacology with the educational aspects of phylobiology is by no means excluded.

Assuring you again of my appreciation of your interest and sympathy in the trend of our investigations, I am

Sincerely yours,

Trigant Burrow

To Mrs. Burrow   Lifwynn Camp, Merrill, N. Y.
Greens Farms, Connecticut   July 2, 1949, 7:30 a.m.

Dear Brownie:

My trunk came yesterday. So now I'm all assembled. I do hope you are not going to fail us this summer, but will definitely be up

here for at least two weeks of rest. *You need it and I need you.*
Don't put it off too long. William Mac will attend to everything
in your absence just as though you were there—Jack's garden as
well as ours. You know that. After all, this camp is a unique and
wonderful spot. Jack loved it and we should love it the more for
his precious sake. There are always plenty of reasons that stand in
the way of one's leaving home, when one is the whole strength and
meaning of it. . . . One has to plan and make a visit like this a part of
one's life-plan. You are necessary at Summer Hill, but you are also
necessary at Lifwynn Camp. Both have an equal place. . . .

Devotedly,

Trigant

To Mrs. John D. Burrow   Lifwynn Camp, Merrill, N. Y.
Westport, Connecticut   July 3, 1949

Dear Helen:

This is a lovely morning here at the Lake. The days have been
unfailingly friendly, and we are glad to be in camp again. It was
good to have at least that moment with you before leaving. You
were troubled and obviously laboring under various cares. I wish
I could help. I wish we could talk of things together more often.
It would not occur to me, dear, to tell you what I think is best for
you to do. That would be presuming of me—of anyone. But
together we could consider this and that aspect, and its relation to
the problem or circumstance as a whole. As you have often said, it
meant so much to you and Jack just to view a situation together
and talk things over from their different angles. Jack was necessarily a closer, more integral part of things than anyone else could
be. Your life was his life. Between you and Jack and Penny there
was an instinctual understanding. No one can fill the breach in
'the little team.' I know that. But something in some small way
akin to the elemental confidence among you might help sustain

the common strength that meant so much to you throughout those precious years. I'd so like to be by and share the burden of the cares that have so suddenly and so ruthlessly descended upon you.

I suppose my very radically altered 'basis of reference' presents difficulty for you. But, as you have so often said, Jack so largely shared that basis with me. Somehow he embodied it. So that you are not a stranger to it, and I might, at a test, prove more understanding than I ordinarily appear. On the other hand, I confess I'm terribly shy of young people. I feel so keenly the hurt I've caused them—I and the rest of my generation with our ignorance and neurosis. But this it is up to you and your generation to dispel! This battle of the generations, for all our camouflaging, is a tragically sorry business. It's the business of phylobiology—of you and Jack, of 'C.D.' and Nell and me.(10) It must be the business of Penny too, of John and Stephan, of George and little Jack.(11) It isn't true that human nature cannot change, that man must be always a fool. Man is only playing a part—an unconscious part. It is incumbent upon him—upon us—to change the false human nature that stage-struck man now everywhere takes to be true.

Clarence too felt the undercurrent of sadness and perplexity the other day. We spoke of it in the train. He said your face had grown maturer, more thoughtful under the stress of unaccustomed responsibilities. But we agreed that it had not taken from, but on the contrary added to your natural loveliness. Never doubt that we think of you, dear.

It will mean very much to have you and Penny with me here in camp. Come whenever convenient for you, and if you decide to send Penny on ahead, you know that she will be in careful hands.

I'm hoping for a letter soon—maybe today. My love, dear.

Devotedly,

Father

(10) Clarence Shields (called 'C.D.' by the children) and Nelly Hölljes, R.N.
(11) Dr. Burrow's grandchildren and the children of Dr. and Mrs. Galt.

To Alys Bentley   Lifwynn Camp, Merrill, N. Y.
New York   July 28, 1949

Dear Allie Ben:

The chair is here, and I am seated in it as I write you. It is really a joy, but even more than the comfort of its sturdy, substantial build is its association with you of whom I am so fond. It was sweet of you to think of me this way.

Thinking of you, and of all you have been through the years to me and to mine, I shall cherish this token of your thought and affection more than I can say. As I use this familiar reminder of you, I shall think of you and of the glad years we used to know. And, if it may be granted me, I shall not fail to identify myself with the courageous spirit whose presence graced this chair over a period of so many years, as you would try, as you would work, often in the silent watches of the night, to understand, to grow closer in thought and feeling to the meaning of this strangely baffling, yet undeniably beautiful world.

As I wrote you once following what was a moment of very poignant anguish for you, as you grow old your comfort must be very, very great in the thought of how much you have meant to so many, how many lives have been the richer for having touched your own. Of no one of your many friends can this be more truly said than of you. I am deeply grateful for it all.

As ever,

Trigant Burrow

To Professor John Dewey   Lifwynn Camp, Merrill, N. Y.
New Alexandria, Pennsylvania   August 15, 1949

Dear Professor Dewey:

I have allowed a whole month to pass since your good letter to me of July 12.

You are very good to plan to read the book and write me about it. This is an honor that I deeply value. I value it the more, as I realize the great demands upon you of your own work and the inevitable slowing of activities with us all as we grow older.

I wish it might have been my privilege over the years to talk with you from time to time, as it has been the great good fortune of other students of science and of life. The spoken word, carrying as it does all the warmth, all the feeling of the personality back of it, necessarily conveys so much more than the written page. What a man *is* so far exceeds what he does, no matter how great his accomplishment may be. This is why I miss, and shall miss the inspiration of having known you personally. May I say, though, that what you are is to an unusual degree conveyed in your letters, and for that I am very grateful. Sensing this, I am the more heartened by what I feel to be the essential sympathies and agreements between us.

Your emphasis upon the cultural factor in man's present-day dilemma does not divide us for a moment. And, incidentally, as I understand prejudice, your emphasis upon the influence of culture possesses no such emotional bias, since your conclusions rest upon the objective analysis and study of the social elements involved. Anyhow, I am in full accord with your position.

I only hope my book will set forth my own position in a sufficiently clear light to leave no doubt that our views in respect to man's present muddle are in no way irreconcilable. The thing that interests me is the question of the origin in man of the tendency to yield more easily to the dictates of prejudice than of reason. This seems to me an artificial condition, artificially created. Some deviate, some abnormal circumstance or conditioning must have intervened, that man should prefer to act counter to what is in his interest as a healthy organism rather than yield to incitements that are sane and clear.

I certainly do not think for a moment that language (which I suppose is, in a sense, coeval with consciousness—with intellectual consciousness) is of itself an impediment to consciousness, and an encouragement to man's substituting for conscious action a pattern of behavior that is narrow or biased. The possibility, though, that coincident with the emergence of language there has occurred a false exaggeration, a false self-centring of the individual's personal identity as over against the larger identity we share in common as a race or species, and that this false identity has blurred man's social vision—this possibility does interest and intrigue me.

But I must let my book present my cause. What really fills me, what is really seeking to find expression in this word to you, is my deep appreciation of your never-failing readiness to help wherever helpfulness lies to your hand. I cannot half say all that I feel when I think of your generous response to my groping efforts on behalf of a saner world, however alien to your accustomed field my own must sometimes appear.

Most gratefully and sincerely yours,

Trigant Burrow

To Dr. C. P. Oberndorf   Lifwynn Camp, Merrill, N. Y.
New York   August 18, 1949

My dear Oberndorf:

It was a real regret to me not to have seen you last winter. I kept promising myself that some blithe day in the spring when I would be motoring in to New York I'd give you a ring in the hope that I might have lunch and a talk with you as you kindly suggested. But, as it happened, my optimism was overborne by the pressure of those commitments that are the fatal routine of us all. We must really try to get together sometime soon. If not in New York, perhaps you will come out some day to Westport and have lunch with us, and see a very pleasant countryside if you have not already known it.

I miss the familiar contacts of past years. And now you and I are among the very few that remain of the old guard. From time to time I have seen Kempf or Hamilton or Glueck at the very occasional Psychopathological Meeting I manage to attend these days, but you seem to be a more confirmed absentee than even I. When I was in Baltimore, I used to keep in rather lively contact with my psychoanalytic confrères because, in addition to the regular meetings twice a year of the A.P.A.(12) and the conferences at St. Elizabeths, there were frequent informal gatherings in New York with August Hoch, Pierce Clark, John MacCurdy, Ramsay Hunt and a few others.

I was greatly pleased and flattered when, this spring, Mr. Whitney notified me that as an ex-President of the American Psychoanalytic Association I was to be the recipient of the Abraham A. Brill Memorial Medal. I much regretted that I was unable to be present at the meeting in Montreal to accept this honor in person. Speaking of that year of my presidency, I wince as I recall my phenomenal inadequacy in my role of presiding officer. But I remember gratefully your goodness in having generously taken me under your parliamentary wing. That helped, but not even your graciousness could save the day!

In writing Mr. Whitney it was a pleasure, as you will understand, to express my high regard for Brill whom I not only knew and admired, as I said, but with whom I shared the special honor of charter membership in the American Psychoanalytic Association.

But the real purport of this note is to let you know that I have not overlooked your kind invitation to lunch with you, and assure you that I am most anxious that we meet sometime in the not too distant future.

With my kind regards,

Sincerely yours,

Trigant Burrow

(12) The American Psychoanalytic Association.

To Professor Anton J. Carlson   Westport, Connecticut
Chicago   September 9, 1949

Dear Dr. Carlson:

I have you to thank, and most heartily, on three counts: for your very kind letter of August 27, for the reprints you recently sent me, but most of all for the copy of the fine review of my book you were generous enough to write for *The Journal of Higher Education.*(13) . . . I am most happy and grateful for your considered estimate of my book.

The reprints were most welcome. I have read (reread some of them) and greatly value the broad scope of their subject matter. As far as I am concerned—as far as concerns my experimental investigations in social groups—your recognition and consistent emphasis upon the solidarity of man as a species is, of all your contributions, the most important. For me, this premise stands preëminent throughout your writings. It is upon this principle that my entire thesis rests. In the absence of it as 'a proved biologic fact,' all the prattle we hear about 'peace in our time' seems to me sheer nonsense. As this 'fact' is intrinsic to the evolution of man, my hope is that with objectively directed measures of education, man's actions will ultimately bear witness to this principle in terms of mutual coöperation and harmony among individuals and communities. . . .

Thank you again for everything.

With my kind regards,

Sincerely yours,

Trigant Burrow

(13) *The Journal of Higher Education*, 1950, vol. 21, pp. 335–6.

To Thomas Sancton Westport, Connecticut
New Orleans September 28, 1949

Dear Mr. Sancton:

I am really quite overwhelmed by your thoughtful and generous letter. There is so much to say in reply to it, and I shall try to say it as well as I can in the time at my disposal. And, of course, I shall send you at once all the material for which you ask.

Let me take up the items of your letter as they come to me. This may not be in the order of their importance or of your major interest. First, I do want to disparage the idea too common among friends or students interested in the thesis of phylobiology, that I alone embody the creative spirit responsible for the work of our organization. This is not said out of a spirit of humility or out of the wish to be generous, though I hope I am not a stranger to these motives. I say it because it is the simple truth. As you may have surmised, the thesis of phylobiology could not arise—it is organically excluded that it should have arisen from the mind of one individual. The 'I'-persona marks a universal dissociation within the species man, because in its interrelational blindness this false self or identity has virtually cut itself off from connection with the biological organism (individual and phylic) which presumably it represents. To expect, therefore, that anyone should come forth from this distorted biological medium and turn with a clear, objective eye upon this subjective disturbance would be comparable to an insane patient on the ward of a mental institution suddenly turning about and presenting a clear analysis of the disordered feeling and thinking characterizing himself and his fellow patients. Mentally, theoretically, I did see very early that normality does not present a dependable criterion of healthy human behavior. But behavior is motivated by feeling; feeling is the basis of behavior, and my own feeling, of course, was compactly interwoven with the feeling-pattern characteristic of the 'normal' mode of adaptation.

The phylobiological thesis did not have its inception until there was the very intensive work, first on the part of Mr. Shields and myself, and later, in conjunction with Mr. Shields, in systematic group-sessions with associates and students. In this experimental setting, you will understand, Mr. Shields and I were patients just as my other associates and students were patients. That is, in our phylobiological premise the organism of man was the physician, and normality (socially unintegrated man) the patient. As you see, this was not and could not be a one-man job. Here was a social disorder involving man at large, and only organismic man could possibly tackle objectively this problem of his own social disorder.

With regard to your very natural comment, it is certainly true, as you say, that no one mind can wholly compass the meaning of mind, and I concede that the effort to do so would in itself involve bias for the mind thus engaged. And I am heartily in sympathy with your feeling of the wide differences in outlook there are, for example, between the southern peasant and the wealthy industrial magnate. But, as a matter of fact, these differences were included in the cross section of society that formed our experimental group. It embraced such wide socio-economic extremes as a woman from the wealthiest and most aristocratic family in Maryland, and a street car conductor. The latter, incidentally, was from the South. Indeed, as far as that goes, my own background and Mr. Shields', a Pennsylvania German of very simple upbringing, stood out in marked contrast to one another.

But the principle of phylobiology is wholly independent of these superficial discriminations. Certainly a brain surgeon does not have a different operation (lobectomy) for the same functional brain-disorder according as it occurs in the aristocrat or the proletarian. Ditention is a functional brain-disorder affecting man throughout. It is a disorder of function that destroys man's sense of his unity and solidarity as a species and, instead, sets each individual, or each ideologically amalgamated group or nation, over against every other individual or nation as a separate and discrete entity. This ditentive mechanism involves the private assumption by each of us that he possesses a valid 'right' or preroga-tive, and that other people are 'right' only in the measure in which they agree with him. In short, each of us is interrelationally, *in actu* or *in posse*, a self-appointed Czar. Each of us is the private arbiter of the moral 'right' he now entertains vicariously in place of the biologically fitting behavior—the basic unity of function—that marks man's primary continuity and solidarity as a species. The 'I'-persona of the man in my book, with a son at the university and a wife with furs, is, of course, fundamentally of precisely the same structure socially as that of the ignorant southern white who is contemptuous of the negro because he is black. They are the same socially (interrelationally) because essentially they stem from the same disordered or partitive pattern of brain-function....

Please know that I do value and agree with your remark about the proprietary attitude people have toward a new idea or method they have advanced, or that they think they have. I realize that be-cause of the 'I'-persona such innovators can be all kinds of a fool, and I cannot claim that I am not involved in just such a social 'I'-persona. But I believe that the communal nature of our approach (I use 'communal' in its biological sense, of course) affords a certain safeguard, or is at least a mitigating circumstance in the group work of my associates and myself. That work has consisted merely in introducing a much needed technique into the field of human behavior. There is a displaced pattern of feeling and think-ing (prejudice) in man. With our effort, as a group, to challenge and discountenance this displaced pattern of feeling and thinking, the physiological substrate of prejudice was accidentally laid bare. In our effort of adjustment we worked for a long time only with our mutual affects, then suddenly and unexpectedly we discovered the physiological conflict lying beneath these affects—a conflict calling for a physiological adjustment. You see, we were faced with a problem in internal orthopedics. But what we were doing only became clear after we had done it. We had, as it were, to explain ourselves to ourselves! We are still doing so, for our work is not completed....

We have not been idle in our efforts to secure the wider financial support of the community for the Foundation's work. We have made a number of applications to philanthropic organizations that we hoped might be interested in assisting in the financial support of our endeavors. . . . Thus far we have been unsuccessful in our quest. But we have not abandoned our attempts. The response we have had could hardly have been otherwise, and in the main we are not disheartened. Our confidence in the intelligence, the consistency and the endurance of phylic man is unlimited, and when our researches have reached the point where we can present them in such a way as to reach this deeper, unconditioned level of man's behavior, we feel sure we shall achieve the needed results. (14) . . .

I most heartily accent your wish that we might have met before your return to New Orleans. The devil was certainly sitting cross-legged when I was denied that pleasure. Perhaps matters incident to the publication of your novel or some other errand will be bringing you to New York. If so, you must certainly come out to us. Westport is not at all a mean base from which to transact one's business in New York.

Your statement that being thirty-four 'it is too late for you to become a scientist,' I cannot accept—certainly not, if this includes the science of phylobiology. This is a field in which you have your material always with you—in your study, in your sleeping room (that's my scientific laboratory, *par excellence*), in the midst of your family, and among your friends. For the tension underlying the 'I'-persona is always at hand. And, from the point of view of professional preparedness, scientific or what-not, do you reckon the enormous asset in relation to behavior adaptation of a happily adjusted home life? Speaking as a behaviorist, I would say that this, in itself, is a most significant equipment. Then, added to it, there is your training and experience as an accomplished writer— and all this at the age of thirty-four. Why, I don't think I know

(14) The income from the Foundation's small endowment was insufficient for its needs and over the years the members of the Foundation contributed funds for the larger part of its operating expenses.

anyone quite as young as you are! With so distinguished a doctorate as you hold in your possession, you shouldn't feel daunted in attempting to tackle any career.

... I have not myself read either Fromm or Horney, but a good many people have spoken of what they felt was the tendency of these authors to borrow rather freely from my thesis. Harry Stack Sullivan helped himself lavishly to my material. I knew him at Hopkins and he received through the years all of my reprints.

And now let me tell you—and this has been uppermost in my mind throughout this letter—how happy I am that you are reviewing my book for *The Nation*. I don't know anyone I would rather have write such a review, or anyone who from his background of feeling and thinking is better prepared to do so....

With my kind regards,

Sincerely yours,

Trigant Burrow

This review did not appear.

To Jean Garrigue
New York

Westport, Connecticut
November 8, 1949

Dear Miss Garrigue:

Your review in *The Tiger's Eye* of my book, *The Neurosis of Man*, interested me greatly. It is most sensitive and understanding. But of still greater meaning to me, it was obviously written from an intuitive feeling for my thesis. So that to say that I am grateful to you for so spontaneous an impression seems almost like an infringement. Realizing though, as I do, how helpful your review will be in furthering the aims of my associates and myself, I feel I must tell you of my deep appreciation.

The matter of my lack of organization does trouble me. I never have planned in advance the order of any piece of writing of mine. I live in the midst of a daily experiment in human behavior, and the quantity of material that might be recorded is overwhelming. This is no excuse. Order is heaven's first law, and I must somehow cultivate a method that is more consistent with our phylobiological thesis.

I should like now to write a small book, and I want to start out with a description of cotention. Such an arrangement may seem like reversing the order of things. But I feel that this time I should set down first things first—that I should say at the outset whatever I can to make clear the primary place of cotention in any attempt to restore order to man's benighted social world. Then I would go on to a theme, 'Emotion and the Social Crisis,' that I discussed at a symposium last fall at The University of Chicago and, for Chapter three, to a study I am preparing now for another symposium-volume.

But I ask myself, 'Can such a schema be brought in line with the sort of organization my writing stands in so great need of?' With *The Neurosis of Man* I held off discussion of the technique—the recovery of the pattern of cotention that is the real crux of my thesis—until as late as the tenth chapter. I felt that the way had to be carefully laid for it, believing as I do that, after all the talk, cotention is the essential bedrock of my thesis. Nevertheless, in this new book I incline to burst in with a description of this sorely-needed orthopedic adjustment and then go on to speak of the consequences of an absence in man of this balanced principle of behavior—the many personal and social symptoms that beset us all. But, as I say, I fear that I am being very unorthodox from the point of view of organized writing.

Thank you again most earnestly for your very generous and sympathetic review.

Sincerely yours,

Trigant Burrow

To Dr. C. Judson Herrick   Westport, Connecticut
Grand Rapids, Michigan   December 10, 1949

Dear Dr. Herrick:

I have really not been as neglectful of your good letter of July 28 as might appear to be the case. In accepting an invitation from Professor Sorokin to contribute an article to his forthcoming Symposium-Volume—a volume in which he is offering the 'prescriptions' of various investigators for the relief of man's disordered behavior—I had your letter very constantly in mind. I had in mind too your book on Coghill's life and work. But I am no little taken aback to discover just this morning that I did not at the time send you at least a word acknowledging your letter and letting you know that I would reply to it more fully in some less crowded moment. I am sure that 'in my mind' I must have written you more than once, and that this explains my false memory of having written you earlier.

As I say, your letter was very much to the fore with me as I wrote the paper for Sorokin—as thoughts of Dr. Coghill too were very much to the fore with me. I have tried in this paper to anticipate what must be criticisms similar to your own on the part of many other colleagues. I have in mind in particular your feeling of the undue weight I appear to lend to the phylic aspects of behavior, to the neglect of the individual factor. My hope is that the present essay whose theme is so largely directed by your letter may serve to reconcile those apparent differences between us in spite of which you are generous enough to feel that 'we come out at about the same place.'

I have just today finished my paper and am taking the liberty of sending a manuscript copy of it to you under separate cover. I believe this study presents certain aspects of my position more succinctly and clearly than I have succeeded in doing in former writings. I am bringing this material before you as soon as possible, as I feel it will indicate much more adequately than any letter could how fully in sympathy I am with your basic concept of our common problem. . . .

I have kept your book, *George Ellett Coghill,* close beside me during the past months and in my not too frequent periods of recess have enjoyed it immensely, and have greatly profited too from the wisdom of your comments. I have now turned it over to my associates, Dr. Syz and Dr. Galt, who are looking forward eagerly to reading it. As I believe I mentioned to you earlier, from the time of my first acquaintance with Coghill in 1932 I admired him greatly and felt that his fresh insights into neuroanatomic function were of fundamental importance. His formulations in regard to total and partial patterns at neuroanatomic levels gave assistance and support to the new formulations I had been developing over the years in respect to human behavior. As you may know, I referred to Coghill extensively in my book, *The Biology of Human Conflict.* . . .

With my thanks again for your good letter of last summer, and for the care and sympathy with which you read my book,

Sincerely yours,

Trigant Burrow

To Dr. S. J. Hayakawa   Westport, Connecticut
Editor, *ETC.*, Chicago   November 16, 1949

Dear Dr. Hayakawa:

Thank you for sending me the copy of *ETC.* for the summer of 1948 containing your article on the Aristotelian structure of language in which you make reference to me. On reading the quotation from me given in the footnote to your article (page 228) I was quite taken aback by the meaning it seemed to convey, and immediately turned to the original passage in *The Biology of Human Conflict*. In so doing, I found that you had omitted the first part of the sentence (the part before the dash), and quoted the second part as though it were complete. In full, the sentence reads: 'It is in his unfamiliarity with the deeper basic factors internal to him that man has failed to come to grips with the actual processes underlying all these spurious abstractions—these mere names that have vicariously become the be-all and the end-all of his existence.'

I know you will not think me unduly meticulous in calling this discrepancy to your attention. It so happens that the omitted portion of the sentence is extremely vital in correctly conveying my position regarding the importance of language in the social dysfunction of man—a point of view which I feel differs fundamentally from that of General Semantics. As I have many times stated, I do not think that man's basic difficulty is in the inadequacy of his words to present reality, or in his faulty response to words. Nor does it seem to me that man can come to grips with his conflict and division by achieving piecemeal a more extensional orientation in regard to the myriad words with which we are surrounded, or by a greater knowledge or awareness of the process of abstracting, however valuable and important such disciplines may be. To our research unit these factors, like much else in the symptomatology of man's behavior, appear to stem from the presence in man of an interpersonally systematized affect-identity (the 'I'-persona, in my terminology) which has overtly replaced the actual self as a freely functioning unit in a species continuum. . . .

It does seem to me that the 'I'-persona developed in man coincidently with the emergence of the function of communication through speech. This is a topic to which I am giving especial emphasis in a paper I am preparing at the moment. It may be that my manner of emphasizing the joint origin of language and man's ditentive behavior has been misleading. I fear, too, that I have not always been explicit enough in my writing. If this is true, I concede that it is up to me as a recalcitrant 'I'-persona to eat humble pie— a dietary régime to which I am not a stranger. In reading passages from *The Biology of Human Conflict* (I have especially in mind portions of the Introduction), I can easily see that I may have given an undue emphasis to the function of language in man's bionomic dilemma. Taken out of the context of my thesis in its entirety, a number of passages could be misleading, and the reader might readily conclude that the theme of phylobiology and that of General Semantics are largely in agreement. . . .

I was very glad to receive a copy of your *Language in Thought and Action* from Harcourt, Brace. Dr. Galt fell upon it before I had had time to examine it with the care I want to give it. He is reading it with keen interest and plans to write a review for one of the psychological journals. I have just read the excellent comments on your book in *The Nation* by Stuart Chase.

Thank you again for your earnest and continued interest in the trend of my research.

With my best regards,

Sincerely yours,

Trigant Burrow

By the end of 1949, Burrow was writing *Science and Man's Behavior* and was also at work on a small volume dealing with the technique of cotention. While thus engaged he was stricken with what appeared to be a severe virus infection. After several weeks the illness failed to yield to treatment, and he entered the New York Hospital. While there, in spite of increasing weakness, he dictated to Mr. Shields a reply to a note from Mrs. William Galt.

To Mrs. William E. Galt New York Hospital
Westport, Connecticut March 12, 1950

Dear Alfreda:

Cotention is *nothing*. That is its difficulty. To people, to a race of people who are at all times, from birth to death, hot after *something*—everything—cotention seems, of course, unattainable.

We have a colossal job. People with a colossal job ordinarily apply their energies accordingly. But people who are hot after *something*—something mental—take a laissez faire attitude toward their job. They play about—giggling, coquetting or grieving, according to the direction in which this mental emotive *something*—this visible addition to me, seems to lie.

Cotention is not the rub. It is ditention—the imaginary mental something man is vainly projecting at every moment.

I would like to go farther. It just isn't possible—not now.

Yours,

Trigant Burrow

When at length it became clear that he was suffering from malignant lymphoma, Dr. Burrow was brought back to his home.

To Dr. Cornelius C. Wholey Westport, Connecticut
Pittsburgh May 3, 1950

Dear Neil:

I am still too ill to write you now. I do want to thank you for your gracious phone call and for your extremely thoughtful offer to come to see me. You were right in sensing the pleasure that would give me. But I fear we must postpone that pleasure for some time to come.

While a viral infection is not just up your 'skyway,' as Laura Portor expressed it the other day, you know me so well, and your interest in medicine has always been so extremely liberal, that you would probably have much valuable information and counsel to pass on to me. I just must somehow get over this thing, and with the systematic blood transfusions things begin to be very encouraging in this direction.

Tomorrow is your birthday. That's the particular reason I wanted to have this word go to you today. I would not want you to think me unmindful of the 4th. This word takes you my heartiest felicitations and best wishes.

Affectionately,

Trigant

To Dr. Hans Syz   Greens Farms, Connecticut
New York Hospital   May 14, 1950

Dear, dear Hans:

I am so very pleased at the prospect of your early return home. We've both had a long hard pull.(15) It is lovely here in the country now, and you cannot fail to respond to all its warmth and beauty and sunshine.

Here's seeing you soon,

With all my love,

Father

(15) Dr. Syz had also been a patient in the hospital.

Dr. Burrow died on May 24, 1950. The day before his death, Mr. Shields, realizing that the end was very close, said to him, 'Dr. Burrow, *we will go on working.*' It was several hours before the sick man could summon the strength to reply. Then Mr. Shields, bending close to him, caught the faint whisper, 'We will go on.' Those who knew him realized that he was speaking not only of his immediate associates. Trigant Burrow was voicing his abiding faith in man.

PUBLISHED WRITINGS

Bibliography

PUBLISHED WRITINGS OF
TRIGANT BURROW, M.D., Ph.D.

BOOKS

The Social Basis of Consciousness—A Study in Organic Psychology, The International Library of Psychology, Philosophy and Scientific Method, New York, Harcourt, Brace; London, Kegan Paul, Trench, Trubner, 1927, pp. XVIII, 256

The Structure of Insanity—A Study in Phylopathology, Psyche Miniatures, London, Kegan Paul, Trench, Trubner, 1932, pp. 80

(Translation) *Die Struktur der Geisteskrankheit—Eine Studie in Phylopathologie*, übersetzt von Miriam Bredow. Leipzig, Georg Thieme, 1933, pp. 52

The Biology of Human Conflict—An Anatomy of Behavior, Individual and Social, New York, Macmillan, 1937, pp. XL, 435

The Neurosis of Man—An Introduction to a Science of Human Behavior, London, Routledge and Kegan Paul; New York, Harcourt, Brace, 1949, pp. XXVI, 428

Science and Man's Behavior—The Contribution of Phylobiology, edited by William E. Galt, Ph.D. (including the full text of *The Neurosis of Man*), New York, Philosophical Library, 1953, pp. XII, 564

PAPERS

Hysterical Defects of Musical Language, *Maryland Medical Journal*, 1909, Vol. 52, pp. 249-50

The Determination of the Position of a Momentary Impression in the Temporal Course of a Moving Visual Impression (Doctoral thesis), *The Johns Hopkins Studies in Philosophy and Psychology*, No. 3, *Psychological Monographs*, 1909, Vol. XI, pp. 1-63

Freud's Psychology in Its Relation to the Neurosis, *American Journal of the Medical Sciences*, 1911, Vol. 141, pp. 873-82

Some Psychological Phases of Medicine, *The Journal of Abnormal Psychology*, 1911, Vol. VI, pp. 205-13

Conscious and Unconscious Mentation from the Psychoanalytic Viewpoint, *Psychological Bulletin*, 1912, Vol. IX, pp. 154-60

Psychoanalysis and Society, *The Journal of Abnormal Psychology*, 1912-13, Vol. VII, pp. 340-46

The Psychotherapeutic Treatment of the Functional Neuroses (with L. F. Barker) in Forchheimer, *Therapeusis of Internal Diseases*, New York, Appleton, 1913, Vol. IV, pp. 569-81

The Method of Psychoanalysis, *The Virginia Medical Semi-Monthly*, 1913, pp. 430-33

Character and the Neuroses, *The Psychoanalytic Review*, 1914, Vol. I, pp. 121-8

The Psychological Analysis of So-called Neurasthenic and Allied States—A Fragment, *The Journal of Abnormal Psychology*, 1913, Vol. VIII, pp. 243-58
(Translation) Die psychologische Analyse der sogenannten Neurasthenie und verwandter Zustände, *Internationale Zeitschrift für ärztliche Psychoanalyse*, 1913, Vol. I, pp. 330-43

The Meaning of the Psychic Factor, *The Journal of Abnormal Psychology*, 1913, Vol. VIII

The Psychanalyst and the Community, *The Journal of the American Medical Association*, 1914, Vol. LXII, pp. 1876-8

The Philology of Hysteria—An A Priori Study of the Neuroses in the Light of Freudian Psychology, *The Journal of the American Medical Association*, 1916, Vol. LXVI, pp. 783-7

Permutations within the Sphere of Consciousness—Or the Factor of Repression and its Influence upon Education, *The Journal of Abnormal Psychology*, 1916, Vol. XI, pp. 178-88

Conceptions and Misconceptions in Psychoanalysis, *The Journal of the American Medical Association*, 1917, Vol. LXVIII, pp. 355-60. Published also in *Contemporary Science*, edited by Benjamin Harrow, Ph.D., New York, Boni and Liveright, 1921, pp. 211-29

The Meaning of Psychoanalysis, *The Journal of Abnormal Psychology*, 1917, Vol. XII, pp. 58-68

The Genesis and Meaning of 'Homosexuality' and Its Relation to the Problem of Introverted Mental State, *The Psychoanalytic Review*, 1917, Vol. 4, pp. 272-84

Notes with Reference to Freud, Jung and Adler, *The Journal of Abnormal Psychology*, 1917, Vol. XII, pp. 161-7

The Origin of the Incest-Awe, *The Psychoanalytic Review*, 1918, Vol. V, pp. 243-54

Social Images versus Reality, *The Journal of Abnormal Psychology and Social Psychology*, 1924, Vol. XIX, pp. 230-35

A Relative Concept of Consciousness—An Analysis of Consciousness in its Ethnic Origin, *The Psychoanalytic Review*, 1925, Vol. XII, pp. 1-15

Psychiatry as an Objective Science, *The British Journal of Medical Psychology*, 1925, Vol. V, pp. 298-309

The Laboratory Method in Psychoanalysis—Its Inception and Development, *The American Journal of Psychiatry*, 1926, Vol. V, pp. 345-55
(Translation) Die Laboratoriumsmethode in der Psychoanalyse—Ihr Anfang und ihre Entwicklung, *Internationale Zeitschrift für Psychoanalyse*, 1928, Vol. XIV, pp. 375-86

Psychoanalytic Improvisations and the Personal Equation, *The Psychoanalytic Review*, 1926, Vol. XIII, pp. 173-86

Our Mass Neurosis, *The Psychological Bulletin*, 1926, Vol. 23, pp. 305-12

Our Social Evasion, *Medical Journal and Record*, 1926, Vol. CXXIII, pp. 793-6

Insanity a Social Problem, *The American Journal of Sociology*, 1926, Vol. XXXII, pp. 80-87

The Heroic Role—An Historical Retrospect, *Psyche* (London), 1926, Vol. VI, pp. 42-54

Psychoanalysis in Theory and in Life, *The Journal of Nervous and Mental Disease*, 1926, Vol. 64, pp. 209-24

The Reabsorbed Affect and Its Elimination, *The British Journal of Medical Psychology*, 1926, Vol. VI, pp. 211-18

The Need of an Analytic Psychiatry, *The American Journal of Psychiatry*, 1927, Vol. VI, pp. 485-92

An Ethnic Aspect of Consciousness, *The Sociological Review* (London), 1927, Vol. XIX, pp. 69-76

Speaking of Resistances, *Psyche* (London), 1927, Vol. VII, pp. 20-27

The Group Method of Analysis, *The Psychoanalytic Review*, 1927, Vol. XIV, pp. 268-80

(Translation) Die Gruppenmethode in der Psychoanalyse, *Imago*, 1926, Vol. XII, pp. 211-22

The Problem of the Transference, *The British Journal of Medical Psychology*, 1927, Vol. VII, pp. 193-202

The Autonomy of the 'I' from the Standpoint of Group Analysis, *Psyche* (London) 1928, Vol. VIII, pp. 35-50

Biological Foundations and Mental Methods, *The British Journal of Medical Psychology*, 1928, Vol. VIII, pp. 49-63

The Basis of Group-Analysis, or the Analysis of the Reactions of Normal and Neurotic Individuals, *The British Journal of Medical Psychology*, 1928, Vol. VIII, 198-206

The Physiological Basis of Neurosis and Dream—A Societal Interpretation of the Sensori-Motor Reactions Reflected in Insanity and Crime, *The Journal of Social Psychology*, 1930, Vol. I, pp. 48-65

(Translation) Ueber Phylopathologie und Phyloanalyse—Eine physiologische Deutung der gestörten sozialen Interreaktionen, *Zentralblatt für Psychotherapie und ihre Grenzgebiete*, 1930, Vol. III, pp. 394-411

So-called 'Normal' Social Relationships Expressed in the Individual and the Group, and Their Bearing on the Problems of Neurotic Disharmonies, *The American Journal of Psychiatry*, 1930, Vol. X, pp. 101-16

(Translation) Sogenannte 'normale' soziale Wechselbeziehungen in Individuum und Gruppe und ihre Bedeutung für das Problem neurotischer Störungen, *Zentralblatt für Psychotherapie und ihre Grenzgebiete*, 1932, Vol. 5, pp. 677-91

Physiological Behavior-Reactions in the Individual and the Community—A Study in Phyloanalysis, *Psyche* (London), 1930, Vol. XI, pp. 67-81

(Translations) Physiologische Verhaltungsreaktionen in Individuum und in der Gesellschaft—Eine Studie in Phyloanalyse (*Schweizer Archiv für Neurologie und Psychiatrie*, 1932, Vol. XXIX, pp. 253-68

Réactions Physiologiques du Comportement Individuel et Collectif— Une Étude en Phyloanalyse, *Journal de Neurologie et de Psychiatrie,* 1932, Vol. XXXII, pp. 442-59

A Phylogenetic Study of Insanity in its Underlying Morphology, *The Journal of the American Medical Association,* 1933, Vol. 100, pp. 648-51

(Translation) Uno Studio Filogenetico della Alienazione Mentale e delle sue Basi Morfologiche, *Archivio Generale di Neurologia Psychiatria e Psicoanalisi,* 1934, Vol. XV, pp. 133-42

Crime and the Social Reaction of Right and Wrong—A Study in Clinical Sociology, *Journal of Criminal Law and Criminology,* 1933, Vol. XXIV, pp. 685-99

(Translation) Le Crime et la force sociale de la notion du bien et du mal—étude clinique de sociologie, *Revue Internationale de Droit Pénal,* 1935, Vol. 12, pp. 265-84

The Morphology of Insanity as a Racial Process—A Study of Attention in Relation to Adaptive Disorders, *The British Journal of Medical Psychology,* 1933, Vol. XIII, pp. 296-312

Neuropathology and the Internal Environment—A Study of the Neuromuscular Factors in Attention and Their Bearing upon Man's Disorders of Adaptation, *Human Biology,* 1935, Vol. 7, pp. 74-94

Behavior Mechanisms and their Phylopathology, *The Psychoanalytic Review,* 1935, Vol. XXII, pp. 169-81

Fallacies of the Senses, '*Scientia,*' 1935, Vol. LVII, pp. 354-65, 431-41

Altering Frames of Reference in the Sphere of Human Behavior, *Journal of Social Philosophy,* 1937, Vol. 2, pp. 118-41

The Law of the Organism—A Neuro-social Approach to the Problems of Human Behavior, *The American Journal of Sociology,* 1937, Vol. XLII, pp. 814-24

The Organismic Factor in Disorders of Behavior, *The Journal of Psychology,* 1937, Vol. 4, pp. 333-41

The Organism as a Whole and Its Phyloanalytic Implications—An Organismic Approach to Disorders of Human Behavior, *The Australasian Journal of Psychology and Philosophy,* 1937, Vol. XV, pp. 259-78

Bio-Physical Factors in Relation to Functional Imbalances, *Human Biology,* 1938, Vol. 10, pp. 93-105

Kymograph Studies of Physiological (Respiratory) Concomitants in Two Types of Attentional Adaptation, *Nature* (London), 1938, Vol. 142, p. 156

The World as Will—A View and a Review, *Journal of Social Philosophy*, 1939, Vol. 4, pp. 162-73

The Economic Factor in Disorders of Behavior, *The American Journal of Orthopsychiatry*, 1939, Vol. IX, pp. 102-8

The Human Equation, *Mental Hygiene*, 1941, Vol. XXV, pp. 210-20

Kymograph Records of Neuromuscular (Respiratory) Patterns in Relation to Behavior Disorders, *Psychosomatic Medicine*, 1941, Vol. III, pp. 174-86

Neurosis and War: A Problem in Human Behavior, *The Journal of Psychology*, 1941, Vol. 12, pp. 235-49

Preliminary Report of Electroencephalographic Recordings in Relation to Behavior Modifications, *The Journal of Psychology*, 1943, Vol. 15, pp. 109-14

The Neurodynamics of Behavior. A Phylobiological Foreword, *Philosophy of Science*, 1943, Vol. 10, pp. 271-88

Electroencephalographic Recordings of Varying Aspects of Attention in Relation to Behavior (with William E. Galt, Ph.D.), *The Journal of General Psychology*, 1945, Vol. 32, pp. 269-88

Phylobiology: Behavior Reactions in the Individual and the Community, *ETC.*, 1946, Vol. III, pp. 265-78 (previously published under the title, Physiological Behavior-Reactions in the Individual and the Community, 1930)

The Social Neurosis: A Study in Clinical Anthropology, *Philosophy of Science*, 1949, Vol. 16, pp. 25-40

Two Modes of Social Adaptation and Their Concomitants in Ocular Movements (with Hans Syz, M.D.), *The Journal of Abnormal and Social Psychology*, 1949, Vol. 44, pp. 191-211

Studies with the Lifwynn Eye-Movement Camera (with Hans Syz, M.D.), *Journal of the Biological Photographic Association*, 1949, Vol. 17, pp. 155-70

(This thesis is more fully developed in Two Modes of Social Adaptation and Their Concomitants in Ocular Movements, 1949)

Emotion and the Social Crisis—A Problem in Phylobiology, in *Feelings and Emotions—The Mooseheart Symposium*, edited by Martin L. Reymert, Ph.D., New York, McGraw-Hill, 1950, pp. 465-86

Prescription for Peace: The Biological Basis of Man's Ideological Conflicts, in *Explorations in Altruistic Love and Behavior*, edited by Pitirim A. Sorokin, Ph.D., Boston, The Beacon Press, 1950, pp. 93-117

INDEX

Index